This book belongs to:

Peschel Press, P.O. Box 132, Hershey, PA 17033

A Dictionary

of Flowers

and Gems

Say What You Mean
~ Even Say It Mean ~
The Victorian Way

A Dictionary of Flowers and Gems

Say What You Mean
~ Even Say It Mean ~
The Victorian Way

Skye Kingsbury

Cover design by Lily Peschel.

www.peschelpress.com

ISBN-13: 978-1-950347-05-6

Library of Congress Control Number: 2018944295

First IngramSpark printing: June 2019, version 1.0

TABLE OF CONTENTS

SNOWDROPS.

INTRODUCTION

Oh, hello, I didn't see you there. So you decided to pick this book up, then? Well then, thank-you! I really do appreciate it.

So, you're probably wondering, "Who are you?"

Excellent question, actually. I tend to go by Skye nowadays, but that's always subject to change.

About a year and a half ago, I became interested in the language of flowers and how each one meant one (or many) things. It became a game, really, to see how many different ways I could tell someone to "Get lost" by using only flowers, herbs, trees, and anything else that fell into the "flora" category. There are even a few mushrooms in here, too.

When I started incorporating them into my stories and art, I became frustrated with the lack of good flower dictionaries. There are several on the market, but they always missed the information that I wanted. They always seemed to be short the particular flower I was looking for, and I became tired very quickly of having to Google the specific flower I was looking for.

So I decided to do something about it.

To be honest, this entire "write your own book" came about when I was told the story of my dad's ex-wife. Upon finding a lack of good rune dictionaries, she wrote her own. So I decided to write my own flower dictionary, but make it as complete as possible.

There are over two thousand flowers in this book, with as many other common names and their Latin name just to be sure of their correct identity — about twenty or so flowers short of twenty two hundred if you wish to be precise—and the bonus gemstone section has approximately three hundred and fifty stones.

It all took way too much research, well over a year of digging through books and eying websites dubiously, but I consider it worth my time.

This book is for all the artists who like to incorporate flowers and gems into their work, using their meanings to add hidden depth to the creation, and for all the writers whose characters give bouquets of flowers to their loved ones.

I've even created a few listings, ranging from all of the flowers that mean some form of love, to the one list that's made up of all the flowers that mean various forms of "get lost."

I had a great time working on this book, and I'm extremely pleased that it's finally finished.

With all my love (and flowers),

Skye

EDITOR'S NOTE

This book combines material on the meaning of flowers from several Victorian sources. Their meanings varied by county, region, language, and culture. Scientific advances since then introduced changes of their own. Flower names were changed or dropped. Scientific names were changed. During the construction of this book, the editors reconciled history, tradition, folklore, and science. The meaning of a flower remains in the eye of the beholder, the heart of the giver, and the arms of its lucky recipient.

PARTS OF THE BOOK

Each section has a unique page border that'll help in finding the section you want.

The **Flowers to Meanings** section describes what meanings are associated with specific flowers. The flower is listed in **bold**, followed by, if any, other names within parentheses (like this), then the Latin name within square brackets [like this]. For example: **Osier** (Willow) [*Salix*]: Frankness.

The **Meanings to Flowers** section is the opposite of the first one. Listed is the meaning, followed by all of the flowers that go with it afterwards. Use this section to find all of the flowers that can mean a specific thing. Love, Luck, and Lust are three examples you will find within this section.

The **Gemstones to Meanings** section is exactly as in the "Flowers to Meanings" section; this one gives you all of the meanings that can be found that are associated with a certain gemstone. Like the previous section, this is best used when you have a specific gemstone in mind and want to know what meanings go with it.

The **Meanings to Gemstones** section is best used when you have a specific meaning in mind, but not the stone that goes with. It is organized similar to the "Meanings to Flowers" section, only with gems instead of flowers.

Flowers

to

Meanings

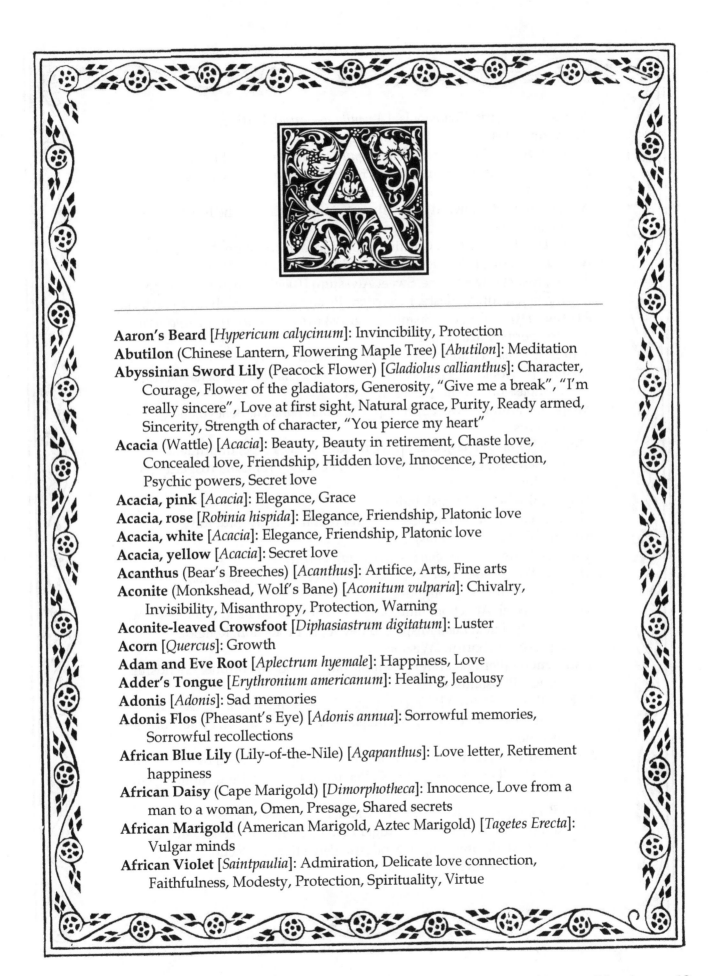

Aaron's Beard [*Hypericum calycinum*]: Invincibility, Protection

Abutilon (Chinese Lantern, Flowering Maple Tree) [*Abutilon*]: Meditation

Abyssinian Sword Lily (Peacock Flower) [*Gladiolus callianthus*]: Character, Courage, Flower of the gladiators, Generosity, "Give me a break", "I'm really sincere", Love at first sight, Natural grace, Purity, Ready armed, Sincerity, Strength of character, "You pierce my heart"

Acacia (Wattle) [*Acacia*]: Beauty, Beauty in retirement, Chaste love, Concealed love, Friendship, Hidden love, Innocence, Protection, Psychic powers, Secret love

Acacia, pink [*Acacia*]: Elegance, Grace

Acacia, rose [*Robinia hispida*]: Elegance, Friendship, Platonic love

Acacia, white [*Acacia*]: Elegance, Friendship, Platonic love

Acacia, yellow [*Acacia*]: Secret love

Acanthus (Bear's Breeches) [*Acanthus*]: Artifice, Arts, Fine arts

Aconite (Monkshead, Wolf's Bane) [*Aconitum vulparia*]: Chivalry, Invisibility, Misanthropy, Protection, Warning

Aconite-leaved Crowsfoot [*Diphasiastrum digitatum*]: Luster

Acorn [*Quercus*]: Growth

Adam and Eve Root [*Aplectrum hyemale*]: Happiness, Love

Adder's Tongue [*Erythronium americanum*]: Healing, Jealousy

Adonis [*Adonis*]: Sad memories

Adonis Flos (Pheasant's Eye) [*Adonis annua*]: Sorrowful memories, Sorrowful recollections

African Blue Lily (Lily-of-the-Nile) [*Agapanthus*]: Love letter, Retirement happiness

African Daisy (Cape Marigold) [*Dimorphotheca*]: Innocence, Love from a man to a woman, Omen, Presage, Shared secrets

African Marigold (American Marigold, Aztec Marigold) [*Tagetes Erecta*]: Vulgar minds

African Violet [*Saintpaulia*]: Admiration, Delicate love connection, Faithfulness, Modesty, Protection, Spirituality, Virtue

Agaric (Fly Agaric, Toadstools) [*Amanita muscaria*]: Fertility

Ageratum (Floss Flower) [*Ageratum*]: Delay, Faithful love

Agnus Castus (Chaste Tree) [*Vitex agnus-castus*]: Fertility, Purity

Agrimony [*Agrimonia*]: Gratitude, Protection, Sleep, Thankfulness

Ague Root [*Aletris farinosa*]: Protection

Ajuga (Bugle, Bugleweed) [*Ajuga*]: Anticipation, Cheers the heart, Most lovable, Rain

Alder Tree [*Alnus*]: Arts, Creativity, Guidance, Inspiration, Music, Poetry

Alfalfa (Lucerne) [*Medicago sativa*]: Anti-hunger, Money, Prosperity

Alison, Sweet (Sweet Alice, Sweet Alyssum) [*Lobularia maritima*]: Anger management, Modesty, Perfection, Protection, "Worth beyond all beauty"

Alkanet (Dyer's Bugloss, Spanish Bugloss) [*Alkanna tinctoria* or *Anchusa*]: Prosperity, Purification

Allium [*Allium*]: Humility, Patience, Prosperity, Unity

Allspice [*Calycanthus*, *Pimenta*, or *Solenostemon amboinicus*]: Benevolence, Compassion, Healing, Luck, Money

Allspice, Carolina (Sweet Shrub) [*Calycanthus floridus*]: Benevolence, Generosity

Almond [*Prunus dulcis*]: Giddiness, Heedlessness, Hope, Imprudence, Indiscretion, Lover's charm, Money, Perfidy, Promise, Prosperity, Wisdom

Almond Blossom [*Prunus*]: Indiscretion

Almond, common [*Prunus dulcis*]: Indiscretion, Perfidy, Stupidity

Almond, flowering [*Prunus*]: Hope

Almond, laurel [*Prunus dulcis* var. *amara*]: Perfidy

Almond Tree [*Prunus dulcis*]: Concealed love, Hope, Indiscretion, Thoughtfulness, Thoughtlessness

Aloe [*Aloe vera*]: Affection, Bitterness, Dejection, Good luck, Grief, Healing, Integrity, Luck, Lust, Misplaced devotion, Protection, Religious superstition, Sorrow, Wisdom

Alstroemeria (Peruvian Lily) [*Alstroemeria*]: Devotion, Fortune, Friendship, Money, Pleasantness

Althea (Rose of Sharon) [*Hibiscus syriacus*]: Consumed by love, Delicate beauty, Fiery love, Love, Mildness, Passion, Persuasion, Protection, Sexual liberation

Althea Frutes (Syrian Mallow) [*Hibiscus syriacus*]: Consumed by love, Healing, Honesty, "I am deeply in love", Persuasion, Purity, Protection, Psychic powers

Alum Root (Coral Bells) [*Heuchera*]: Challenge, Protection

Alyssum (Madwort) [*Alyssum*]: Anger management, Excellence beyond beauty, Moderating anger, Modesty, Perfection, Protection, "Worth beyond all beauty"

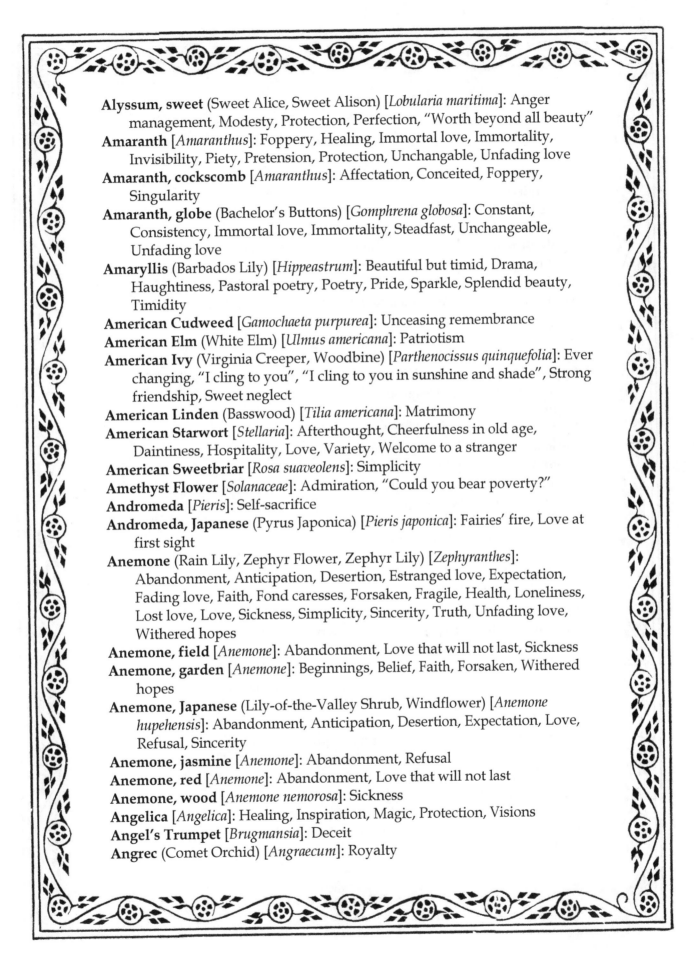

Alyssum, sweet (Sweet Alice, Sweet Alison) [*Lobularia maritima*]: Anger management, Modesty, Protection, Perfection, "Worth beyond all beauty"

Amaranth [*Amaranthus*]: Foppery, Healing, Immortal love, Immortality, Invisibility, Piety, Pretension, Protection, Unchangable, Unfading love

Amaranth, cockscomb [*Amaranthus*]: Affectation, Conceited, Foppery, Singularity

Amaranth, globe (Bachelor's Buttons) [*Gomphrena globosa*]: Constant, Consistency, Immortal love, Immortality, Steadfast, Unchangeable, Unfading love

Amaryllis (Barbados Lily) [*Hippeastrum*]: Beautiful but timid, Drama, Haughtiness, Pastoral poetry, Poetry, Pride, Sparkle, Splendid beauty, Timidity

American Cudweed [*Gamochaeta purpurea*]: Unceasing remembrance

American Elm (White Elm) [*Ulmus americana*]: Patriotism

American Ivy (Virginia Creeper, Woodbine) [*Parthenocissus quinquefolia*]: Ever changing, "I cling to you", "I cling to you in sunshine and shade", Strong friendship, Sweet neglect

American Linden (Basswood) [*Tilia americana*]: Matrimony

American Starwort [*Stellaria*]: Afterthought, Cheerfulness in old age, Daintiness, Hospitality, Love, Variety, Welcome to a stranger

American Sweetbriar [*Rosa suaveolens*]: Simplicity

Amethyst Flower [*Solanaceae*]: Admiration, "Could you bear poverty?"

Andromeda [*Pieris*]: Self-sacrifice

Andromeda, Japanese (Pyrus Japonica) [*Pieris japonica*]: Fairies' fire, Love at first sight

Anemone (Rain Lily, Zephyr Flower, Zephyr Lily) [*Zephyranthes*]: Abandonment, Anticipation, Desertion, Estranged love, Expectation, Fading love, Faith, Fond caresses, Forsaken, Fragile, Health, Loneliness, Lost love, Love, Sickness, Simplicity, Sincerity, Truth, Unfading love, Withered hopes

Anemone, field [*Anemone*]: Abandonment, Love that will not last, Sickness

Anemone, garden [*Anemone*]: Beginnings, Belief, Faith, Forsaken, Withered hopes

Anemone, Japanese (Lily-of-the-Valley Shrub, Windflower) [*Anemone hupehensis*]: Abandonment, Anticipation, Desertion, Expectation, Love, Refusal, Sincerity

Anemone, jasmine [*Anemone*]: Abandonment, Refusal

Anemone, red [*Anemone*]: Abandonment, Love that will not last

Anemone, wood [*Anemone nemorosa*]: Sickness

Angelica [*Angelica*]: Healing, Inspiration, Magic, Protection, Visions

Angel's Trumpet [*Brugmansia*]: Deceit

Angrec (Comet Orchid) [*Angraecum*]: Royalty

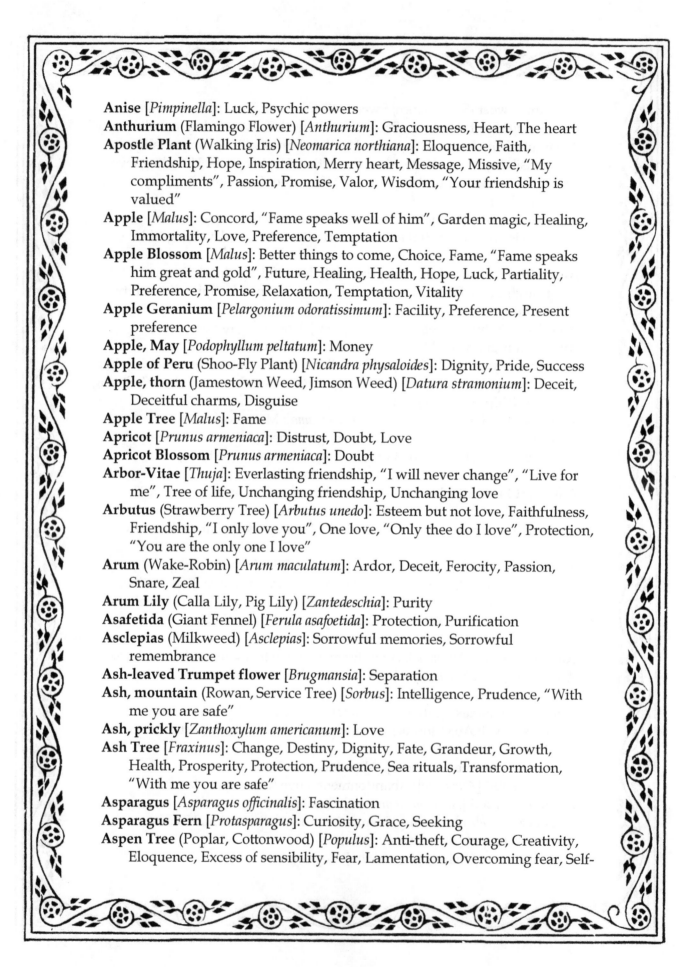

Anise [*Pimpinella*]: Luck, Psychic powers

Anthurium (Flamingo Flower) [*Anthurium*]: Graciousness, Heart, The heart

Apostle Plant (Walking Iris) [*Neomarica northiana*]: Eloquence, Faith, Friendship, Hope, Inspiration, Merry heart, Message, Missive, "My compliments", Passion, Promise, Valor, Wisdom, "Your friendship is valued"

Apple [*Malus*]: Concord, "Fame speaks well of him", Garden magic, Healing, Immortality, Love, Preference, Temptation

Apple Blossom [*Malus*]: Better things to come, Choice, Fame, "Fame speaks him great and gold", Future, Healing, Health, Hope, Luck, Partiality, Preference, Promise, Relaxation, Temptation, Vitality

Apple Geranium [*Pelargonium odoratissimum*]: Facility, Preference, Present preference

Apple, May [*Podophyllum peltatum*]: Money

Apple of Peru (Shoo-Fly Plant) [*Nicandra physaloides*]: Dignity, Pride, Success

Apple, thorn (Jamestown Weed, Jimson Weed) [*Datura stramonium*]: Deceit, Deceitful charms, Disguise

Apple Tree [*Malus*]: Fame

Apricot [*Prunus armeniaca*]: Distrust, Doubt, Love

Apricot Blossom [*Prunus armeniaca*]: Doubt

Arbor-Vitae [*Thuja*]: Everlasting friendship, "I will never change", "Live for me", Tree of life, Unchanging friendship, Unchanging love

Arbutus (Strawberry Tree) [*Arbutus unedo*]: Esteem but not love, Faithfulness, Friendship, "I only love you", One love, "Only thee do I love", Protection, "You are the only one I love"

Arum (Wake-Robin) [*Arum maculatum*]: Ardor, Deceit, Ferocity, Passion, Snare, Zeal

Arum Lily (Calla Lily, Pig Lily) [*Zantedeschia*]: Purity

Asafetida (Giant Fennel) [*Ferula asafoetida*]: Protection, Purification

Asclepias (Milkweed) [*Asclepias*]: Sorrowful memories, Sorrowful remembrance

Ash-leaved Trumpet flower [*Brugmansia*]: Separation

Ash, mountain (Rowan, Service Tree) [*Sorbus*]: Intelligence, Prudence, "With me you are safe"

Ash, prickly [*Zanthoxylum americanum*]: Love

Ash Tree [*Fraxinus*]: Change, Destiny, Dignity, Fate, Grandeur, Growth, Health, Prosperity, Protection, Prudence, Sea rituals, Transformation, "With me you are safe"

Asparagus [*Asparagus officinalis*]: Fascination

Asparagus Fern [*Protasparagus*]: Curiosity, Grace, Seeking

Aspen Tree (Poplar, Cottonwood) [*Populus*]: Anti-theft, Courage, Creativity, Eloquence, Excess of sensibility, Fear, Lamentation, Overcoming fear, Self-

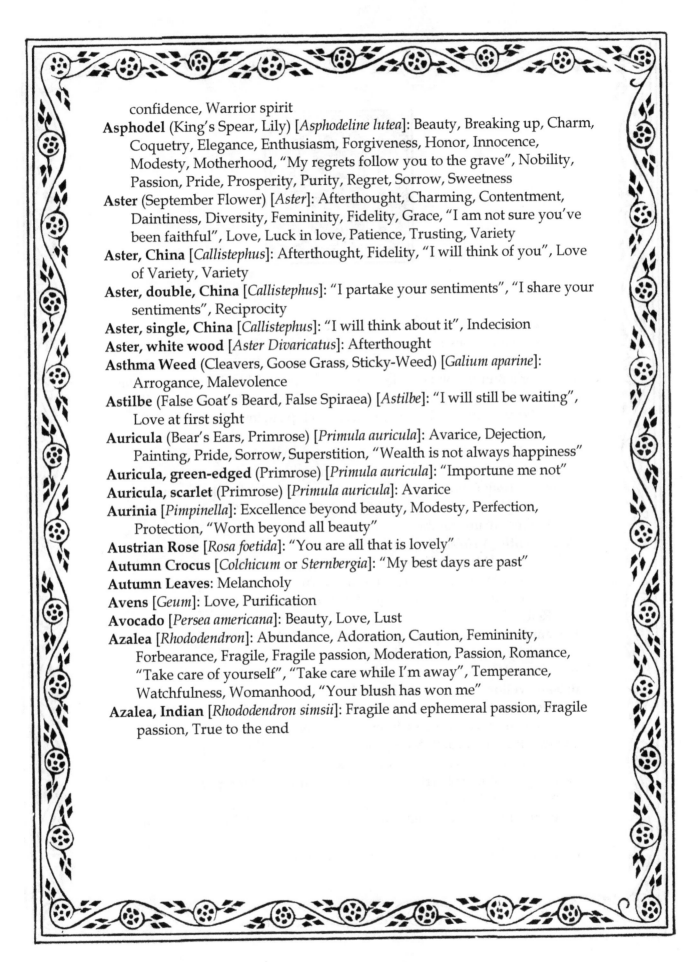

confidence, Warrior spirit

Asphodel (King's Spear, Lily) [*Asphodeline lutea*]: Beauty, Breaking up, Charm, Coquetry, Elegance, Enthusiasm, Forgiveness, Honor, Innocence, Modesty, Motherhood, "My regrets follow you to the grave", Nobility, Passion, Pride, Prosperity, Purity, Regret, Sorrow, Sweetness

Aster (September Flower) [*Aster*]: Afterthought, Charming, Contentment, Daintiness, Diversity, Femininity, Fidelity, Grace, "I am not sure you've been faithful", Love, Luck in love, Patience, Trusting, Variety

Aster, China [*Callistephus*]: Afterthought, Fidelity, "I will think of you", Love of Variety, Variety

Aster, double, China [*Callistephus*]: "I partake your sentiments", "I share your sentiments", Reciprocity

Aster, single, China [*Callistephus*]: "I will think about it", Indecision

Aster, white wood [*Aster Divaricatus*]: Afterthought

Asthma Weed (Cleavers, Goose Grass, Sticky-Weed) [*Galium aparine*]: Arrogance, Malevolence

Astilbe (False Goat's Beard, False Spiraea) [*Astilbe*]: "I will still be waiting", Love at first sight

Auricula (Bear's Ears, Primrose) [*Primula auricula*]: Avarice, Dejection, Painting, Pride, Sorrow, Superstition, "Wealth is not always happiness"

Auricula, green-edged (Primrose) [*Primula auricula*]: "Importune me not"

Auricula, scarlet (Primrose) [*Primula auricula*]: Avarice

Aurinia [*Pimpinella*]: Excellence beyond beauty, Modesty, Perfection, Protection, "Worth beyond all beauty"

Austrian Rose [*Rosa foetida*]: "You are all that is lovely"

Autumn Crocus [*Colchicum* or *Sternbergia*]: "My best days are past"

Autumn Leaves: Melancholy

Avens [*Geum*]: Love, Purification

Avocado [*Persea americana*]: Beauty, Love, Lust

Azalea [*Rhododendron*]: Abundance, Adoration, Caution, Femininity, Forbearance, Fragile, Fragile passion, Moderation, Passion, Romance, "Take care of yourself", "Take care while I'm away", Temperance, Watchfulness, Womanhood, "Your blush has won me"

Azalea, Indian [*Rhododendron simsii*]: Fragile and ephemeral passion, Fragile passion, True to the end

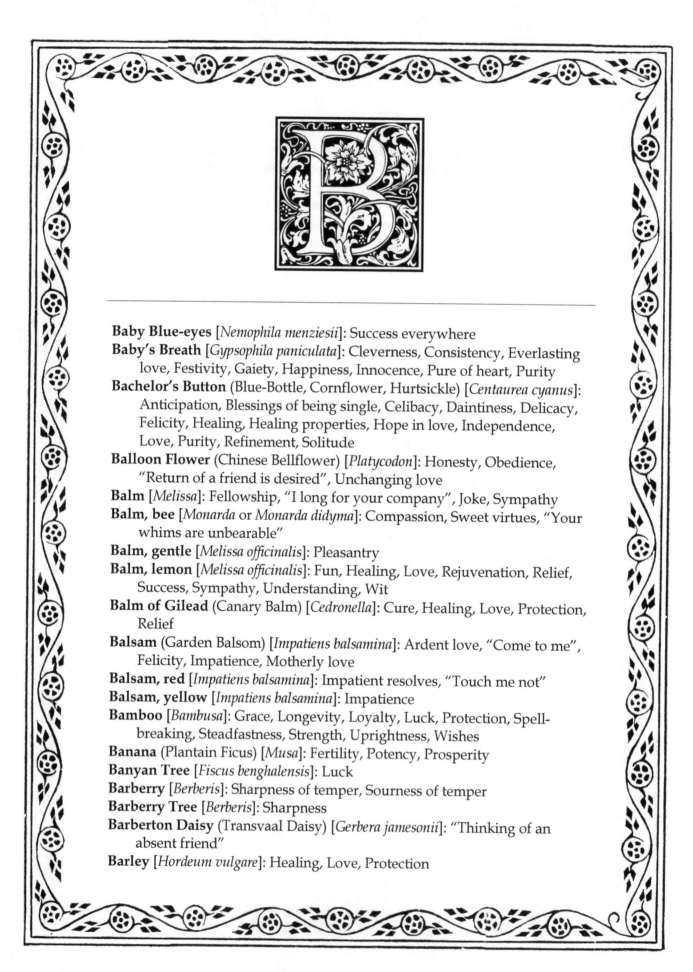

Baby Blue-eyes [*Nemophila menziesii*]: Success everywhere

Baby's Breath [*Gypsophila paniculata*]: Cleverness, Consistency, Everlasting love, Festivity, Gaiety, Happiness, Innocence, Pure of heart, Purity

Bachelor's Button (Blue-Bottle, Cornflower, Hurtsickle) [*Centaurea cyanus*]: Anticipation, Blessings of being single, Celibacy, Daintiness, Delicacy, Felicity, Healing, Healing properties, Hope in love, Independence, Love, Purity, Refinement, Solitude

Balloon Flower (Chinese Bellflower) [*Platycodon*]: Honesty, Obedience, "Return of a friend is desired", Unchanging love

Balm [*Melissa*]: Fellowship, "I long for your company", Joke, Sympathy

Balm, bee [*Monarda* or *Monarda didyma*]: Compassion, Sweet virtues, "Your whims are unbearable"

Balm, gentle [*Melissa officinalis*]: Pleasantry

Balm, lemon [*Melissa officinalis*]: Fun, Healing, Love, Rejuvenation, Relief, Success, Sympathy, Understanding, Wit

Balm of Gilead (Canary Balm) [*Cedronella*]: Cure, Healing, Love, Protection, Relief

Balsam (Garden Balsom) [*Impatiens balsamina*]: Ardent love, "Come to me", Felicity, Impatience, Motherly love

Balsam, red [*Impatiens balsamina*]: Impatient resolves, "Touch me not"

Balsam, yellow [*Impatiens balsamina*]: Impatience

Bamboo [*Bambusa*]: Grace, Longevity, Loyalty, Luck, Protection, Spell-breaking, Steadfastness, Strength, Uprightness, Wishes

Banana (Plantain Ficus) [*Musa*]: Fertility, Potency, Prosperity

Banyan Tree [*Fiscus benghalensis*]: Luck

Barberry [*Berberis*]: Sharpness of temper, Sourness of temper

Barberry Tree [*Berberis*]: Sharpness

Barberton Daisy (Transvaal Daisy) [*Gerbera jamesonii*]: "Thinking of an absent friend"

Barley [*Hordeum vulgare*]: Healing, Love, Protection

Basil [*Ocimum*]: Animosity, Best wishes, Creativity, Flying, "Give me your good wishes", Hatred, Healing, Love, Protection, Self-esteem, Wealth

Basil, sweet [*Ocimum basilicum*]: Good wishes

Basket Flower (Peruvian Daffodil) [*Hymenocallis narcissiflora*]: Anticipation, Blessings of being single, Celibacy, Independence, Solitude

Basket Lily (Spider Flower, Spider Plant) [*Hymenocallis*]: Elopement, "Elope with me", "Not as bad as I seem"

Bay (Bay Laurel, Laurel Tree, Sweet Bay) [*Laurus nobilis*]: Accomplishment, Achievement in the arts, Civil service, Courage, Creation of beauty, Glory, Glory and success, Healing, Perfidy, Personal achievement, Protection, Psychic powers, Purification, Reward of merit, Sharpness, Strength, Success

Bay Leaf [*Laurus nobilis*]: Faithfulness, Healing, "I change but in death", "No change until death", Psychic powers

Bay Wreath [*Laurus nobilis*]: Reward of merit

Bayberry (Wax Myrtle) [*Myrica cerifera*]: Discipline, Good luck, Instruction

Bean [*Phaseolus*]: Love, Poetry, Potency, Protection, Reconciliation

Bearded Crepis (Purple-Eyed Succory-Hawkweed) [*Crepis barbata*]: Protection

Bearded Iris [*Iris*]: Ardor

Beardtongue [*Penstemon*]: Creativity, Pleasure without alloy (e.g., anything debasing it)

Bear's Ears (Auricula) [*Primula suricula*]: Avarice, Dejection, Painting, Pride, Sorrow, Superstition, "Wealth is not always happiness"

Bedstraw [*Galium*]: Love, Patience

Bee Balm [*Melissa officinalis* or *Monarda didyma*]: Compassion, Sweet virtues, "Your whims are unbearable"

Beech Tree [*Fagus*]: Affluence, Lovers' tryst, Prosperity, Wishes

Beet [*Beta*]: Love

Begonia [*Begonia*]: Beware, Caution, Dark thoughts, Deep thoughts, Deformity, Fame, Fanciful nature, Long beautiful, Many interests, Popular favor, Spontaneous, "Take care while I'm away", Unrequited love, Warning

Begonia, strawberry (Mother of Thousands) [*Saxifraga stolonifera*]: Cleverness

Belladonna (Deadly Nightshade) [*Atropa belladonna*]: Astral projection, Drama, Death, Hush, Silence

Belladonna Lily (Naked Lady) [*Amaryllis belladonna*]: "Dance with me", Drama

Bellflower (Bluebell) [*Campanula*]: Acknowledgment, Aspiring, Consistency, Gratitude, Grief, Humility, "I wish to speak to you", Indiscretion, "Return of a friend is desired", Thankfulness, "Thinking of you", Warning

Bellflower, Chinese (Balloon Flower) [*Platycodon*]: Honesty, Obedience, Unchanging love

Bellflower, pyramidal [*Campanula pyramidalis*]: Constancy

Bellflower, small, white [*Campanula*]: Gratitude

Bells of Ireland (Shell Flower) [*Moluccella laevis*]: Good luck, Luck, Whimsy

Belvedere: (Summer Cypress) [*Chenopodium scoparia*]"I declare war against you"

Benzion (Benjamin Bush, Spice Bush) [*Lindera benzoin*]: Protection, Purification

Bergamot (Horsemint) [*Monarda*]: Money, "Your whims are unbearable", "Your wiles are irresistible"

Berry Wreath: Reward

Betony (Hedge Nettle, Woundwort) [*Stachys*]: Surprise

Betsy, Sweet [*Calycanthus floridus*]: Benevolence, Generosity

Bi-colored Carnation [*Dianthus caryophyllus*]: No!

Bilberry (Whortleberry) [*Vaccinium myrtillus*]: Calmness, Clarity, Communication, Peace, Treachery, Wisdom

Bindweed (Minor Convolvulus) [*Convolvulus*]: Bonds, Despondency, Eminence, Extinguished hopes, Humility, Insinuation, Inspiration, Night, Profuseness, Uncertainty

Bindweed, blue [*Convolvulus*]: Repose

Bindweed, great [*Calystegia silvatica*]: Importunity, Insinuation

Bindweed, small [*Calystegia*]: Humility

Birch Tree [*Betula*]: Beginnings, Change, Elegance, Grace, Protection, Purification

Birch Tree, Paper (Canoe Birch) [*Betula papyrifera*]: Good fortune, Meekness, Tree of mothers

Birch Tree, Weeping White [*Betula*]: Beauty

Bird of Paradise (Crane Flower) [*Strelitzia reginae*]: Faithfulness, Good perspective, Liberty, Magnificence

Bird's Nest Fern [*Asplenium australasicum* or *Aplenium nidus*]: Confidence, Magic, Shelter, Sincerity

Birdsfoot Trefoil [*Lotus corniculatus*]: Resilience, Revenge, Vengeance

Bistort [*Persicaria*]: Fertility, Psychic powers

Bittersweet [*Celastrus* or *Solanum dulcamara*]: Healing, Platonic love, Protection, Truth

Bittersweet Nightshade (Poisonus Nightshade) [*Solanum dulcamara*]: Truth

Bitterweed (Bitter Sneezeweed) [*Helenium amarum*]: Love returned, "Your love is returned"

Black Bryony [*Dioscorea communis*]: "Be my support", Helpfulness, Support

Black Cohosh (Black Snakeroot, Squawroot) [*Cimicifuga racemosa*]: Courage, Love, Potency, Protection

Black-eyed Susan (Rudbeckia) [*Rudbeckia hirta*]: Encouragement, Impartiality, Justice

Black False Hellebore [*Veratrum nigrum*]: Protection

Black Locust Tree (False Acacia) [*Robinia pseudoacacia*]: Platonic love

Black Mulberry Tree [*Morus nigra*]: "I shall not survive you"

Black Poplar Tree [*Populus nigra*]: Courage

Black Prince Geranium [*Pelargonium x domesticum*]: Delusive hopes

Black Rose [*Rosa*]: Death, Farewell, Hatred, Obsession, Rebirth

Black Samson [*Echinacea angustifolia*]: Healing

Black Snakeroot [*Actaea racemosa*]: Love, Lust, Money

Blackberry [*Rubus fruticosus*]: Dangerous pride, Envy, Healing, Money, Protection

Blackthorn (Sloe) [*Prunus spinosa*]: Adversity, Conflict, Difficulty, Pain, Separation

Bladder Nut Tree [*Staphylea*]: Amusement, Frivolity

Blanket Flower [*Gaillardia*]: Joy

Blazing Star [*Liatris*]: Enthusiasm, "I will try again"

Bleeding Heart (Lyre Flower, Venus' Car) [*Dicentra spectabilis*]: Elegance, Fidelity, "Fly with me", Love, Love attraction, Unrequited love

Blood Drops (Adonis Flos, Pheasant's Eye) [*Adonis annua*]: Sorrowful memories, Sorrowful recollections

Blood Flower (Bloedblom) [*Asclepias curassavica*]: Glory, "Let me go", Splendor

Blood Lily [*Haemanthus*]: Glory, Splendor

Bloodroot [*Sanguinaria*]: Love, Protection, Purification

Bloodweed [*Ambrosia trifida*]: Love returned, "Your love is returned"

Bloom (Chrysanthemum, Mum) [*Chrysanthemum*]: Abundance, Cheerfulness, Cheerfulness in old age, Cheerfulness under adversity, Desolate heart, Friendship, Innocence, Joviality, Joy, Long life, Loyal love, Mirth, Optimism, Protection, Restfulness, Riches, Truth, Wealth, "With love", "You are a wonderful friend"

Bloom, white [*Chrysanthemum*]: Truth

Blooming Sally (Purple Loosestrife) [*Lythrum salicaria*]: Peace, Protection

Blue Bindweed [*Convolvulus*]: Repose

Blue-bottle (Bachelor's Button, Cornflower) [*Centaurea cyanus*]: Anticipation, Blessings of being single, Celibacy, Constancy, Delicacy, Felicity, Independence, Solitude

Blue-flowered Greek Valerian [*Polemonium reptans*]: Repose

Blue Ginger (Brazilian Ginger) [*Dichorisandra thyrsiflora*]: Health, Lust, Money, Protection, Psychic powers

Blue Hyacinth [*Hyacinthus*]: Consistency, Constancy

Blue Iris [*Iris*]: Money

Blue minor Convolvulus [*Convolvulus*]: Night, Repose

Blue Periwinkle [*Vinca*]: Early attachment, Early friendship

Blue Rose [*Rosa*]: Mystery, Wistfulness

Blue Salvia (Blue Sage) [*Saliva azurea*]: "I think of you", Wisdom

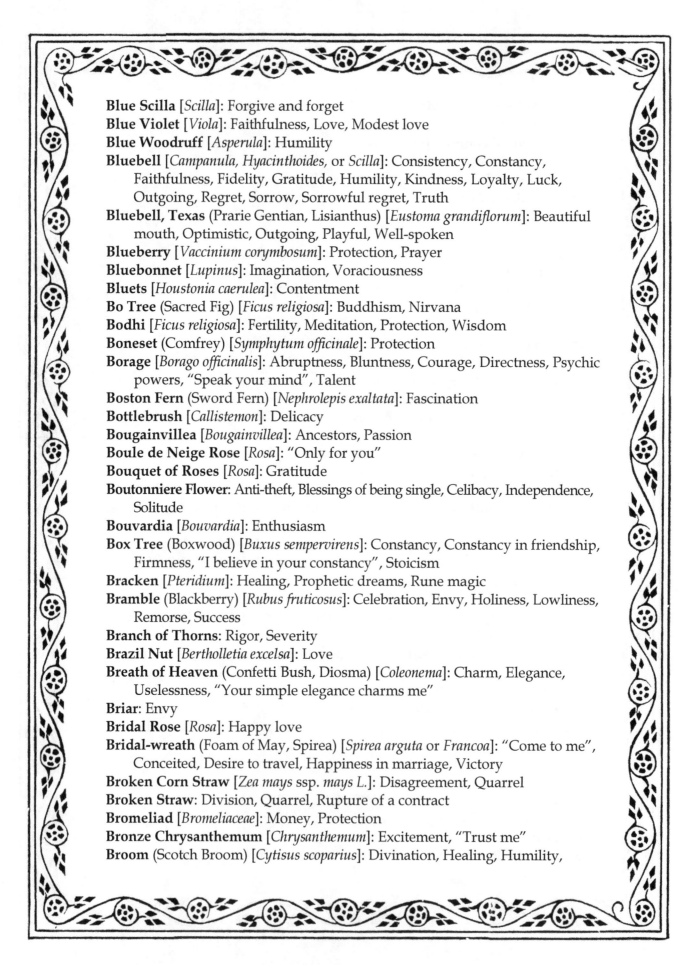

Blue Scilla [*Scilla*]: Forgive and forget

Blue Violet [*Viola*]: Faithfulness, Love, Modest love

Blue Woodruff [*Asperula*]: Humility

Bluebell [*Campanula, Hyacinthoides,* or *Scilla*]: Consistency, Constancy, Faithfulness, Fidelity, Gratitude, Humility, Kindness, Loyalty, Luck, Outgoing, Regret, Sorrow, Sorrowful regret, Truth

Bluebell, Texas (Prarie Gentian, Lisianthus) [*Eustoma grandiflorum*]: Beautiful mouth, Optimistic, Outgoing, Playful, Well-spoken

Blueberry [*Vaccinium corymbosum*]: Protection, Prayer

Bluebonnet [*Lupinus*]: Imagination, Voraciousness

Bluets [*Houstonia caerulea*]: Contentment

Bo Tree (Sacred Fig) [*Ficus religiosa*]: Buddhism, Nirvana

Bodhi [*Ficus religiosa*]: Fertility, Meditation, Protection, Wisdom

Boneset (Comfrey) [*Symphytum officinale*]: Protection

Borage [*Borago officinalis*]: Abruptness, Bluntness, Courage, Directness, Psychic powers, "Speak your mind", Talent

Boston Fern (Sword Fern) [*Nephrolepis exaltata*]: Fascination

Bottlebrush [*Callistemon*]: Delicacy

Bougainvillea [*Bougainvillea*]: Ancestors, Passion

Boule de Neige Rose [*Rosa*]: "Only for you"

Bouquet of Roses [*Rosa*]: Gratitude

Boutonniere Flower: Anti-theft, Blessings of being single, Celibacy, Independence, Solitude

Bouvardia [*Bouvardia*]: Enthusiasm

Box Tree (Boxwood) [*Buxus sempervirens*]: Constancy, Constancy in friendship, Firmness, "I believe in your constancy", Stoicism

Bracken [*Pteridium*]: Healing, Prophetic dreams, Rune magic

Bramble (Blackberry) [*Rubus fruticosus*]: Celebration, Envy, Holiness, Lowliness, Remorse, Success

Branch of Thorns: Rigor, Severity

Brazil Nut [*Bertholletia excelsa*]: Love

Breath of Heaven (Confetti Bush, Diosma) [*Coleonema*]: Charm, Elegance, Uselessness, "Your simple elegance charms me"

Briar: Envy

Bridal Rose [*Rosa*]: Happy love

Bridal-wreath (Foam of May, Spirea) [*Spirea arguta* or *Francoa*]: "Come to me", Conceited, Desire to travel, Happiness in marriage, Victory

Broken Corn Straw [*Zea mays* ssp. *mays L.*]: Disagreement, Quarrel

Broken Straw: Division, Quarrel, Rupture of a contract

Bromeliad [*Bromeliaceae*]: Money, Protection

Bronze Chrysanthemum [*Chrysanthemum*]: Excitement, "Trust me"

Broom (Scotch Broom) [*Cytisus scoparius*]: Divination, Healing, Humility,

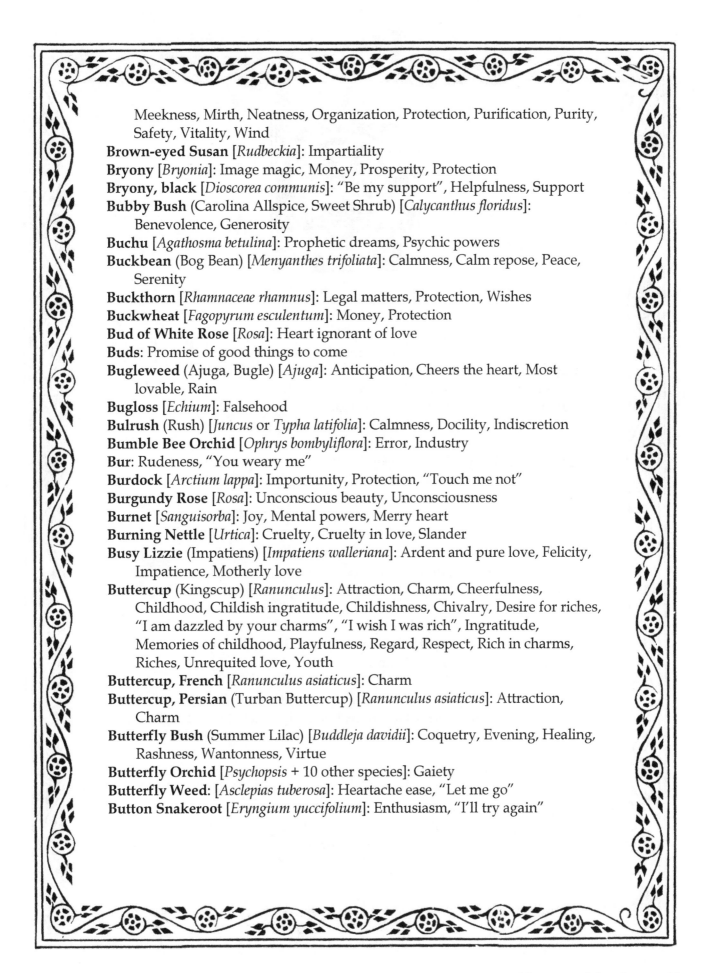

Meekness, Mirth, Neatness, Organization, Protection, Purification, Purity, Safety, Vitality, Wind

Brown-eyed Susan [*Rudbeckia*]: Impartiality

Bryony [*Bryonia*]: Image magic, Money, Prosperity, Protection

Bryony, black [*Dioscorea communis*]: "Be my support", Helpfulness, Support

Bubby Bush (Carolina Allspice, Sweet Shrub) [*Calycanthus floridus*]: Benevolence, Generosity

Buchu [*Agathosma betulina*]: Prophetic dreams, Psychic powers

Buckbean (Bog Bean) [*Menyanthes trifoliata*]: Calmness, Calm repose, Peace, Serenity

Buckthorn [*Rhamnaceae rhamnus*]: Legal matters, Protection, Wishes

Buckwheat [*Fagopyrum esculentum*]: Money, Protection

Bud of White Rose [*Rosa*]: Heart ignorant of love

Buds: Promise of good things to come

Bugleweed (Ajuga, Bugle) [*Ajuga*]: Anticipation, Cheers the heart, Most lovable, Rain

Bugloss [*Echium*]: Falsehood

Bulrush (Rush) [*Juncus* or *Typha latifolia*]: Calmness, Docility, Indiscretion

Bumble Bee Orchid [*Ophrys bombyliflora*]: Error, Industry

Bur: Rudeness, "You weary me"

Burdock [*Arctium lappa*]: Importunity, Protection, "Touch me not"

Burgundy Rose [*Rosa*]: Unconscious beauty, Unconsciousness

Burnet [*Sanguisorba*]: Joy, Mental powers, Merry heart

Burning Nettle [*Urtica*]: Cruelty, Cruelty in love, Slander

Busy Lizzie (Impatiens) [*Impatiens walleriana*]: Ardent and pure love, Felicity, Impatience, Motherly love

Buttercup (Kingscup) [*Ranunculus*]: Attraction, Charm, Cheerfulness, Childhood, Childish ingratitude, Childishness, Chivalry, Desire for riches, "I am dazzled by your charms", "I wish I was rich", Ingratitude, Memories of childhood, Playfulness, Regard, Respect, Rich in charms, Riches, Unrequited love, Youth

Buttercup, French [*Ranunculus asiaticus*]: Charm

Buttercup, Persian (Turban Buttercup) [*Ranunculus asiaticus*]: Attraction, Charm

Butterfly Bush (Summer Lilac) [*Buddleja davidii*]: Coquetry, Evening, Healing, Rashness, Wantonness, Virtue

Butterfly Orchid [*Psychopsis* + 10 other species]: Gaiety

Butterfly Weed: [*Asclepias tuberosa*]: Heartache ease, "Let me go"

Button Snakeroot [*Eryngium yuccifolium*]: Enthusiasm, "I'll try again"

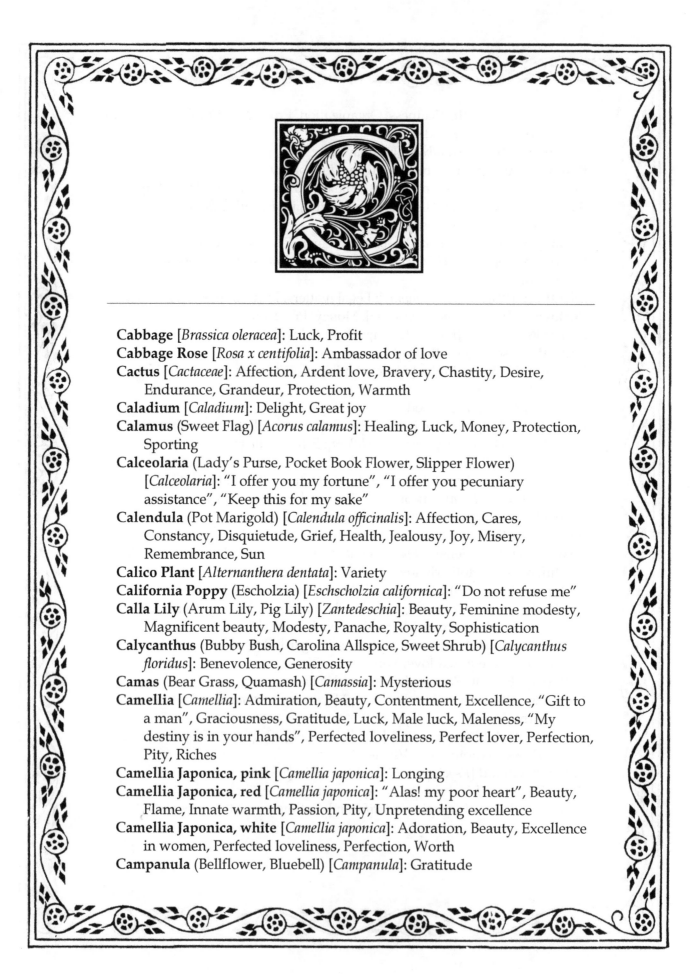

Cabbage [*Brassica oleracea*]: Luck, Profit

Cabbage Rose [*Rosa x centifolia*]: Ambassador of love

Cactus [*Cactaceae*]: Affection, Ardent love, Bravery, Chastity, Desire, Endurance, Grandeur, Protection, Warmth

Caladium [*Caladium*]: Delight, Great joy

Calamus (Sweet Flag) [*Acorus calamus*]: Healing, Luck, Money, Protection, Sporting

Calceolaria (Lady's Purse, Pocket Book Flower, Slipper Flower) [*Calceolaria*]: "I offer you my fortune", "I offer you pecuniary assistance", "Keep this for my sake"

Calendula (Pot Marigold) [*Calendula officinalis*]: Affection, Cares, Constancy, Disquietude, Grief, Health, Jealousy, Joy, Misery, Remembrance, Sun

Calico Plant [*Alternanthera dentata*]: Variety

California Poppy (Escholzia) [*Eschscholzia californica*]: "Do not refuse me"

Calla Lily (Arum Lily, Pig Lily) [*Zantedeschia*]: Beauty, Feminine modesty, Magnificent beauty, Modesty, Panache, Royalty, Sophistication

Calycanthus (Bubby Bush, Carolina Allspice, Sweet Shrub) [*Calycanthus floridus*]: Benevolence, Generosity

Camas (Bear Grass, Quamash) [*Camassia*]: Mysterious

Camellia [*Camellia*]: Admiration, Beauty, Contentment, Excellence, "Gift to a man", Graciousness, Gratitude, Luck, Male luck, Maleness, "My destiny is in your hands", Perfected loveliness, Perfect lover, Perfection, Pity, Riches

Camellia Japonica, pink [*Camellia japonica*]: Longing

Camellia Japonica, red [*Camellia japonica*]: "Alas! my poor heart", Beauty, Flame, Innate warmth, Passion, Pity, Unpretending excellence

Camellia Japonica, white [*Camellia japonica*]: Adoration, Beauty, Excellence in women, Perfected loveliness, Perfection, Worth

Campanula (Bellflower, Bluebell) [*Campanula*]: Gratitude

Campanula Pyramida [*Campanula pyramidalis*]: Aspiring

Camphor [*Cinnamomum camphora*]: Chastity, Cleansing, Divination, Health, Life direction

Campion Rose [*Rosa*]: "Dance with me", "You only deserve my love"

Canary Grass [*Phalaris canariensis*]: Cleansing, Determination, Life direction, Perseverance

Candytuft [*Iberis sempervirens*]: Architecture, Balance, Indifference

Candytuft, everflowering [*Iberis*]: Indifference

Canna Lily [*Canna*]: Great beauty

Canterbury Bells [*Campanula medium*]: Acknowledgment, Consistency, Constancy, Fascination, Gossip, Gratitude, Grief, Humility, Indiscretion, Love, Obligation, Thankfulness, Warning

Canterbury Bells, green [*Campanula medium*]: Secret followers of Oscar Wilde

Canterbury Bells, red [*Campanula medium*]: Deep romance, Passion

Cape Jasmine (Common Gardenia) [*Gardenia augusta*]: Anticipation, "I am too happy", Transport of joy

Cape Lily, red [*Crinum x powellii*]: Glory, Splendor

Cape Marigold (African Daisy) [*Dimorphotheca*]: Innocence, Love from a man to a woman, Omen, Presage, Shared secrets

Cape Myrtle [*Myrsine africana* or *Phylica*]: Eloquence

Cape Tulip [*Homeria*]: Glory, Splendor

Capers [*Capparis spinosa*]: Luck, Lust, Potency

Caraway [*Carum carvi*]: Anti-theft, Health, Infidelity prevented, Lust, Mental powers, Protection

Cardamom [*Zingiberaceae*]: Love, Lust, Paternal error

Cardinal Creeper (Ipomoea Quamoclit) [*Ipomoea horsfalliae*]: Busybody

Cardinal Flower (Scarlet Lobelia) [*Lobelia cardinalis*]: Distinction, Honor, Splendor

Carnation (Pinks) [*Dianthus*]: Admiration, Ardent and pure love, Beauty, Boldness, Bonds of love, Chivalry, Devotion, Faithfulness, Fascination, Finesse, Gallantry, Goodness, "Grant me a smile", Healing, "My heart aches for you", Perfection, Price, Protection, Pure and deep love, Scorn, Strength, Unfading beauty, Woman's love

Carnation, bi-colored [*Dianthus*]: No!

Carnation, deep red [*Dianthus*]: "Alas! for my poor heart"

Carnation, laced [*Dianthus*]: Passion

Carnation, mauve [*Dianthus*]: Dreams of fantasy

Carnation, mixed colors [*Dianthus*]: Beauty, Health and energy, Pride and beauty

Carnation, pink [*Dianthus*]: "Always on my mind", Beauty, Encouragement, Friendship, Gratitude, "I will never forget you", Lively and pure affection, Maternal affection, Pride, Remembrance, Sexual liberation, Unforgettable, Woman's love

Carnation, purple [*Dianthus*]: Capriciousness, Unreliable, Whimsical

Carnation, red [*Dianthus*]: Admiration, "Alas! my poor heart", Ardor, Beauty, Betrothal, Deep pure love, Fascination, Flame, Flashy, Innate warmth, "My heart aches for you", "My heart breaks", Passion, Pity, Pure love, Unpretending excellence

Carnation, solid-colored [*Dianthus*]: Yes!

Carnation, striped [*Dianthus*]: Extremes, "I cannot be with you", Indecision, Refusal, Rejection, "Sorry I can't be with you"

Carnation, white [*Dianthus*]: Democracy, Devotion, Endearment, "I am still available", Innocence, Living for love, Lovely, Pure and ardent love, Purity, Remembrance, Sweet and lovely, Sweetness

Carnation, yellow [*Dianthus*]: Admiration, Cheerful, Contempt, Disappointment, Disdain, Fascination, "I do not believe you", No!, Rejection, Rue, "You have disappointed me"

Carob (St. John's Bread) [*Ceratonia*]: Health, Protection

Carolina Allspice (Sweet Shrub) [*Calycanthus floridus*]: Benevolence, Generosity

Carolina Jasmine [*Gelsemium sempervirens*]: Amiability, Elegance, Gracefulness, Separation

Carolina Rose [*Rosa carolina*]: "Love is dangerous"

Carolina Syringa (Mock Orange) [*Philadelphus inodorus*]: Disappointment

Carrot [*Daucus carota* subsp. *sativus*]: Fertility, Lust

Carrot Flower [*Daucus carota* subsp. *sativus*]: "Do not refuse me"

Cascara (Bearberry) [*Rhamnus purshiana*]: Legal matters, Money, Protection

Cashew Nut [*Anacardium occidentale*]: Money

Castor Bean [*Ricinus communis*]: Protection

Catalpa Tree [*Catalpa*]: Beware of the coquette

Catchfly (Campion) [*Lychnis* or *Silene*]: Pretend to love, Snare, Unchanging friendship, Youth

Catchfly, red [*Lychnis* or *Silene*]: "I fall into a trap laid for me", Youthful love

Catchfly, white [*Lychnis* or *Silene*]: Betrayed

Catherine Wheel Pincushion [*Leucospermum*]: Glory, Splendor

Catnip (Catmint) [*Nepeta cataria*]: Beauty, Cat magic, Happiness, Love

Cattail [*Typha*]: Lust, Peace, Prosperity

Cattleya Orchid [*Cattleya*]: Mature charm, Mature grace

Cedar Leaf [*Cedrus*]: "I live for you", "Think of me"

Cedar of Lebanon [*Cedrus libani*]: Incorruptible

Cedar Tree [*Cedrus*]: Constancy, Constancy in love, Everlasting love, Healing, "I live for you", Incorruptible, Money, Protection, Purification, Strength, "Think of me"

Celandine (Swallowwort) [*Chelidonium*]: Education, Escape, Future joys, Happiness, Joys to come, Legal matters, Protection

Celandine, creeping [*Chelidonium*]: Modest genius

Celandine, lesser [*Ficaria verna*]: Joy, Joys to come

Celery [*Apium*]: Lust, Mental powers, Psychic powers

Celosia (Cockscomb, Chinese Woolflower) [*Celosia*]: Affection, Humor, Silliness, Singularity

Century Plant [*Agave americana*]: Anticipation, Celibacy, Constancy, Delicacy, Delicate, Felicity, Snake removing

Cereus, creeping [*Cereus Flagelliformis*]: Horror, Modest genius

Cereus, night-blooming [*Epiphyllum oxypetalum*]: Transient beauty

Chamomile [*Chamaemelum nobile*]: Action, Comfort, Emotional balance, Energy, Energy in adversity, Fortitude, Help against weariness, Logical functioning, Love, Meditation, Money, Patience, Physician plant, Purification, Serenity, Sleep, Sunny disposition

Champignon (Mushroom) [*Agaricus bisporus*]: Mistrust, Suspicion

Charles le Fievree Rose [*Rosa*]: "Speak low if you speak love"

Chaste Bush [*Vitex agnus-castus*]: Coldness, Indifference

Chaste Tree (Agnus castus) [*Vitex agnus-castus*]: Fertility, Purity

Checkered Fritillary (Checkered Lily, Snake's Head Fritillary) [*Fritillaria meleagris*]: Persecution

Chelone (Turtlehead) [*Chelone*]: Courage, Pleasure without alloy

Cherry [*Prunus cerasus*]: Chivalry, Divination, Good education, Good works, Insincerity, Love, Nobility, Sweetness of character

Cherry Blossom [*Prunus*]: Beauty, Education, Impermanence, Kindness, Learning, Spiritual beauty, Spirituality

Cherry Tree: [*Prunus*]: Deception, Duration, Education, Good education

Cherry Tree, white [*Prunus*]: Deception

Cherry, winter [*Withania somnifera*]: Deception

Chervil, garden [*Anthriscus cerefolium*]: Sincerity

Chestnut [*Castanea*]: Affluence, "Do me justice"

Chestnut, horse (Buckeye) [*Aesculus*]: Healing, Luxury, Money

Chestnut Tree [*Castanea*]: "Do me justice", Love, Luxury

Chickweed (Starwort) [*Stellaria*]: Assignation, Favors, Fertility, Frigidity, "Give an account of yourself", "I cling to you", Ingenious simplicity, Invisibility, Love, Removing obstacles, Rendezvous

Chickweed, mouse-eared [*Stellaria*]: Ingenious simplicity

Chicory (Radicchio) [*Cichorium intybus*]: Economy, Favors, Frigidity, Frugality, Invisibility, Removing obstacles

Chilli Pepper [*Capsicum frutescens*]: Fidelity, Love

China Aster [*Callistephus*]: Afterthought, Fidelity, "I will think of you", Love of variety, Variety

China Aster, double [*Callistephus*]: "I partake your sentiments", "I share your sentiments", Reciprocity

China Aster, single [*Callistephus*]: "I will think about it", Indecision
China Pink (Indian pink) [*Dianthus chinensis*]: Aversion
China Primrose [*Primula*]: Lasting love
China Rose (Chinese Hibiscus) [*Hibiscus rosa-sinensis*]: Beauty always new, Grace
Chinaberry [*Melia*]: Death, Love
Chinese Bellflower (Balloon Flower) [*Platycodon*]: Honesty, Obedience, Unchanging love
Chinese Chrysanthemum [*Chrysanthemum*]: Cheerfulness under adversity
Chinese Ground Orchid [*Bletilla ochracea*]: Beauty
Chinese Parsley (Cilantro, Coriander) [*Coriandrum sativum*]: Concealed merit, Healing, Health, Hidden worth, Love, "Never judge solely on appearances"
Chives [*Allium schoenoprasum*]: Courage, Protection, Strength
Christmas Rose [*Helleborus niger*]: Anxiety relief, "Relieve my anxiety", Tranquilize my anxiety"
Chrysanthemum (Bloom, Mum) [*Chrysanthemum*]: Abundance, Cheerfulness, Cheerfulness in old age, Cheerfulness under adversity, Desolate heart, Friendship, Innocence, Joy, Joviality, Long life, Loyal love, Mirth, Optimism, Protection, Restfulness, Riches, Truth, Wealth, "With love", "You are a wonderful friend"
Chrysanthemum, bronze [*Chrysanthemum*]: Excitement, "Trust me"
Chrysanthemum, Chinese [*Chrysanthemum*]: Cheerfulness under adversity
Chrysanthemum, red [*Chrysanthemum*]: "I love", "I love you", "I love you too"
Chrysanthemum, white [*Chrysanthemum*]: Remembrance, Trust, Truth
Chrysanthemum, yellow [*Chrysanthemum*]: Cheerfulness, Dejection, Secret admirer, Slighted, Slighted love
Cicely (Myrrh, Sweet Cicely) [*Myrrhis odorata*]: Gladness, Rejoices and comforts the heart, Simplicity, Sincerity
Cilantro (Chinese Parsley, Coriander) [*Coriandrum sativum*]: Concealed merit, Healing, Health, Hidden worth, Love, "Never judge solely on appearances"
Cinchona [*Rubiaceae*]: Delightful, Luck, Protection
Cineraria [*Pericallis x Hybrida*]: A star, Always delightful, Delightful, Ever bright
Cinnamon [*Cinnamomum zeylanicum*]: Beauty, Forgiveness of injuries, Healing, Love, Lust protection, "My fortune is yours", Power, Psychic powers, Spirituality
Cinquefoil [*Potentilla*]: Beloved child, Beloved daughter, Cherished, Maternal affection, Money, Prophetic dreams, Protection, Sleep
Circaea [*Ciracaea*]: Spell
Cistus (Rook Rose) [*Cistus*]: Popular favor

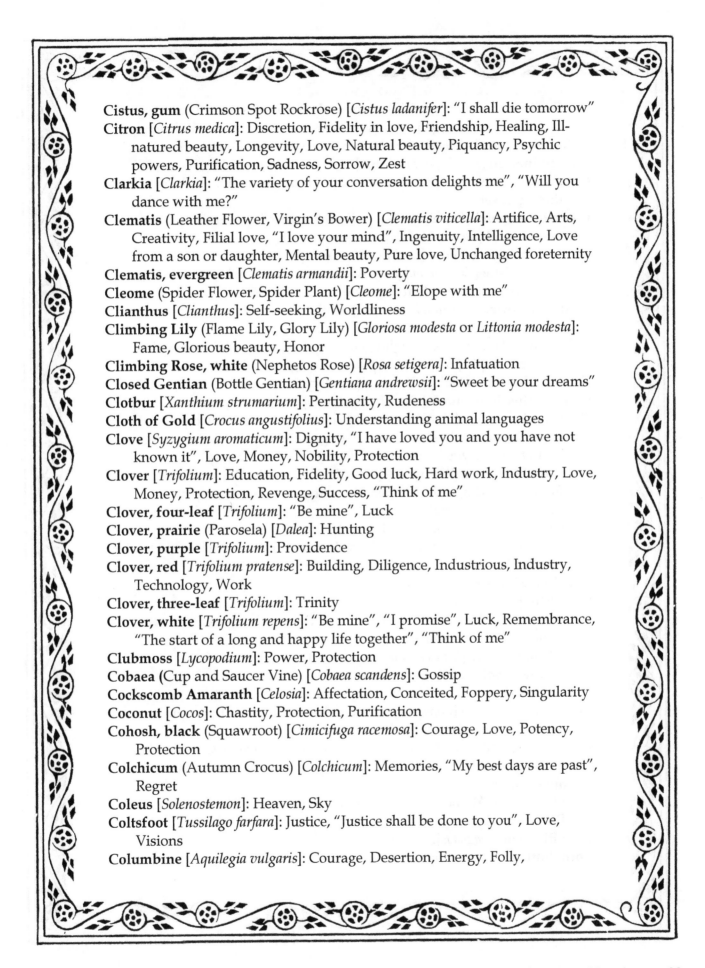

Cistus, gum (Crimson Spot Rockrose) [*Cistus ladanifer*]: "I shall die tomorrow"

Citron [*Citrus medica*]: Discretion, Fidelity in love, Friendship, Healing, Ill-natured beauty, Longevity, Love, Natural beauty, Piquancy, Psychic powers, Purification, Sadness, Sorrow, Zest

Clarkia [*Clarkia*]: "The variety of your conversation delights me", "Will you dance with me?"

Clematis (Leather Flower, Virgin's Bower) [*Clematis viticella*]: Artifice, Arts, Creativity, Filial love, "I love your mind", Ingenuity, Intelligence, Love from a son or daughter, Mental beauty, Pure love, Unchanged foreternity

Clematis, evergreen [*Clematis armandii*]: Poverty

Cleome (Spider Flower, Spider Plant) [*Cleome*]: "Elope with me"

Clianthus [*Clianthus*]: Self-seeking, Worldliness

Climbing Lily (Flame Lily, Glory Lily) [*Gloriosa modesta* or *Littonia modesta*]: Fame, Glorious beauty, Honor

Climbing Rose, white (Nephetos Rose) [*Rosa setigera*]: Infatuation

Closed Gentian (Bottle Gentian) [*Gentiana andrewsii*]: "Sweet be your dreams"

Clotbur [*Xanthium strumarium*]: Pertinacity, Rudeness

Cloth of Gold [*Crocus angustifolius*]: Understanding animal languages

Clove [*Syzygium aromaticum*]: Dignity, "I have loved you and you have not known it", Love, Money, Nobility, Protection

Clover [*Trifolium*]: Education, Fidelity, Good luck, Hard work, Industry, Love, Money, Protection, Revenge, Success, "Think of me"

Clover, four-leaf [*Trifolium*]: "Be mine", Luck

Clover, prairie (Parosela) [*Dalea*]: Hunting

Clover, purple [*Trifolium*]: Providence

Clover, red [*Trifolium pratense*]: Building, Diligence, Industrious, Industry, Technology, Work

Clover, three-leaf [*Trifolium*]: Trinity

Clover, white [*Trifolium repens*]: "Be mine", "I promise", Luck, Remembrance, "The start of a long and happy life together", "Think of me"

Clubmoss [*Lycopodium*]: Power, Protection

Cobaea (Cup and Saucer Vine) [*Cobaea scandens*]: Gossip

Cockscomb Amaranth [*Celosia*]: Affectation, Conceited, Foppery, Singularity

Coconut [*Cocos*]: Chastity, Protection, Purification

Cohosh, black (Squawroot) [*Cimicifuga racemosa*]: Courage, Love, Potency, Protection

Colchicum (Autumn Crocus) [*Colchicum*]: Memories, "My best days are past", Regret

Coleus [*Solenostemon*]: Heaven, Sky

Coltsfoot [*Tussilago farfara*]: Justice, "Justice shall be done to you", Love, Visions

Columbine [*Aquilegia vulgaris*]: Courage, Desertion, Energy, Folly,

Foolishness, Frivolous, Gifts of the Holy Spirit, Healing, "I cannot give you up", Inconstancy, Inspiration, Love, Resolved to win, Warrior spirit

Columbine, purple [*Aquilegia vulgaris*]: Resolved to win, Resolution

Columbine, red [*Aquilegia canadensis*]: Anxious and trembling, Worried

Comfrey (Boneset) [*Symphytum officinale*]: "Home sweet home", Money, Safety during travel

Common Almond [*Prunus dulcis*]: Indiscretion, Perfidy, Stupidity

Common Laurel [*Kalmia latifolia*]: Perfidy

Common Stinging Nettle [*Urtica*]: "You are spiteful"

Common Thistle [*Cirsium vulgare*]: Austerity, Grief, Harshness, Healing, Independence, Protection, Strength

Compass Flower [*Silphium laciniatum*]: Faith

Cone Fir [*Conifer*]: Order

Coneflower [*Echinacea*]: Capability, Healing, Immunity, Skill, Strength

Coneflower, purple [*Echinacea purpurea*]: Strength and health

Convolvulus [*Convolvulus*]: Bonds, Quandary, Uncertainty

Convolvulus, blue minor [*Convolvulus tricolor*]: Night, Repose

Convolvulus, major (Morning Glory) [*Ipomoea*]: Affectation, Coquetry, Dead hope, Departure, Despondency, Extinguished hopes, Gladness, Glorious beauty, "I love you", Insincerity, Transience, Uncertainty

Convolvulus, minor (Bindweed) [*Convolvulus*]: Bonds, Despondency, Eminence, Extinguished hopes, Humility, Insinuation, Inspiration, Night, Profuseness, Uncertainty

Convolvulus, night [*Convolvulus*]: Night

Convolvulus, pink [*Convolvulus*]: "Worth sustained by judicious and tender affection"

Copal Tree [*Burseraceae*]: Love, Purification

Coppertip [*Crocosmia*]: "Wishes come true"

Coral Bells [*Heuchera sanguinea*]: Challenge, Dainty pleasures, Hard work, Protection, Scholarship

Coral Honeysuckle [*Lonicera sempervirens*]: "The color of my fate"

Coral Rose [*Rosa*]: Desire, Enthusiasm

Corchorus [*Malvaceae Grewioideae*]: Impatient of absence, Return quickly

Coreopsis (Tickseed) [*Coreopsis*]: Always cheerful, Cheerful, Happiness, Joy

Coreopsis Arkansa [*Coreopsis*]: Love at first sight

Coriander (Chinese Parsley, Cilantro) [*Coriandrum sativum*]: Concealed merit, Healing, Health, Hidden worth, Love, "Never judge solely on appearances"

Corn [*Zea mays*]: Abundance, Divination, Gift of Mother Nature, Luck, Protection, Riches

Corn Blossom [*Zea mays*]: Riches

Corn Bottle [*Zea mays*]: Delicacy

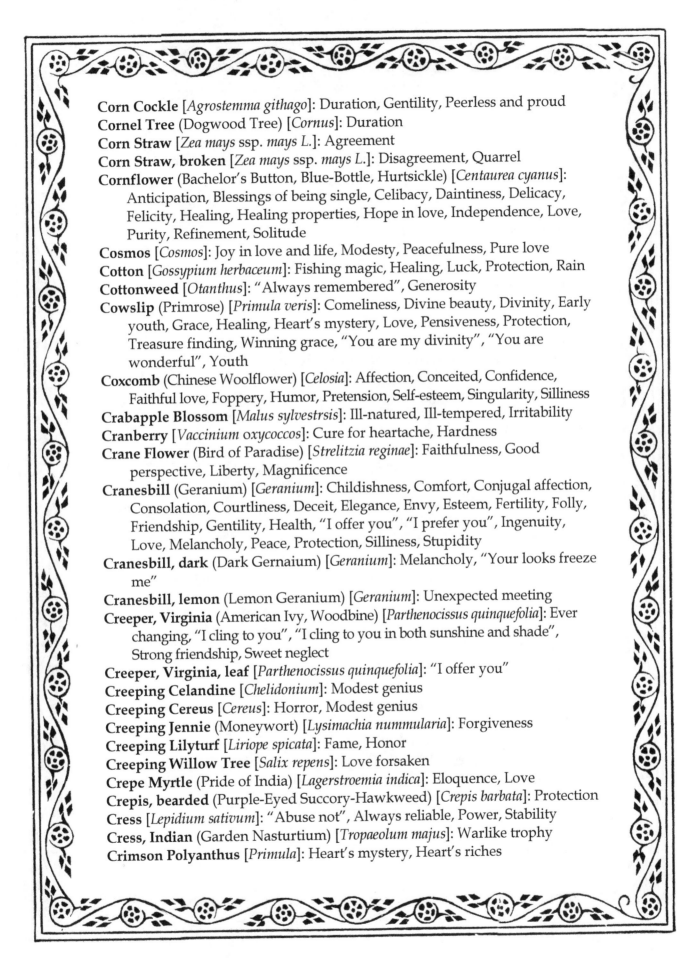

Corn Cockle [*Agrostemma githago*]: Duration, Gentility, Peerless and proud

Cornel Tree (Dogwood Tree) [*Cornus*]: Duration

Corn Straw [*Zea mays* ssp. *mays L.*]: Agreement

Corn Straw, broken [*Zea mays* ssp. *mays L.*]: Disagreement, Quarrel

Cornflower (Bachelor's Button, Blue-Bottle, Hurtsickle) [*Centaurea cyanus*]: Anticipation, Blessings of being single, Celibacy, Daintiness, Delicacy, Felicity, Healing, Healing properties, Hope in love, Independence, Love, Purity, Refinement, Solitude

Cosmos [*Cosmos*]: Joy in love and life, Modesty, Peacefulness, Pure love

Cotton [*Gossypium herbaceum*]: Fishing magic, Healing, Luck, Protection, Rain

Cottonweed [*Otanthus*]: "Always remembered", Generosity

Cowslip (Primrose) [*Primula veris*]: Comeliness, Divine beauty, Divinity, Early youth, Grace, Healing, Heart's mystery, Love, Pensiveness, Protection, Treasure finding, Winning grace, "You are my divinity", "You are wonderful", Youth

Coxcomb (Chinese Woolflower) [*Celosia*]: Affection, Conceited, Confidence, Faithful love, Foppery, Humor, Pretension, Self-esteem, Singularity, Silliness

Crabapple Blossom [*Malus sylvestrsis*]: Ill-natured, Ill-tempered, Irritability

Cranberry [*Vaccinium oxycoccos*]: Cure for heartache, Hardness

Crane Flower (Bird of Paradise) [*Strelitzia reginae*]: Faithfulness, Good perspective, Liberty, Magnificence

Cranesbill (Geranium) [*Geranium*]: Childishness, Comfort, Conjugal affection, Consolation, Courtliness, Deceit, Elegance, Envy, Esteem, Fertility, Folly, Friendship, Gentility, Health, "I offer you", "I prefer you", Ingenuity, Love, Melancholy, Peace, Protection, Silliness, Stupidity

Cranesbill, dark (Dark Gernaium) [*Geranium*]: Melancholy, "Your looks freeze me"

Cranesbill, lemon (Lemon Geranium) [*Geranium*]: Unexpected meeting

Creeper, Virginia (American Ivy, Woodbine) [*Parthenocissus quinquefolia*]: Ever changing, "I cling to you", "I cling to you in both sunshine and shade", Strong friendship, Sweet neglect

Creeper, Virginia, leaf [*Parthenocissus quinquefolia*]: "I offer you"

Creeping Celandine [*Chelidonium*]: Modest genius

Creeping Cereus [*Cereus*]: Horror, Modest genius

Creeping Jennie (Moneywort) [*Lysimachia nummularia*]: Forgiveness

Creeping Lilyturf [*Liriope spicata*]: Fame, Honor

Creeping Willow Tree [*Salix repens*]: Love forsaken

Crepe Myrtle (Pride of India) [*Lagerstroemia indica*]: Eloquence, Love

Crepis, bearded (Purple-Eyed Succory-Hawkweed) [*Crepis barbata*]: Protection

Cress [*Lepidium sativum*]: "Abuse not", Always reliable, Power, Stability

Cress, Indian (Garden Nasturtium) [*Tropaeolum majus*]: Warlike trophy

Crimson Polyanthus [*Primula*]: Heart's mystery, Heart's riches

Crimson Poppy [*Papaver*]: Fantasy

Crocosmia [*Crocosmia*]: "Wishes come true"

Crocus [*Crocus*]: "Abuse not", Attachment, Cheerfulness, Exuberance, Foresight, Gladness, Jovial, Joy, Love, Mirth, Pleasure of hope, Visions, Youthful gladness

Crocus, autumn [*Colchicum* or *Sternbergia*]: "My best days are past"

Crocus, saffron [*Crocus sativus*]: Mirth

Crocus, spring [*Crocus*]: Youthful gladness

Croton [*Codiaeum variegatum*]: Faithful

Crown Imperial [*Fritillaria imperialis*]: Arrogance, Majesty, Power, Pride of birth

Crown of Roses [*Rosa*]: Reward of virtue

Crown Vetch [*Coronilla varia*]: Success, "Success to you"

Crowsbill (Airplant) [*Tillandsia*]: Envy

Crowsfoot [*Diphasiastrum digitatum*]: Ingratitude, Luster

Crowsfoot, aconite-leaved [*Diphasiastrum digitatum*]: Luster

Cuckoo Flower (Lady's Smock) [*Cardamine pratensis*]: Acceptance, Ardor, Fertility, Grounding, Lover, Paternal error, Protection, Tolerance

Cucumber [*Cucumis sativus*]: Chastity, Criticism, Fertility, Healing

Cudweed, American [*Gamochaeta purpurea*]: Unceasing remembrance

Cumin [*Cuminum cyminum*]: Happiness, Peace, Protection

Cup-and-Saucer Vine (Cobaea) [*Cobaea scandens*]: Gossip

Cupid's Bower (Hot Water Plant) [*Achimenes*]: Suffer from cold

Currant [*Ribes*]: Heals conflict, Joy, Peace, Relaxation, Serenity, "You please all", "Your frown will kill me"

Curry [*Murraya koenigii*]: Protection

Cuscuta [*Cuscuteae*]: Meanness

Cushion Spurge (Euphorbia, Spurge) [*Euphorbia polychroma*]: Persistence, Protection, Purification, Welcome

Cyclamen [*Cyclamen*]: Diffidence, Endings, Farewell, Fertility, Good-bye, Happiness, "I understand you", Lust, Modesty, Protection, Resignation, Timid hope

Cyclamen, red [*Cyclamen*]: "I will not economize"

Cyclamen, white [*Cyclamen*]: Warmth of heart

Cymbidium Orchid [*Cymbidium*]: Beauty, Love, Luxury, Magnificence, Scholarship

Cypress, Summer (Belvedere) [*Bassia scoparia*]: "I declare war against you"

Cypress Tree [*Cupressus*]: Death, Deceit, Despair, Healing, Longevity, Mourning, Protection, Regard, Unrequited love, Vanity, Without hope

Cypress Tree and Marigold [*Cupressus and Tagetes*]: Despair, Great despair

Cypress Tree, Irish [*Cupressus*]: Death

Cypress Tree, Italian [*Cupressus sempervirens*]: Death

Czar Violet (Sweet violet) [*Viola odorata*]: Kindness, Kindness and worth, Worth

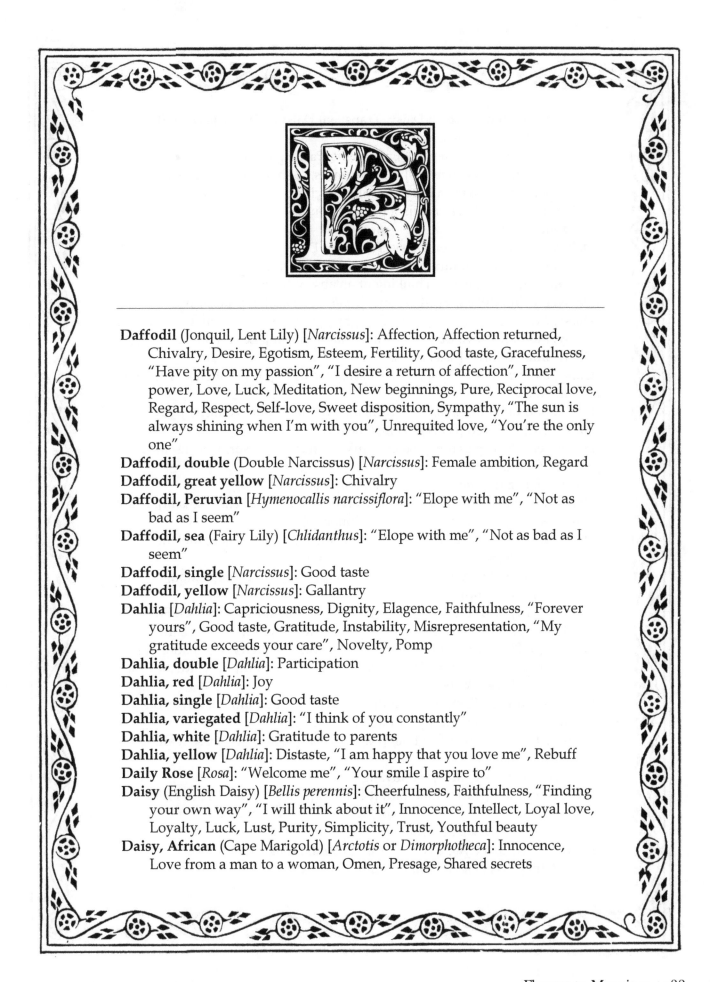

Daffodil (Jonquil, Lent Lily) [*Narcissus*]: Affection, Affection returned, Chivalry, Desire, Egotism, Esteem, Fertility, Good taste, Gracefulness, "Have pity on my passion", "I desire a return of affection", Inner power, Love, Luck, Meditation, New beginnings, Pure, Reciprocal love, Regard, Respect, Self-love, Sweet disposition, Sympathy, "The sun is always shining when I'm with you", Unrequited love, "You're the only one"

Daffodil, double (Double Narcissus) [*Narcissus*]: Female ambition, Regard

Daffodil, great yellow [*Narcissus*]: Chivalry

Daffodil, Peruvian [*Hymenocallis narcissiflora*]: "Elope with me", "Not as bad as I seem"

Daffodil, sea (Fairy Lily) [*Chlidanthus*]: "Elope with me", "Not as bad as I seem"

Daffodil, single [*Narcissus*]: Good taste

Daffodil, yellow [*Narcissus*]: Gallantry

Dahlia [*Dahlia*]: Capriciousness, Dignity, Elagence, Faithfulness, "Forever yours", Good taste, Gratitude, Instability, Misrepresentation, "My gratitude exceeds your care", Novelty, Pomp

Dahlia, double [*Dahlia*]: Participation

Dahlia, red [*Dahlia*]: Joy

Dahlia, single [*Dahlia*]: Good taste

Dahlia, variegated [*Dahlia*]: "I think of you constantly"

Dahlia, white [*Dahlia*]: Gratitude to parents

Dahlia, yellow [*Dahlia*]: Distaste, "I am happy that you love me", Rebuff

Daily Rose [*Rosa*]: "Welcome me", "Your smile I aspire to"

Daisy (English Daisy) [*Bellis perennis*]: Cheerfulness, Faithfulness, "Finding your own way", "I will think about it", Innocence, Intellect, Loyal love, Loyalty, Luck, Lust, Purity, Simplicity, Trust, Youthful beauty

Daisy, African (Cape Marigold) [*Arctotis* or *Dimorphotheca*]: Innocence, Love from a man to a woman, Omen, Presage, Shared secrets

Daisy, barberton (Gerbera Daisy, Transvaal Daisy) [*Gerbera jamesonii*]: "Thinking of an absent friend"

Daisy, double [*Bellis perennis*]: Enjoyment, Participation

Daisy, English [*Bellis perennis*]: Cheerfulness, "I share your sentiments", Innocence, Newborn baby, Popular oracle, Simplicity

Daisy, garden [*Bellis perennis*]: "I partake your sentiments", "I share your sentiments"

Daisy, gerbera (Barberton Daisy, Transvaal Daisy) [*Gerbera jamisonii*]: Beauty, Cheerfulness, Enduring purity, Friendship, Innocence, Needing protection, Sadness, "Thinking of an absent friend"

Daisy, gloriosa (Black-Eyed Susans) [*Rudbeckia hirta*]: Impartiality

Daisy, Michaelmas [*Aster*]: Afterthought, Daintiness, Farewell, Love, Variety

Daisy, moon (Ox-Eye Daisy) [*Leucanthemum vulgare*]: Love's oracle

Daisy, multicolored [*Asteraceae*]: Beauty

Daisy, ox-eye (Moon Daisy) [*Leucanthemum vulgare*]: Joy, Patience, Token of affection

Daisy, painted [*Chrysanthemum carinatum* or *Tanacetum coccineum*]: Joy

Daisy, parti-colored [*Bellis perennis*]: Beauty

Daisy, red [Bellis perennis]: Beauty unknown to possessor, Unconscious, Uselessness

Daisy, Shasta [*Leucanthemum x superbum*]: Patience

Daisy, Transvaal (Barberton Daisy, Gerbera Daisy) [*Gerbera jamesonii*]: Beauty

Daisy, white [*Bellis perennis*]: Beauty, Innocence

Daisy, wild [*Bellis perennis*]: "I will think about it", Indecision, Melancholy

Daisy, wreath [*Bellis perennis*]: "I will think about it"

Damask Rose [*Rosa x damascena*]: Bashful love, Brilliant complexion, Freshness, Youth

Dame's Gillyflower (Dame's Rocket, Dame's Violet, Dame's Wort, Sweet Rocket) [*Hesperis matronalis*]: Coquetry, Evening, Virtue, Watchfulness

Dandelion [*Taraxacum officinale*]: Calling spirits, Coquetry, Divination, Energy, Faithfulness, Flirting, Happiness, Lover's oracle, Prophecy, Rustic oracle, Stress release, Wishes

Daphne [*Daphne*]: Fame, Gilding the Lily, Glory, "I would not have you otherwise", Immortality, Ornament, Tolerance

Daphne Odora (Winter Daphne) [*Daphne odora*]: Desire to please, Painting the Lily, Sweetness

Dark crimson Rose [*Rosa*]: Mourning

Dark Geranium (Dark Cranesbill) [*Geranium*]: Melancholy, "Your looks freeze me"

Dark red Rose [*Rosa*]: Mourning

Darnel (Perennial Ryegrass, Ray-grass) [*Lolium temulentum*]: Vice

Date Palm [*Phoenix dactylifera*]: Fertility, Potency

Datura (Devil's Trumpet) [*Datura*]: Deceitful charms, Protection, Separation, Sleep

Daylily [*Hemerocallis*]: Breaking up, Coquetry, Enthusiasm, Flirting, Loss of what could have been, Motherhood

Dead leaves: Melancholy, Sadness, Sorrow

Deep pink Rose [*Rosa*]: "Thank you"

Deep red Carnation [*Dianthus caryophyllus*]: "Alas! for my poor heart"

Deep red Rose [*Rosa*]: Bashfulness, Bashful shame

Deer's Tongue [*Erythronium albidum*]: Lust, Protection

Delphinium [*Delphinium*]: Airy, Ardent attachment, Beauty, Boldness, Fickleness, Flights of fancy, Fun, Gaiety, Haughtiness, Humor, Inner beauty, Levity, Magnanimous, Playfulness, "Return of a friend is desired", Sweetness of character, Well-being

Devil's Bit [*Chamaelirium luteum*]: Love, Lust, Protection

Devil's Cucumber (Jimson Weed, Jamestownweed, Common Thorn Apple) [*Datura stramonium*]: Deceit

Devil's Potato [*Echites umbellata*]: Be warned in time

Devil's Shoestring (Dodder) [*Cuscuta*]: Employment, Gambling, Luck, Power, Protection

Devil's Trumpet [*Datura*]: Deceit

Dew Plant [*Aptenia cordifolia*]: "A serenade"

Dianthus (Carnation, Pinks) [*Dianthus*]: Admiration, Affection, Aversion, Beauty, Boldness, Chivalry, Devotion, Faithfulness, Fascination, Finesse, Gallantry, "Grant me a smile", Make haste, "My heart aches for you", Perfection, Pride, Pure affection, Pure and deep love, Scorn, Woman's love

Dianthus, white [*Dianthus*]: Talent

Digitalis (Foxglove) [*Digitalis*]: Charm, Decisions, Healing, Healing and charm, Hypocrisy, Insincerity, Protection, Stateliness, Wishes, Youth, "You are false"

Dill [*Anethum*]: Irresistible, Luck, Lust, Money, Protection, Soothing

Diosma (Breath of Heaven, Confetti Bush) [*Coleonema*]: Charm, Elegance, Uselessness, "Your simple elegance charms me"

Dittany of Crete [*Origanum dictamnus*]: Astral projection, Birth, Divination, Manifestations, Passion

Dittany, white (Burning Bush, Gas Plant) [*Dictamnus albus*]: Passion

Dock (Sorrel) [*Rumex*]: Endurance, Fertility, Healing, Money, Patience

Dodder (Devil's Shoestring) [*Cuscuta*]: Baseness, Divination, Knot magic, Love

Dodder of Thyme [*Thymus vulgaris*]: Baseness, Meanness

Dogbane (Apocynum) [*Apocynum cannabinum*]: Deceit, Divination, Durability, Falsehood, Figment, "I doubt you"

Dog Fennel [*Eupatorium capillifolium*]: Action, Energy

Dog Rose [*Rosa canina*]: Mixed feelings, Pleasure and pain
Dogwood, flowering [*Cornus*]: Durability, Love undiminished by adversity
Dogwood Tree (Cornel Tree) [*Cornus*]: "Am I indifferent to you?", Constancy, Crucifixion, Durability, Faith, Faithfulness, Indifferent, Loveliness, Protection, Steadfastness, Success, Wishes
Double China Aster [*Callistephus*]: "I partake your sentiments", "I share your sentiments", Reciprocity
Double Daffodil [*Narcissus*]: Female ambition, Regard
Double Dahlia [*Dahlia*]: Participation
Double Daisy [*Bellis perennis*]: Enjoyment, Participation
Double Indian Pink [*Dianthus chinensis*]: Always lovely
Double Narcissus (Double Daffodil) [*Narcissus*]: Female ambition, Regard
Double red Pink [*Dianthus*]: Pure and ardent love
Dracaena [*Dracaena*]: Inner power
Dragon Plant (Stink Lily, Dragon Lily) [*Dracunculus vulgaris*]: Dread, Snare
Dragon Root (Jack in the Pulpit) [*Arisaema dracontium*]: Ardor
Dragon's Blood [*Croton*]: Love, Potency, Protection
Dragonwort (Tarragon) [*Artemisia dracunculus*]: Ardor, Astonishment, Horror
Dried Flax [*Linum*]: Industry, Utility
Dried white Rose [*Rosa*]: "Death preferable to loss of innocence"
Dundee Rambler Rose [*Rosa*]: "Only deserve my love"
Dusty Miller [*Artemisia stelleriana, Centaurea cineraria, Lychnis coronaria, Senecio cineraria, Senecio viravira,* or *Tanacetum ptarmiciflorum*]: Delicacy, Felicity, Happiness, Industriousness, Venerable
Dutchman's Breeches [*Dicentra cucullaria*]: Elegance, Fidelity, Love, Love attraction
Dwarf Morning Glory [*Convolvulus tricolor*]: Bonds of affection
Dwarf Sunflower [*Helianthus annuus*]: Adoration, Infatuation

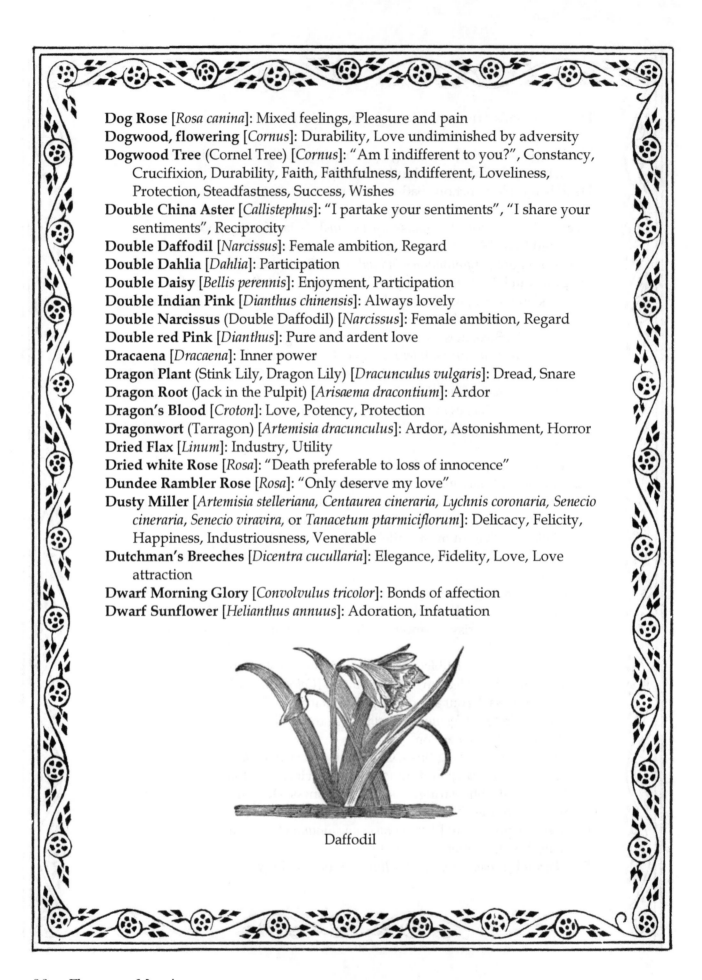

Daffodil

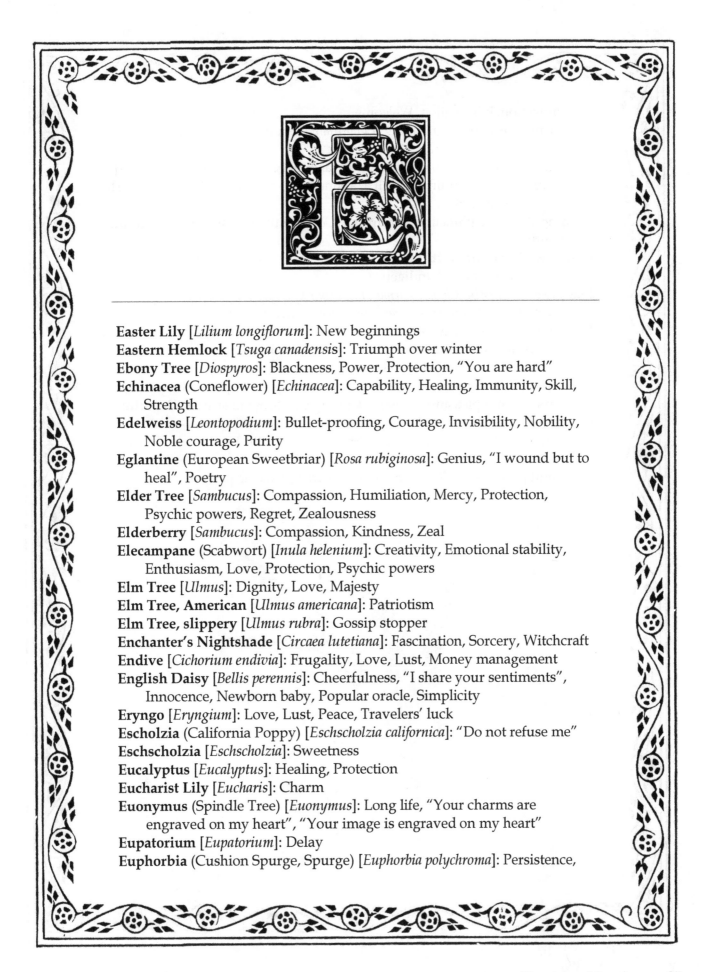

Easter Lily [*Lilium longiflorum*]: New beginnings

Eastern Hemlock [*Tsuga canadensis*]: Triumph over winter

Ebony Tree [*Diospyros*]: Blackness, Power, Protection, "You are hard"

Echinacea (Coneflower) [*Echinacea*]: Capability, Healing, Immunity, Skill, Strength

Edelweiss [*Leontopodium*]: Bullet-proofing, Courage, Invisibility, Nobility, Noble courage, Purity

Eglantine (European Sweetbriar) [*Rosa rubiginosa*]: Genius, "I wound but to heal", Poetry

Elder Tree [*Sambucus*]: Compassion, Humiliation, Mercy, Protection, Psychic powers, Regret, Zealousness

Elderberry [*Sambucus*]: Compassion, Kindness, Zeal

Elecampane (Scabwort) [*Inula helenium*]: Creativity, Emotional stability, Enthusiasm, Love, Protection, Psychic powers

Elm Tree [*Ulmus*]: Dignity, Love, Majesty

Elm Tree, American [*Ulmus americana*]: Patriotism

Elm Tree, slippery [*Ulmus rubra*]: Gossip stopper

Enchanter's Nightshade [*Circaea lutetiana*]: Fascination, Sorcery, Witchcraft

Endive [*Cichorium endivia*]: Frugality, Love, Lust, Money management

English Daisy [*Bellis perennis*]: Cheerfulness, "I share your sentiments", Innocence, Newborn baby, Popular oracle, Simplicity

Eryngo [*Eryngium*]: Love, Lust, Peace, Travelers' luck

Escholzia (California Poppy) [*Eschscholzia californica*]: "Do not refuse me"

Eschscholzia [*Eschscholzia*]: Sweetness

Eucalyptus [*Eucalyptus*]: Healing, Protection

Eucharist Lily [*Eucharis*]: Charm

Euonymus (Spindle Tree) [*Euonymus*]: Long life, "Your charms are engraved on my heart", "Your image is engraved on my heart"

Eupatorium [*Eupatorium*]: Delay

Euphorbia (Cushion Spurge, Spurge) [*Euphorbia polychroma*]: Persistence,

Protection, Purification, Welcome

European Sweetbriar (Eglantine) [*Eglantine*]: Genius, "I wound but to heal", Poetry

Eustoma (Lisianthus, Prairie Gentian, Texas Bluebell) [*Eustoma grandiflorum*]: Appreciation, Beautiful mouth, Calmness, Optimistic, Outgoing, Playful, Showy, Well-spoken

Evening Primrose (Suncups, Sundrops) [*Oenothera*]: Inconstancy, Unfaithful, Youth

Everflowering Candytuft [*Iberis Sempervirens*]: Indifference

Evergreen [*Sempervirens*]: Indigence

Evergreen Clematis [*Clematis armandii*]: Poverty

Evergreen Thorn [*Crataegus oxyacantha*]: Solace in adversity

Everlasting (Paper Daisy, Strawflower) [*Helichrysum*]: "Always remembered", Cheerfulness under adversity, Eternity, "I think of you", Immortality, Memories, Never-ceasing remembrance, Remembrance

Everlasting Pea (Perennial Pea) [*Lathyrus latifolius*]: An appointed meeting, Bliss, Blissful pleasure, Chastity, Courage, Delicate pleasures, Departure, Friendship, Good-bye, Lasting pleasure, "Let's meet", Never-ceasing remembrance, "Remember me", Shyness, Strength, Tenderness, "Thank you for a good time"

Eyebright [*Euphrasia*]: Cheer up, Mental powers, Psychic powers

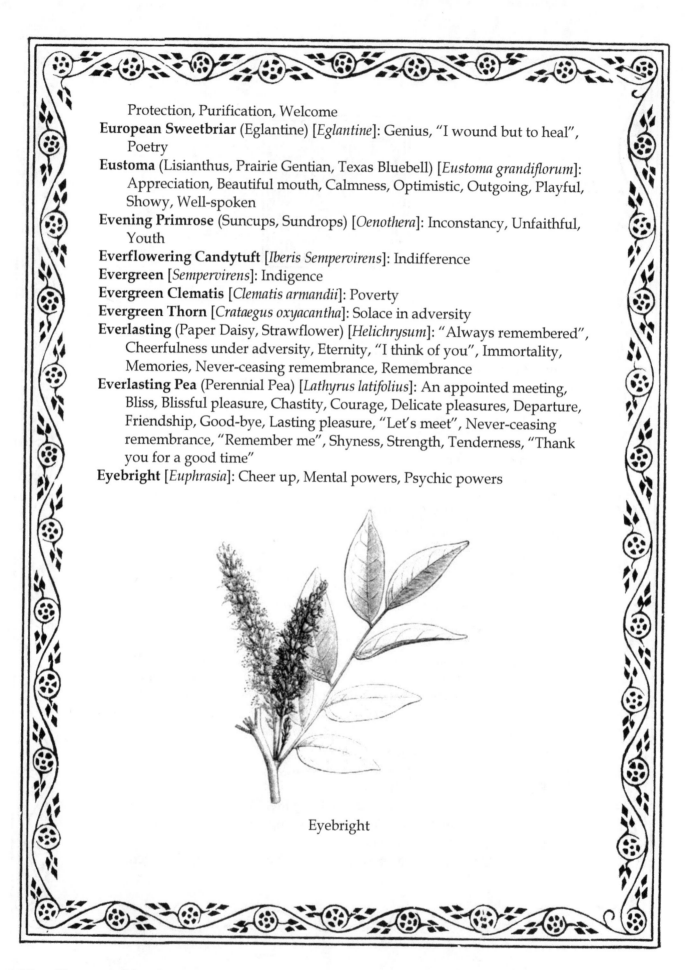

Eyebright

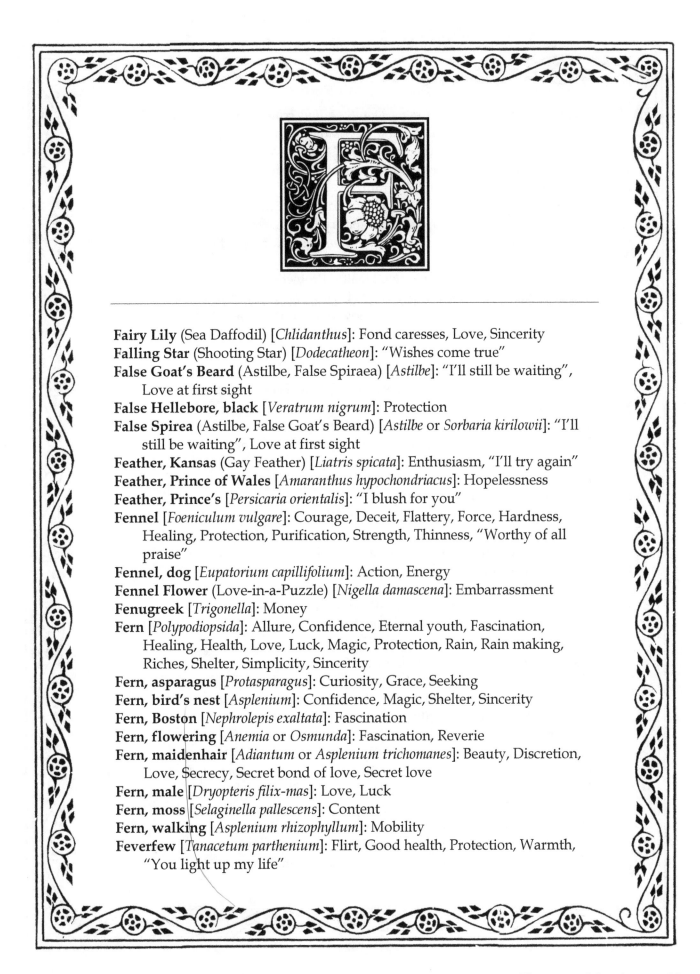

Fairy Lily (Sea Daffodil) [*Chlidanthus*]: Fond caresses, Love, Sincerity

Falling Star (Shooting Star) [*Dodecatheon*]: "Wishes come true"

False Goat's Beard (Astilbe, False Spiraea) [*Astilbe*]: "I'll still be waiting", Love at first sight

False Hellebore, black [*Veratrum nigrum*]: Protection

False Spirea (Astilbe, False Goat's Beard) [*Astilbe* or *Sorbaria kirilowii*]: "I'll still be waiting", Love at first sight

Feather, Kansas (Gay Feather) [*Liatris spicata*]: Enthusiasm, "I'll try again"

Feather, Prince of Wales [*Amaranthus hypochondriacus*]: Hopelessness

Feather, Prince's [*Persicaria orientalis*]: "I blush for you"

Fennel [*Foeniculum vulgare*]: Courage, Deceit, Flattery, Force, Hardness, Healing, Protection, Purification, Strength, Thinness, "Worthy of all praise"

Fennel, dog [*Eupatorium capillifolium*]: Action, Energy

Fennel Flower (Love-in-a-Puzzle) [*Nigella damascena*]: Embarrassment

Fenugreek [*Trigonella*]: Money

Fern [*Polypodiopsida*]: Allure, Confidence, Eternal youth, Fascination, Healing, Health, Love, Luck, Magic, Protection, Rain, Rain making, Riches, Shelter, Simplicity, Sincerity

Fern, asparagus [*Protasparagus*]: Curiosity, Grace, Seeking

Fern, bird's nest [*Asplenium*]: Confidence, Magic, Shelter, Sincerity

Fern, Boston [*Nephrolepis exaltata*]: Fascination

Fern, flowering [*Anemia* or *Osmunda*]: Fascination, Reverie

Fern, maidenhair [*Adiantum* or *Asplenium trichomanes*]: Beauty, Discretion, Love, Secrecy, Secret bond of love, Secret love

Fern, male [*Dryopteris filix-mas*]: Love, Luck

Fern, moss [*Selaginella pallescens*]: Content

Fern, walking [*Asplenium rhizophyllum*]: Mobility

Feverfew [*Tanacetum parthenium*]: Flirt, Good health, Protection, Warmth, "You light up my life"

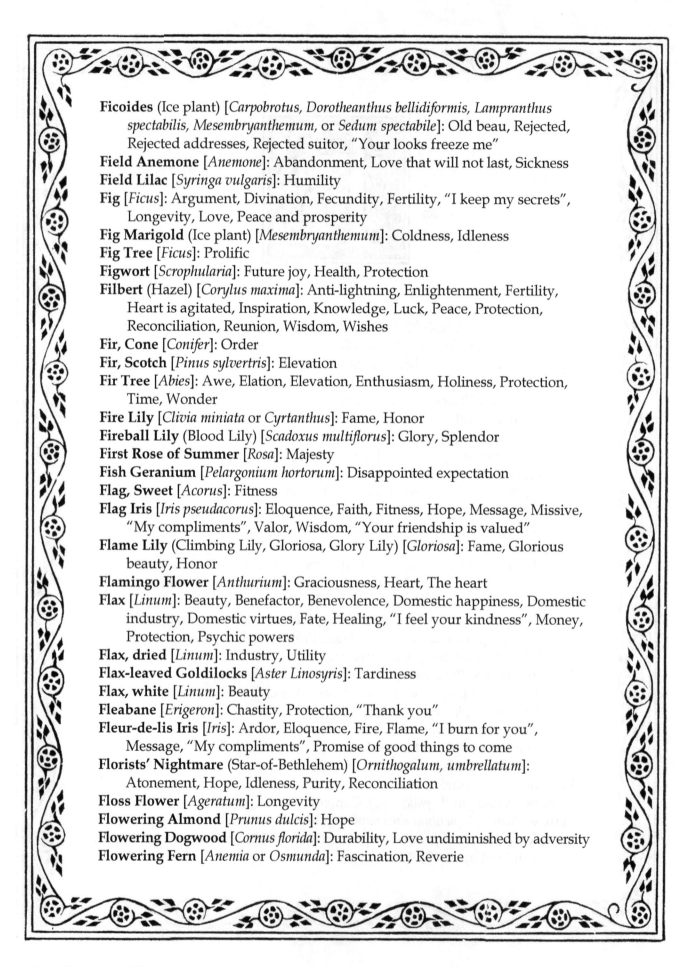

Ficoides (Ice plant) [*Carpobrotus, Dorotheanthus bellidiformis, Lampranthus spectabilis, Mesembryanthemum,* or *Sedum spectabile*]: Old beau, Rejected, Rejected addresses, Rejected suitor, "Your looks freeze me"

Field Anemone [*Anemone*]: Abandonment, Love that will not last, Sickness

Field Lilac [*Syringa vulgaris*]: Humility

Fig [*Ficus*]: Argument, Divination, Fecundity, Fertility, "I keep my secrets", Longevity, Love, Peace and prosperity

Fig Marigold (Ice plant) [*Mesembryanthemum*]: Coldness, Idleness

Fig Tree [*Ficus*]: Prolific

Figwort [*Scrophularia*]: Future joy, Health, Protection

Filbert (Hazel) [*Corylus maxima*]: Anti-lightning, Enlightenment, Fertility, Heart is agitated, Inspiration, Knowledge, Luck, Peace, Protection, Reconciliation, Reunion, Wisdom, Wishes

Fir, Cone [*Conifer*]: Order

Fir, Scotch [*Pinus sylvertris*]: Elevation

Fir Tree [*Abies*]: Awe, Elation, Elevation, Enthusiasm, Holiness, Protection, Time, Wonder

Fire Lily [*Clivia miniata* or *Cyrtanthus*]: Fame, Honor

Fireball Lily (Blood Lily) [*Scadoxus multiflorus*]: Glory, Splendor

First Rose of Summer [*Rosa*]: Majesty

Fish Geranium [*Pelargonium hortorum*]: Disappointed expectation

Flag, Sweet [*Acorus*]: Fitness

Flag Iris [*Iris pseudacorus*]: Eloquence, Faith, Fitness, Hope, Message, Missive, "My compliments", Valor, Wisdom, "Your friendship is valued"

Flame Lily (Climbing Lily, Gloriosa, Glory Lily) [*Gloriosa*]: Fame, Glorious beauty, Honor

Flamingo Flower [*Anthurium*]: Graciousness, Heart, The heart

Flax [*Linum*]: Beauty, Benefactor, Benevolence, Domestic happiness, Domestic industry, Domestic virtues, Fate, Healing, "I feel your kindness", Money, Protection, Psychic powers

Flax, dried [*Linum*]: Industry, Utility

Flax-leaved Goldilocks [*Aster Linosyris*]: Tardiness

Flax, white [*Linum*]: Beauty

Fleabane [*Erigeron*]: Chastity, Protection, "Thank you"

Fleur-de-lis Iris [*Iris*]: Ardor, Eloquence, Fire, Flame, "I burn for you", Message, "My compliments", Promise of good things to come

Florists' Nightmare (Star-of-Bethlehem) [*Ornithogalum, umbrellatum*]: Atonement, Hope, Idleness, Purity, Reconciliation

Floss Flower [*Ageratum*]: Longevity

Flowering Almond [*Prunus dulcis*]: Hope

Flowering Dogwood [*Cornus florida*]: Durability, Love undiminished by adversity

Flowering Fern [*Anemia* or *Osmunda*]: Fascination, Reverie

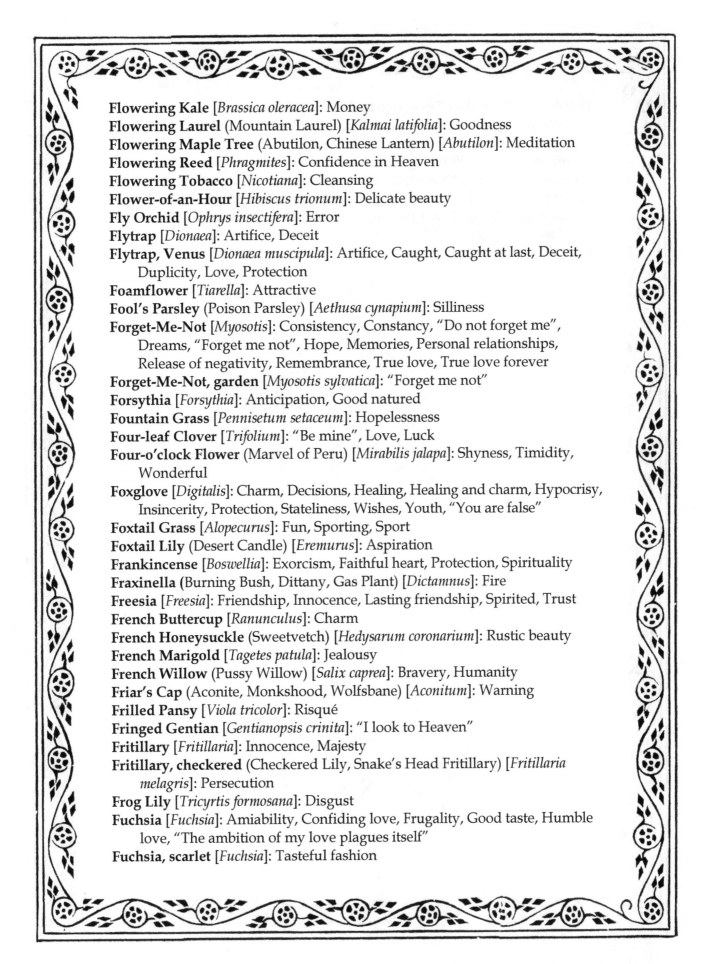

Flowering Kale [*Brassica oleracea*]: Money

Flowering Laurel (Mountain Laurel) [*Kalmai latifolia*]: Goodness

Flowering Maple Tree (Abutilon, Chinese Lantern) [*Abutilon*]: Meditation

Flowering Reed [*Phragmites*]: Confidence in Heaven

Flowering Tobacco [*Nicotiana*]: Cleansing

Flower-of-an-Hour [*Hibiscus trionum*]: Delicate beauty

Fly Orchid [*Ophrys insectifera*]: Error

Flytrap [*Dionaea*]: Artifice, Deceit

Flytrap, Venus [*Dionaea muscipula*]: Artifice, Caught, Caught at last, Deceit, Duplicity, Love, Protection

Foamflower [*Tiarella*]: Attractive

Fool's Parsley (Poison Parsley) [*Aethusa cynapium*]: Silliness

Forget-Me-Not [*Myosotis*]: Consistency, Constancy, "Do not forget me", Dreams, "Forget me not", Hope, Memories, Personal relationships, Release of negativity, Remembrance, True love, True love forever

Forget-Me-Not, garden [*Myosotis sylvatica*]: "Forget me not"

Forsythia [*Forsythia*]: Anticipation, Good natured

Fountain Grass [*Pennisetum setaceum*]: Hopelessness

Four-leaf Clover [*Trifolium*]: "Be mine", Love, Luck

Four-o'clock Flower (Marvel of Peru) [*Mirabilis jalapa*]: Shyness, Timidity, Wonderful

Foxglove [*Digitalis*]: Charm, Decisions, Healing, Healing and charm, Hypocrisy, Insincerity, Protection, Stateliness, Wishes, Youth, "You are false"

Foxtail Grass [*Alopecurus*]: Fun, Sporting, Sport

Foxtail Lily (Desert Candle) [*Eremurus*]: Aspiration

Frankincense [*Boswellia*]: Exorcism, Faithful heart, Protection, Spirituality

Fraxinella (Burning Bush, Dittany, Gas Plant) [*Dictamnus*]: Fire

Freesia [*Freesia*]: Friendship, Innocence, Lasting friendship, Spirited, Trust

French Buttercup [*Ranunculus*]: Charm

French Honeysuckle (Sweetvetch) [*Hedysarum coronarium*]: Rustic beauty

French Marigold [*Tagetes patula*]: Jealousy

French Willow (Pussy Willow) [*Salix caprea*]: Bravery, Humanity

Friar's Cap (Aconite, Monkshood, Wolfsbane) [*Aconitum*]: Warning

Frilled Pansy [*Viola tricolor*]: Risqué

Fringed Gentian [*Gentianopsis crinita*]: "I look to Heaven"

Fritillary [*Fritillaria*]: Innocence, Majesty

Fritillary, checkered (Checkered Lily, Snake's Head Fritillary) [*Fritillaria melagris*]: Persecution

Frog Lily [*Tricyrtis formosana*]: Disgust

Fuchsia [*Fuchsia*]: Amiability, Confiding love, Frugality, Good taste, Humble love, "The ambition of my love plagues itself"

Fuchsia, scarlet [*Fuchsia*]: Tasteful fashion

Full-blown Rose placed over two buds [*Rosa*]: Secrecy

Fuller's Teasel [*Dipsacus sativus*]: Importunity, Misanthropy

Fuller's Thistle [*Cirsium vulgare*]: Misanthropy

Fumitory [*Fumaria officinalis*]: Exorcism, Hatred, Money, Spleen

Fungus [*Eulcaryotic*]: Disgust, Loneliness, Resilience, Solitude

Furze (Gorse) [*Ulex europaeus*]: Affection, Anger, Attraction, Enduring affection, General love, Health, Ire, Love for all seasons, Lust, Money, Passion, Protection, Vitality

Fuzzy Weed [*Artemisia dracunculoides*]: Hunting, Love

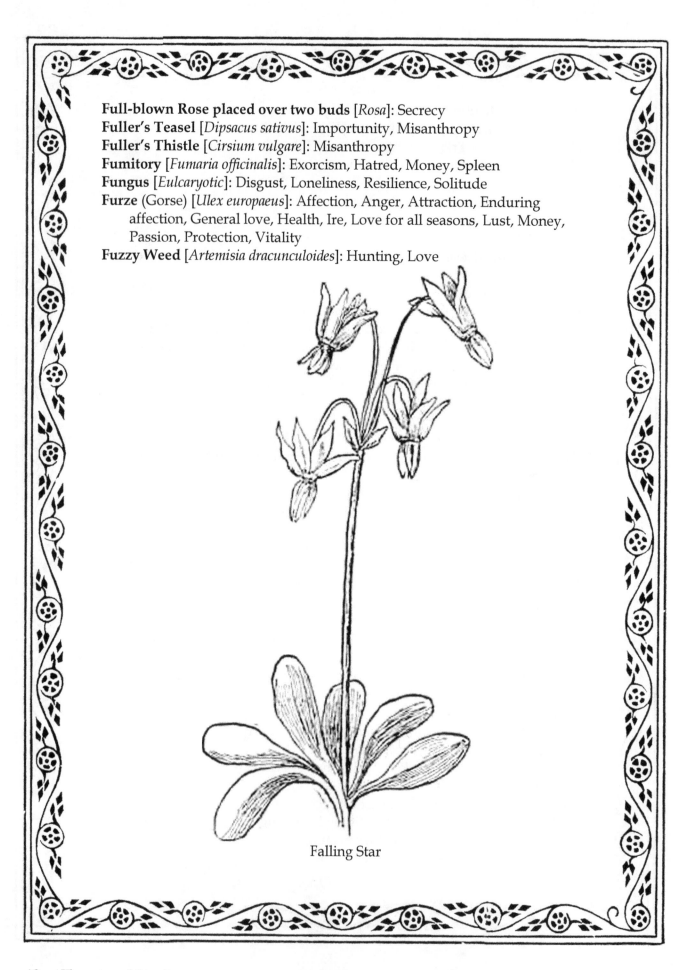

Falling Star

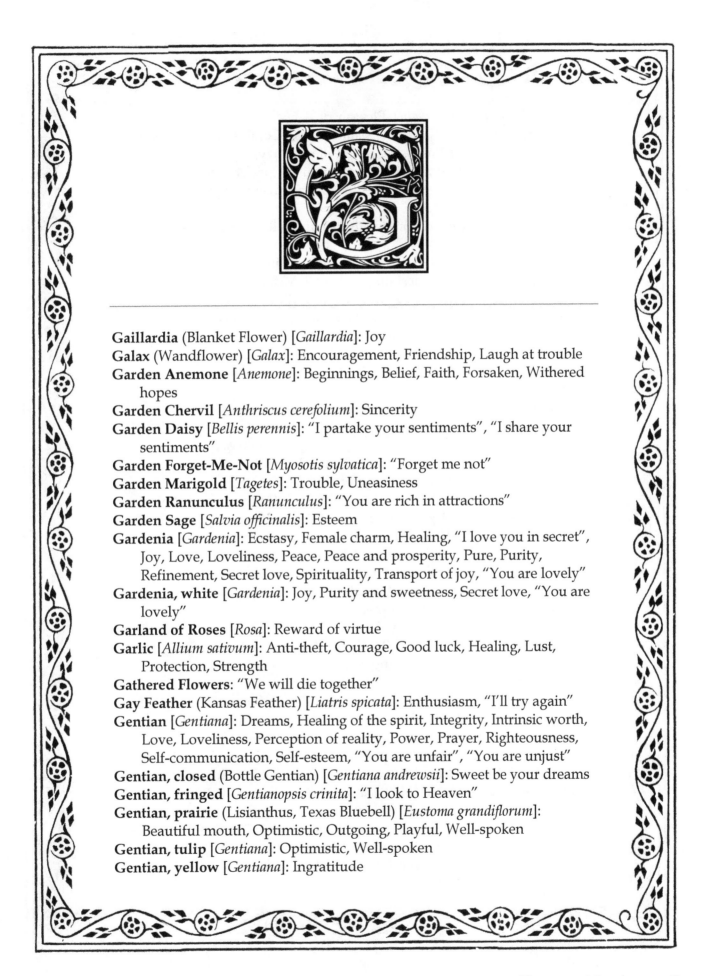

Gaillardia (Blanket Flower) [*Gaillardia*]: Joy

Galax (Wandflower) [*Galax*]: Encouragement, Friendship, Laugh at trouble

Garden Anemone [*Anemone*]: Beginnings, Belief, Faith, Forsaken, Withered hopes

Garden Chervil [*Anthriscus cerefolium*]: Sincerity

Garden Daisy [*Bellis perennis*]: "I partake your sentiments", "I share your sentiments"

Garden Forget-Me-Not [*Myosotis sylvatica*]: "Forget me not"

Garden Marigold [*Tagetes*]: Trouble, Uneasiness

Garden Ranunculus [*Ranunculus*]: "You are rich in attractions"

Garden Sage [*Salvia officinalis*]: Esteem

Gardenia [*Gardenia*]: Ecstasy, Female charm, Healing, "I love you in secret", Joy, Love, Loveliness, Peace, Peace and prosperity, Pure, Purity, Refinement, Secret love, Spirituality, Transport of joy, "You are lovely"

Gardenia, white [*Gardenia*]: Joy, Purity and sweetness, Secret love, "You are lovely"

Garland of Roses [*Rosa*]: Reward of virtue

Garlic [*Allium sativum*]: Anti-theft, Courage, Good luck, Healing, Lust, Protection, Strength

Gathered Flowers: "We will die together"

Gay Feather (Kansas Feather) [*Liatris spicata*]: Enthusiasm, "I'll try again"

Gentian [*Gentiana*]: Dreams, Healing of the spirit, Integrity, Intrinsic worth, Love, Loveliness, Perception of reality, Power, Prayer, Righteousness, Self-communication, Self-esteem, "You are unfair", "You are unjust"

Gentian, closed (Bottle Gentian) [*Gentiana andrewsii*]: Sweet be your dreams

Gentian, fringed [*Gentianopsis crinita*]: "I look to Heaven"

Gentian, prairie (Lisianthus, Texas Bluebell) [*Eustoma grandiflorum*]: Beautiful mouth, Optimistic, Outgoing, Playful, Well-spoken

Gentian, tulip [*Gentiana*]: Optimistic, Well-spoken

Gentian, yellow [*Gentiana*]: Ingratitude

Gentle Balm [*Melissa officinalis*]: Pleasantry

Geranium (Cranesbill) [*Geranium*]: Childishness, Comfort, Conjugal affection, Consolation, Courtliness, Deceit, Elegance, Envy, Esteem, Fertility, Folly, Friendship, Gentility, Health, "I offer you", "I prefer you", Ingenuity, Love, Melancholy, Peace, Protection, Silliness, Stupidity, Unexpected meeting

Geranium, apple [*Pelargonium odoratissimum*]: Facility, Preference, Present preference

Geranium, Black Prince [*Pelargonium x domesticum*]: Delusive hopes

Geranium, dark (Dark Cranesbill) [*Geranium*]: Melancholy, "Your looks freeze me"

Geranium, fish [*Pelargonium hortorum*]: Disappointed expectation

Geranium, ivy [*Pelargonium peltatum*]: Bridal favor, "Your hand for the next dance"

Geranium, lemon (Lemon Cranesbill) [*Pelargonium crispum*]: Unexpected meeting

Geranium, nutmeg [*Pelargonium fragrans*]: Expected meeting

Geranium, oak-leaf [*Pelargonium quercifolium*]: Deign to smile, Lady, True friendship

Geranium, pencil-leaf [*Pelargonium*]: Genius, Ingenuity

Geranium, pink [*Pelargonium*]: "I prefer you", Preference

Geranium, rose-scented [*Pelargonium graveolens*]: "I prefer you", Preference

Geranium, scarlet [*Pelargonium*]: Comfort, Silliness, Stupidity

Geranium, silver-leaf [*Pelargonium*]: Recall, Retrospection

Geranium, variegated [*Pelargonium*]: Charms of women

Geranium, white [*Pelargonium*]: Gracefulness, Refinement

Geranium, wild [*Pelargonium*]: Availability, Constancy, Envy, "I desire to please", Steadfast, Steadfast piety

Gerbera Daisy (Barberton Daisy, Transvaal Daisy) [*Gerbera jamesonii*]: Beauty, Cheerfulness, Enduring purity, Friendship, Innocence, Needing protection, Sadness, "Thinking of an absent friend"

Germander Speedwell [*Teucrium*]: Facility

German Iris [*Iris germanica*]: Aflame, Flame, "I burn for you"

Gillyflower (Stock) [*Matthiola*]: Bonds of affection, Enduring beauty, Faithfulness, Lasting beauty, Promptness, "You are fair"

Gillyflower, Dame's (Dame's Rocket, Dame's Violet, Dame's Wort, Sweet Rocket) [*Hesperis matronalis*]: Coquetry, Evening, Watchfulness, Virtue

Gillyflower, night-scented [*Matthiola longipetala*]: Coquetry, Evening, Virtue

Gillyflower, Rogue's [*Hesperis matronalis*]: Coquetry, Evening, Virtue

Ginger [*Zingiber officinale*]: Comforting, Love, Money, Pleasant, Power, Pride, Safe, Strength, Success, Warming, Wishes

Ginger, blue (Brazilian Ginger) [*Dichorisandra thyrsiflora*]: Health, Lust,

Money, Protection, Psychic powers

Ginkgo Tree (Maidenhair Tree) [*Ginkgo biloba*]: Fond memories

Ginseng [*Panax*]: Beauty, Healing, Love, Lust, Protection, Wishes

Gladiolus (Abyssinian Sword Lily, Peacock Flower) [*Gladiolus callianthus*]: Character, Courage, Flower of the gladiators, Generosity, "Give me a break", "I'm really sincere", Love at first sight, Natural grace, Purity, Ready armed, Sincerity, Strength of character, Sweetness, "You pierce my heart"

Glasswort (Salicornia) [*Salicornia*]: Pretension

Glastum (Woad) [*Isatis tinctoria*]: Modesty

Globe Amaranth [*Gomphrena globosa*]: Constant, Constancy, Immortal love, Immortality, Steadfast, Unchangeable, Unfading love

Globe Ranunculus [*Trollius*]: "I am dazzled by your charms"

Globeflower (Trollius) [*Trollius*]: Generosity, Gratitude, Solitude

Glorie de Dijon Rose [*Rosa*]: Growing old, Old age, Winter

Gloriosa (Climbing Lily, Flame Lily, Glory Lily) [*Gloriosa*]: Fame, Glorious beauty, Honor

Gloriosa Daisy (Black-eyed Susan) [*Rudbeckia hirta*]: Impartiality

Glory Lily (Climbing Lily, Flame Lily, Gloriosa) [*Gloriosa*]: Fame, Glorious beauty, Honor

Gloxinia [*Sinningia speciosa*]: "A proud spirit", Love at first sight

Goat's Beard, false (Astilbe, False Spiraea) [*Astilbe*]: "I'll still be waiting"

Goat's Rue [*Galega*]: Healing, Health, Reason

Gold Rose [*Rosa*]: Absolute achievement, Achievement

Golden Chain Tree [*Laburnum*]: Pensive beauty

Goldenrod (Solidago) [*Solidago*]: "Be cautious", Careful encouragement, Divination, Divine guidance, Encouragement, Good fortune, Money, Precaution, Success, Support, Warning, "You will succeed"

Goldenseal [*Hydrastis canadensis*]: Healing, Money

Gooseberry [*Ribes uva-crispa*]: Anticipation, Ease, Energy, Enjoyment, Expectation, Goodness, Peace, Protection, Relaxation

Goosefoot (Arrowhead Vine) [*Syngonium podophyllum*]: Goodness

Gooseneck (Japanese Loosestrife) [*Lysimachia clethroides*]: Peace, Protection

Gooseneck Loosestrife [*Lythrum*]: Forgiveness

Gorse (Furze) [*Ulex europaeus*]: Affection, Anger, Attraction, Enduring affection, General love, Health, Ire, Love for all seasons, Lust, Money, Passion, Protection, Vitality

Gotu-Kola (Indian Pennywort) [*Centella asiatica*]: Meditation

Gourd [*Cucumis* or *Cucurbita*]: Bulk, Extent, Protection, Spirituality

Grain [*Poaceae*]: Plenty, Protection

Grains of Paradise (Grass of Paradise) [*Aframomum melegueta*]: Love, Luck, Lust, Money, Wishes

Grape [*Vitis*]: Abandonment, Carousing, Domestic happiness, Fertility,

Garden magic, Intoxication, Mental powers, Money, Plenty, Prosperity

Grape Hyacinth [*Muscari*]: Encouragement, Engagement, Romantic love, Unobtrusive loveliness

Grape, Oregon (Holly Grape) [*Mahonia aquifolium*]: Money, Prosperity

Grapevine [*Vitis*]: Abundance, Intoxication

Grape, wild [*Vitis vinifera* subsp. *Sylvestris vitis californica*]: Charity, Mirth

Grass [*Poaceae*]: Fleeting life, Humility, Protection, Psychic powers, Submission, Utility

Grass of Paradise (Grains of Paradise) [*Aframomum melegueta*]: Love

Grass Pea [*Lathyrus nissolia* or *Lathyrus sativus*]: Bliss, Blissful pleasure, Chastity, Courage, Delicate pleasures, Departure, Friendship, Good-bye, "Let's meet", "Remember me", Shyness, Strength, Tenderness, "Thank you for a good time"

Grass, purple [*Enneapogon desvauxii*]: Sport

Great Bindweed [*Calystegia silvatica*]: Importunity, Insinuation

Greek Valerian, blue-flowered [*Polemonium reptans*]: Rupture

Green Canterbury Bells [*Campanula medium*]: Secret followers of Oscar Wilde

Green-edged Auricula [*Primula Auricula*]: "Importune me not"

Green Locust Tree [*Gleditsia*]: "Affection beyond the grave"

Ground Ivy (Runaway Robin) [*Glechoma hederacea*]: Divination, Humility

Ground Laurel [*Laurus nobilis*]: Perseverance

Groundseal [*Senecio*]: Objectivity

Guelder Rose (European Cranberry Bush) [*Viburnum opulus*]: Age, Boredom, Bound, Ennui, Good news, Thoughts of Heaven, Winter

Gum Arabic [*Acacia*]: Purifies negativity and evil

Gum Cistus [*Cistaceae*]: "I shall die tomorrow"

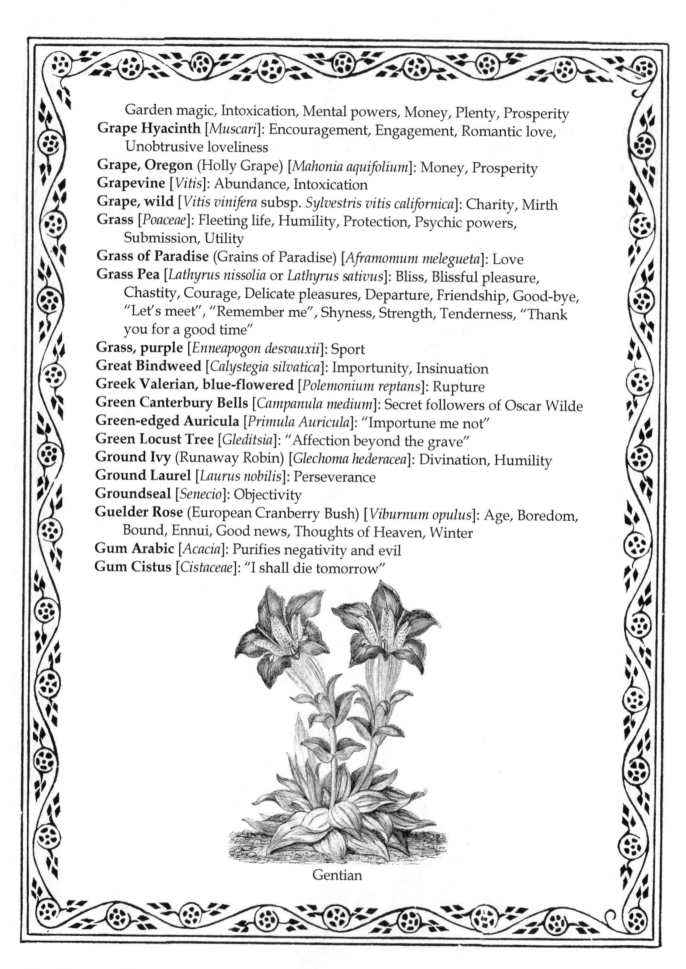

Gentian

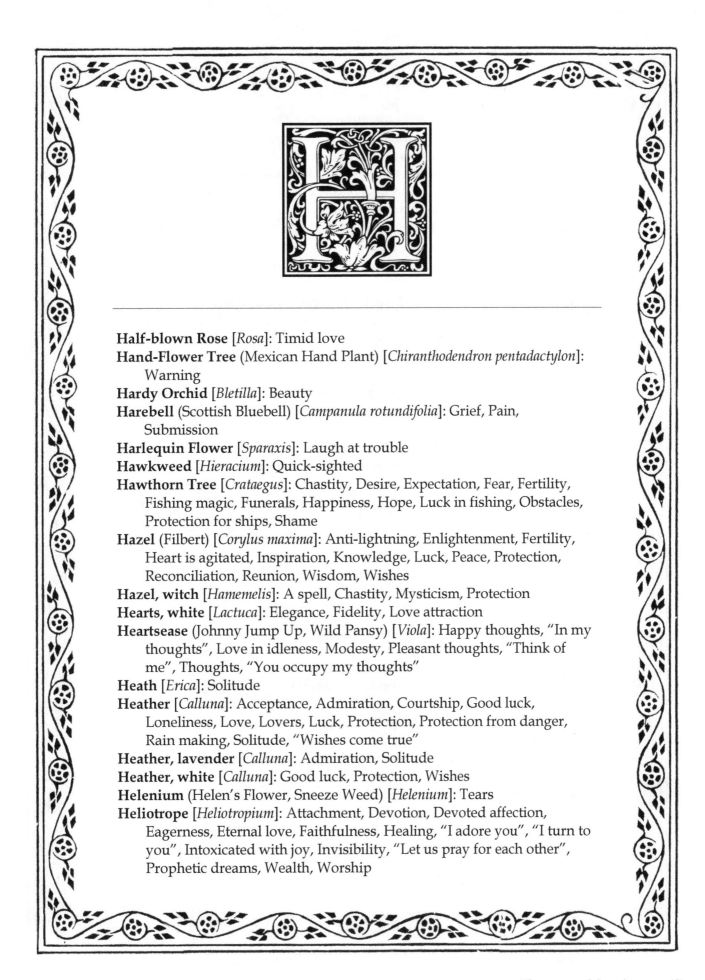

Half-blown Rose [*Rosa*]: Timid love

Hand-Flower Tree (Mexican Hand Plant) [*Chiranthodendron pentadactylon*]: Warning

Hardy Orchid [*Bletilla*]: Beauty

Harebell (Scottish Bluebell) [*Campanula rotundifolia*]: Grief, Pain, Submission

Harlequin Flower [*Sparaxis*]: Laugh at trouble

Hawkweed [*Hieracium*]: Quick-sighted

Hawthorn Tree [*Crataegus*]: Chastity, Desire, Expectation, Fear, Fertility, Fishing magic, Funerals, Happiness, Hope, Luck in fishing, Obstacles, Protection for ships, Shame

Hazel (Filbert) [*Corylus maxima*]: Anti-lightning, Enlightenment, Fertility, Heart is agitated, Inspiration, Knowledge, Luck, Peace, Protection, Reconciliation, Reunion, Wisdom, Wishes

Hazel, witch [*Hamemelis*]: A spell, Chastity, Mysticism, Protection

Hearts, white [*Lactuca*]: Elegance, Fidelity, Love attraction

Heartsease (Johnny Jump Up, Wild Pansy) [*Viola*]: Happy thoughts, "In my thoughts", Love in idleness, Modesty, Pleasant thoughts, "Think of me", Thoughts, "You occupy my thoughts"

Heath [*Erica*]: Solitude

Heather [*Calluna*]: Acceptance, Admiration, Courtship, Good luck, Loneliness, Love, Lovers, Luck, Protection, Protection from danger, Rain making, Solitude, "Wishes come true"

Heather, lavender [*Calluna*]: Admiration, Solitude

Heather, white [*Calluna*]: Good luck, Protection, Wishes

Helenium (Helen's Flower, Sneeze Weed) [*Helenium*]: Tears

Heliotrope [*Heliotropium*]: Attachment, Devotion, Devoted affection, Eagerness, Eternal love, Faithfulness, Healing, "I adore you", "I turn to you", Intoxicated with joy, Invisibility, "Let us pray for each other", Prophetic dreams, Wealth, Worship

Heliotrope, Peruvian [*Heliotropium arborescens*]: Devotion

Hellebore, black, false [*Veratrum nigrum*]: Protection

Helleborus (Hellebore, Lenten Rose) [*Helleborus*]: Anxiety relief, Balance, Calumny, Goals, Malicious representation, Poise, Relieve my anxiety, Scandal, Self-assurance, Shyness reduction, Slander, Stress relief, Tension relief, "You have listened to scandal", Wit

Helleborus, Oriental [*Helleborus orientalis*]: Goals, Poise, Self-assurance, Shyness reduction, Tension relief

Hemlock [*Tsuga*]: Black magic, Chastity, Evil, Triumph over winter, "You will be my death"

Hemlock, Eastern [*Tsuga canadensis*]: Triumph over winter

Hemp [*Cannabis sativa* subsp. *sativa*]: Fate, Healing, Love, Meditation, Visions

Henbane (Henbit) [*Hyoscyamus niger*]: Beware, Danger, Fault, Female attraction, Imperfection

Henna [*Lawsonia*]: Healing

Hens and Chicks (Sedum) [*Echeveria*]: Motherly love, Tranquility, "Welcome home, drunk husband"

Hepatica [*Hepatica*]: Confidence

Hibiscus [*Hibiscus*]: Change, Delicate beauty, Divination, Love, Lust, Mildness, Passion, Sexual passion, Sweet disposition

Hickory Tree [*Carya*]: Legal matters

High John the Conqueror [*Ipomoea jalapa*]: Happiness, Love, Money, Success

Himalayan Moringa (Tree of Life) [*Moringa oleifera*]: Age, Old age

Holly [*Ilex*]: "Am I forgotten?", Anti-lightning, Challenge, Defense, Domestic happiness, Dream magic, Enchantment, Farsightedness, Foresight, Good will, Good wishes, Lightning protection, Luck, Protection, Strengthening, Testing, Transformation, Trials

Holly Berries [*Ilex*]: Christmas joy, Greeting, Protection

Holly, variegated [*Ilex*]: Always cheerful

Hollyhock [*Alcea*]: Ambition, Ambition of a scholar, Aspiration, Farsightedness, Fecundity, Female ambition, Fertility, Fruitfulness, "I seek glory"

Hollyhock, white [*Alcea rosea*]: Female ambition

Honesty (Lunaria) [*Lunaria*]: Accept change, Accepting change in life, Fascination, Flexibility, Forgetfulness, Honesty, Money, Relationships, Self-knowledge, Simplicity, Sincerity, Trustworthiness

Honeyflower (Honeybush, Touch-Me-Not) [*Melianthus major*]: Love sweet and secret

Honeysuckle [*Lonicera*]: Affection, Bonds of love, Devoted love, "Do you love me?", Domestic happiness, Fidelity, Fraternal affection, Generosity, Generous and devoted love, Happiness, Inconstancy, Love, Money, Protection, Psychic powers, Sweet disposition, "Wedding will follow shortly"

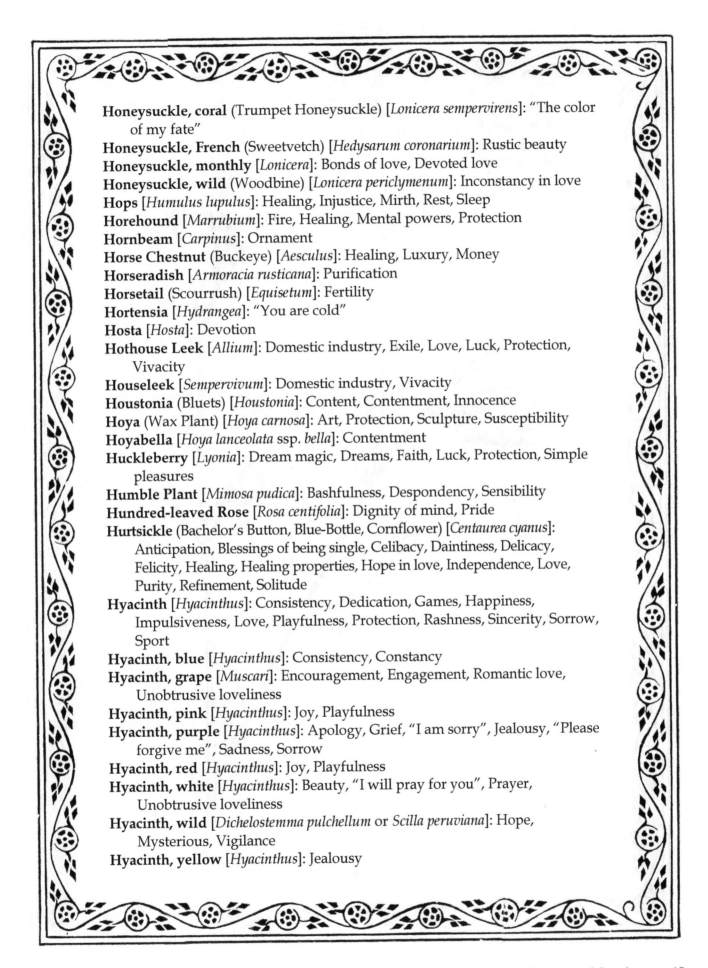

Honeysuckle, coral (Trumpet Honeysuckle) [*Lonicera sempervirens*]: "The color of my fate"

Honeysuckle, French (Sweetvetch) [*Hedysarum coronarium*]: Rustic beauty

Honeysuckle, monthly [*Lonicera*]: Bonds of love, Devoted love

Honeysuckle, wild (Woodbine) [*Lonicera periclymenum*]: Inconstancy in love

Hops [*Humulus lupulus*]: Healing, Injustice, Mirth, Rest, Sleep

Horehound [*Marrubium*]: Fire, Healing, Mental powers, Protection

Hornbeam [*Carpinus*]: Ornament

Horse Chestnut (Buckeye) [*Aesculus*]: Healing, Luxury, Money

Horseradish [*Armoracia rusticana*]: Purification

Horsetail (Scourrush) [*Equisetum*]: Fertility

Hortensia [*Hydrangea*]: "You are cold"

Hosta [*Hosta*]: Devotion

Hothouse Leek [*Allium*]: Domestic industry, Exile, Love, Luck, Protection, Vivacity

Houseleek [*Sempervivum*]: Domestic industry, Vivacity

Houstonia (Bluets) [*Houstonia*]: Content, Contentment, Innocence

Hoya (Wax Plant) [*Hoya carnosa*]: Art, Protection, Sculpture, Susceptibility

Hoyabella [*Hoya lanceolata* ssp. *bella*]: Contentment

Huckleberry [*Lyonia*]: Dream magic, Dreams, Faith, Luck, Protection, Simple pleasures

Humble Plant [*Mimosa pudica*]: Bashfulness, Despondency, Sensibility

Hundred-leaved Rose [*Rosa centifolia*]: Dignity of mind, Pride

Hurtsickle (Bachelor's Button, Blue-Bottle, Cornflower) [*Centaurea cyanus*]: Anticipation, Blessings of being single, Celibacy, Daintiness, Delicacy, Felicity, Healing, Healing properties, Hope in love, Independence, Love, Purity, Refinement, Solitude

Hyacinth [*Hyacinthus*]: Consistency, Dedication, Games, Happiness, Impulsiveness, Love, Playfulness, Protection, Rashness, Sincerity, Sorrow, Sport

Hyacinth, blue [*Hyacinthus*]: Consistency, Constancy

Hyacinth, grape [*Muscari*]: Encouragement, Engagement, Romantic love, Unobtrusive loveliness

Hyacinth, pink [*Hyacinthus*]: Joy, Playfulness

Hyacinth, purple [*Hyacinthus*]: Apology, Grief, "I am sorry", Jealousy, "Please forgive me", Sadness, Sorrow

Hyacinth, red [*Hyacinthus*]: Joy, Playfulness

Hyacinth, white [*Hyacinthus*]: Beauty, "I will pray for you", Prayer, Unobtrusive loveliness

Hyacinth, wild [*Dichelostemma pulchellum* or *Scilla peruviana*]: Hope, Mysterious, Vigilance

Hyacinth, yellow [*Hyacinthus*]: Jealousy

Hydrangea [*Hydrangea*]: A boaster, Boastfulness, Braggart, Devotion, Dispassion, Frigidity, Heartlessness, Perseverance, Remembrance, Understanding, "You are cold"
Hypericum [*Hypericum*]: Protection, Superstition, "You are a prophet"
Hyssop [*Hyssopus officinalis*]: Cleanliness, Protection, Purification, Purity

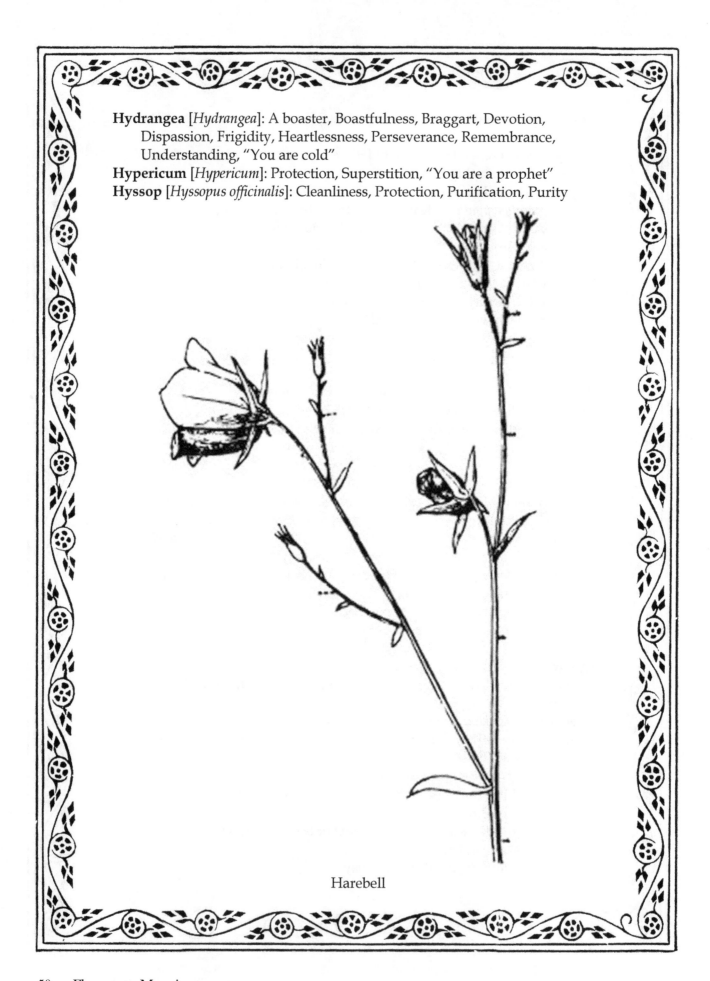

Harebell

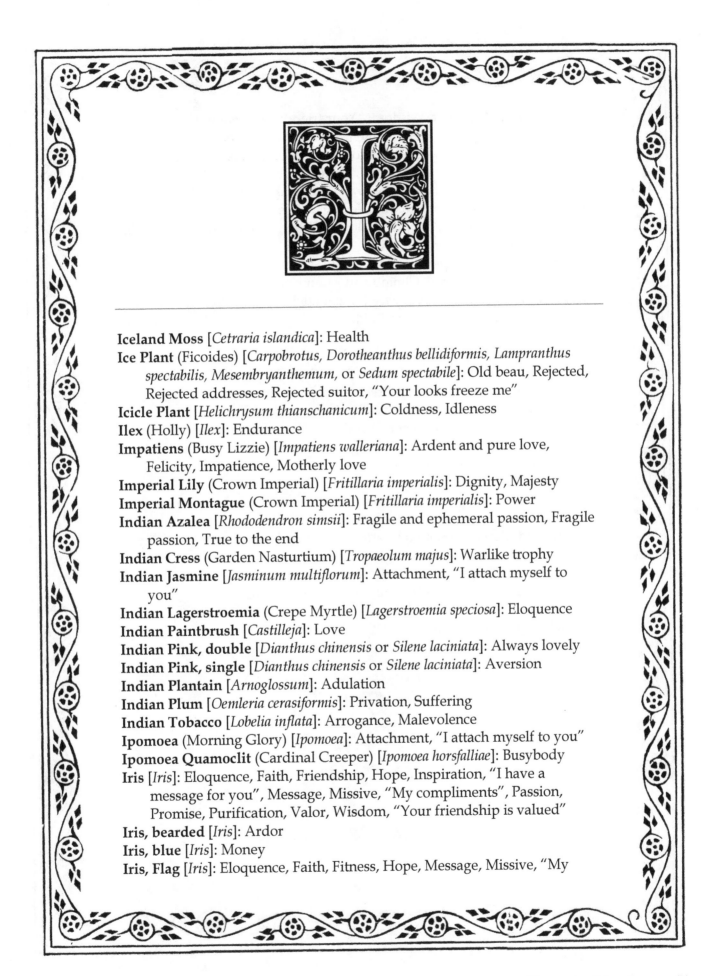

Iceland Moss [*Cetraria islandica*]: Health

Ice Plant (Ficoides) [*Carpobrotus, Dorotheanthus bellidiformis, Lampranthus spectabilis, Mesembryanthemum,* or *Sedum spectabile*]: Old beau, Rejected, Rejected addresses, Rejected suitor, "Your looks freeze me"

Icicle Plant [*Helichrysum thianschanicum*]: Coldness, Idleness

Ilex (Holly) [*Ilex*]: Endurance

Impatiens (Busy Lizzie) [*Impatiens walleriana*]: Ardent and pure love, Felicity, Impatience, Motherly love

Imperial Lily (Crown Imperial) [*Fritillaria imperialis*]: Dignity, Majesty

Imperial Montague (Crown Imperial) [*Fritillaria imperialis*]: Power

Indian Azalea [*Rhododendron simsii*]: Fragile and ephemeral passion, Fragile passion, True to the end

Indian Cress (Garden Nasturtium) [*Tropaeolum majus*]: Warlike trophy

Indian Jasmine [*Jasminum multiflorum*]: Attachment, "I attach myself to you"

Indian Lagerstroemia (Crepe Myrtle) [*Lagerstroemia speciosa*]: Eloquence

Indian Paintbrush [*Castilleja*]: Love

Indian Pink, double [*Dianthus chinensis* or *Silene laciniata*]: Always lovely

Indian Pink, single [*Dianthus chinensis* or *Silene laciniata*]: Aversion

Indian Plantain [*Arnoglossum*]: Adulation

Indian Plum [*Oemleria cerasiformis*]: Privation, Suffering

Indian Tobacco [*Lobelia inflata*]: Arrogance, Malevolence

Ipomoea (Morning Glory) [*Ipomoea*]: Attachment, "I attach myself to you"

Ipomoea Quamoclit (Cardinal Creeper) [*Ipomoea horsfalliae*]: Busybody

Iris [*Iris*]: Eloquence, Faith, Friendship, Hope, Inspiration, "I have a message for you", Message, Missive, "My compliments", Passion, Promise, Purification, Valor, Wisdom, "Your friendship is valued"

Iris, bearded [*Iris*]: Ardor

Iris, blue [*Iris*]: Money

Iris, Flag [*Iris*]: Eloquence, Faith, Fitness, Hope, Message, Missive, "My compliments", Valor, Wisdom, "Your friendship is valued"

Iris, Fleur-de-lis [*Iris*]: Ardor, Eloquence, Fire, Flame, "I burn for you", Message, "My compliments", Promise of good things to come

Iris, German [*Iris germanica*]: Aflame, Flame, "I burn for you"

Iris, walking (Apostle Plant) [*Neomarica northiana*]: Eloquence, Faith, Friendship, Hope, Inspiration, Message, Missive, "My compliments", Passion, Promise, Protection, Valor, Wisdom, "Your friendship is valued"

Iris, yellow [*Iris*]: Passion, Sorrow

Irish Cypress Tree [*Cupressus x leylandii*]: Death

Irish Ivy [*Hedera hibernica*]: Clinging affection

Irish Moss (Scotch Moss) [*Sagina subulata*]: Luck, Money, Protection

Ismene (Sacred Lily of the Incas, Spider Lily) [*Hymenocallis*]: "Elope with me", "Not as bad as I seem"

Italian Cypress [*Cupressus sempervirens*]: Death

Ivy [*Hedera*]: Achievement, Affection, Ambition, Conjugal affection, Constancy, Fealty, Fidelity, Friendship, Growth, Healing, Loyalty, Marriage, Protection, Tenacity, Trustfulness, Wedded love

Ivy, American (Virginia Creeper, Woodbine) [*Parthenocissus quinquefolia*]: Ever changing, "I cling to you", "I cling to you in sunshine and shade", Strong friendship, Sweet neglect

Ivy, berry [*Hedera*]: Warning

Ivy Geranium [*Pelargonium peltatum*]: Bridal favor, "Your hand for the next dance"

Ivy, ground (Runaway Robin) [*Glechoma hederacea*]: Divination, Humility

Ivy, Irish [*Hedera hibernica*]: Clinging affection

Ivy Leaf, folded together [*Hedera*]: "I have…"

Ivy, sprig of, with tendrils [*Hedera*]: Assiduous to please

Ivy, variegated [*Hedera*]: Brightness

Ivy, white [*Hedera*]: Rarity

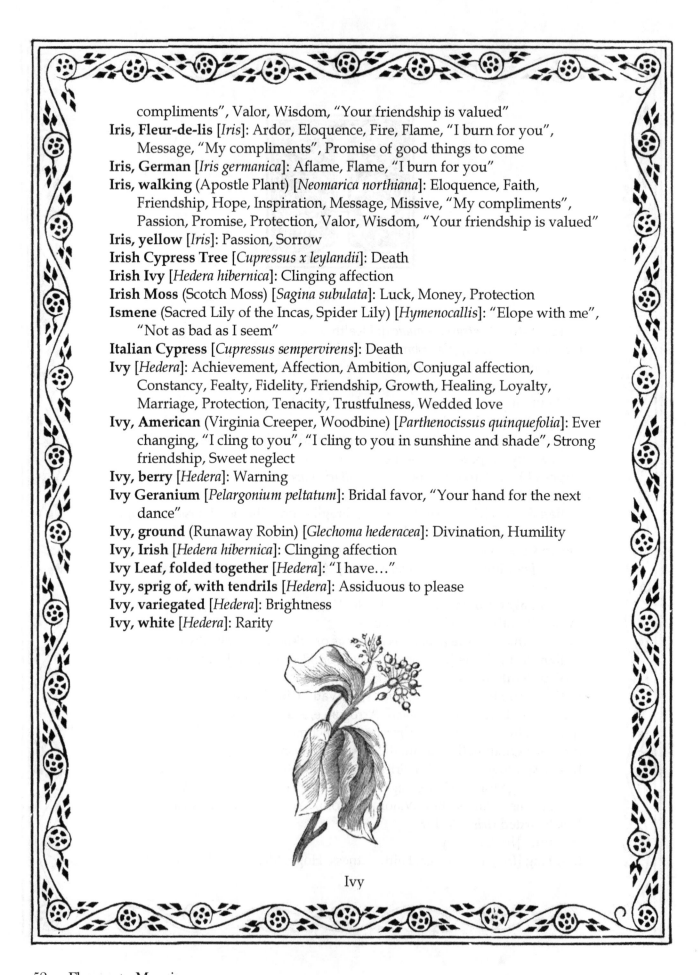

Ivy

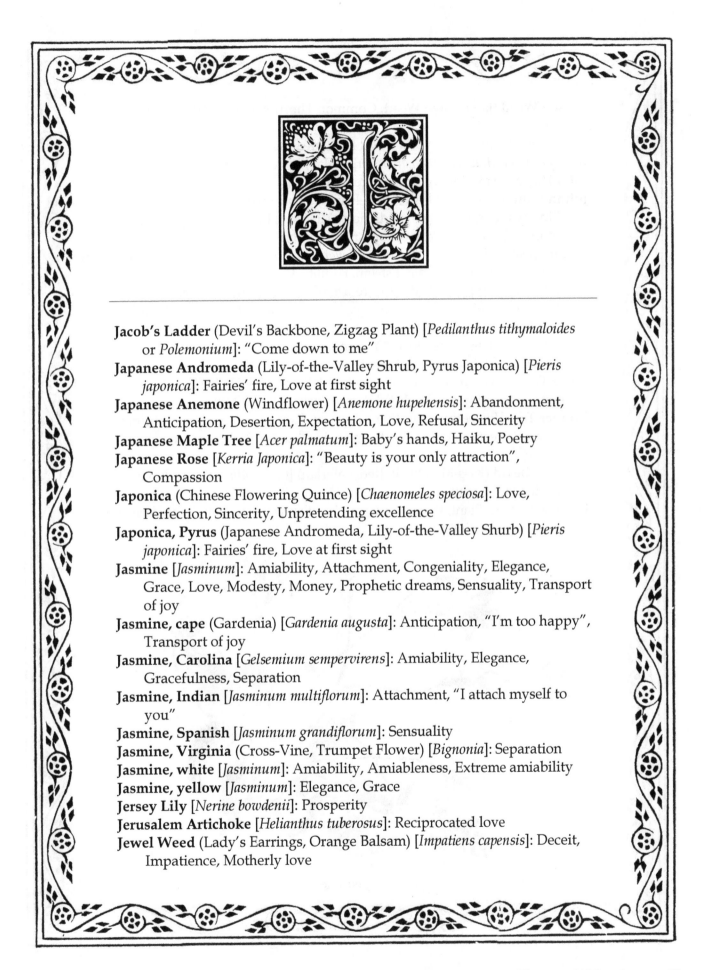

Jacob's Ladder (Devil's Backbone, Zigzag Plant) [*Pedilanthus tithymaloides* or *Polemonium*]: "Come down to me"

Japanese Andromeda (Lily-of-the-Valley Shrub, Pyrus Japonica) [*Pieris japonica*]: Fairies' fire, Love at first sight

Japanese Anemone (Windflower) [*Anemone hupehensis*]: Abandonment, Anticipation, Desertion, Expectation, Love, Refusal, Sincerity

Japanese Maple Tree [*Acer palmatum*]: Baby's hands, Haiku, Poetry

Japanese Rose [*Kerria Japonica*]: "Beauty is your only attraction", Compassion

Japonica (Chinese Flowering Quince) [*Chaenomeles speciosa*]: Love, Perfection, Sincerity, Unpretending excellence

Japonica, Pyrus (Japanese Andromeda, Lily-of-the-Valley Shurb) [*Pieris japonica*]: Fairies' fire, Love at first sight

Jasmine [*Jasminum*]: Amiability, Attachment, Congeniality, Elegance, Grace, Love, Modesty, Money, Prophetic dreams, Sensuality, Transport of joy

Jasmine, cape (Gardenia) [*Gardenia augusta*]: Anticipation, "I'm too happy", Transport of joy

Jasmine, Carolina [*Gelsemium sempervirens*]: Amiability, Elegance, Gracefulness, Separation

Jasmine, Indian [*Jasminum multiflorum*]: Attachment, "I attach myself to you"

Jasmine, Spanish [*Jasminum grandiflorum*]: Sensuality

Jasmine, Virginia (Cross-Vine, Trumpet Flower) [*Bignonia*]: Separation

Jasmine, white [*Jasminum*]: Amiability, Amiableness, Extreme amiability

Jasmine, yellow [*Jasminum*]: Elegance, Grace

Jersey Lily [*Nerine bowdenii*]: Prosperity

Jerusalem Artichoke [*Helianthus tuberosus*]: Reciprocated love

Jewel Weed (Lady's Earrings, Orange Balsam) [*Impatiens capensis*]: Deceit, Impatience, Motherly love

Jimson Weed (Jamestown Weed, Common Thorn Apple) [*Datura stramonium*]: Deceit

Job's Tears [*Coix lacryma-jobi*]: Good luck, Healing, Luck, Wishes

Joe Pye Weed [*Eupatorium fistulosum*]: Delay, Love, Respect

John Hopper Rose [*Rosa*]: Encouragement

Johnny Jump Up (Heartsease, Wild Pansy) [*Viola tricolor*]: Happy thoughts, "In my thoughts", Love in idleness, Modesty, Pleasant thoughts, "Think of me", Thoughts, "You occupy my thoughts"

Jonquil (Daffodil, Lent Lily) [*Narcissus jonquilla*]: Affection, Affection returned, Chivalry, Desire, Egotism, Esteem, Fertility, Good taste, Gracefulness, "Have pity on my passion", "I desire a return of affection", Inner power, Love, Luck, Meditation, New beginnings, Pure, Reciprocal love, Regard, Respect, Self-love, Sweet disposition, Sympathy, "The sun is always shining when I'm with you", Unrequited love, "You're the only one"

Joseph's Coat [*Alternanthera*]: Hopelessness

Judas Tree (Love Tree) [*Cercis siliquastrum*]: Betrayal, Unbelief

Julienne, white (Dame's Rocket) [*Hesperis matronalis*]: "Despair not"

Juniper Tree [*Juniperus*]: Anti-theft, Asylum, Exorcism, Health, Helpfulness, Love, Protection, Protection from snakes, Succor, "Welcome to a new home"

Jupiter's Beard (Kiss-Me-Quick, Red Valerian) [*Centranthus ruber*]: Love, Protection, Purity

Justicia (Shrimp Plant, Water Willow) [*Acanthaceae*]: Freedom, "The perfection of female loveliness"

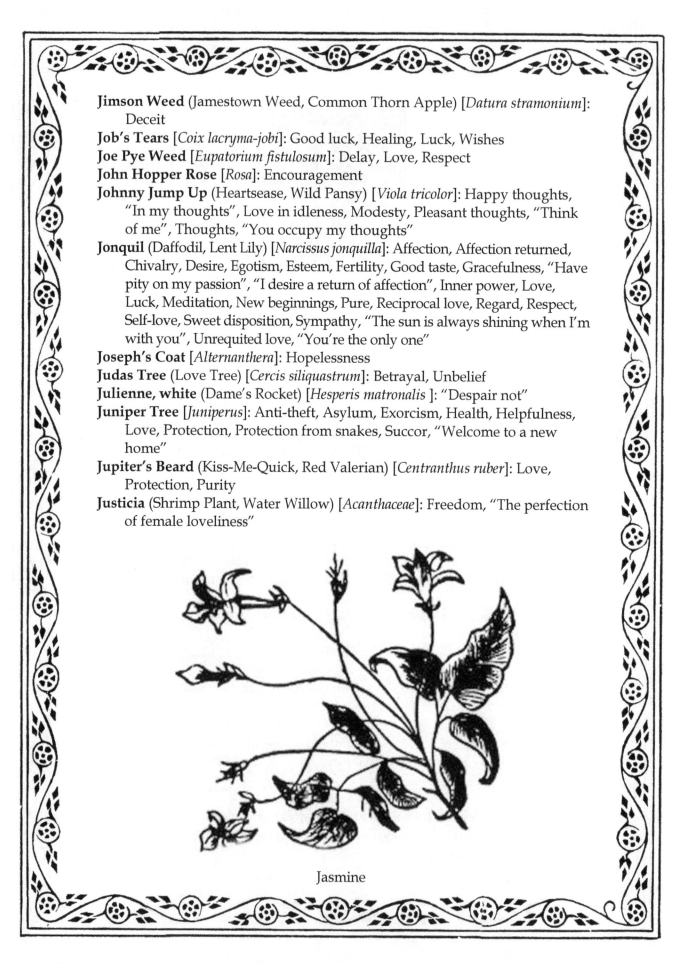

Jasmine

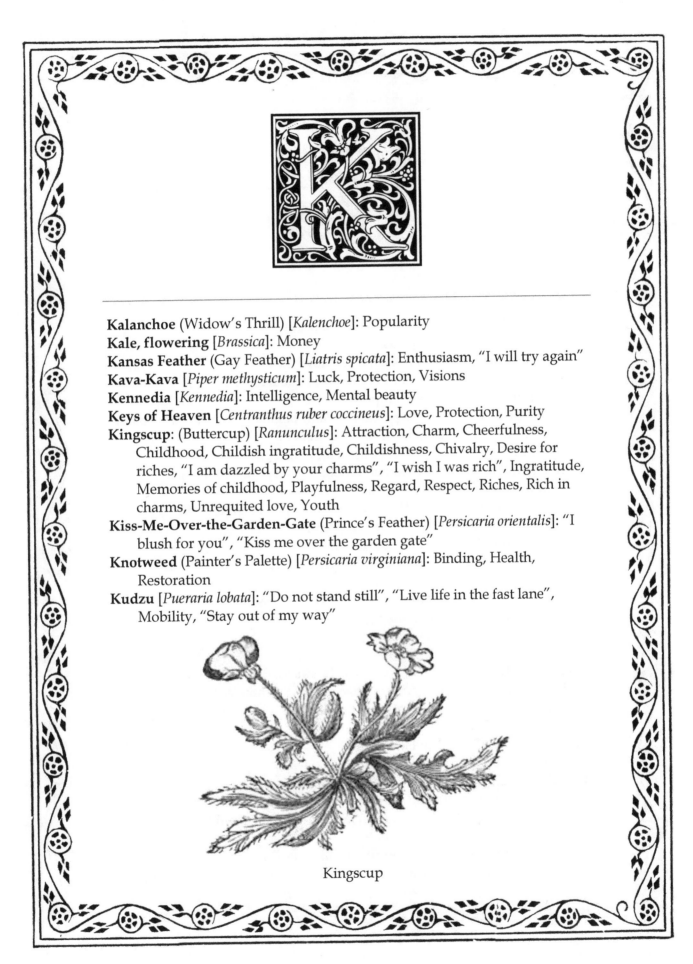

Kalanchoe (Widow's Thrill) [*Kalenchoe*]: Popularity

Kale, flowering [*Brassica*]: Money

Kansas Feather (Gay Feather) [*Liatris spicata*]: Enthusiasm, "I will try again"

Kava-Kava [*Piper methysticum*]: Luck, Protection, Visions

Kennedia [*Kennedia*]: Intelligence, Mental beauty

Keys of Heaven [*Centranthus ruber coccineus*]: Love, Protection, Purity

Kingscup: (Buttercup) [*Ranunculus*]: Attraction, Charm, Cheerfulness, Childhood, Childish ingratitude, Childishness, Chivalry, Desire for riches, "I am dazzled by your charms", "I wish I was rich", Ingratitude, Memories of childhood, Playfulness, Regard, Respect, Riches, Rich in charms, Unrequited love, Youth

Kiss-Me-Over-the-Garden-Gate (Prince's Feather) [*Persicaria orientalis*]: "I blush for you", "Kiss me over the garden gate"

Knotweed (Painter's Palette) [*Persicaria virginiana*]: Binding, Health, Restoration

Kudzu [*Pueraria lobata*]: "Do not stand still", "Live life in the fast lane", Mobility, "Stay out of my way"

Kingscup

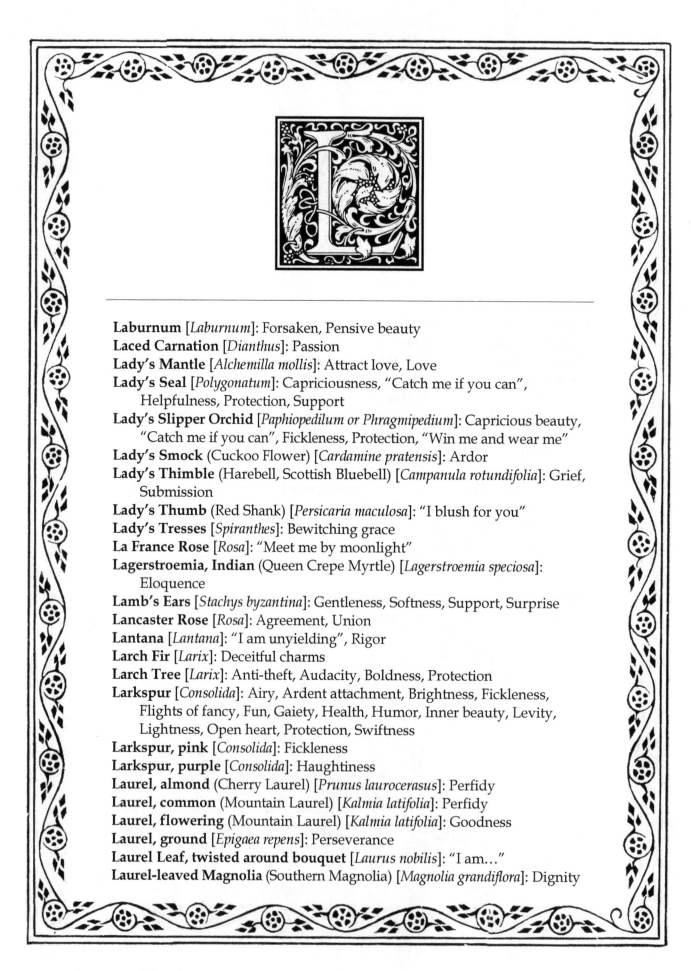

Laburnum [*Laburnum*]: Forsaken, Pensive beauty

Laced Carnation [*Dianthus*]: Passion

Lady's Mantle [*Alchemilla mollis*]: Attract love, Love

Lady's Seal [*Polygonatum*]: Capriciousness, "Catch me if you can",
    Helpfulness, Protection, Support

Lady's Slipper Orchid [*Paphiopedilum or Phragmipedium*]: Capricious beauty,
    "Catch me if you can", Fickleness, Protection, "Win me and wear me"

Lady's Smock (Cuckoo Flower) [*Cardamine pratensis*]: Ardor

Lady's Thimble (Harebell, Scottish Bluebell) [*Campanula rotundifolia*]: Grief,
    Submission

Lady's Thumb (Red Shank) [*Persicaria maculosa*]: "I blush for you"

Lady's Tresses [*Spiranthes*]: Bewitching grace

La France Rose [*Rosa*]: "Meet me by moonlight"

Lagerstroemia, Indian (Queen Crepe Myrtle) [*Lagerstroemia speciosa*]:
    Eloquence

Lamb's Ears [*Stachys byzantina*]: Gentleness, Softness, Support, Surprise

Lancaster Rose [*Rosa*]: Agreement, Union

Lantana [*Lantana*]: "I am unyielding", Rigor

Larch Fir [*Larix*]: Deceitful charms

Larch Tree [*Larix*]: Anti-theft, Audacity, Boldness, Protection

Larkspur [*Consolida*]: Airy, Ardent attachment, Brightness, Fickleness,
    Flights of fancy, Fun, Gaiety, Health, Humor, Inner beauty, Levity,
    Lightness, Open heart, Protection, Swiftness

Larkspur, pink [*Consolida*]: Fickleness

Larkspur, purple [*Consolida*]: Haughtiness

Laurel, almond (Cherry Laurel) [*Prunus laurocerasus*]: Perfidy

Laurel, common (Mountain Laurel) [*Kalmia latifolia*]: Perfidy

Laurel, flowering (Mountain Laurel) [*Kalmia latifolia*]: Goodness

Laurel, ground [*Epigaea repens*]: Perseverance

Laurel Leaf, twisted around bouquet [*Laurus nobilis*]: "I am…"

Laurel-leaved Magnolia (Southern Magnolia) [*Magnolia grandiflora*]: Dignity

Laurel, mountain (Common Laurel, Flowering Laural) [*Kalmia latifolia*]: Ambition, Ambition of a hero, Treachery, Victory

Laurel, Texas mountain (Mescal Bean) [*Sophora secundiflora*]: Dreams, Psychic power

Laurel Tree (Bay, Sweet Bay) [*Laurus nobilis*]: Accomplishment, Achievement in the arts, Civil service, Courage, Creation of beauty, Glory, Glory and success, Healing, Perfidy, Personal achievement, Protection, Psychic powers, Purification, Reward of merit, Sharpness, Strength, Success

Laurel, variegated [*Laurus nobilis*]: Attractive

Lauresina (Airplant) [*Tillandsia*]: "I die if neglected"

Laurustinus [*Viburnurn tinus*]: Cheerful, "I die if neglected", Token of affection

Lavatera (Annual Mallow) [*Lavatera trimestris* syn. Althaea trimestris]: Delicate beauty, Sweet disposition, Sweetness

Lavender [*Lavandula*]: Acknowledgment, Ardent attachment, Blocks emotional conflicts, Chastity, Devotion, Distrust, Failure, Happiness, "I like you only as a friend", Longevity, Love, Luck, Mistrust, Peace, Protection, Purification, Refusal, Sensitivity, Sleep, "Soothes the heart", Success, Suspicion

Lavender Heather [*Calluna Vulgaris*]: Admiration, Solitude

Lavender Rose [*Rosa*]: Enchantment, Love at first sight

Lavender, sea (Sea Pinks, Sea Thrift, Statice) [*Limonium*]: Success, Sympathy

Leadwort [*Plumbago*]: Antidote, Holy wishes, Success, Sympathy

Leather Flower (Virgin's Bower) [*Clematis viticella*]: Artifice, Arts, Creativity, Filial love, "I love your mind", Ingenuity, Intelligence, Love from a son or daughter, Mental beauty, Pure love, Unchanged for eternity

Leaves, autumn: Melancholy

Leaves, dead: Melancholy, Sadness, Sorrow

Leek [*Allium porrum*]: Exorcism, Love, Protection

Leek, Hothouse [*Allium*]: Domestic industry, Exile, Love, Luck, Protection, Vivacity

Lemon Balm (Bee Balm) [*Melissa officinalis*]: Fun, Healing, Love, Rejuvenation, Relief, Success, Sympathy, Understanding, Wit

Lemon Blossom [*Citrus limon*]: Discretion, Faithfulness, Fidelity, Fidelity in love

Lemon Geranium (Lemon Cranesbill) [*Pelargonium crispum*]: Unexpected meeting

Lemon Verbena [*Aloysia triphylla*]: Attractive to the opposite sex, Love, Purification, Responsibility

Lemongrass [*Cymbopogon citratus*]: Lust, Psychic powers, Snake repelling

Lent Lily (Daffodil, Jonquil) [*Narcissus pseudonarcissus*]: Affection, Affection returned, Chivalry, Desire, Egotism, Esteem, Fertility, Good taste, Gracefulness, "Have pity on my passion", "I desire a return of affection",

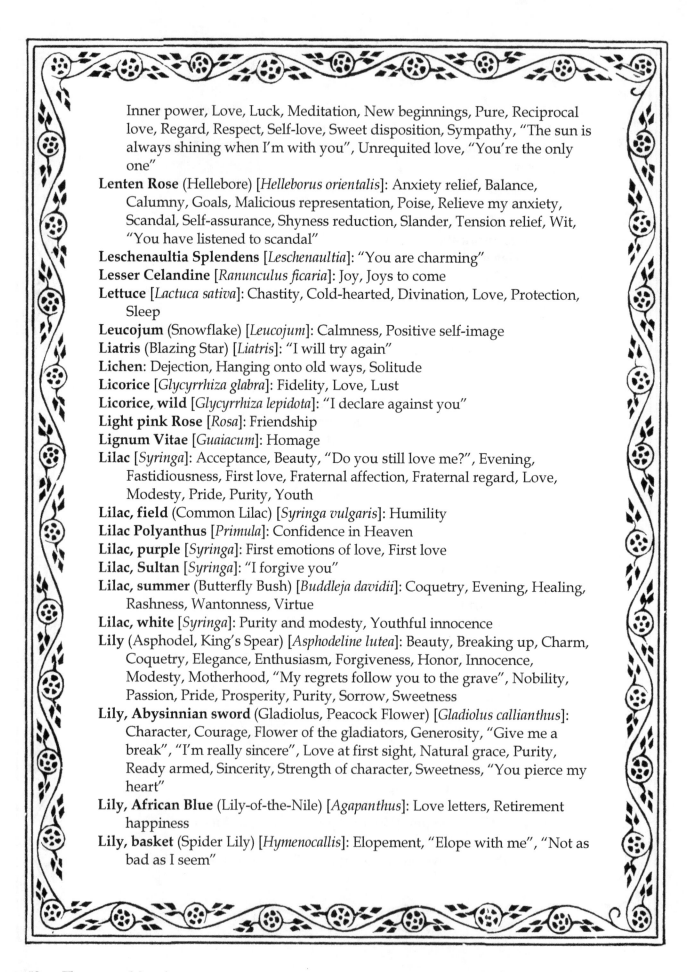

Inner power, Love, Luck, Meditation, New beginnings, Pure, Reciprocal love, Regard, Respect, Self-love, Sweet disposition, Sympathy, "The sun is always shining when I'm with you", Unrequited love, "You're the only one"

Lenten Rose (Hellebore) [*Helleborus orientalis*]: Anxiety relief, Balance, Calumny, Goals, Malicious representation, Poise, Relieve my anxiety, Scandal, Self-assurance, Shyness reduction, Slander, Tension relief, Wit, "You have listened to scandal"

Leschenaultia Splendens [*Leschenaultia*]: "You are charming"

Lesser Celandine [*Ranunculus ficaria*]: Joy, Joys to come

Lettuce [*Lactuca sativa*]: Chastity, Cold-hearted, Divination, Love, Protection, Sleep

Leucojum (Snowflake) [*Leucojum*]: Calmness, Positive self-image

Liatris (Blazing Star) [*Liatris*]: "I will try again"

Lichen: Dejection, Hanging onto old ways, Solitude

Licorice [*Glycyrrhiza glabra*]: Fidelity, Love, Lust

Licorice, wild [*Glycyrrhiza lepidota*]: "I declare against you"

Light pink Rose [*Rosa*]: Friendship

Lignum Vitae [*Guaiacum*]: Homage

Lilac [*Syringa*]: Acceptance, Beauty, "Do you still love me?", Evening, Fastidiousness, First love, Fraternal affection, Fraternal regard, Love, Modesty, Pride, Purity, Youth

Lilac, field (Common Lilac) [*Syringa vulgaris*]: Humility

Lilac Polyanthus [*Primula*]: Confidence in Heaven

Lilac, purple [*Syringa*]: First emotions of love, First love

Lilac, Sultan [*Syringa*]: "I forgive you"

Lilac, summer (Butterfly Bush) [*Buddleja davidii*]: Coquetry, Evening, Healing, Rashness, Wantonness, Virtue

Lilac, white [*Syringa*]: Purity and modesty, Youthful innocence

Lily (Asphodel, King's Spear) [*Asphodeline lutea*]: Beauty, Breaking up, Charm, Coquetry, Elegance, Enthusiasm, Forgiveness, Honor, Innocence, Modesty, Motherhood, "My regrets follow you to the grave", Nobility, Passion, Pride, Prosperity, Purity, Sorrow, Sweetness

Lily, Abysinnian sword (Gladiolus, Peacock Flower) [*Gladiolus callianthus*]: Character, Courage, Flower of the gladiators, Generosity, "Give me a break", "I'm really sincere", Love at first sight, Natural grace, Purity, Ready armed, Sincerity, Strength of character, Sweetness, "You pierce my heart"

Lily, African Blue (Lily-of-the-Nile) [*Agapanthus*]: Love letters, Retirement happiness

Lily, basket (Spider Lily) [*Hymenocallis*]: Elopement, "Elope with me", "Not as bad as I seem"

Lily, belladonna (Naked Lady) [*Amaryllis belladonna*]: "Dance with me", Drama

Lily, blood [*Haemanthus coccineus* or *Scadoxus*]: Glory, Splendor

Lily, Calla (Arum Lily, Pig Lily) [*Zantedeschia*]: Beauty, Feminine modesty, Magnificent beauty, Modesty, Panache, Royalty, Sophistication

Lily, canna [*Canna*]: Great beauty

Lily, climbing (Flame Lily, Glory Lily) [*Gloriosa* or *Littonia modesta*]: Fame, Glorious beauty, Honor

Lily, Easter [*Lilium longiflorum*]: New beginnings

Lily, Eucharist (Amazon Lily) [*Eucharis*]: Charm

Lily, fairy (Sea Daffodil) [*Chlidanthus*]: Fond caresses, Love, Sincerity

Lily, fire [*Clivia miniata* or *Cyrtanthus*]: Fame, Honor

Lily, fireball (Blood Lily) [*Scadoxus*]: Glory, Splendor

Lily, flame (Climbing Lily, Glory Lily) [*Gloriosa* or *Littonia modesta*]: Fame, Glorious beauty, Honor

Lily, foxtail (Desert Candle) [*Eremurus*]: Aspiration

Lily, frog [*Tricyrtis formosana*]: Disgust

Lily, glory (Climbing Lily, Flame Lily) [*Gloriosa* or *Littonia modesta*]: Fame, Glorious beauty, Honor

Lily, Imperial (Crown Imperial) [*Fritillaria imperialis*]: Dignity, Majesty

Lily, Jersey [*Nerine bowdenii*]: Prosperity

Lily, Lent (Daffodil, Jonquil) [*Narcissus pesudonarcissus*]: Affection, Affection returned, Chivalry, Desire, Egotism, Esteem, Fertility, Good taste, Gracefulness, "Have pity on my passion", "I desire a return of affection", Inner power, Love, Luck, Meditation, New beginnings, Pure, Reciprocal love, Regard, Respect, Self-love, Sweet disposition, Sympathy, "The sun is always shining when I'm with you", Unrequited love, "You're the only one"

Lily, magic [*Lycoris squamigera*]: "Dance with me"

Lily of the Incas [*Alstroemeria*]: Prosperity

Lily of the Nile [*Agapanthus africanus*]: Love letters, Retirement happiness

Lily-of-the-Valley [*Convallaria majalis*]: Happiness, Humility, Mental ability, Purity, Retirement happiness, Return of happiness, Sweetness, "You have made my life complete"

Lily, orange [*Lilium bulbiferum*]: Enemy, Hatred, Passion

Lily, Peruvian [*Alstroemeria*]: Devotion, Fortune, Friendship, Money, Pleasantness

Lily, purple [*Lilium*]: First love

Lily, rain (Zephyr Lily) [*Zephyranthes*]: Fond caresses, Love, Sincerity

Lily, red cape [*Crinum x powellii*]: Glory, Splendor

Lily, scarlet [*Lilium*]: High of soul

Lily, spider [*Hymenocallis, Lycoris,* or *Nerine*]: "Dance with me", "Elope with me", "Not as bad as I seem"

Lily, tiger [*Lilium lancifolium*]: Fun, "I dare you to love me", Riches

Lily, torch (Red-Hot Poker) [*Kniphofia*]: Dangerous, Determined

Lily, white [*Lilium*]: Beauty, Modesty, Purity, Sweetness

Lily, yellow [*Lilium*]: Coquetry, Falsehood, Flirtation, Gaiety, Happiness, Lies

Lilyturf, creeping [*Liriope spicata*]: Fame, Honor

Lime [*Citrus aurantifolia*]: Marital affection

Lime Blossom [*Citrus aurantifolia*]: Fornication, Lust

Lime Tree [*Tilia*]: Conjugal affection, Conjugal love, Marriage, Yielding

Linaria (Toadflax) [*Linaria*]: Deception

Linden, American (Basswood) [*Tilia americana*]: Matrimony

Linden Tree [*Tilia*]: Conjugal affection, Conjugal love, Judgment, Lenient, Marriage, Prophecies, Yielding

Lint [*Linum usitatissimum*]: "I feel my obligations", Obligation

Lisianthus (Eustoma, Prairie Gentian, Texas Bluebell) [*Eustoma*]: Appreciation, Beautiful mouth, Calmness, Optimistic, Outgoing, Playful, Showy, Well-spoken

Live Oak [*Quercus virginiana*]: Liberty

Liverwort [*Marchantiophyta*]: Confidence, Love, Protection

Lobelia [*Lobelia*]: Arrogance, Malevolence

Lobelia, scarlet (Cardinal flower) [*Lobelia cardinalis*]: Distinction, Honor

Locust Tree [*Gleditsia*]: Elegance

Locust Tree, black (False Acacia) [*Robinia pseudoacacia*]: Platonic love

Locust Tree, green [*Gleditsia* or *Robinia*]: Affection beyond the grave

London Pride [*Saxifraga x urbium*]: Frivolity, "Look up and kiss me", Whimsy

Long Purples [*Orchis mascula*]: Sporting

Long-stemmed Rose [*Rosa*]: "I will always remember you"

Loosestrife [*Lysimachia* or *Lythrum*]: Forgiveness, Peace, Pretension, Protection, Wishes granted

Lote tree (European Hackberry, Nettle Tree) [*Celtis australis*]: Concert, Concord

Lotus [*Nelumbo* or *Nymphaea lotus*]: Birth, Elegance, Enlightenment, Estranged love, Fertility, Protection, Purity

Lotus Flower [*Nelumbo* or *Nymphaea lotus*]: Estranged love

Lotus Leaf [*Nelumbo* or *Nymphaea lotus*]: Recantation

Lovage [*Levisticum*]: Love, Strength

Love-in-a-Mist (Nigella) [*Nigella damascena*]: Calmness, Delicacy, Embarrassment, Independence, "Kiss me twice before I rise", Love, Motivation, Perplexity, Prosperity and plenty, Questioning

Love-in-a-Puzzle (Fennel Flower) [*Nigella damascena*]: Embarrassment

Love-in-Idleness (Johnny Jump-Up, Wild Pansy) [*Viola tricolor*]: Love at first sight

Love-Lies-Bleeding (Tassel Flower) [*Amaranthus caudatus*]: Heartless, Hopeless, Hopelessness, Hopeless not heartless

Lucerne (Alfalfa) [*Medicago sativa*]: Life

Lucky Hand [*Orchis mascula* or *Orchis militaris*]: Employment, Friendship,

Luck, Money, Protection, Travel

Lucky Seed, red [*Adenanthera pavonina*]: Friendship, Love

Lunaria (Honesty) [*Lunaria*]: Accept change, Accepting change in life, Fascination, Flexibility, Forgetfulness, Honesty, Money, Relationships, Self-knowledge, Sincerity, Trustworthiness

Lungwort [*Pulmonaria*]: Life, Success, "You are my life"

Lupine [*Lupinus*]: Dejection, Imagination, Voraciousness

Lupine, rose [*Lupinus*]: Fanciful

Lupine, white [*Lupinus*]: Always happy

Lychnis (Campion, Catch Fly) [*Lychnis*]: Religion, Religious enthusiasm, Wit

Lychnis, meadow [*Lychnis*]: Wit

Lychnis, scarlet [*Lychnis*]: Sunbeaming eyes

Lyre Flower (Bleeding Heart, Venus' Car) [*Lamprocapnos spectabilis*]: Elegance, Fidelity, Fly with me, Love, Love attraction, Unrequited love

Lysimachia (Loosestrife) [*Lysimachia*]: Forgiveness

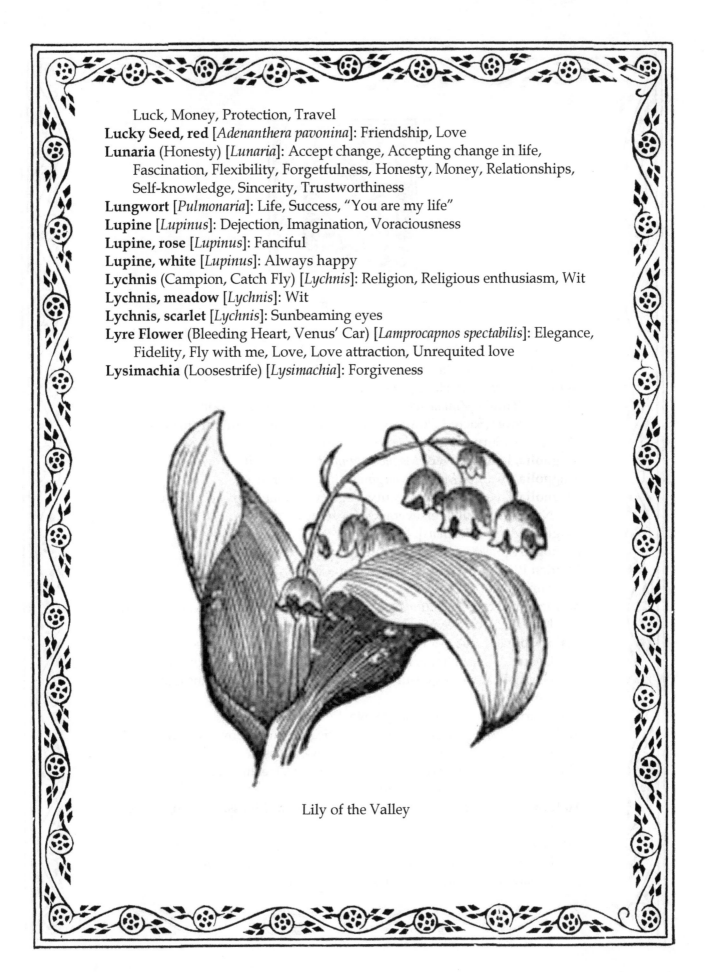

Lily of the Valley

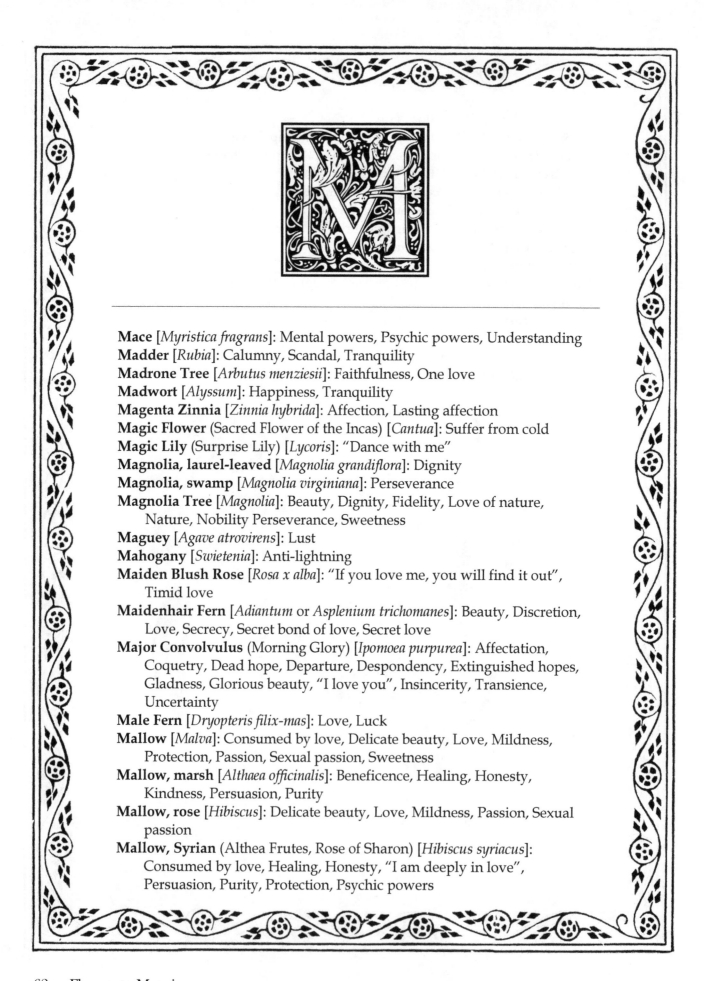

Mace [*Myristica fragrans*]: Mental powers, Psychic powers, Understanding

Madder [*Rubia*]: Calumny, Scandal, Tranquility

Madrone Tree [*Arbutus menziesii*]: Faithfulness, One love

Madwort [*Alyssum*]: Happiness, Tranquility

Magenta Zinnia [*Zinnia hybrida*]: Affection, Lasting affection

Magic Flower (Sacred Flower of the Incas) [*Cantua*]: Suffer from cold

Magic Lily (Surprise Lily) [*Lycoris*]: "Dance with me"

Magnolia, laurel-leaved [*Magnolia grandiflora*]: Dignity

Magnolia, swamp [*Magnolia virginiana*]: Perseverance

Magnolia Tree [*Magnolia*]: Beauty, Dignity, Fidelity, Love of nature, Nature, Nobility Perseverance, Sweetness

Maguey [*Agave atrovirens*]: Lust

Mahogany [*Swietenia*]: Anti-lightning

Maiden Blush Rose [*Rosa x alba*]: "If you love me, you will find it out", Timid love

Maidenhair Fern [*Adiantum* or *Asplenium trichomanes*]: Beauty, Discretion, Love, Secrecy, Secret bond of love, Secret love

Major Convolvulus (Morning Glory) [*Ipomoea purpurea*]: Affectation, Coquetry, Dead hope, Departure, Despondency, Extinguished hopes, Gladness, Glorious beauty, "I love you", Insincerity, Transience, Uncertainty

Male Fern [*Dryopteris filix-mas*]: Love, Luck

Mallow [*Malva*]: Consumed by love, Delicate beauty, Love, Mildness, Protection, Passion, Sexual passion, Sweetness

Mallow, marsh [*Althaea officinalis*]: Beneficence, Healing, Honesty, Kindness, Persuasion, Purity

Mallow, rose [*Hibiscus*]: Delicate beauty, Love, Mildness, Passion, Sexual passion

Mallow, Syrian (Althea Frutes, Rose of Sharon) [*Hibiscus syriacus*]: Consumed by love, Healing, Honesty, "I am deeply in love", Persuasion, Purity, Protection, Psychic powers

Mallow, Venetian [*Hibiscus trionum*]: Delicate beauty

Maltese Cross [*Lychnis chalcedonica*]: "Dance with me", Religion

Malva Rose (Island Mallow) [*Lavatera assurgentiflora*]: Delicate beauty, Love, Mildness, Sexual passion

Manchineel Tree [*Hippomane mancinella*]: Betrayal, Falsehood, "Little apple of death"

Mandevilla [*Mandevilla*]: Reckless, Thoughtlessness, "Voice of the heart"

Mandrake [*Mandragora*]: Fertility, Health, Honor, Horror, Love, Money, Protection, Rarity

Maple Tree [*Acer*]: Beauty, Elegance, Keys, Longevity, Love, Money, Reserve, Success

Maple Tree, flowering (Abutilon, Chinese Lantern) [*Abutilon*]: Meditation

Maple Tree, Japanese [*Acer palmatum*]: Baby's hands, Haiku, Poetry

Marguerite [*Argyranthemum*]: Action, Energy

Marianthus [*Marianthus*]: Hope for better days

Marigold [*Calendula* or *Tagetes*]: Chagrin, Cruelty, Cruelty in love, Despair, Despondency, Distress, Grief, Health, Heart's comfort, "I have cause", Inquietude, Jealousy, Legal matters, Prophetic dreams, Protection, Psychic powers, Remembrance, Restlessness, Riches, Sacred affection, Sadness, Sun, Trouble, Uneasiness

Marigold, African (American Marigold, Aztek Marigold) [*Tagetes erecta*]: Vulgar minds

Marigold and Cypress [*Tagetes* and *Cupressus*]: Despair, Great despair

Marigold, cape (African Daisy) [*Castalis tragus* or *Dimorphotheca*]: Innocence, Love from a man to a woman, Omen, Presage, Shared secrets

Marigold, Fig (Ice Plant) [*Mesembryanthemum*]: Coldness, Idleness

Marigold, French [*Tagetes patula*]: Jealousy

Marigold, garden [*Tagetes*]: Trouble, Uneasiness

Marigold, marsh [*Caltha palustris*]: Desire for riches

Marigold, placed face-down [*Tagetes*]: Mental anguish

Marigold, placed face-up [*Tagetes*]: Indifference

Marigold, pot (Calendula, English Marrow) [*Calendula officinalis*]: Affection, Cares, Constancy, Disquietude, Grief, Health, Jealousy, Joy, Misery, Remembrance, Sun

Marigold, prophetic [*Calendula officinalis*]: Prediction

Marigold, red-flowering [*Tagetes*]: "The varying course of life"

Marjoram [*Origanum majorana*]: Blushes, Delusion, Happiness, Health, Humor, Illusion, Love, Money, Protection

Marsh Mallow [*Althaea officinalis*]: Beneficence, Healing, Honesty, Kindness, Persuasion, Purity

Marsh Marigold [*Caltha palustris*]: Desire for riches

Marsh Rosemary (Sea Lavender, Statice) [*Limonium* or *Rhododendron*

tomentosum]: Success, Sympathy

Marvel of Peru (Four O'clock Flower) [*Mirabilis jalapa*]: Shyness, Timidity, Wonderful

Masterwort [*Astrantia*]: Courage, Protection, Strength

Mastic Tree [*Pistacia lentiscus*]: Lust, Manifestations, Psychic powers

Mauve Carnation (Clove Pink, Wild Carnation) [*Dianthus caryophyllus*]: Dreams of fantasy

May Apple [*Podophyllum peltatum*]: Money

Mayflower [*Maianthemum canadense*]: Budding beauty, Coming of age, Welcome

Mayweed (Stinking Chamomile) [*Anthemis cotula*]: Action, Energy

Meadow Lychnis (Maltese Cross) [*Lychnis chalcedonica*]: Wit

Meadow Saffron (Autumn Crocus) [*Colchicum autumnale*]: Cherished, Domestic duties, Domestic virtue, Esteem, Growing old, Long life, Memories, "My best days are past", Past, Regret, Wisdom

Meadow Sage (Autumn Crocus, Meadow Clary) [*Salvia pratensis*]: Cherished, Domestic duties, Domestic virtue, Esteem, Long life, Wisdom

Meadowsweet (Queen-of-the-Meadow) [*Filipendula ulmaria*]: Divination, Happiness, Love, Peace, Uselessness

Melissa (Bee Balm, Lemon Balm) [*Melissa officinalis*]: Fellowship, Joke, Sympathy

Mercury [*Mercurialis*]: Goodness

Mesquite [*Prosopis*]: Healing

Mexican Sage [*Salvia mexicana*]: Eloquence, Spectacular

Mezereon (February Daphne) [*Daphne mezereum*]: Desire to please, Flirt

Michaelmas Daisy [*Aster*]: Afterthought, Daintiness, Farewell, Love, Variety

Mignonette [*Reseda*]: Excellence, Healing, "I live for you", "Your qualities surpass your charms"

Milfoil (Sneezewort, Yarrow) [*Achillea millefolium* or *Myriophyllum*]: Courage, Cure for heartache, Healing, Heartache ease, Love, Psychic powers, War, Warning

Milk Vetch [*Astrgalus*]: Soothing, "Your presence softens my pains"

Milkwort (Seneca, Snakeroot) [*Polygala*]: Hermitage

Millet [*Milium effusum*]: Money

Mimosa (Sensitive plant) [*Acacia dealbata*]: Bashfulness, Delicate feelings, "Do not hurt me", Love, Modesty, Prophetic dreams, Protection, Purification, Secret love, Sensibility, Sensitiveness, Sensitivity, Shyness

Minor Convolvulus (Bindweed) [*Convolvulus*]: Bonds, Despondency, Eminence, Extinguished hopes, Humility, Insinuation, Inspiration, Night, Profuseness, Uncertainty

Minor Convolvulus, blue [*Convolvulus tricolor*]: Night, Repose

Mint [*Mentha*]: Healing, Love, Lust, Money, Protection, Travel, Virtue

Mission Bells [*Fritillaria*]: Persecution

Mistletoe [*Viscum album*]: Affection, Balance, Creativity, Fertility, Health, Holiness, "I surmount all difficulties/obstacles", Kiss me, Love, Obstacles, Overcoming difficulties, Peace, Protection, Sense of self, Warding, Welcome

Mixed-colors Carnation [*Dianthus caryophyllus*]: Beauty, Health and energy, Pride and beauty

Mixed Zinnia [*Zinnia elegans*]: Thinking of an absent friend, "Thinking of you"

Mock Orange [*Murraya paniculata* or *Philadelphus*]: Balance, Counterfeit, Creativity, Deceit, Sense of self, Uncertainty

Molukka Bean [*Moringa ovalifolia*]: Protection

Monarda (Bee Balm) [*Monarda didyma*]: Compassion, Sweet virtues, "Your whims are unbearable"

Money Plant (Sweetheart Vine) [*Philodendron scandens* subsp. *oxycardium*]: Fascination, Forgetfulness, Honesty, Sincerity

Monk's Head [*Aconitum*]: Elegance, Fidelity, Love attraction

Monkshood (Aconite) [*Aconitum napellus*]: "A foe is near", Chivalry, Deadly foe is near, Deception, Warning

Montbretia [*Crocosima*]: "Wishes come true"

Monthly Honeysuckle (Woodbine) [*Lonicera*]: Bond of love, Devoted love

Monthly Rose [*Rosa*]: Beauty ever new

Monthly Rosebud [*Rosa*]: Enchantment

Moon Daisy (Ox-Eye Daisy) [*Leucanthemum vulgare*]: Love's oracle

Moonflower (Moon Vine) [*Ipomoea alba*]: Attachment, Breath of an angel, "I only dream of you", Instability, Moonlight, Night

Moonwort [*Botrychium lunaria*]: Forgetfulness, Love, Money

Moringa, Himalayan (Tree of Life) [*Moringa oleifera*]: Age, Old age

Morning Glory (Major Convolvulus) [*Ipomoea purpurea*]: Affectation, Coquetry, Dead hope, Despondency, Departure, Extinguished hopes, Gladness, Glorious beauty, "I love you", Insincerity, Transience, Uncertainty

Morning Glory, dwarf [*Convolvulus*]: Bonds of affection

Morning Glory, red [*Ipomoea coccinea*]: Attachment

Moschatel [*Adoxa moschatellina*]: "Weak but winning", Weakness

Moss [*Bryophyta*]: Ennui, Luck, Maternal love, Money

Moss Fern [*Selaginella pallescens*]: Content

Moss, Iceland [*Cetraria islandica*]: Health

Moss, Irish (Scotch Moss) [*Sagina subulata*]: Luck, Money, Protection

Moss Rose [*Portulaca grandiflora*]: Confession of love, Love, Superior merit, Voluptuous love, Voluptuousness

Moss Rosebud [*Portulaca grandiflora*]: Confessed love, Confession of love

Moss, Spanish [*Tillandsia usneoides*]: Protection

Mosses [*Bryophyta*]: Ennui, Seclusion

Mossy Saxifrage [*Saxifraga*]: Affection

Mother of the Evening (Dame's Rocket, Sweet Rocket) [*Hesperis matronalis*]: Coquetry, Evening, Virtue

Motherwort [*Leonurus cardiaca*]: Concealed love, Secret love

Mountain Ash [*Eucalyptus regnans* or *Sorbus*]: Intelligence, Prudence, "With me you are safe"

Mountain Laurel [*Kalmia latifolia*]: Ambition, Ambition of a hero, Treachery, Victory

Mountain Laurel, Texas [*Dermatophyllum secundiflorum*]: Dreams, Psychic powers

Mountain Pink [*Dianthus armeria*]: Ambition, Aspiring

Mourning Bride [*Scabiosa*]: "I have lost all", Unfortunate attachment

Mouse-eared Chickweed [*Cerastium*]: Ingenious simplicity

Mouse-eared Scorpion Grass [*Myosotis*]: "Do not forget me", "Forget me not"

Moving Plant (Sensitive Plant, Touch-Me-Not) [*Mimosa pudica*]: Agitation

Mudwort [*Limosella*]: Tranquility

Mugwort [*Artemisia vulgaris*]: Absence, Astral projection, Conception, Encouragement, Good luck, Happiness, Healing, Prophetic dreams, Protection, Psychic powers, Strength, Tranquility

Mulberry Tree [*Morus*]: Protection, Strength

Mulberry Tree, black [*Morus nigra*]: "I shall not survive you"

Mulberry Tree, white [*Morus alba*]: Wisdom

Mullein [*Verbascum*]: Communication, Courage, Divination, Good natured, Health, Love, Protection, Self-empowerment, Self-knowledge, "Take courage"

Mullein, white [*Verbascum lychnitis*]: Good nature

Multicolored Daisy [*Asteraceae*]: Beauty

Multiflora Rose [*Rosa multiflora*]: Grace, Gracefulness

Mum (Bloom, Chrysanthemum) [*Chrysanthemum*]: Abundance, Cheerfulness, Cheerfulness in old age, Cheerfulness under adversity, Desolate heart, Friendship, Innocence, Joy, Joviality, Long life, Loyal love, Mirth, Optimism, Protection, Restfulness, Riches, Truth, Wealth, "With love", "You are a wonderful friend"

Mum, yellow [*Chrysanthemum*]: Slighted love

Mundi Rose [*Rosa gallica*]: Variety, "You are merry"

Mushroom (Champignon) [*Agaricus*]: Mistrust, Suspicion

Musk-mallow [*Abelmoschus moschatus* or *Malva moschata*]: Delicate beauty

Musk Plant (Monkey Musk) [*Mimulus moschatus*]: Weakness

Musk Rose [*Rosa moschata*]: Capricious beauty

Musk Rose cluster [*Rosa moschata*]: Charming

Mustard [*Brassica*]: Fertility, "I am hurt", Indifference, Mental powers, Protection

Mustard Seed [*Brassica*]: Faith, Indifference

Myosotis (Forget-Me-Not) [*Myosotis*]: Consistency, Constancy, "Do not forget me", Dreams, "Forget me not", Hope, Memories, Personal relationships, Release of negativity, Remembrance, True love, True love forever

Myrobalan (Cherry Plum, Purple-Leafed Plum) [*Prunus cerasifera*]: Privation

Myrrh (Sweet Cicely) [*Myrrhis odorata*]: Gladness, Healing, Protection, Spirituality

Myrtle [*Myrtus*]: Joy, Love, Love in absence

Myrtle, cape [*Myrsine africana*]: Eloquence

Myrtle, crepe [*Lagerstroemia*]: Eloquence, Love

Myrtle, wax [*Myrica cerifera*]: Discipline, Good luck, Instruction

Mimosa

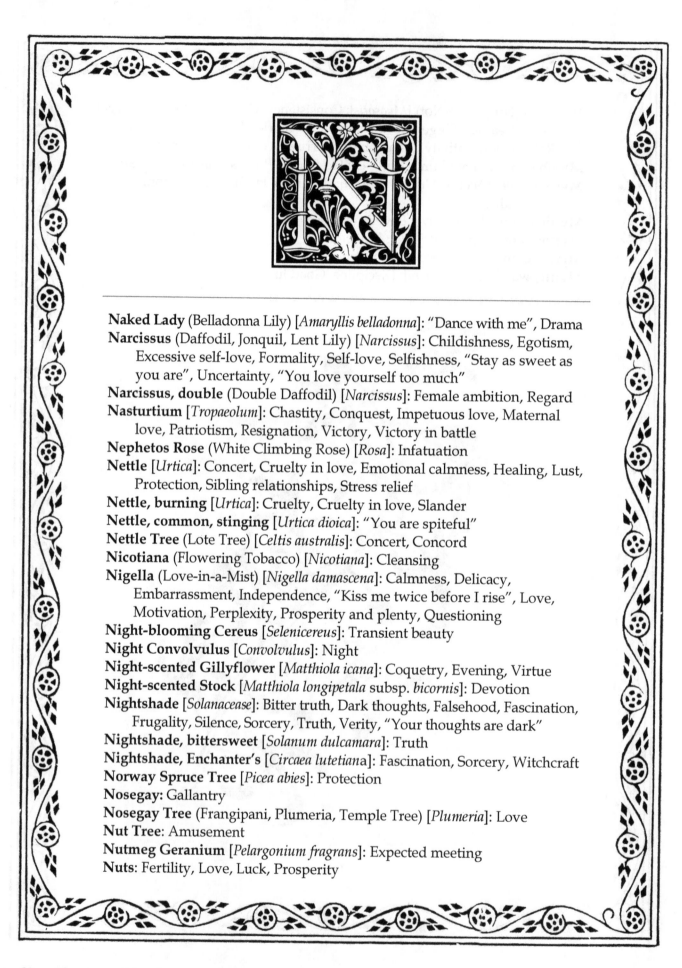

Naked Lady (Belladonna Lily) [*Amaryllis belladonna*]: "Dance with me", Drama

Narcissus (Daffodil, Jonquil, Lent Lily) [*Narcissus*]: Childishness, Egotism, Excessive self-love, Formality, Self-love, Selfishness, "Stay as sweet as you are", Uncertainty, "You love yourself too much"

Narcissus, double (Double Daffodil) [*Narcissus*]: Female ambition, Regard

Nasturtium [*Tropaeolum*]: Chastity, Conquest, Impetuous love, Maternal love, Patriotism, Resignation, Victory, Victory in battle

Nephetos Rose (White Climbing Rose) [*Rosa*]: Infatuation

Nettle [*Urtica*]: Concert, Cruelty in love, Emotional calmness, Healing, Lust, Protection, Sibling relationships, Stress relief

Nettle, burning [*Urtica*]: Cruelty, Cruelty in love, Slander

Nettle, common, stinging [*Urtica dioica*]: "You are spiteful"

Nettle Tree (Lote Tree) [*Celtis australis*]: Concert, Concord

Nicotiana (Flowering Tobacco) [*Nicotiana*]: Cleansing

Nigella (Love-in-a-Mist) [*Nigella damascena*]: Calmness, Delicacy, Embarrassment, Independence, "Kiss me twice before I rise", Love, Motivation, Perplexity, Prosperity and plenty, Questioning

Night-blooming Cereus [*Selenicereus*]: Transient beauty

Night Convolvulus [*Convolvulus*]: Night

Night-scented Gillyflower [*Matthiola icana*]: Coquetry, Evening, Virtue

Night-scented Stock [*Matthiola longipetala* subsp. *bicornis*]: Devotion

Nightshade [*Solanacease*]: Bitter truth, Dark thoughts, Falsehood, Fascination, Frugality, Silence, Sorcery, Truth, Verity, "Your thoughts are dark"

Nightshade, bittersweet [*Solanum dulcamara*]: Truth

Nightshade, Enchanter's [*Circaea lutetiana*]: Fascination, Sorcery, Witchcraft

Norway Spruce Tree [*Picea abies*]: Protection

Nosegay: Gallantry

Nosegay Tree (Frangipani, Plumeria, Temple Tree) [*Plumeria*]: Love

Nut Tree: Amusement

Nutmeg Geranium [*Pelargonium fragrans*]: Expected meeting

Nuts: Fertility, Love, Luck, Prosperity

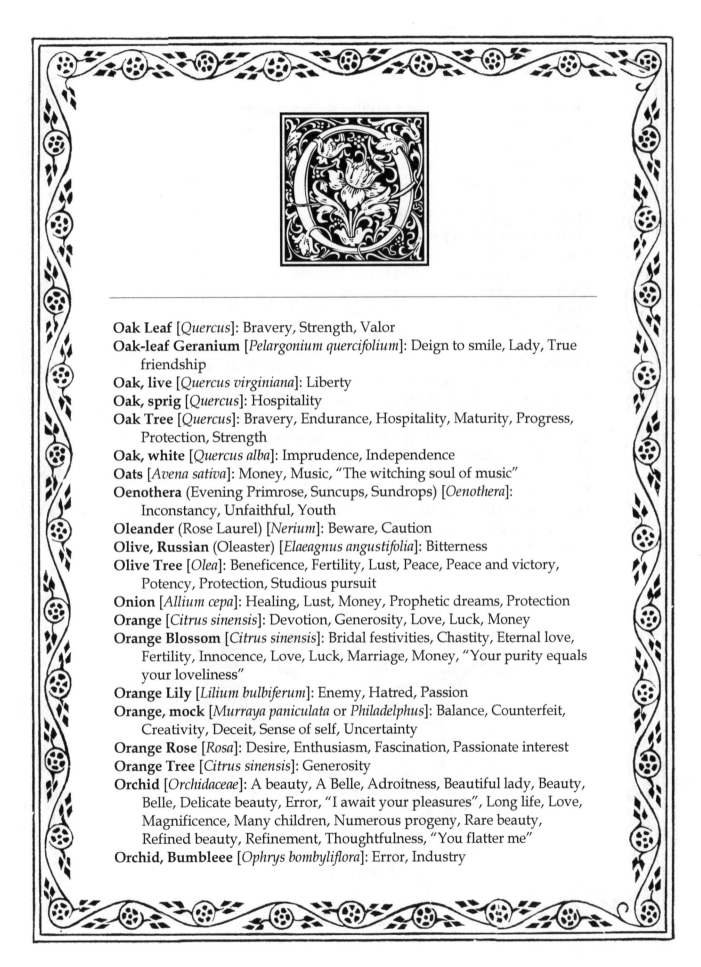

Oak Leaf [*Quercus*]: Bravery, Strength, Valor

Oak-leaf Geranium [*Pelargonium quercifolium*]: Deign to smile, Lady, True friendship

Oak, live [*Quercus virginiana*]: Liberty

Oak, sprig [*Quercus*]: Hospitality

Oak Tree [*Quercus*]: Bravery, Endurance, Hospitality, Maturity, Progress, Protection, Strength

Oak, white [*Quercus alba*]: Imprudence, Independence

Oats [*Avena sativa*]: Money, Music, "The witching soul of music"

Oenothera (Evening Primrose, Suncups, Sundrops) [*Oenothera*]: Inconstancy, Unfaithful, Youth

Oleander (Rose Laurel) [*Nerium*]: Beware, Caution

Olive, Russian (Oleaster) [*Elaeagnus angustifolia*]: Bitterness

Olive Tree [*Olea*]: Beneficence, Fertility, Lust, Peace, Peace and victory, Potency, Protection, Studious pursuit

Onion [*Allium cepa*]: Healing, Lust, Money, Prophetic dreams, Protection

Orange [*Citrus sinensis*]: Devotion, Generosity, Love, Luck, Money

Orange Blossom [*Citrus sinensis*]: Bridal festivities, Chastity, Eternal love, Fertility, Innocence, Love, Luck, Marriage, Money, "Your purity equals your loveliness"

Orange Lily [*Lilium bulbiferum*]: Enemy, Hatred, Passion

Orange, mock [*Murraya paniculata* or *Philadelphus*]: Balance, Counterfeit, Creativity, Deceit, Sense of self, Uncertainty

Orange Rose [*Rosa*]: Desire, Enthusiasm, Fascination, Passionate interest

Orange Tree [*Citrus sinensis*]: Generosity

Orchid [*Orchidaceae*]: A beauty, A Belle, Adroitness, Beautiful lady, Beauty, Belle, Delicate beauty, Error, "I await your pleasures", Long life, Love, Magnificence, Many children, Numerous progeny, Rare beauty, Refined beauty, Refinement, Thoughtfulness, "You flatter me"

Orchid, Bumbleee [*Ophrys bombyliflora*]: Error, Industry

Orchid, Butterfly [*Psychopsis* + 10 other species]: Gaiety

Orchid, Cattleya [*Cattleya*]: Mature charm, Mature grace

Orchid, Chinese ground [*Bletilla*]: Beauty

Orchid, comet (Angrec) [*Angraecum*]: Royalty

Orchid, Cymbidium [*Cymbidium*]: Beauty, Love, Luxury, Magnificence, Scholarship

Orchid, Fly [*Ophrys insectifera*]: Error

Orchid, hardy [*Bletilla*]: Beauty

Orchid, Lady's Slipper [*Paphiopedilum* or *Phragmipedium*]: Capricious beauty, "Catch me if you can", Fickleness, Protection, "Win me and wear me"

Orchid, scorpion [*Arachnis*]: Elopement

Orchid, spider [*Dendrobium tetragonum*]: Adroitness, Skill

Oregano [*Origanum*]: Birth, Joy, Peace

Oregon Grape (Holly Grape) [*Mahonia aquifolium*]: Money, Prosperity

Oriental Helleborus (Lenten Rose) [*Helleborus orientalis*]: Goals, Poise, Self-assurance, Shyness reduction, Tension relief

Ornithogalum (Florists' Nightmare, Star-of-Bethlehem) [*Ornithogalum umbellatum*]: Atonement, Hope, Idleness, Purity, Reconciliation

Orris Root [*Iris pallida* or *Iris germanica*]: Divination, Love, Protection

Osier (Willow) [*Salix*]: Frankness

Osmunda [*Osmunda*]: Dreams, "I dream of you", Reverie

Our Lady's Earrings [*Impatiens walleriana*]: Impatience, Motherly love

Oxalis (Sorrel) [*Oxalis*]: Affection, Funny, Healing, Health, Joy, Not funny, Parental affection, Secret sweetness

Ox-eye Daisy [*Leucanthemum vulgare*]: Joy, Patience, Token of affection

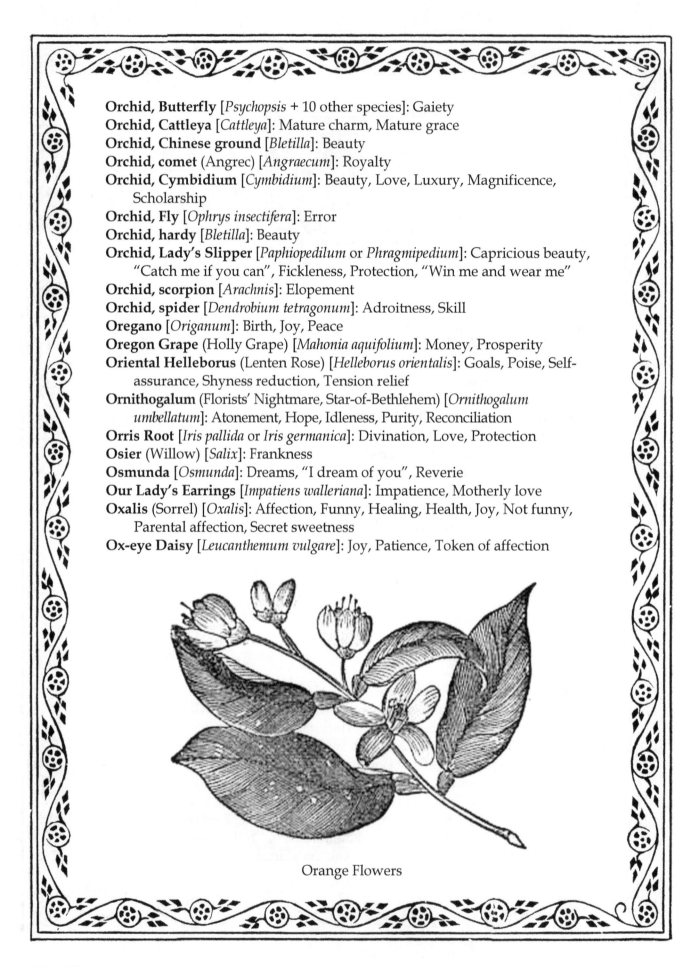

Orange Flowers

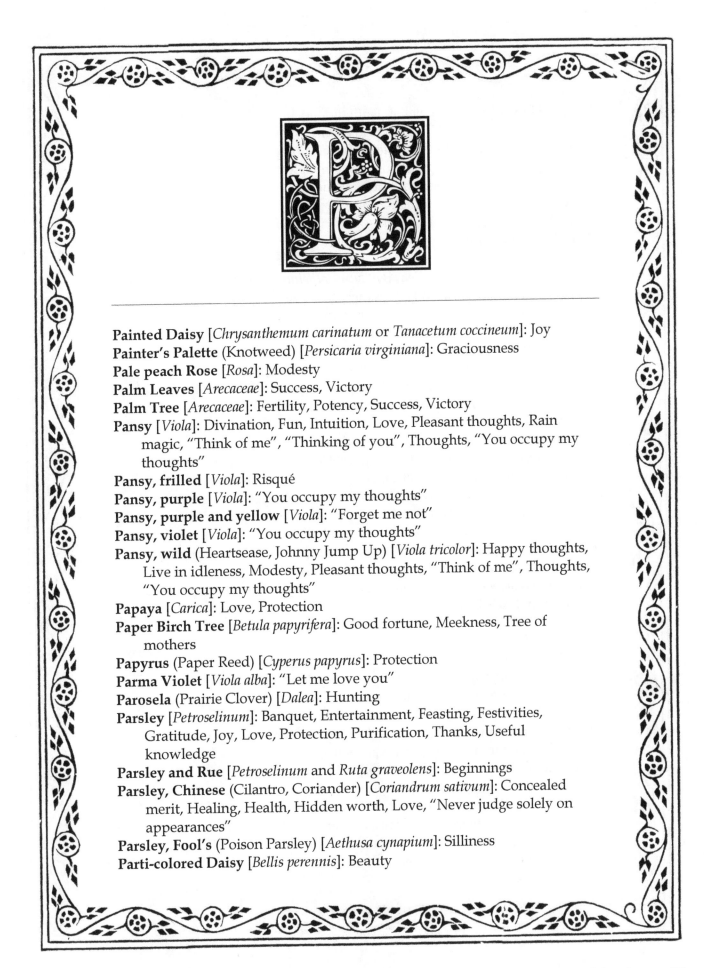

Painted Daisy [*Chrysanthemum carinatum* or *Tanacetum coccineum*]: Joy

Painter's Palette (Knotweed) [*Persicaria virginiana*]: Graciousness

Pale peach Rose [*Rosa*]: Modesty

Palm Leaves [*Arecaceae*]: Success, Victory

Palm Tree [*Arecaceae*]: Fertility, Potency, Success, Victory

Pansy [*Viola*]: Divination, Fun, Intuition, Love, Pleasant thoughts, Rain magic, "Think of me", "Thinking of you", Thoughts, "You occupy my thoughts"

Pansy, frilled [*Viola*]: Risqué

Pansy, purple [*Viola*]: "You occupy my thoughts"

Pansy, purple and yellow [*Viola*]: "Forget me not"

Pansy, violet [*Viola*]: "You occupy my thoughts"

Pansy, wild (Heartsease, Johnny Jump Up) [*Viola tricolor*]: Happy thoughts, Live in idleness, Modesty, Pleasant thoughts, "Think of me", Thoughts, "You occupy my thoughts"

Papaya [*Carica*]: Love, Protection

Paper Birch Tree [*Betula papyrifera*]: Good fortune, Meekness, Tree of mothers

Papyrus (Paper Reed) [*Cyperus papyrus*]: Protection

Parma Violet [*Viola alba*]: "Let me love you"

Parosela (Prairie Clover) [*Dalea*]: Hunting

Parsley [*Petroselinum*]: Banquet, Entertainment, Feasting, Festivities, Gratitude, Joy, Love, Protection, Purification, Thanks, Useful knowledge

Parsley and Rue [*Petroselinum* and *Ruta graveolens*]: Beginnings

Parsley, Chinese (Cilantro, Coriander) [*Coriandrum sativum*]: Concealed merit, Healing, Health, Hidden worth, Love, "Never judge solely on appearances"

Parsley, Fool's (Poison Parsley) [*Aethusa cynapium*]: Silliness

Parti-colored Daisy [*Bellis perennis*]: Beauty

Pasque Flower [*Pulsatilla*]: Belief, Faith, Friendship, Religion, Sleep, Unpretentiousness, "You have no claims"

Passionflower (Grandilla) [*Passiflora*]: Belief, Compassion, Faith, Friendship, Religious fervor, Religious superstition, Spirituality

Patchouli [*Pogostemon*]: Fertility, Lust, Money

Patience Dock [*Rumex patientia*]: Patience

Patient Lucy (Busy Lizzie) [*Impatiens walleriana*]: Impatience, Motherly love

Pea [*Pisum sativum*]: An appointed meeting, Departure, Happiness in marriage, Love, Money, Profits in business, Respect

Pea, everlasting (Perennial Pea) [*Lathyrus latifolius*]: Appointed meeting, Bliss, Blissful pleasure, Chastity, Courage, Delicate pleasures, Departure, Friendship, Good-bye, Lasting pleasure, "Let's meet", Never-ceasing remembrance, "Remember me", Shyness, Strength, Tenderness, "Thank you for a good time"

Pea, grass [*Lathyrus nissolia* or *Lathyrus sativus*]: Bliss, Blissful pleasure, Chastity, Courage, Delicate pleasures, Departure, Friendship, Good-bye, "Let's meet", "Remember me", Shyness, Strength, Tenderness, "Thank you for a good time"

Pea, sweet [*Lathyrus odoratus*]: Appointed meeting, Bliss, Blissful pleasure, Chastity, Courage, Delicate pleasures, Departure, "Do not go away", Friendship, Good-bye, "Let's meet", "Meet me", "Remember me", Shyness, Strength, Tender memories, Tenderness, "Thank you for a good time"

Peach [*Prunus persica*]: Fertility, Longevity, Love, Submission, Wishes, "Your qualities, like your charms, are unequaled"

Peach Blossom [*Prunus persica*]: "I am your captive", "My heart is yours"

Peach Rose [*Rosa*]: Desire, Enthusiasm, Shyness

Pear [*Pyrus communis*]: Affection, Benevolent justice, Good government, Health, Love, Lust, Wise administration

Pear Blossom [*Pyrus*]: Comfort

Pear, prickly [*Opuntia*]: "I burn for you", Satire

Pear Tree [*Pyrus*]: Affection, Comfort, Health

Pecan Tree [*Carya illinoinensis*]: Employment, Money

Pelargonium [*Pelargonium*]: Eagerness

Pelargonium, red [*Pelargonium*]: Gracefulness

Pelargonium, white [*Pelargonium*]: "Her smile is the soul of witchery"

Pencil-leaf Geranium [*Pelargonium*]: Genius, Ingenuity

Penstemon (Beardtongue) [*Penstemon*]: Creativity, Pleasure without alloy

Pennyroyal [*Mentha pulegium*]: Clarity of thought, "Flee away", Peace, Positive thoughts, Protection, Strength

Peony [*Paeonia*]: Anger, Bashfulness, Bravery, Contrition, "Hands full of cash", Happiness, Healing, Indignation, Marriage, Ostentation, Prosperity, Protection, Shame, Shyness

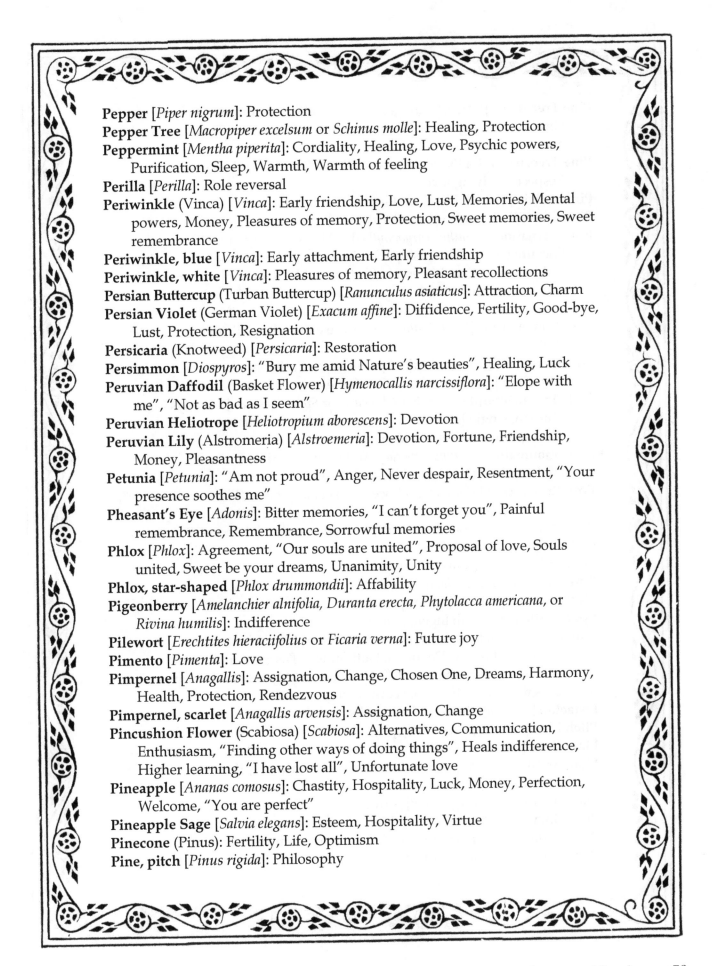

Pepper [*Piper nigrum*]: Protection

Pepper Tree [*Macropiper excelsum* or *Schinus molle*]: Healing, Protection

Peppermint [*Mentha piperita*]: Cordiality, Healing, Love, Psychic powers, Purification, Sleep, Warmth, Warmth of feeling

Perilla [*Perilla*]: Role reversal

Periwinkle (Vinca) [*Vinca*]: Early friendship, Love, Lust, Memories, Mental powers, Money, Pleasures of memory, Protection, Sweet memories, Sweet remembrance

Periwinkle, blue [*Vinca*]: Early attachment, Early friendship

Periwinkle, white [*Vinca*]: Pleasures of memory, Pleasant recollections

Persian Buttercup (Turban Buttercup) [*Ranunculus asiaticus*]: Attraction, Charm

Persian Violet (German Violet) [*Exacum affine*]: Diffidence, Fertility, Good-bye, Lust, Protection, Resignation

Persicaria (Knotweed) [*Persicaria*]: Restoration

Persimmon [*Diospyros*]: "Bury me amid Nature's beauties", Healing, Luck

Peruvian Daffodil (Basket Flower) [*Hymenocallis narcissiflora*]: "Elope with me", "Not as bad as I seem"

Peruvian Heliotrope [*Heliotropium aborescens*]: Devotion

Peruvian Lily (Alstromeria) [*Alstroemeria*]: Devotion, Fortune, Friendship, Money, Pleasantness

Petunia [*Petunia*]: "Am not proud", Anger, Never despair, Resentment, "Your presence soothes me"

Pheasant's Eye [*Adonis*]: Bitter memories, "I can't forget you", Painful remembrance, Remembrance, Sorrowful memories

Phlox [*Phlox*]: Agreement, "Our souls are united", Proposal of love, Souls united, Sweet be your dreams, Unanimity, Unity

Phlox, star-shaped [*Phlox drummondii*]: Affability

Pigeonberry [*Amelanchier alnifolia*, *Duranta erecta*, *Phytolacca americana*, or *Rivina humilis*]: Indifference

Pilewort [*Erechtites hieraciifolius* or *Ficaria verna*]: Future joy

Pimento [*Pimenta*]: Love

Pimpernel [*Anagallis*]: Assignation, Change, Chosen One, Dreams, Harmony, Health, Protection, Rendezvous

Pimpernel, scarlet [*Anagallis arvensis*]: Assignation, Change

Pincushion Flower (Scabiosa) [*Scabiosa*]: Alternatives, Communication, Enthusiasm, "Finding other ways of doing things", Heals indifference, Higher learning, "I have lost all", Unfortunate love

Pineapple [*Ananas comosus*]: Chastity, Hospitality, Luck, Money, Perfection, Welcome, "You are perfect"

Pineapple Sage [*Salvia elegans*]: Esteem, Hospitality, Virtue

Pinecone (Pinus): Fertility, Life, Optimism

Pine, pitch [*Pinus rigida*]: Philosophy

Pine Tree [*Pinus*]: Awe, Courage, Daring, Elation, Endurance, Enthusiasm, Fertility, Healing, Hope, Mobility, Money, Protection, Time, Spiritual energy, Wonder

Pine Tree, umbrella [*Sciadopitys verticillata*]: "Honoring the dead", Joy, Respect, Undying love

Pink Acacia [*Acacia*]: Elegance, Grace

Pink Camellia Japonica [*Camellia japonica*]: Longing

Pink Carnation [*Dianthus caryophyllus*]: "Always on my mind", Beauty, Encouragement, Friendship, Gratitude, "I will never forget you", Lively and pure affection, Maternal affection, Pride, Remembrance, Sexual liberation, Unforgettable, Woman's love

Pink, China [*Dianthus chinensis*]: Aversion

Pink Convolvulus [*Convolvulus*]: Worth sustained by judicious and tender affection

Pink Geranium [*Pelargonium*]: "I prefer you", Preference

Pink Hyacinth [*Hyacinthus*]: Joy, Playfulness

Pink, Indian, double [*Dianthus Chinensis* or *Silene laciniata*]: Always lovely

Pink, Indian, single [*Dianthus Chinensis* or *Silene laciniata*]: Aversion

Pink Larkspur [*Consolida*]: Fickleness

Pink, mountain [*Dianthus armeria*]: Ambition, Aspiring

Pink, red, double [*Dianthus*]: Pure and ardent love

Pink Rose [*Rosa*]: Friendship, Grace, Perfect happiness, "Please believe me", Secret love, Sweetness

Pink, sea (Sea Lavender, Sea Thrift) [*Armeria maritima*]: Success, Sympathy

Pink, single [*Dianthus*]: Pure love

Pink Tulip [*Tulipa*]: Caring, Dreaminess

Pink, variegated [*Dianthus*]: Refusal

Pink Verbena [*Verbena*]: Family union

Pink, white [*Dianthus*]: Ingeniousness, Talent

Pinks (Carnation, Dianthus) [*Dianthus*]: Admiration, Affection, Aversion, Boldness, Chivalry, Devotion, Faithfulness, Fascination, Finesse, Gallantry, "Grant me a smile", Make haste, "My heart aches for you", Perfection, Pure affection, Scorn, Woman's love

Pistachio [*Pistacia*]: Breaking love spells

Pitch Pine [*Pinus rigida*]: Philosophy

Plane Tree [*Platanus*]: Genius

Plantain [*Arnoglossum*]: Adulation, Healing, Pilgrimage, Protection, Strength, Well-trodden path

Plantain, Indian [*Arnoglossum*]: Adulation

Plantain, white [*Plantago major*]: Man's footsteps

Plum [*Prunus domestica*]: Healing, "Keep your promises", Promises

Plum Blossom [*Prunus*]: Fidelity

Plum, Indian [*Flacourtia jangomas* or *Oemleria cerasiformis*]: Privation, Suffering

Plum Tree [*Prunus domestica*]: Fidelity, Genius, Imprudence, Independence

Plum, wild [*Prunus americana*]: Independence

Plumbago (Leadwort) [*Plumbago*]: Antidote, Holy wishes, Success, Sympathy

Plumeria (Frangipani, Nosegay Tree) [*Plumeria*]: Love

Poinsettia [*Euphorbia pulcherrima*]: Be of good cheer, Celebration, Good cheer, Mirth, Success

Poison Root [*Scadoxus multiflorus*]: Glory, Splendor

Poke (Pokeweed) [*Phytolacca americana*]: Courage

Polonium (Empress Tree, Princess Tree) [*Paulownia tomentosa*]: Breaking

Policeman's Helmet [*Impatiens glandulifera*]: Impatience, Motherly love

Polyanthus [*Primula polyantha*]: Pride of riches

Polyanthus, crimson [*Primula polyantha*]: Heart's mystery, Heart's riches

Polyanthus, lilac [*Primula polyantha*]: Confidence in heaven

Pomegranate [*Punica grantum*]: Conceited, Divination, Elegance, Fertility, Folly, Foolishness, Luck, Wealth, Wishes

Pomegranate Flower [*Punica grantum*]: Mature elegance, Perfection

Poor Robin [*Geranium robertianum*]: Compensation, "Of an equivalent"

Poplar Tree [*Populus*]: Flying, Money

Poplar Tree, black [*Populus nigra*]: Courage

Poplar Tree, white [*Populus alba*]: Time

Poplar, tulip [*Liriodendron tulipifera*]: Among the nobles, Fame, Retirement, Rural happiness

Poppy [*Papaver*]: Consolation, Death, Dreaminess, Eternal sleep, Evanescent pleasure, Extravagance, Fertility, Imagination, Invisibility, Love, Luck, Money, Oblivion, Sleep

Poppy, California (Escholzia) [*Eschscholzia californica*]: "Do not refuse me"

Poppy, crimson [*Papaver*]: Fantasy

Poppy, red [*Papaver*]: Consolation, Passion, Pleasure

Poppy, red field [*Papaver rhoeas*]: Consolation

Poppy, scarlet [*Papaver*]: Fantastic extravagance

Poppy, variegated [*Papaver*]: Dreaminess, Flirtation

Poppy, white [*Papaver*]: Consolation, Dormant affection, Forgetfulness, Oblivion, "Sleep - my bane, my antidote"

Poppy, yellow [*Papaver*]: Success, Wealth

Portulaca (Moss Roses, Purslane) [*Portulaca*]: "It's time"

Pot Marigold (Calendula, English Marigold) [*Calendula officinalis*]: Affection, Cares, Constancy, Disquietude, Grief, Health, Jealousy, Joy, Misery, Remembrance, Sun

Potato [*Solanum tuberosum*]: Beneficence, Benevolence, Healing, Image magic

Potato Vine [*Solanum jasminoides* or *Solanum wendlandii*]: "You are delicious"

Prairie Clover (Parosela) [*Dalea*]: Hunting

Prairie Gentian (Lisianthus, Texas Bluebell) [*Eustoma grandiflorum*]: Beautiful mouth, Optimistic, Outgoing, Playful, Well-spoken

Prairie Rose [*Rosa setigera*]: Beautiful mouth, Optimistic, Outgoing, Playful, Well-spoken

Prayer Plant [*Maranta leuconeura*]: Bashfulness, Sensibility

Pretty Face [*Triteleia ixioides*]: Hope, Vigilance, Watchfulness

Prickly Ash [*Zanthoxylum americanum*]: Love

Prickly Burr [*Acaena magellanica*]: Deceit

Prickly Pear [*Opuntia*]: "I burn for you", Satire

Pride of China [*Incarvillea delavayi* or *Koelreuteria bipinnata*]: Dissension

Primrose (Cowslip) [*Primula veris*]: Comeliness, Divine beauty, Divinity, Early youth, Grace, Healing, Heart's mystery, Love, Pensiveness, Protection, Treasure finding, Winning grace, "You are my divinity", "You are wonderful", Youth

Primrose, China [*Primula*]: Lasting love

Primrose, evening (Suncups, Sundrops) [*Oenothera*]: Inconstancy, Unfaithful, Youth

Primrose, red [*Primula*]: Unpatronized merit

Primrose, yellow [*Primula*]: Hunting

Prince of Wales Feather [*Amaranthus hypochondriacus*]: Hopelessness

Prince's Feather (Kiss-Me-Over-the-Garden-Gate) [*Persicaria orientalis*]: "I blush for you"

Privet Hedge [*Ligustrum*]: Prohibition

Prophetic Marigold [*Calendula officinalis*]: Prediction

Protea (Sugarbush) [*Protea*]: Courage

Provence Rose [*Rosa centifolia*]: Gentleness

Pukeweed [*Lobelia inflata*]: Arrogance

Pumpkin [*Cucurbita*]: Coarseness, Vulgarity

Purple and yellow Pansy [*Viola*]: "Forget me not"

Purple Carnation [*Dianthus caryophyllus*]: Capriciousness, Unreliable, Whimsical

Purple Clover [*Trifolium purpureum*]: Providence

Purple Columbine [*Aquilegia*]: Resolved to win, Resolution

Purple Coneflower (Echinacea) [*Echinacea purpurea*]: Strength and health

Purple Grass (Fountain Grass) [*Pennisetum setaceum*]: Sport

Purple Hyacinth [*Hyacinthus*]: Apology, Grief, "I'm sorry", Jealousy, "Please forgive me", Sadness, Sorrow

Purple Larkspur [*Consolida* or *Delphinium*]: Haughtiness

Purple-leaf Sage [*Salvia blepharophylla* or *Salvia purpurea*]: Gratitude

Purple Lilac (Syringa) [*Synnga*]: First emotions of love, First love

Purple Lily [*Syringa vulgaris*]: First love

Purple Pansy [*Viola*]: "You occupy my thoughts"

Purple Rose [*Rosa*]: Enchantment, Lust, Passion
Purple Tulip [*Tulipa*]: Royalty
Purple Verbena [*Verbena*]: "I weep for you", Regret
Purple Violet [*Viola*]: "You occupy my thoughts"
Purple Willow Herb [*Epilobium coloratum*]: Sporting
Purslane [*Portulaca oleracea*]: Happiness, Love, Luck, Protection, Sleep
Pussy Willow [*Salix caprea*]: Friendship, Mother, Recovery from illness
Pyramidal Bellflower [*Campanula pyramidalis*]: Constancy
Pyrus Japonica (Japanese Andromeda, Lily-of-the-Valley Shrub) [*Pieris japonica*]: Fairies' fire, Love at first sight
Pyxie [*Pyxidanthera barbulata*]: "Life is sweet"

Poppy

Quaking Grass [*Briza media*]: Agitation

Quamash (Camas) [*Camassia*]: Mysterious

Queen Anne's Lace [*Daucus carota*]: "Do not refuse me", Fantasy, Femininity, "I will return"

Queen Anne's Thimbles [*Gilia capitata*]: Enduring beauty, Promptness

Queen of the Meadows (Meadowsweet) [*Filipendula ulmaria*]: Uselessness

Queen's Rocket (Dame's Rocket, Sweet Rocket) [*Hesperis matronalis*]: Fashion, "You are the queen of coquettes"

Quince [*Cydonia oblonga*]: "Cheers my soul", Happiness, Love, Protection, Temptation, Triteness

Quince

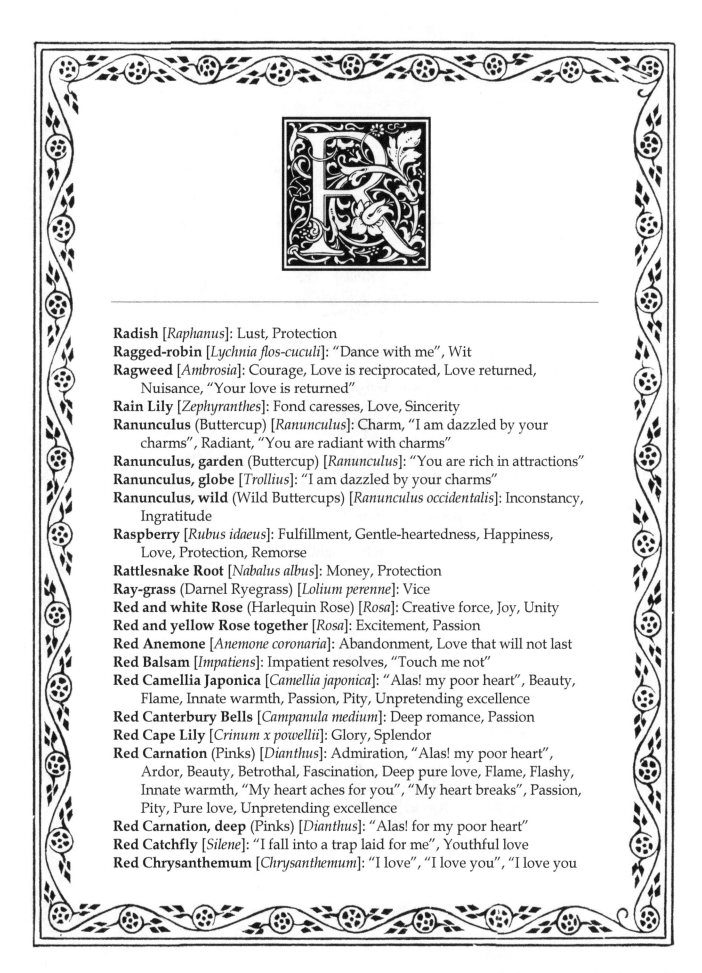

Radish [*Raphanus*]: Lust, Protection

Ragged-robin [*Lychnia flos-cuculi*]: "Dance with me", Wit

Ragweed [*Ambrosia*]: Courage, Love is reciprocated, Love returned, Nuisance, "Your love is returned"

Rain Lily [*Zephyranthes*]: Fond caresses, Love, Sincerity

Ranunculus (Buttercup) [*Ranunculus*]: Charm, "I am dazzled by your charms", Radiant, "You are radiant with charms"

Ranunculus, garden (Buttercup) [*Ranunculus*]: "You are rich in attractions"

Ranunculus, globe [*Trollius*]: "I am dazzled by your charms"

Ranunculus, wild (Wild Buttercups) [*Ranunculus occidentalis*]: Inconstancy, Ingratitude

Raspberry [*Rubus idaeus*]: Fulfillment, Gentle-heartedness, Happiness, Love, Protection, Remorse

Rattlesnake Root [*Nabalus albus*]: Money, Protection

Ray-grass (Darnel Ryegrass) [*Lolium perenne*]: Vice

Red and white Rose (Harlequin Rose) [*Rosa*]: Creative force, Joy, Unity

Red and yellow Rose together [*Rosa*]: Excitement, Passion

Red Anemone [*Anemone coronaria*]: Abandonment, Love that will not last

Red Balsam [*Impatiens*]: Impatient resolves, "Touch me not"

Red Camellia Japonica [*Camellia japonica*]: "Alas! my poor heart", Beauty, Flame, Innate warmth, Passion, Pity, Unpretending excellence

Red Canterbury Bells [*Campanula medium*]: Deep romance, Passion

Red Cape Lily [*Crinum x powellii*]: Glory, Splendor

Red Carnation (Pinks) [*Dianthus*]: Admiration, "Alas! my poor heart", Ardor, Beauty, Betrothal, Fascination, Deep pure love, Flame, Flashy, Innate warmth, "My heart aches for you", "My heart breaks", Passion, Pity, Pure love, Unpretending excellence

Red Carnation, deep (Pinks) [*Dianthus*]: "Alas! for my poor heart"

Red Catchfly [*Silene*]: "I fall into a trap laid for me", Youthful love

Red Chrysanthemum [*Chrysanthemum*]: "I love", "I love you", "I love you

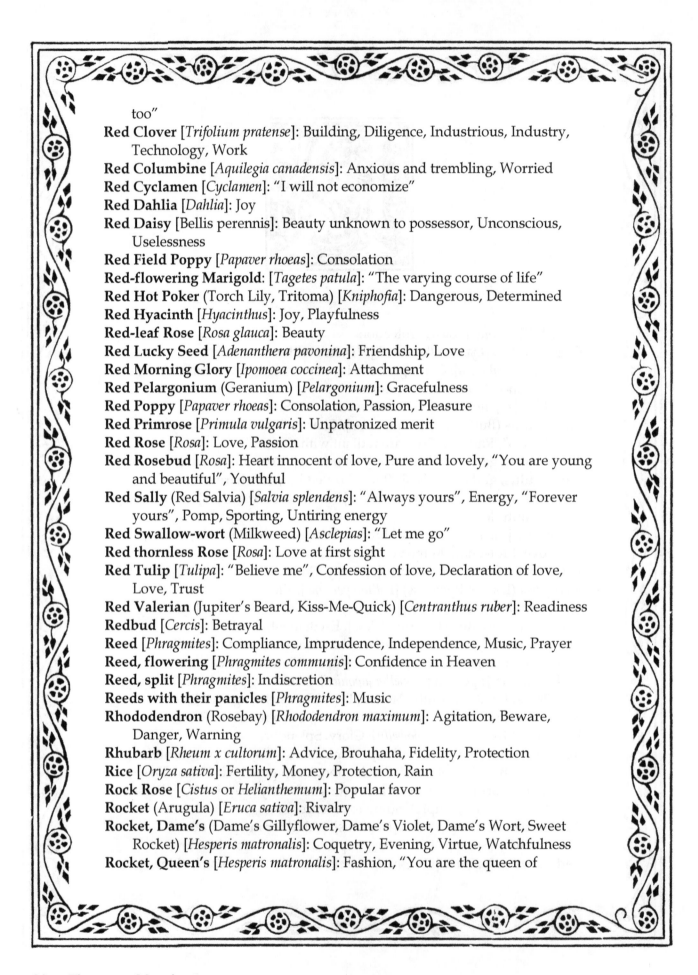

too"

Red Clover [*Trifolium pratense*]: Building, Diligence, Industrious, Industry, Technology, Work

Red Columbine [*Aquilegia canadensis*]: Anxious and trembling, Worried

Red Cyclamen [*Cyclamen*]: "I will not economize"

Red Dahlia [*Dahlia*]: Joy

Red Daisy [Bellis perennis]: Beauty unknown to possessor, Unconscious, Uselessness

Red Field Poppy [*Papaver rhoeas*]: Consolation

Red-flowering Marigold: [*Tagetes patula*]: "The varying course of life"

Red Hot Poker (Torch Lily, Tritoma) [*Kniphofia*]: Dangerous, Determined

Red Hyacinth [*Hyacinthus*]: Joy, Playfulness

Red-leaf Rose [*Rosa glauca*]: Beauty

Red Lucky Seed [*Adenanthera pavonina*]: Friendship, Love

Red Morning Glory [*Ipomoea coccinea*]: Attachment

Red Pelargonium (Geranium) [*Pelargonium*]: Gracefulness

Red Poppy [*Papaver rhoeas*]: Consolation, Passion, Pleasure

Red Primrose [*Primula vulgaris*]: Unpatronized merit

Red Rose [*Rosa*]: Love, Passion

Red Rosebud [*Rosa*]: Heart innocent of love, Pure and lovely, "You are young and beautiful", Youthful

Red Sally (Red Salvia) [*Salvia splendens*]: "Always yours", Energy, "Forever yours", Pomp, Sporting, Untiring energy

Red Swallow-wort (Milkweed) [*Asclepias*]: "Let me go"

Red thornless Rose [*Rosa*]: Love at first sight

Red Tulip [*Tulipa*]: "Believe me", Confession of love, Declaration of love, Love, Trust

Red Valerian (Jupiter's Beard, Kiss-Me-Quick) [*Centranthus ruber*]: Readiness

Redbud [*Cercis*]: Betrayal

Reed [*Phragmites*]: Compliance, Imprudence, Independence, Music, Prayer

Reed, flowering [*Phragmites communis*]: Confidence in Heaven

Reed, split [*Phragmites*]: Indiscretion

Reeds with their panicles [*Phragmites*]: Music

Rhododendron (Rosebay) [*Rhododendron maximum*]: Agitation, Beware, Danger, Warning

Rhubarb [*Rheum x cultorum*]: Advice, Brouhaha, Fidelity, Protection

Rice [*Oryza sativa*]: Fertility, Money, Protection, Rain

Rock Rose [*Cistus* or *Helianthemum*]: Popular favor

Rocket (Arugula) [*Eruca sativa*]: Rivalry

Rocket, Dame's (Dame's Gillyflower, Dame's Violet, Dame's Wort, Sweet Rocket) [*Hesperis matronalis*]: Coquetry, Evening, Virtue, Watchfulness

Rocket, Queen's [*Hesperis matronalis*]: Fashion, "You are the queen of coquettes"

Rocket, sweet [*Hesperis matronalis*]: Coquetry, Evening, Virtue

Rogue's Gillyflower [*Hesperis matronalis*]: Coquetry, Evening, Virtue

Roots: Divination, Power, Protection

Rose [*Rosa*]: Always, Desire, Divination, Eternal love, Friendship, Gladness, Happiness, Healing, "I love you", Joy, Love, Love at first sight, Passion, Perfect happiness, "Please believe me", Psychic powers, "Thy smile I aspire to", Unity, Warmth of heart, "You are everything to me"

Rose Acacia [*Robinia hispida*]: Elegance, Friendship, Platonic love

Rose, Austrian [*Rosa foetida*]: "You are all that is lovely"

Rose, black [*Rosa*]: Death, Farewell, Hatred, Obsession, Rebirth

Rose, blue [*Rosa*]: Mystery, Wistfulness

Rose Bouquet [*Rosa*]: Gratitude

Rose, Boule de Neige [*Rosa*]: "Only for you"

Rose, bridal [*Rosa*]: Happy love

Rose, burgundy [*Rosa*]: Unconscious beauty, Unconsciousness

Rose, cabbage [*Rosa centifolia*]: Ambassador of love

Rose, Campion [*Lychnis coronaria*]: "Dance with me", "You only deserve my love"

Rose, Carolina [*Rosa carolina*]: Love is dangerous

Rose, Charles le Fievree [*Rosa*]: "Speak low if you speak love"

Rose, China [*Hibiscus rosa-sinensis*]: Beauty always new, Grace

Rose, Christmas [*Helleborus niger*]: Anxiety relief, "Relieve my anxiety", "Tranquilize my anxiety"

Rose, climbing white (Nephetos Rose) [*Rosa*]: Infatuation

Rose Cluster, musk [*Rosa moschata*]: Charming

Rose, coral [*Rosa*]: Desire, Enthusiasm

Rose, daily [*Rosa*]: "Welcome me", "Your smile I aspire to"

Rose, damask [*Rosa gallica x Rosa phoenicea, or Rosa gallica x Rosa moschata*]: Bashful love, Brilliant complexion, Freshness, Youth

Rose, dark crimson [*Rosa*]: Mourning

Rose, dark red [*Rosa*]: Mourning

Rose, deep pink [*Rosa*]: "Thank you"

Rose, deep red [*Rosa*]: Bashful shame, Bashfulness

Rose, dog [*Rosa canina*]: Mixed feelings, Pleasure and pain

Rose, Dundee Rambler [*Rosa*]: Only deserve my love

Rose, dried white [*Rosa*]: "Death preferable to loss of innocence"

Rose, Eglantine [*Rosa rubiginosa*]: Poetry

Rose, first of summer [*Rosa*]: Majesty

Rose, full-blown, placed over two buds [*Rosa*]: Secrecy

Rose garland [*Rosa*]: Reward of virtue

Rose, Gloire de Dijon [*Rosa*]: Growing old, Old age, Winter

Rose, gold [*Rosa*]: Absolute achievement, Achievement

Rose, Guelder (European Cranberry Bush) [*Viburnum opulus*]: Age, Boredom, Bound, Ennui, Good news, Thoughts of Heaven, Winter

Rose, half-blown [*Rosa*]: Timid love

Rose, hundred-leaved: [*Rosa centifolia*]: Dignity of mind, Pride

Rose, Japanese [*Kerria Japonica*]: "Beauty is your only attraction", Compassion

Rose, John Hopper [*Rosa*]: Encouragement

Rose, la France [*Rosa*]: "Meet me by moonlight"

Rose, Lancaster [*Rosa damascena*]: Agreement, Union

Rose, lavender [*Rosa*]: Enchantment, Love at first sight

Rose, leaf [*Rosa*]: "You may hope"

Rose, lenten (Helleborus) [*Helleborus orientalis*]: Anxiety relief, Balance, Calumny, Gods, Malicious representation, Poise, Relieve my anxiety, Scandal, Self-assurance, Shyness reduction, Slander, Tension relief, Wit, "You have listened to scandal"

Rose, light pink [*Rosa*]: Friendship

Rose, long-stemmed [*Rosa*]: "I will always remember you"

Rose Lupine [*Lupinus*]: Fanciful

Rose, maiden blush [*Rosa*]: "If you love me you will find it out", Timid love

Rose Mallow [*Hibiscus*]: Delicate beauty, Love, Mildness, Passion, Sexual passion

Rose, malva [*Lavatera assurgentiflora*]: Delicate beauty, Love, Mildness, Sexual passion

Rose, monthly [*Rosa*]: Beauty ever new

Rose, moss [*Portulaca grandiflora*]: Confession of love, Love, Superior merit, Voluptuous love, Voluptuousness

Rose, multiflora [*Rosa multiflora*]: Grace, Gracefulness

Rose, mundi [*Rosa*]: Variety, "You are merry"

Rose, musk [*Rosa moschata*]: Capricious beauty

Rose, musk, cluster [*Rosa moschata*]: Charming

Rose, Nephitos (White Climbing Rose) [*Rosa*]: Infatuation

Rose of Sharon (Althea) [*Hibiscus syriacus*]: Consumed by love, Delicate beauty, Fiery love, Love, Mildness, Passion, Persuasion, Sexual passion

Rose, orange [*Rosa*]: Desire, Enthusiasm, Fascination, Passionate interest

Rose, pale peach [*Rosa*]: Modesty

Rose, peach [*Rosa*]: Desire, Enthusiasm, Shyness

Rose, pink [*Rosa*]: Friendship, Grace, Perfect happiness, "Please believe me", Secret love, Sweetness

Rose, prairie [*Rosa setigera*]: Beautiful mouth, Optimistic, Outgoing, Playful, Well-spoken

Rose, Provence [*Rosa x centifolia*]: Gentleness

Rose, purple [*Rosa*]: Enchantment, Lust, Passion

Rose, red-leaf [*Rosa glauca*]: Beauty

Rose, red [*Rosa*]: Love, Passion

Rose, red and white [*Rosa*]: Creative force, Joy, Unity

Rose, red and yellow [*Rosa*]: Excitement, Passion

Rose, rock [*Cistus* or *Helianthemum*]: Popular favor

Rose, santana [*Rosa*]: Pride

Rose-scented Geranium [*Pelargonium graveolens*]: "I prefer you", Preference

Rose, short-stemmed [*Rosa*]: Girlhood, Sweetheart

Rose, single [*Rosa*]: "I love you", "I still love you", Simplicity

Rose, single, red [*Rosa*]: True love

Rose, tea [*Rosa*]: Always lovely, "I'll always remember", Remembrance

Rose, thornless [*Rosa*]: Early attachment

Rose, thornless red [*Rosa*]: Love at first sight

Rose, unique [*Rosa*]: "Call me not beautiful", Modesty

Rose, white [*Rosa*]: "A heart unacquainted with love", Eternal love, False love, Heavenly, "I am worthy of you", Innocence, Pure, Secrecy, Silence

Rose, white, dried [*Rosa*]: "Death preferable to loss of innocence"

Rose, white, withered [*Rosa*]: Transient impressions

Rose, wild [*Rosa*]: Charming simplicity, Poetry, Purity, Simplicity

Rose, yellow [*Rosa*]: Betrayal, Broken heart, Decreased love, Departure of love, Dying love, Extreme betrayal, Forgive and forget, Infidelity, Intense emotions, Jealousy, Joy

Rose, York and Lancaster [*Rosa versicolor*]: War

Rosebay (Rhododendron) [*Rhododendrum maximum*]: Agitation, Beware, Danger, Warning

Rosebud [*Rosa*]: Beauty, Heart ignorant of love, New love, Pure, Youth

Rosebud, monthly [*Rosa*]: Enchantment

Rosebud, moss [*Portulaca grandiflora*]: Confessed love, Confession of love

Rosebud, red [*Rosa*]: Heart innocent of love, Pure and lovely, "You are young and beautiful", Youthful

Rosebud, thornless with leaves [*Rosa*]: "I fear no longer; I hope"

Rosebud, thornless without leaves [*Rosa*]: "There is nothing to hope or fear"

Rosebud, white [*Rosa*]: Girlhood, "Heart ignorant of love", Innocence

Rosemary [*Rosmarinus officinalis*]: Fidelity, Good luck in the new year, Happiness in marriage, Healing, Love, Memory, Mental powers, Protection, Purification, Remembrance, Sleep, Success, Youth

Rosemary, marsh [*Statice limonium* or *Rhododendron tomentosum*]: Success, Sympathy

Roses, crown of [*Rosa*]: Reward of virtue

Rosy Strife (Purple Loosestrife) [*Lythrum salicaria*]: Sporting

Rowan Tree [*Sorbus*]: Defense, Healing, Protection, Psychic powers, Sanctuary, Success

Rudbeckia (Black-eyed Susan) [*Rudbeckia fulgida*]: Encouragement, Impartiality, Justice

Rue [*Ruta*]: Beware of excess pleasures, Contempt, Disdain, Divination, Emotions, Go, Healing, Health, Love, Manners, Mental powers, Never return, Self-expression, Self-image, Sensitivity

Rush (Bulrush) [*Juncus* or *Typha latifolia*]: Calmness, Docility, Indiscretion

Russian Olive (Oleaster) [*Elaeagnus angustifolia*]: Bitterness

Rye Skullcap [*Scutellaria galericulata*]: Fidelity

Ryegrass [*Lolium*]: Changeable disposition, Fidelity, Love

Rhododendron

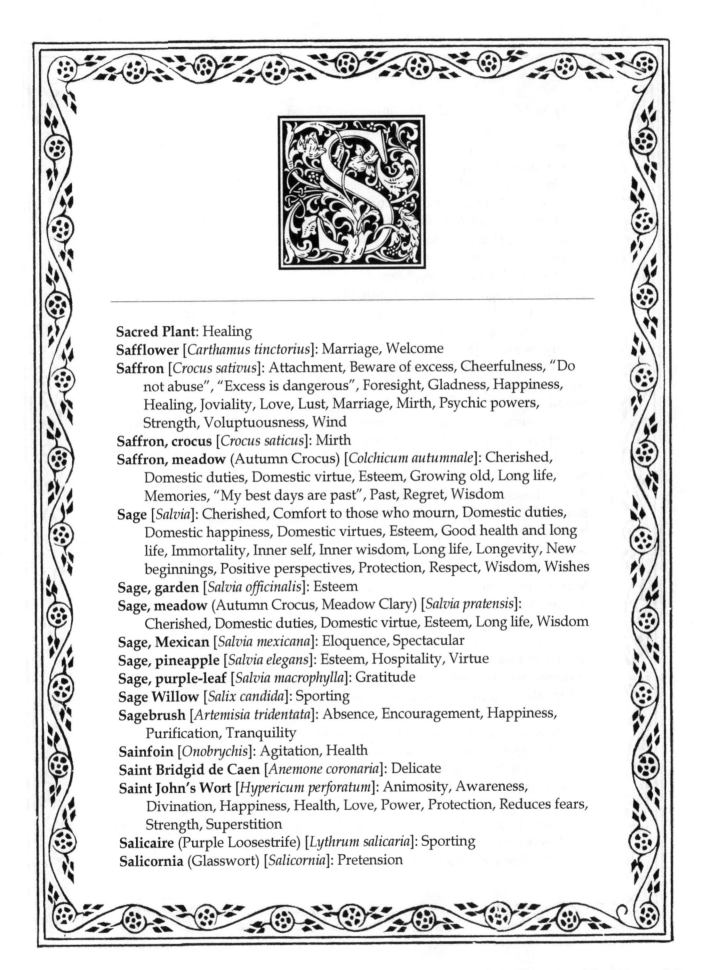

Sacred Plant: Healing

Safflower [*Carthamus tinctorius*]: Marriage, Welcome

Saffron [*Crocus sativus*]: Attachment, Beware of excess, Cheerfulness, "Do not abuse", "Excess is dangerous", Foresight, Gladness, Happiness, Healing, Joviality, Love, Lust, Marriage, Mirth, Psychic powers, Strength, Voluptuousness, Wind

Saffron, crocus [*Crocus saticus*]: Mirth

Saffron, meadow (Autumn Crocus) [*Colchicum autumnale*]: Cherished, Domestic duties, Domestic virtue, Esteem, Growing old, Long life, Memories, "My best days are past", Past, Regret, Wisdom

Sage [*Salvia*]: Cherished, Comfort to those who mourn, Domestic duties, Domestic happiness, Domestic virtues, Esteem, Good health and long life, Immortality, Inner self, Inner wisdom, Long life, Longevity, New beginnings, Positive perspectives, Protection, Respect, Wisdom, Wishes

Sage, garden [*Salvia officinalis*]: Esteem

Sage, meadow (Autumn Crocus, Meadow Clary) [*Salvia pratensis*]: Cherished, Domestic duties, Domestic virtue, Esteem, Long life, Wisdom

Sage, Mexican [*Salvia mexicana*]: Eloquence, Spectacular

Sage, pineapple [*Salvia elegans*]: Esteem, Hospitality, Virtue

Sage, purple-leaf [*Salvia macrophylla*]: Gratitude

Sage Willow [*Salix candida*]: Sporting

Sagebrush [*Artemisia tridentata*]: Absence, Encouragement, Happiness, Purification, Tranquility

Sainfoin [*Onobrychis*]: Agitation, Health

Saint Bridgid de Caen [*Anemone coronaria*]: Delicate

Saint John's Wort [*Hypericum perforatum*]: Animosity, Awareness, Divination, Happiness, Health, Love, Power, Protection, Reduces fears, Strength, Superstition

Salicaire (Purple Loosestrife) [*Lythrum salicaria*]: Sporting

Salicornia (Glasswort) [*Salicornia*]: Pretension

Sally, red (Red Salvia) [*Salvia splendens*]: "Always yours", Energy, "Forever yours", Pomp, Sporting, Untiring energy

Salvia [*Salvia*]: Cherished

Salvia, blue [*Salvia*]: "I think of you", Wisdom

Salvia, red (Red Sally) [*Salvia splendens*]: "Always yours", Energy, "Forever yours", Pomp, Sporting, Untiring energy

Sandalwood [*Santalum album*]: Healing, Protection, Spirituality

Santana Rose [*Rosa*]: Pride

Sardonyx [*Sempervivum sardonyx*]: Irony

Sarsaparilla [*Smilax*]: Love, Money

Sassafras [*Sassafras albidum*]: Health, Money

Satin Flower [*Romulea bulbocodium* or *Sisyrinchium striatum*]: "Am I forgotten?", Sincerity

Savory, summer [*Satureja hortensis*]: Mental powers

Saxifrage [*Saxifraga*]: Affection, Balance, Cleverness, New ideas, Peace

Saxifrage, mossy [*Saxifraga*]: Affection

Scabiosa (Pincushion Flower) [*Scabiosa*]: Alternatives, Communication, Enthusiasm, "Finding other ways of doing things", Heals indifference, Higher learning, "I have lost all", Unfortunate love

Scabiosa, sweet (Sweet William) [*Scabiosa*]: Widowhood

Scarlet Auricula (Bear's Ears) [*Primula auricula*]: Avarice

Scarlet Fuschia [*Fuchsia*]: Taste in fashion

Scarlet Geranium [*Pelargonium*]: Comfort, Silliness, Stupidity

Scarlet Lily [*Lilium*]: High of soul

Scarlet Lobelia [*Lobelia splendens*]: Distinction, Honor

Scarlet Lychnis (Maltese Cross) [*Lychnis chalcedonica*]: Sunbeaming eyes

Scarlet Pimpernel [*Anagellis arvensis*]: Assignation, Change

Scarlet Poppy [*Papaver*]: Fantastic extravagance

Scarlet Verbena [*Verbena*]: Church unity, Sensibility, Sensitivity, Unite against evil

Scarlet Zinnia [*Zinnia elegans*]: Constancy, Consistency, Steadfast

Schinus [*Schinus*]: Religious enthusiasm

Scilla, blue (Squill) [*Scilla*]: Forgive and forget

Scilla, Siberia (Siberian Squill) [*Scilla siberica*]: Pleasure without alloy

Scilla, white (Squill) [*Scilla*]: Sweet innocence

Scorpion grass, mouse-eared [*Myosotis*]: "Do not forget me", "Forget me not"

Scorpion Orchid [*Arachnis*]: Elopement

Scotch Fir [*Pinus sylvestris*]: Elevation

Scotch Thistle (Cotton Thistle) [*Onopordum acanthium*]: Retaliation

Sea Daffodil (Fairy Lily) [*Chlidanthus*]: "Elope with me", "Not as bad as I seem"

Sea Pinks (Sea Lavender, Sea Thrift) [*Armeria maritima*]: Success, Sympathy

Sedum (Hens and Chicks) [*Echeveria*]: Motherly love, Tranquility, "Welcome home, drunk husband"

Seeds, winged: Message

Sensitive plant (Humble Plant, Mimosa, Touch-Me-Not) [*Mimosa pudica*]:
Bashfulness, Delicate feelings, "Do not hurt me", Love, Modesty,
Prophetic dreams, Protection, Purification, Secret love, Sensibility,
Sensitiveness, Sensitivity, Shyness

Senvy (Mustard) [*Brassica*]: Indifference

September Flower (Aster) [*Aster*]: Afterthought, Charming, Contentment,
Daintiness, Diversity, Femininity, Fidelity, Grace, "I'm not sure you've
been faithful", Love, Luck in love, Patience, Trusting, Variety

Service Tree [*Sorbus domestica*]: Prudence

Sesame [*Sesamum orientale*]: Lust, Money

Shallot [*Allium cepa*]: Purification

Shameplant [*Mimosa*]: Bashfulness

Shamrock [*Oxalis*]: Joy, Joy in sorrow, Light-heartedness, Loyalty

Shasta Daisy [*Leucanthemum superbum*]: Patience

Shepherd's Purse [*Capsella bursa-pastoris*]: "I offer you my all"

Shoo-Fly Plant (Apple of Peru) [*Nicandra physaloides*]: Dignity, Pride, Success

Shooting Stars [*Dodecatheon*]: "You are my divinity"

Short-stemmed Rose [*Rosa*]: Girlhood, Sweetheart

Shrimp Plant (Water Willow) [*Justicia*]: Freedom, "The perfection of female
loveliness"

Siberian Squill [*Scilla Siberica*]: Pleasure without alloy

Silver-leaf Geranium [*Kalwerbossie geranium*]: Recall, Retrospection

Single China Aster [*Callistephus chinensis*]: "I will think about it", Indecision

Single Dahlia [*Dahlia*]: Good taste

Single Daffodil [*Narcissus*]: Good taste

Single Pink (Carnation) [*Dianthus*]: Pure love

Single red Rose [*Rosa*]: True love

Single Rose [*Rosa*]: "I love you", "I still love you", Simplicity

Skullcap [*Scutellaria*]: Calming thoughts, Fidelity, Letting go, Love, Peace

Skullcap, Rye [*Scutellaria galericulata*]: Fidelity

Skunk Cabbage [*Lysichiton* or *Symplocarpus*]: Legal matters

Sleeping Grass [*Mimosa pudica*]: Bashfulness, Sensibility

Slippery Elm Tree [*Ulmus rubra*]: Gossip stopper

Smilax (Sarsaparilla) [*Smilax*]: Loveliness

Snakefoot [*Rauvolfia serpentina*]: Horror

Snakeroot [*Liatris punctata* or *Polygala*]: Enthusiasm, "I will try again", Luck,
Money

Snakeroot, black [*Actaea racemosa*]: Love, Lust, Money

Snakeroot, button [*Eryngium yuccifolium*]: Enthusiasm, "I will try again"

Snakeroot, white [*Ageratina altissima*]: Delay

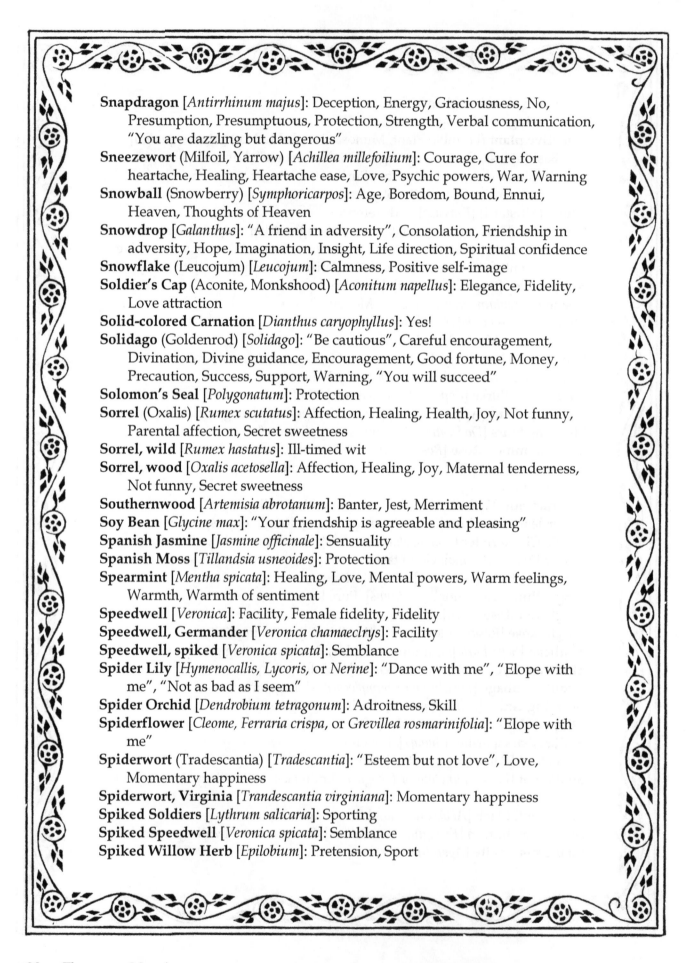

Snapdragon [*Antirrhinum majus*]: Deception, Energy, Graciousness, No, Presumption, Presumptuous, Protection, Strength, Verbal communication, "You are dazzling but dangerous"

Sneezewort (Milfoil, Yarrow) [*Achillea millefoilium*]: Courage, Cure for heartache, Healing, Heartache ease, Love, Psychic powers, War, Warning

Snowball (Snowberry) [*Symphoricarpos*]: Age, Boredom, Bound, Ennui, Heaven, Thoughts of Heaven

Snowdrop [*Galanthus*]: "A friend in adversity", Consolation, Friendship in adversity, Hope, Imagination, Insight, Life direction, Spiritual confidence

Snowflake (Leucojum) [*Leucojum*]: Calmness, Positive self-image

Soldier's Cap (Aconite, Monkshood) [*Aconitum napellus*]: Elegance, Fidelity, Love attraction

Solid-colored Carnation [*Dianthus caryophyllus*]: Yes!

Solidago (Goldenrod) [*Solidago*]: "Be cautious", Careful encouragement, Divination, Divine guidance, Encouragement, Good fortune, Money, Precaution, Success, Support, Warning, "You will succeed"

Solomon's Seal [*Polygonatum*]: Protection

Sorrel (Oxalis) [*Rumex scutatus*]: Affection, Healing, Health, Joy, Not funny, Parental affection, Secret sweetness

Sorrel, wild [*Rumex hastatus*]: Ill-timed wit

Sorrel, wood [*Oxalis acetosella*]: Affection, Healing, Joy, Maternal tenderness, Not funny, Secret sweetness

Southernwood [*Artemisia abrotanum*]: Banter, Jest, Merriment

Soy Bean [*Glycine max*]: "Your friendship is agreeable and pleasing"

Spanish Jasmine [*Jasmine officinale*]: Sensuality

Spanish Moss [*Tillandsia usneoides*]: Protection

Spearmint [*Mentha spicata*]: Healing, Love, Mental powers, Warm feelings, Warmth, Warmth of sentiment

Speedwell [*Veronica*]: Facility, Female fidelity, Fidelity

Speedwell, Germander [*Veronica chamaeclrys*]: Facility

Speedwell, spiked [*Veronica spicata*]: Semblance

Spider Lily [*Hymenocallis, Lycoris,* or *Nerine*]: "Dance with me", "Elope with me", "Not as bad as I seem"

Spider Orchid [*Dendrobium tetragonum*]: Adroitness, Skill

Spiderflower [*Cleome, Ferraria crispa,* or *Grevillea rosmarinifolia*]: "Elope with me"

Spiderwort (Tradescantia) [*Tradescantia*]: "Esteem but not love", Love, Momentary happiness

Spiderwort, Virginia [*Trandescantia virginiana*]: Momentary happiness

Spiked Soldiers [*Lythrum salicaria*]: Sporting

Spiked Speedwell [*Veronica spicata*]: Semblance

Spiked Willow Herb [*Epilobium*]: Pretension, Sport

Spindle Tree (Euonymus, European Sandle Tree) [*Euonymus europaeus*]: Long life, "Your charms are engraved on my heart", "Your image is engraved on my heart"

Spirea (Bridal-wreath, Foam of May) [*Francoa* or *Spiraea arguta*]: "Come to me", Conceited, Desire to travel, Happiness in marriage, Victory

Spirea, False [*Astilbe* or *Sorbaria kirilowii*]: "I'll still be waiting"

Split Reed [*Phragmite*]: Indiscretion

Sprig of Ivy with tendrils [*Hedera*]: Assiduous to please

Spring Crocus [*Crocus*]: Youthful gladness

Spruce Tree [*Picea*]: Farewell, Hope in adversity, Protection

Spruce Tree, Norway [*Picea abies*]: Protection

Spurge (Cushion Spurge, Euphorbia) [*Euphorbia polychroma*]: Persistence, Protection, Purification, Welcome

Squirrel Corn [*Dicentra canadensis*]: Elegance, Fidelity, Love attraction

Staghorn Sumac [*Rhus typhina*]: Communication with spirits

Star of Bethlehem (Florists' Nightmare) [*Ornithogalum umbellatum*]: Atonement, Hope, Idleness, Purity, Reconciliation

Star-shaped Phlox [*Phlox*]: Affability

Starflower [*Mentzelia* or *Smilacina stellata*]: Hope, Vigilance

Starwort, American [*Stellaria*]: Afterthought, Cheerfulness in old age, Daintiness, Hospitality, Love, Variety, Welcome to a stranger

Statice [*Limonium* or *Psylliostachys*]: Dauntlessness, Gratitude, Never-ceasing remembrance, Remembrance, Success, Sympathy

Stephanotis [*Stephanotis*]: Good luck, Happiness in marriage, Marriage, Travel, Wedding, "Will you accompany me?", "You boast too much"

Sticky-Weed (Asthma Weed, Cleavers, Goose Grass) [*Galium aparine*]: Arrogance, Malevolence

Stitchwort [*Stellaria holostea*]: Eases cares and worries, Joy, Relaxation

Stock (Gillyflower) [*Matthiola*]: Affection, Bonds of affection, Lasting beauty, Promptness, Vows, "You will always be beautiful to me"

Stock, night-scented [*Matthiola longipetala* subsp. *bicornis*]: Devotion

Stock, ten-week [*Matthiola incana*]: Promptitude, Promptness

Stonecrop [*Sedum*]: Tranquility

Straw: Agreement, Image magic, Luck, Union

Straw, broken: Division, Quarrel, Rupture of a contract

Strawberry [*Fragaria*]: Foresight, Future promise, Goodness, Love, Luck, Perfect excellence, Perfect goodness, "You are delicious"

Strawberry Begonia [*Saxifraga stolonifera*]: Cleverness

Strawberry Blossoms [*Fragaria*]: Foresight

Strawberry Tree (Arbutus) [*Arbutus unedo*]: Esteem but not love, Faithfulness, Friendship, "I only love you", One love, Protection, "Thee only do I love", "You're the only one I love"

Strawflower [*Bracteantha, Helichrysum,* or *Rhodanthe*]: Agreement

Striped Carnation [*Dianthus caryophyllus*]: Extremes, "I cannot be with you", Indecision, Refusal, Rejection, "Sorry I can't be with you"

Sugar Cane [*Saccharum officinarum*]: Love, Lust

Sugarbush [*Protea repens*]: Courage

Sultan Lilac [*Syringa*]: "I forgive you"

Sultan, sweet [*Amberboa moschata* or *Centaurea moschata*]: Daintiness, Delicacy, Felicity, Happiness, Refinement

Sultan, white [*Scabiosa caucasica alba*]: Sweetness

Sultan, yellow [*Centaurea imperialis suaveolens*]: Contempt

Sultana [*Impatiens*]: Impatience, Motherly love

Sumac [*Rhus*]: Intellectual excellence, Resoluteness

Sumac, staghorn [*Rhus typhina*]: Communication with spirits

Sumac, Venetian (Smoke Tree) [*Cotinus coggygria*]: Intellectual excellence, Splendor

Summer Cypress (Belvedere) [*Chenopodium Scoparia* or *Bassia scoparia*]: "I declare war against you"

Summer Lilac (Butterfly Bush) [*Buddleja davidii*]: Coquetry, Evening, Healing, Rashness, Wantonness, Virtue

Summer Savory [*Satureja hortensis*]: Mental powers

Suncups (Evening Primrose, Sundrops) [*Oenothera*]: Inconstancy, Unfaithful, Youth

Sunflower [*Helianthus annuus*]: Adoration, Arrogance, Devotion, False riches, Fertility, Happiness, Haughtiness, Health, Homage, Loyalty, Sun, Vigilance, Wisdom, Wishes

Sunflower, dwarf [*Helianthus annuus*]: Adoration, Infatuation

Sunflower, tall [*Helianthus annuus*]: Arrogance, Haughtiness, Pride, "You are splendid"

Swallowwort (Greater Celandine) [*Chelidonium majus*]: Cure for heartache

Swallowwort, red (Greater Celandine) [*Chelidonium majus*]: "Let me go"

Swamp Magnolia [*Magnolia virginiana*]: Perseverance

Sweet Alyssum (Sweet Alice, Sweet Alison) [*Lobularia maritima*]: Anger management, Modesty, Perfection, Protection, Worth beyond all beauty

Sweet Basil [*Ocimum basilicum*]: Good wishes

Sweet Bay (Bay, Laurel) [*Laurus nobilis* or *Magnolia virginiana*]: Accomplishment, Achievement in the arts, Civil service, Courage, Creation of beauty, Glory, Glory and success, Healing, Perfidy, Personal achievement, Protection, Psychic powers, Purification, Reward of merit, Sharpness, Strength, Success

Sweet Betsy [*Calycanthus floridus*]: Benevolence, Generosity

Sweet Briar, yellow [*Rosa foetida*]: Decrease of love, "Let us forget"

Sweet Flag [*Acorus*]: Fitness

Sweet Gum Tree [*Liquidambar styraciflua*]: Protection

Sweet Pea [*Lathyrus odoratus*]: Appointed meeting, Bliss, Blissful pleasure, Chastity, Courage, Delicate pleasures, Departure, Friendship, "Do not go away", Good-bye, "Let's meet", "Meet me", "Remember me", Shyness, Strength, Tender memory, Tenderness, "Thank you for a good time"

Sweet Rocket (Dame's Rocket, Queen's Rocket) [*Hesperis matronalis*]: Coquetry, Evening, Virtue

Sweet Scabiosa [*Scabiosa*]: Widowhood

Sweet-scented Tussilage (Coltsfoot) [*Tussilago farfara*]: "Justice shall be done to you"

Sweet Shrub (Carolina Allspice, Sweet Shrub) [*Calycanthus floridus*]: Benevolence, Generosity

Sweet Sultan [*Amberboa moschata* or *Centaurea moschata*]: Daintiness, Delicate, Felicity, Happiness, Refinement

Sweet Violet [*Viola odorata*]: Modesty

Sweet William [*Dianthus barbatus*]: Artifice, Boldness, Childhood, Chivalry, Dexterity, Finesse, Gallantry, "Grant me a smile", Memories, Perfection, Scorn

Sweetbriar, American [*Rosa suaveolens*]: Simplicity

Sweetbriar, European (Eglantine) [*Rosa rubiginosa*]: Genius, "I wound but to heal", Poetry

Sweetgrass [*Hierochloe odorata*]: Spirit calling

Sycamore Tree [*Platanus*]: Curiosity, Genius, Reserve, Resolve

Syrian Mallow (Althea Frutes, Rose of Sharon) [*Hibiscus syricus*]: Consumed by love, Healing, Honesty, "I am deeply in love", Persuasion, Purity, Protection, Psychic powers

Syringa (Lilac) [*Syringa*]: Memory

Syringa, Carolina [*Philadelphus grandiflorus*]: Disappointment

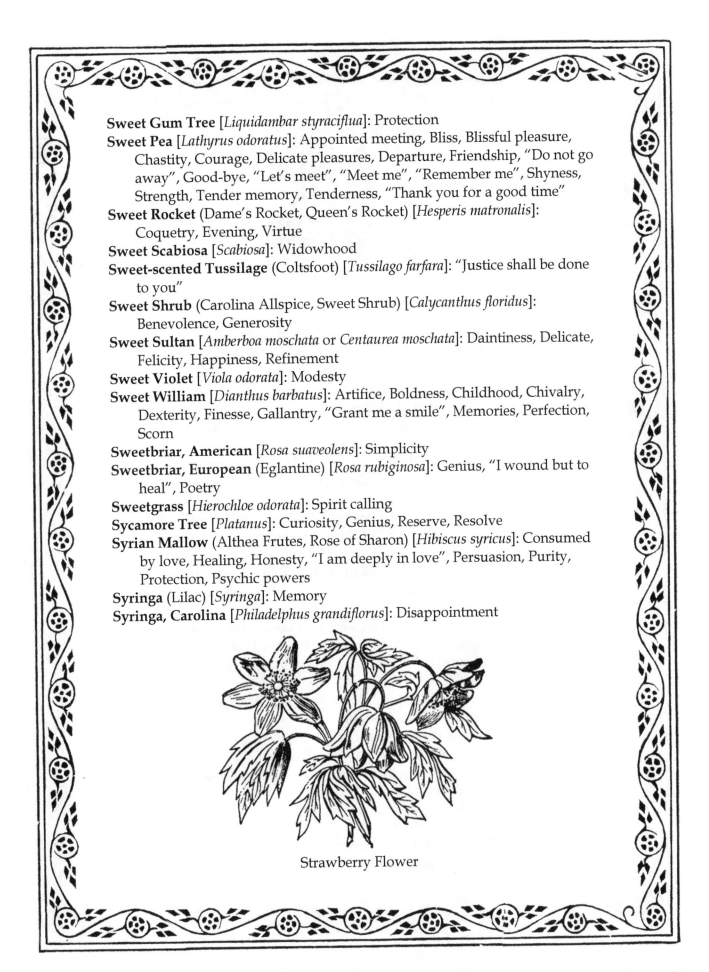

Strawberry Flower

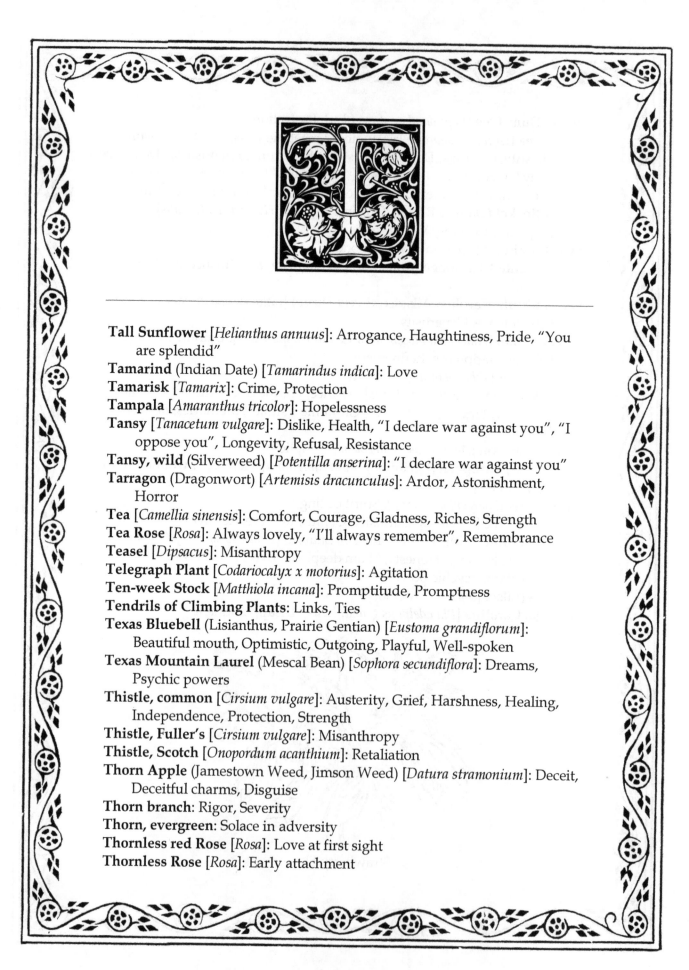

Tall Sunflower [*Helianthus annuus*]: Arrogance, Haughtiness, Pride, "You are splendid"

Tamarind (Indian Date) [*Tamarindus indica*]: Love

Tamarisk [*Tamarix*]: Crime, Protection

Tampala [*Amaranthus tricolor*]: Hopelessness

Tansy [*Tanacetum vulgare*]: Dislike, Health, "I declare war against you", "I oppose you", Longevity, Refusal, Resistance

Tansy, wild (Silverweed) [*Potentilla anserina*]: "I declare war against you"

Tarragon (Dragonwort) [*Artemisis dracunculus*]: Ardor, Astonishment, Horror

Tea [*Camellia sinensis*]: Comfort, Courage, Gladness, Riches, Strength

Tea Rose [*Rosa*]: Always lovely, "I'll always remember", Remembrance

Teasel [*Dipsacus*]: Misanthropy

Telegraph Plant [*Codariocalyx x motorius*]: Agitation

Ten-week Stock [*Matthiola incana*]: Promptitude, Promptness

Tendrils of Climbing Plants: Links, Ties

Texas Bluebell (Lisianthus, Prairie Gentian) [*Eustoma grandiflorum*]: Beautiful mouth, Optimistic, Outgoing, Playful, Well-spoken

Texas Mountain Laurel (Mescal Bean) [*Sophora secundiflora*]: Dreams, Psychic powers

Thistle, common [*Cirsium vulgare*]: Austerity, Grief, Harshness, Healing, Independence, Protection, Strength

Thistle, Fuller's [*Cirsium vulgare*]: Misanthropy

Thistle, Scotch [*Onopordum acanthium*]: Retaliation

Thorn Apple (Jamestown Weed, Jimson Weed) [*Datura stramonium*]: Deceit, Deceitful charms, Disguise

Thorn branch: Rigor, Severity

Thorn, evergreen: Solace in adversity

Thornless red Rose [*Rosa*]: Love at first sight

Thornless Rose [*Rosa*]: Early attachment

Thornless Rosebud with leaves [*Rosa*]: "I fear no longer; I hope"

Thornless Rosebud without leaves [*Rosa*]: "There is nothing to hope or fear"

Three-leaf Clover [*Trifolium*]: Trinity

Thrift [*Armeria*]: Sympathy

Thrift, sea (Sea Lavender, Sea Pinks) [*Armeria maritime* or *Limonium*]: Success, Sympathy

Throatwort (Trachelium) [*Trachelium caeruleum*]: Modest beauty, Neglected beauty

Thyme [*Thymus vulgaris*]: Activity, Allure, Courage, Energy, Healing, Health, Love, Psychic powers, Purification, Sleep, Thriftiness

Thyme, dodder of [*Thymus*]: Baseness, Meanness

Tickseed (Coreopsis) [*Coreopsis grandiflora*]: Always cheerful, Cheerful, Happiness, Joy

Tiger Flower [*Tigridia pavonia*]: "For once may pride befriend me"

Tiger Lily [*Lilium lancifolium*]: Fun, "I dare you to love me", Riches

Toadflax [*Linaria maroccana*]: Deception, Hex breaking, Presumption, Presumptuous, Protection, Strength

Toadstool [*Agaricomycetes, Amanita muscaria* or *Basidiomycota*]: Rain-making

Tobacco [*Nicotiana tabacum*]: Arrogance, Healing, Malevolence, Purification

Tobacco, flowering [*Nicotiana*]: Cleansing

Tobacco, Indian [*Lobelia inflata*]: Arrogance, Malevolence

Torch Lily (Red Hot Poker) [*Kniphofia*]: Dangerous, Determined

Touch-Me-Not [*Impatiens noli-tangere, Melianthus major,* or *Mimosa pudica*]: Bashfulness, Impatience, Motherly love, Sensibility, "Touch me not"

Trachelium (Throatwort) [*Trachelium caeruleum*]: Modest beauty, Neglected beauty

Tradescantia (Spiderwort) [*Tradescantia*]: "Esteem but not love", Love, Momentary happiness

Transvaal Daisy (Barberton Daisy, Gerbera Daisy) [*Gerbera jamesonii*]: Beauty

Traveler's Joy [*Clematis microphylla*]: Safety

Tree of Life (Himalayan Moringa) [*Moringa oleifera*]: Age, Old age

Trefoil [*Lotus*]: Providence, Revenge

Trefoil, bird's foot [*Lotus corniculatus*]: Resilience, Revenge, Vengeance

Tremella Nestoc [*Tremellaceae*]: Resistance

Trillium Pictum [*Trillium undulatum*]: Modest beauty

Trollius (Globeflower) [*Trollius*]: Generosity, Gratitude, Solitude

Truffle [*Tuber melanosporum*]: Surprise

Trumpet Flower [*Bignonia capreolata*]: Fame, Separation

Trumpet Flower, ash-leaved [*Brugmansia*]: Separation

Tuberose [*Polianthes tuberosa*]: Dangerous, Dangerous pleasures, Pleasure, Voluptuousness

Tulip [*Tulipa*]: Fame, Happy years, Love, Memory, Passion, Perfect lover

Tulip, cape [*Moraea flaccida* or *Morara miniata*]: Glory, Splendor

Tulip Gentian [*Gentiana*]: Optimistic, Well-spoken

Tulip, pink [*Tulipa*]: Caring, Dreaminess

Tulip Poplar [*Liriodendron tulipifera*]: Among the noblest, Fame, Retirement, Rural happiness

Tulip, purple [*Tulipa*]: Royalty

Tulip, red [*Tulipa*]: "Believe me", Confession of love, Declaration of love, Love, Trust

Tulip, variegated [*Tulipa*]: Beautiful eyes

Tulip, white [*Tulipa*]: "Let's take a chance", Literary debut, Lost love

Tulip, yellow [*Tulipa*]: Hope in love, Hopeless love, Joy, "There's sunshine in your smile"

Tumeric [*Curcuma domestica*]: Purification

Turban Buttercup (Persian Buttercup) [*Ranunculus asiaticus*]: Attraction, Charm

Turk's Cap Cactus [*Melocactus*]: Splendor

Turnip [*Brassica rapa*]: Charity, Ending relationships, Protection

Turtlehead (Chelone) [*Chelone*]: Courage, Pleasure without alloy

Tussie Mussie: Fragrance remembered

Tussilage, sweet-scented (Coltsfoot) [*Tussilago farfara*]: "Justice shall be done to you"

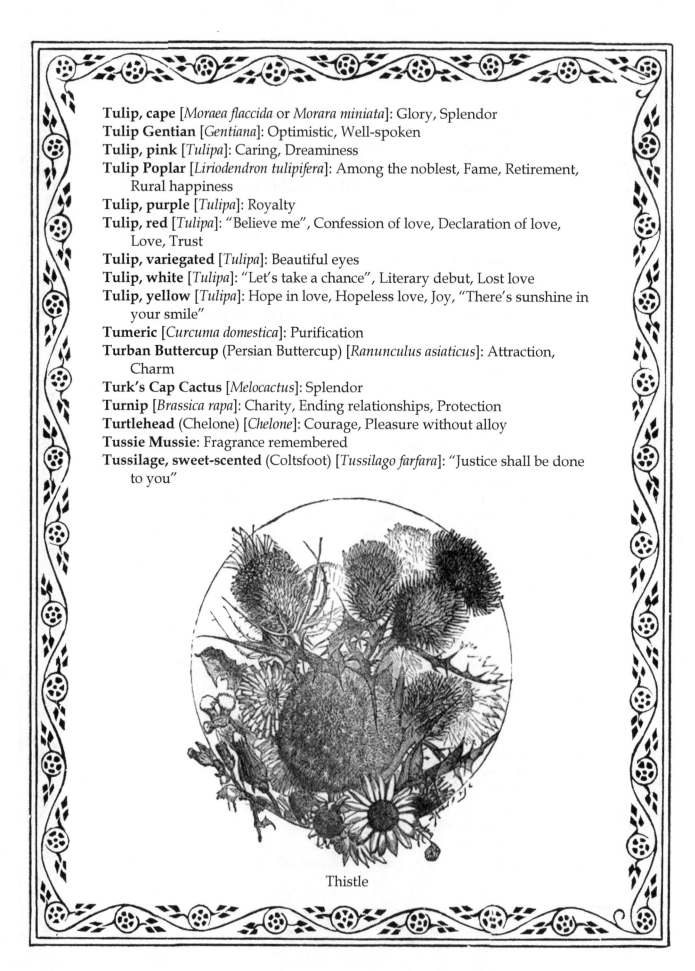

Thistle

Ulster Mary (Peruvian Lily) [*Alstroemeria*]: Wealth

Umbrella Pine Tree [*Sciadopitys verticillata*]: "Honoring the dead", Joy, Respect, Undying love

Unique Rose [*Rosa*]: "Call me not beautiful", Modesty

Uva Ursi (Bearberry, Kinnikinnick) [*Arctostaphylos uva-ursi*]: Psychic workings

Ulex

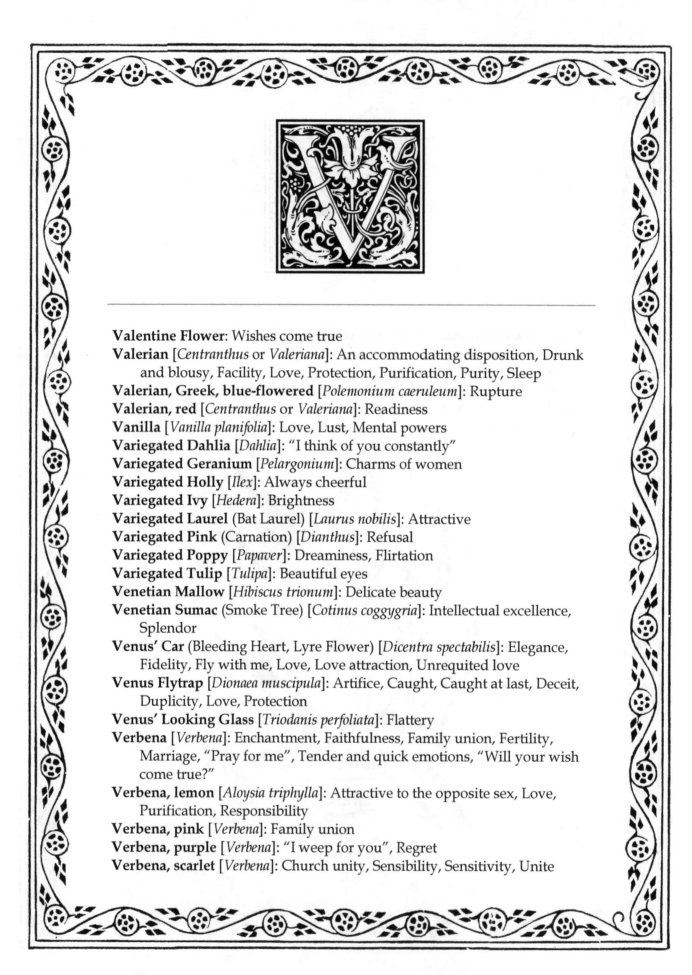

Valentine Flower: Wishes come true

Valerian [*Centranthus* or *Valeriana*]: An accommodating disposition, Drunk and blousy, Facility, Love, Protection, Purification, Purity, Sleep

Valerian, Greek, blue-flowered [*Polemonium caeruleum*]: Rupture

Valerian, red [*Centranthus* or *Valeriana*]: Readiness

Vanilla [*Vanilla planifolia*]: Love, Lust, Mental powers

Variegated Dahlia [*Dahlia*]: "I think of you constantly"

Variegated Geranium [*Pelargonium*]: Charms of women

Variegated Holly [*Ilex*]: Always cheerful

Variegated Ivy [*Hedera*]: Brightness

Variegated Laurel (Bat Laurel) [*Laurus nobilis*]: Attractive

Variegated Pink (Carnation) [*Dianthus*]: Refusal

Variegated Poppy [*Papaver*]: Dreaminess, Flirtation

Variegated Tulip [*Tulipa*]: Beautiful eyes

Venetian Mallow [*Hibiscus trionum*]: Delicate beauty

Venetian Sumac (Smoke Tree) [*Cotinus coggygria*]: Intellectual excellence, Splendor

Venus' Car (Bleeding Heart, Lyre Flower) [*Dicentra spectabilis*]: Elegance, Fidelity, Fly with me, Love, Love attraction, Unrequited love

Venus Flytrap [*Dionaea muscipula*]: Artifice, Caught, Caught at last, Deceit, Duplicity, Love, Protection

Venus' Looking Glass [*Triodanis perfoliata*]: Flattery

Verbena [*Verbena*]: Enchantment, Faithfulness, Family union, Fertility, Marriage, "Pray for me", Tender and quick emotions, "Will your wish come true?"

Verbena, lemon [*Aloysia triphylla*]: Attractive to the opposite sex, Love, Purification, Responsibility

Verbena, pink [*Verbena*]: Family union

Verbena, purple [*Verbena*]: "I weep for you", Regret

Verbena, scarlet [*Verbena*]: Church unity, Sensibility, Sensitivity, Unite against evil

Verbena, white [*Verbena*]: Honesty, "Pray for me", Pure and guileless

Vernal grass [*Anthoxanthum*]: Poor but happy

Veronica [*Hebe, Parahebe* or *Veronica*]: Female fidelity, Fidelity

Veronica Speciosa [*Hebe speciosa*]: "Keep this for my sake"

Vervain [*Verbena*]: Chastity, Enchantment, Healing, Love, Money, Peace, Protection, Purification, Sleep, Youth

Vetch [*Vicia*]: Fidelity, "I cling to you"

Vetiver [*Chrysopogon zizanioides*]: Anti-theft, Love, Luck, Money

Viburnum [*Viburnum*]: "I die if neglected", Thoughts of Heaven, Token of affection

Vinca (Periwinkle) [*Vinca*]: Early friendship, Love, Lust, Memories, Mental powers, Money, Pleasures of memory, Protection, Sweet memories, Sweet remembrance

Vine: Drunkenness, Head over heels in love, Intoxication

Violet [*Viola*]: Affection, Faith, Faithfulness, Healing, Love, Luck, Lust, Modesty, Peace, Shyness, Watchfulness, Wishes

Violet, African [*Saintpaulia*]: Admiration, Delicate love connection, Faithfulness, Modesty, Protection, Spirituality, Virtue

Violet, blue [*Viola*]: Faithfulness, Love, Modest love

Violet, Czar (Sweet Violet) [*Viola odorata*]: Kindness and worth

Violet, Dame's (Dame's Gillyflower, Dame's Rocket, Dame's Wort) [*Hesperis matronalis*]: Coquetry, Evening, Virtue, Watchfulness

Violet, Parma [*Viola alba*]: "Let me love you"

Violet, Persian [*Exacum affine*]: Diffidence, Fertility, Good-bye, Lust, Protection, Resignation

Violet, purple [*Viola*]: "You occupy my thoughts"

Violet, sweet (Czar Violet) [*Viola odorata*]: Modesty

Violet, white [*Viola odorata*]: Balance, Imagination, Innocence, "Let's take a chance on happiness", Modesty, Purity, "Take a chance together"

Violet, wild [*Viola canadensis*]: Goals, Love, Love in idleness, Positive outlook, Self-understanding

Violet, yellow [*Viola*]: Rural happiness

Virgin's Bower (Clematis, Leather Flower) [*Clematis viticella*]: Artifice, Arts, Creativity, Filial love, "I love your mind", Ingenuity, Intelligence, Love from a son or daughter, Mental beauty, Pure love, Unchanged for eternity

Virginia Creeper (American Ivy, Woodbine) [*Parthenocissus quinquefolia*]: Ever changing, "I cling to you", "I cling to you in both sunshine and shade", Strong friendship, Sweet neglect

Virginia Creeper, leaf [*Parthenocissus quinquefolia*]: "I offer you…"

Virginia Jasmine (Cross-Vine, Trumpet Flower) [*Bignonia*]: Separation

Virginia Spiderwort [*Tradescantia virginiana*]: Momentary happiness

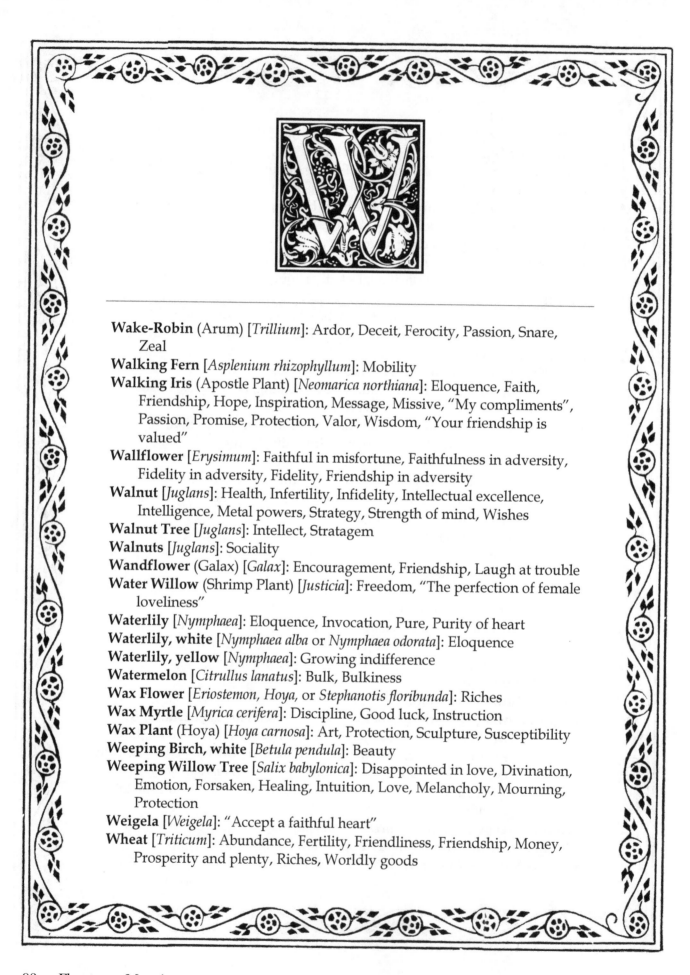

Wake-Robin (Arum) [*Trillium*]: Ardor, Deceit, Ferocity, Passion, Snare, Zeal

Walking Fern [*Asplenium rhizophyllum*]: Mobility

Walking Iris (Apostle Plant) [*Neomarica northiana*]: Eloquence, Faith, Friendship, Hope, Inspiration, Message, Missive, "My compliments", Passion, Promise, Protection, Valor, Wisdom, "Your friendship is valued"

Wallflower [*Erysimum*]: Faithful in misfortune, Faithfulness in adversity, Fidelity in adversity, Fidelity, Friendship in adversity

Walnut [*Juglans*]: Health, Infertility, Infidelity, Intellectual excellence, Intelligence, Metal powers, Strategy, Strength of mind, Wishes

Walnut Tree [*Juglans*]: Intellect, Stratagem

Walnuts [*Juglans*]: Sociality

Wandflower (Galax) [*Galax*]: Encouragement, Friendship, Laugh at trouble

Water Willow (Shrimp Plant) [*Justicia*]: Freedom, "The perfection of female loveliness"

Waterlily [*Nymphaea*]: Eloquence, Invocation, Pure, Purity of heart

Waterlily, white [*Nymphaea alba* or *Nymphaea odorata*]: Eloquence

Waterlily, yellow [*Nymphaea*]: Growing indifference

Watermelon [*Citrullus lanatus*]: Bulk, Bulkiness

Wax Flower [*Eriostemon, Hoya,* or *Stephanotis floribunda*]: Riches

Wax Myrtle [*Myrica cerifera*]: Discipline, Good luck, Instruction

Wax Plant (Hoya) [*Hoya carnosa*]: Art, Protection, Sculpture, Susceptibility

Weeping Birch, white [*Betula pendula*]: Beauty

Weeping Willow Tree [*Salix babylonica*]: Disappointed in love, Divination, Emotion, Forsaken, Healing, Intuition, Love, Melancholy, Mourning, Protection

Weigela [*Weigela*]: "Accept a faithful heart"

Wheat [*Triticum*]: Abundance, Fertility, Friendliness, Friendship, Money, Prosperity and plenty, Riches, Worldly goods

Wheat Stalk [*Triticum*]: Prosperity

Whin (Borse) [*Ulex*]: Anger

White Acacia [*Acacia*]: Elegance, Friendship, Platonic love

White and red Rose [*Rosa*]: Creative force, Joy, Unity

White Aster [*Aster*]: Afterthought

White Bloom [*Chrysanthemum*]: Truth

White Camellia Japonica [*Camellia japonica*]: Adoration, Beauty, Excellence in women, Perfected loveliness, Perfection, Worth

White Carnation [*Dianthus caryophyllus*]: Democracy, Devotion, Endearment, "I am still available", Innocence, Living for love, Lovely, Pure and ardent love, Purity, Remembrance, Sweet and lovely, Sweetness

White Catchfly [*Silene*]: Betrayed

White Cherry Tree [*Prunus*]: Deception

White Chrysanthemum [*Chrysanthemum*]: Remembrance, Truth, Trust

White Climbing Rose (Nephetos Rose) [*Rosa*]: Infatuation

White Clover [*Trifolium repens*]: "Be mine", "I promise", Luck, Remembrance, "The start of a long and happy life together", "Think of me"

White Cyclamen [*Cyclamen*]: Warmth of heart

White Dahlia [*Dahlia*]: Gratitude to parents

White Daisy [*Bellis perennis*]: Beauty, Innocence

White Dittany (Burning Bush, Gas Plant) [*Dictamnus albus*]: Passion

White Flax [*Linum usitatissimum*]: Beauty

White Gardenia [*Gardenia*]: Joy, Purity and sweetness, Secret love, "You are lovely"

White Geranium [*Pelargonium*]: Gracefulness, Refinement

White Hearts [*Dicentra spectabilis 'alba'*]: Elegance, Fidelity, Love attraction

White Heather [*Cassiope mertensiana*]: Good luck, Protection, Wishes

White Hollyhock [*Alcea*]: Female ambition

White Hyacinth [*Hyacinthus*]: Beauty, "I'll pray for you", Prayer, Unobtrusive loveliness

White Jasmine [*Jasminum*]: Amiability, Amiableness, Extreme amiability

White Julienne [*Hesperis matronalis*]: "Despair not"

White Ivy [*Hedera*]: Rarity

White Lilac [*Syringa*]: Purity and modesty, Youthful innocence

White Lily [*Lilium*]: Beauty, Modesty, Purity, Sweetness

White Lupine [*Lupinus*]: Always happy

White Mulberry Tree [*Morus alba*]: Wisdom

White Mullein [*Verbascum*]: Good nature

White Oak [*Quercus alba*]: Imprudence, Independence

White Pelargonium [*Pelargonium*]: "Her smile is the soul of witchery"

White Periwinkle [*Vinca*]: Pleasures of memory, Pleasant recollections

White Pink [*Dianthus*]: Ingeniousness, Talent

White Plantain [*Plantago*]: Man's footsteps

White Poplar [*Populus alba*]: Time

White Poppy [*Papaver*]: Consolation, Dormant affection, Forgetfulness, Oblivion, "Sleep - my bane, my antidote"

White Rose [*Rosa*]: "A heart unacquainted with love", Eternal love, False love, Heavenly, "I am worthy of you", Innocence, Pure, Secrecy, Silence

White Rosebud [*Rosa*]: "Heart ignorant of love", Innocence, Girlhood

White Rose, dried [*Rosa*]: "Death preferable to loss of innocence"

White Rose, withered [*Rosa*]: Transient impressions

White Scilla (Squill) [*Scilla*]: Sweet innocence

White Snakeroot [*Ageratina altissima*]: Delay

White Sultan [*Scabiosa caucasica alba*]: Sweetness

White Tulip [*Tulipa*]: "Let's take a chance", Literary debut, Lost love

White Waterlily [*Nymphara odorata* or *Nymphara alba*]: Eloquence

White Weeping Birch [*Betula pendula*]: Beauty

White Wood Aster [*Aster divaricatus*]: Afterthought

White Verbena [*Verbena*]: Honesty, "Pray for me", Pure and guileless

White Violet [*Viola odorata*]: Balance, Imagination, Innocence, "Let's take a chance on happiness", Modesty, Purity, "Take a chance together"

White Zinnia [*Zinnia acerosa*]: Goodness

Whortleberry [*Vaccinium myrtillus*]: Treachery, Treason

Widow's Tears [*Tradescantia*]: Suffers from cold

Widow's Thrill (Kalanchoe) [*Kalenchoe*]: Popularity

Wild Daisy [*Bellis perennis*]: Indecision, "I will think about it", Melancholy

Wild Geranium (Cranesbill) [*Geranium*]: Availability, Constancy, Envy, "I desire to please", Steadfast, Steadfast piety

Wild Grape [*Vitis vinifera*]: Charity, Mirth

Wild Honeysuckle [*Lonicera*]: Inconstancy in love

Wild Hyacinth [*Dichelostemma pulchellum*]: Hope, Mysterious, Vigilance

Wild Licorice [*Glycyrrhiza lepidota*]: "I declare against you"

Wild Pansy (Heartsease, Johnny Jump Up) [*Viola tricolor*]: Happy thoughts, "In my thoughts", Love in idleness, Modesty, Pleasant thoughts, "Think of me", Thoughts, "You occupy my thoughts"

Wild Plum [*Prunus americana*]: Independence

Wild Ranunculus [*Ranunculus occidentalis*]: Inconstancy, Ingratitude

Wild Rose [*Rosa*]: Charming simplicity, Poetry, Purity, Simplicity

Wild Sorrel [*Rumex hastatus*]: Ill-timed wit

Wild Tansy (Goose Grass, Silverweed) [*Potentilla anserina*]: "I declare war against you"

Wild Violet [*Viola canadensis*]: Goals, Love, Love in idleness, Positive outlooks, Self-understanding

Willow Herb, purple [*Epilobium*]: Sporting

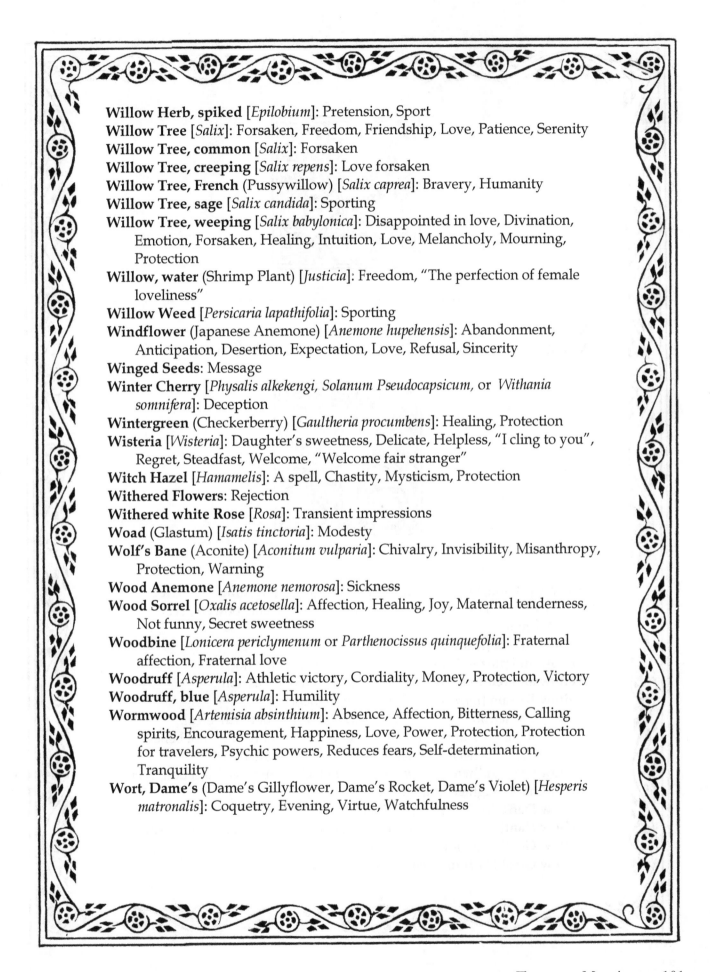

Willow Herb, spiked [*Epilobium*]: Pretension, Sport

Willow Tree [*Salix*]: Forsaken, Freedom, Friendship, Love, Patience, Serenity

Willow Tree, common [*Salix*]: Forsaken

Willow Tree, creeping [*Salix repens*]: Love forsaken

Willow Tree, French (Pussywillow) [*Salix caprea*]: Bravery, Humanity

Willow Tree, sage [*Salix candida*]: Sporting

Willow Tree, weeping [*Salix babylonica*]: Disappointed in love, Divination, Emotion, Forsaken, Healing, Intuition, Love, Melancholy, Mourning, Protection

Willow, water (Shrimp Plant) [*Justicia*]: Freedom, "The perfection of female loveliness"

Willow Weed [*Persicaria lapathifolia*]: Sporting

Windflower (Japanese Anemone) [*Anemone hupehensis*]: Abandonment, Anticipation, Desertion, Expectation, Love, Refusal, Sincerity

Winged Seeds: Message

Winter Cherry [*Physalis alkekengi, Solanum Pseudocapsicum,* or *Withania somnifera*]: Deception

Wintergreen (Checkerberry) [*Gaultheria procumbens*]: Healing, Protection

Wisteria [*Wisteria*]: Daughter's sweetness, Delicate, Helpless, "I cling to you", Regret, Steadfast, Welcome, "Welcome fair stranger"

Witch Hazel [*Hamamelis*]: A spell, Chastity, Mysticism, Protection

Withered Flowers: Rejection

Withered white Rose [*Rosa*]: Transient impressions

Woad (Glastum) [*Isatis tinctoria*]: Modesty

Wolf's Bane (Aconite) [*Aconitum vulparia*]: Chivalry, Invisibility, Misanthropy, Protection, Warning

Wood Anemone [*Anemone nemorosa*]: Sickness

Wood Sorrel [*Oxalis acetosella*]: Affection, Healing, Joy, Maternal tenderness, Not funny, Secret sweetness

Woodbine [*Lonicera periclymenum* or *Parthenocissus quinquefolia*]: Fraternal affection, Fraternal love

Woodruff [*Asperula*]: Athletic victory, Cordiality, Money, Protection, Victory

Woodruff, blue [*Asperula*]: Humility

Wormwood [*Artemisia absinthium*]: Absence, Affection, Bitterness, Calling spirits, Encouragement, Happiness, Love, Power, Protection, Protection for travelers, Psychic powers, Reduces fears, Self-determination, Tranquility

Wort, Dame's (Dame's Gillyflower, Dame's Rocket, Dame's Violet) [*Hesperis matronalis*]: Coquetry, Evening, Virtue, Watchfulness

Xanthium [*Xanthium*]: Pertinacity, Rudeness
Xeranthemum (Immortelle) [*Xeranthemum*]: Cheerfulness under adversity

Yarrow (Milfoil, Sneezewort) [*Achillea millefoilum*]: Courage, Cure for
   heartache, Healing, Heartache ease, Love, Psychic powers, War,
   Warning
Yellow Acacia [*Acacia*]: Secret love
Yellow and purple Pansy [*Viola tricolor*]: "Forget me not"
Yellow and red Rose together [*Rosa*]: Excitement, Passion
Yellow Balsam [*Impatiens balsamina*]: Impatience
Yellow Carnation [*Dianthus caryophyllus*]: Admiration, Cheerful,
   Contempt, Disappointment, Disdain, Fascination, "I do not believe
   you", No!, Rejection, Rue, "You have disappointed me"
Yellow Chrysanthemum [*Chrysanthemum*]: Cheerfulness, Dejection, Secret
   admirer, Slighted, Slighted love
Yellow Daffodil [*Narcissus*]: Gallantry
Yellow Dahlia [*Dahlia*]: Distaste, "I am happy that you love me", Rebuff
Yellow Gentian [*Gentiana*]: Ingratitude
Yellow Great Daffodil [*Narcissus*]: Chivalry

Yellow Hyacinth [*Hyacinthus*]: Jealousy

Yellow Iris [*Iris*]: Passion, Sorrow

Yellow Jasmine [*Jasminum mesnyi*]: Elegance, Grace

Yellow Lily [*Lilium*]: Coquetry, Falsehood, Flirtation, Gaiety, Happiness, Lies

Yellow Poppy [*Papaver*]: Success, Wealth

Yellow Primrose [*Primula*]: Hunting

Yellow Rose [*Rosa*]: Betrayal, Broken heart, Decrease of love, Departure of love, Dying love, Extreme betrayal, Forgive and forget, Infidelity, Intense emotions, Jealousy, Joy

Yellow Sultan [*Centaurea imperialis suaveolens*]: Contempt

Yellow Sweet Briar [*Rosa foetida*]: Decrease of love, "Let us forget"

Yellow Tulip [*Tulipa*]: Hope in love, Hopeless love, Joy, "There's sunshine in your smile"

Yellow Violet [*Viola*]: Rural happiness

Yellow Waterlily [*Nymphaea*]: Growing indifference

Yellow Zinnia [*Zinnia grandiflora*]: Daily remembrance, Remembrance

Yew [*Taxus*]: Beginnings, Endings, Immutability, Patience, Perseverance, Renewal, Sadness, Sorrow, Transitions

York and Lancaster Rose [*Rosa versicolor*]: War

Yucca [*Yucca*]: Protection, Purification, Transmutation

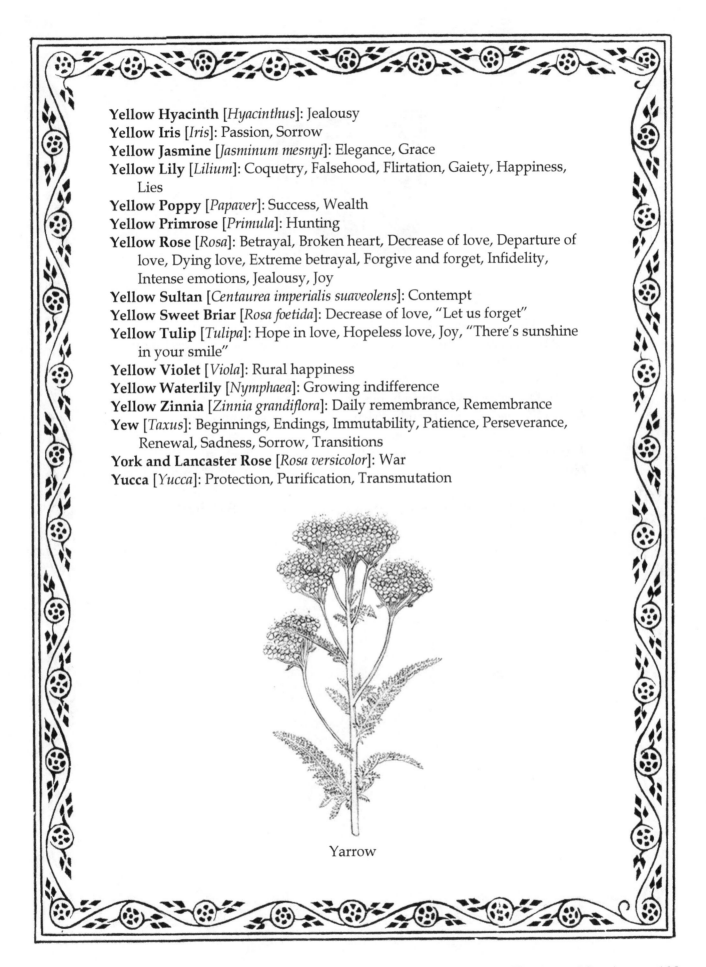

Yarrow

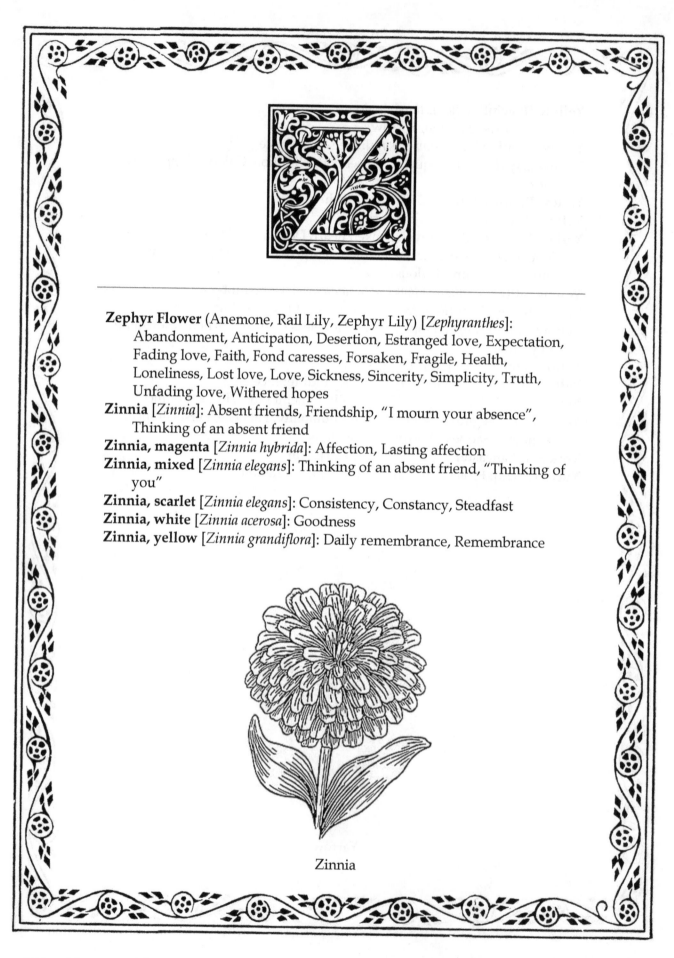

Zephyr Flower (Anemone, Rail Lily, Zephyr Lily) [*Zephyranthes*]:
Abandonment, Anticipation, Desertion, Estranged love, Expectation,
Fading love, Faith, Fond caresses, Forsaken, Fragile, Health,
Loneliness, Lost love, Love, Sickness, Sincerity, Simplicity, Truth,
Unfading love, Withered hopes

Zinnia [*Zinnia*]: Absent friends, Friendship, "I mourn your absence",
Thinking of an absent friend

Zinnia, magenta [*Zinnia hybrida*]: Affection, Lasting affection

Zinnia, mixed [*Zinnia elegans*]: Thinking of an absent friend, "Thinking of
you"

Zinnia, scarlet [*Zinnia elegans*]: Consistency, Constancy, Steadfast

Zinnia, white [*Zinnia acerosa*]: Goodness

Zinnia, yellow [*Zinnia grandiflora*]: Daily remembrance, Remembrance

Zinnia

Meanings to Flowers

A beauty: Orchid
A belle: Orchid
A boaster: Hydrangea
A friend in adversity: Snowdrop
A foe is near: Monkshood
A heart ignorant of love: White Rosebud
A heart unacquainted with love: White Rose
A proud spirit: Gloxinia
A serenade: Dew Plant
A spell: Witch Hazel
A star: Cineraria
Abandonment: Anemone (Zephyr Flower), Field Anemone, Grape, Japanese
    Anemone (Windflower), Red Anemone
Abruptness: Borage
Absence: Mugwort, Sagebrush, Wormwood
Absolute achievement: Gold Rose
Absent friends: Zinnia
Abundance: Azalea, Chrysanthemum (Bloom, Mum), Corn, Grapevine, Wheat
Abuse not: Cress, Crocus
Accept a faithful heart: Weigela
Accept change: Honesty (Lunaria)
Acceptance: Cuckoo Flower, Heather, Lilac
Accepting change in life: Honesty (Lunaria)
Accomplishment: Laurel Tree (Bay, Sweet Bay)
Achievement: Gold Rose, Ivy
Achievement in the arts: Laurel Tree (Bay, Sweet Bay)
Acknowledgment: Bellflower, Canterbury Bells, Lavender
Action: Chamomile, Dog Fennel, Marguerite, Mayweed
Activity: Thyme
Admiration: African Violet, Amethyst Flower, Camellia, Carnation, Dianthus
    (Pinks), Heather, Lavender Heather, Red Carnation, Yellow Carnation
Adoration: Azalea, Dwarf Sunflower, Sunflower, White Camellia Japonica
Adroitness: Orchid, Spider Orchid

Adulation: Indian Plantain, Plantain

Adversity: Blackthorn

Advice: Rhubarb

Affability: Star-shaped Phlox

Affectation: Cockscomb Amaranth, Morning Glory (Major Convolvulus)

Affection: Aloe, Cactus, Calendula (Pot Marigold), Celosia, Coxcomb, Daffodil (Jonquil, Lent Lily), Dianthus (Pinks), Furze (Gorse), Honeysuckle, Ivy, Magenta Zinnia, Mistletoe, Mossy Saxifrage, Oxalis (Sorrel), Pear, Pear Tree, Saxifrage, Stock, Violet, Wood Sorrel, Wormwood

Affection beyond the grave: Green Locust Tree

Affection returned: Jonquil (Daffodil, Lent Lily)

Affluence: Beech Tree, Chestnut

Aflame: German Iris

Afterthought: American Starwort, Aster (September Flower), China Aster, Michaelmas Daisy, White Wood Aster

Age: Guelder Rose, Snowball (Snowberry), Tree of Life (Himalayan Moringa)

Agitation: Moving Plant, Quaking Grass, Rhododendron (Rosebay), Sainfoin, Telegraph Plant

Agreement: Corn Straw, Lancaster Rose, Phlox, Straw, Strawflower

Airy: Delphinium, Larkspur

Alas! my poor heart: Deep red Carnation, Red Camellia Japonica, Red Carnation

Allure: Fern, Thyme

Alternatives: Scabiosa (Pincushion Flower)

Always: Rose

Always cheerful: Coreopsis (Tickseed), Variegated Holly

Always delightful: Cineraria

Always happy: White Lupine

Always lovely: Double Indian Pink, Tea Rose

Always on my mind: Pink Carnation

Always reliable: Cress

Always remembered: Cottonweed, Everlasting

Always yours: Red Sally

Am I forgotten?: Holly, Satin Flower

Am I indifferent to you?: Dogwood Tree

Am not proud: Petunia

Ambassador of love: Cabbage Rose

Ambition: Hollyhock, Ivy, Mountain Laurel, Mountain Pink

Ambition of a hero: Mountain Laurel

Ambition of a scholar: Hollyhock

Amiability: Carolina Jasmine, Fuchsia, Jasmine, White Jasmine

Amiableness: White Jasmine

Among the nobles: Tulip Poplar

Amusement: Bladder Nut Tree, Nut Tree

An accommodating disposition: Valerian

An appointed meeting: Everlasting Pea

Ancestors: Bougainvillea

Anger: Furze (Gorse), Peony, Petunia, Whin

Anger management: Alyssum, Sweet Alyssum (Sweet Alison)

Animosity: Basil, Saint John's Wort

Anti-hunger: Alfalfa

Anti-lightning: Hazel (Filbert), Holly, Mahogany

Anti-theft: Aspen Tree, Boutonniere Flower, Caraway, Garlic, Juniper Tree, Larch Tree, Vetivert

Anticipation: Ajuga (Bugleweed), Anemone (Zephyr Flower), Bachelor's Button (Cornflower, Hurtsickle), Basket Flower, Bluebottle, Cape Jasmine, Century Plant, Forsythia, Gooseberry, Japanese Anemone (Windflower)

Antidote: Plumbago (Leadwort)

Anxiety relief: Christmas Rose, Helleborus (Lenten Rose)

Anxious and trembling: Red Columbine

Apology: Purple Hyacinth

Appointed meeting: Pea, Sweet Pea

Appreciation: Eustoma (Lisianthus)

Architecture: Candytuft

Ardent and pure love: Carnation, Impatiens (Busy Lizzie)

Ardent attachment: Delphinium, Larkspur, Lavender

Ardent love: Balsam, Cactus

Ardor: Arum (Wake-robin), Bearded Iris, Cuckoo flower, Dragon Root, Dragonwort (Tarragon), Fleur-de-Lis Iris, Lady's Smock, Red Carnation

Argument: Fig

Arrogance: Asthma Weed (Sticky-Weed), Crown Imperial, Indian Tobacco, Lobelia, Pukeweed, Sunflower, Tall Sunflower, Tobacco

Art/Arts: Acanthus, Alder Tree, Clematis (Leatherflower, Virgin's Bower), Hoya (Wax Plant)

Artifice: Acanthus, Clematis, Flytrap, Sweet William, Venus Flytrap

Aspiration/Aspiring: Bellflower, Campanula Pyramida, Foxtail Lily, Hollyhock, Mountain Pink

Assiduous to please: Sprig of Ivy with tendrils

Assignation: Chickweed, Pimpernel, Scarlet Pimpernel

Astonishment: Dragonwort (Tarragon)

Astral projection: Belladonna, Dittany of Crete, Mugwort

Asylum: Juniper

Athletic victory: Woodruff

Atonement: Florists' Nightmare (Star of Bethlehem)

Attachment: Crocus, Heliotrope, Indian Jasmine, Ipomaea, Jasmine, Moonflower (Moon Vine), Red Morning Glory, Saffron

Attraction: Buttercup (Kingscup), Furze (Gorse), Turban Buttercup (Persian Buttercup)

Attractive: Foamflower, Variegated Laurel

Attractive to the opposite sex: Lemon Verbena
Attract love: Lady's Mantle
Audacity: Larch Tree
Austerity: Common Thistle
Availability: Wild Geranium
Avarice: Auricula (Bear's Ears), Scarlet Auricula
Aversion: China Pink, Dianthus (Pinks), Single Indian Pink
Awareness: Saint John's Wort
Awe: Fir Tree, Pine Tree

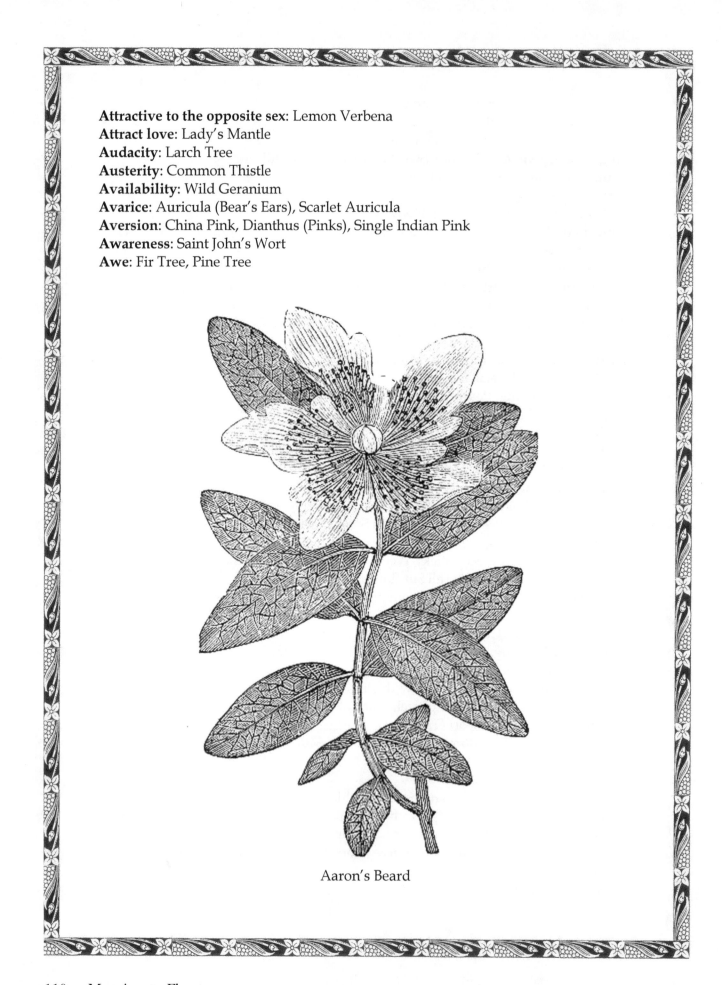

Aaron's Beard

Baby's hands: Japanese Maple

Balance: Candytuft, Helleborus (Lenten Rose), Mistletoe, Mock Orange, Saxifrage, White Violet

Banquet: Parsley

Banter: Southernwood

Baseness: Dodder, Dodder of Thyme

Bashful love: Damask Rose

Bashfulness: Deep Red Rose, Humble Plant, Mimosa Tree (Sensitive Plant), Peony, Prayer Plant, Shame Plant, Sleeping Grass, Touch-Me-Not

Bashful shame: Deep Red Rose

Beautiful but timid: Amaryllis

Beautiful eyes: Variegated Tulip

Beautiful lady: Orchid

Beautiful mouth: Eustoma (Lisanthus), Prairie Gentian, Prairie Rose, Texas Bluebell

Beauty: Acacia, Asphodel (Lily), Avocado, Calla Lily, Camellia, Carnation, Catnip, Cherry Blossom, Chinese Ground Orchid, Cinnamon, Cymbidium Orchid, Delphinium, Dianthus (Pinks), Flax, Gerbera Daisy, Ginseng, Hardy Orchid, Lilac, Magnolia Tree, Maidenhair Fern, Maple Tree, Mixed-colors Carnation, Multicolored Daisy, Orchid, Parti-colored Daisy, Pink Carnation, Red-leaf Rose, Red Camellia Japonica, Red Carnation, Rosebud, Transvaal Daisy, White Camellia Japonica, White Daisy, White Flax, White Hyacinth, White Lily, White Weeping Birch

Beauty always new: China Rose

Beauty ever new: Monthly Rose

Beauty in retirement: Acacia

Beauty is your only attraction: Japanese Rose

Beauty unknown to possessor: Red Daisy

Be cautious: Goldenrod

Beginnings: Birch Tree, Garden Anemone, Parsley and Rue, Yew

Belief: Garden Anemone, Pasque Flower, Passionflower

Believe me: Red Tulip

Belle: Orchid
Beloved child: Cinquefoil
Beloved daughter: Cinquefoil
Be mine: Four-leaved Clover, White Clover
Be my support: Black Bryony
Benefactor: Flax
Beneficence: Marsh Mallow, Olive Tree, Potato
Benevolence: Allspice, Bubby Bush (Calycanthus), Carolina Allspice, Flax, Potato, Sweet Betsy, Sweet Shrub
Benevolent justice: Pear
Be of good cheer: Poinsettia
Best wishes: Basil
Betrayal: Judas Tree, Manchineel Tree, Redbud, Yellow Rose
Betrayed: White Catchfly
Betrothal: Red Carnation
Better things to come: Apple Blossom
Beware: Begonia, Henbane (Henbit), Oleander, Rosebay (Rhododendron)
Beware of excess: Saffron
Beware of excess pleasures: Rue
Beware the coquette: Catalpa Tree
Be warned in time: Devil's Potato
Bewitching grace: Lady's Tresses
Binding: Knotweed (Painter's Palette)
Birth: Dittany of Crete, Lotus, Oregano
Bitter memories: Pheasant's Eye
Bitterness: Aloe, Russian Olive, Wormwood
Bitter truth: Nightshade
Black magic: Hemlock
Blackness: Ebony Tree
Blessings of being single: Bachelor's Button (Cornflower, Hurtsickle), Basket Flower, Bluebottle, Boutonniere Flower
Bliss: Everlasting Pea, Grass Pea, Sweet Pea
Blissful pleasure: Everlasting Pea, Grass Pea, Sweet Pea
Blocks emotional conflicts: Lavender
Bluntness: Borage
Blushes: Marjoram
Boaster/Boastfulness: Hydrangea
Boldness: Carnation, Delphinium, Dianthus (Pinks), Larch Tree, Sweet William
Bonds: Bindweed (Minor Convolvulus), Convolvulus
Bonds of affection: Dwarf Morning Glory, Gillyflower, Stock
Bonds of love: Carnation, Honeysuckle, Monthly Honeysuckle
Boredom: Guelder Rose, Snowball (Snowberry)
Bound: Guelder Rose, Snowball (Snowberry)
Braggart: Hydrangea

Bravery: Cactus, French Willow, Oak Leaf, Oak Tree, Peony
Breaking love spells: Pistachio
Breaking: Polonium
Breaking up: Asphodel (Lily), Daylily
Breath of an angel: Moon Vine (Moonflower)
Bridal favor: Ivy Geranium
Bridal festivities: Orange Blossom
Brightness: Larkspur, Variegated Ivy
Brilliant complexion: Damask Rose
Broken heart: Yellow Rose
Brouhaha: Rhubarb
Buddhism: Bo Tree
Budding beauty: Mayflower
Building: Red Clover
Bulk: Gourd, Watermelon
Bulkiness: Watermelon
Bullet-proofing: Edelweiss
Bury me amid Nature's beauties: Persimmon
Busybody: Cardinal Creeper (Ipomoea Quamoclit)

Boneset

Calling spirits: Dandelion, Wormwood
Call me not beautiful: Unique Rose
Calming thoughts: Skullcap
Calmness: Bilberry, Buckbean, Eustoma (Lisianthus), Love-in-a-Mist (Nigella), Rush (Bulrush), Snowflake (Leucojum)
Calm repose: Buckbean
Calumny: Helleborus (Lenten Rose), Madder
Capability: Coneflower (Echinacea)
Capricious beauty: Lady's Slipper Orchid, Musk Rose
Capriciousness: Dahlia, Lady's Seal, Purple Carnation
Cares: Calendula (Pot Marigold)
Careful encouragement: Goldenrod
Caring: Pink Tulip
Carousing: Grape
Catch me if you can: Lady's Seal, Lady's Slipper Orchid
Cat magic: Catnip
Caught/Caught at last: Venus Flytrap
Caution: Azalea, Begonia, Oleander
Celebration: Bramble, Poinsettia
Celibacy: Bachelor's Button (Cornflower, Hurtsickle), Basket Flower, Bluebottle, Boutonniere Flower, Century Plant
Chagrin: Marigold
Challenge: Alum Root, Coral Bells, Holly
Change: Ash Tree, Birch Tree, Hibiscus, Pimpernel, Scarlet Pimpernel
Changeable disposition: Ryegrass
Character: Gladiolus (Abyssinian Sword Lily)
Charity: Turnip, Wild Grape
Charm: Buttercup (Kingscup), Diosma (Breath of Heaven), Eucharist Lily, Foxglove (Digitalis), French Buttercup, Lily (Asphodel), Persian Buttercup (Turban Buttercup), Ranunculus
Charming: Aster (September Flower), Musk Rose cluster
Charming simplicity: Wild Rose
Charms of women: Variegated Geranium

Chaste love: Acacia

Chastity: Cactus, Camphor, Coconut, Cucumber, Everlasting Pea, Fleabane, Grass Pea, Hawthorn Tree, Hemlock, Lavender, Lettuce, Nasturtium, Orange Blossom, Pineapple, Sweet Pea, Vervain, Witch Hazel

Cheerful/Cheerfulness: Buttercup (Kingscup), Chrysanthemum (Bloom, Mum), Coreopsis (Tickseed), Crocus, Daisy, English Daisy, Gerbera Daisy, Laurustinus, Saffron, Yellow Carnation, Yellow Chrysanthemum

Cheerfulness in old age: American Starwort, Chrysanthemum (Bloom, Mum)

Cheerfulness under adversary: Chinese Chrysanthemum, Chrysanthemum (Bloom, Mum), Everlasting, Xeranthemum

Cheers my soul: Quince

Cheers the heart: Bugleweed (Ajuga)

Cheer up: Eyebright

Cherished: Cinquefoil, Meadow Saffron, Meadow Sage, Sage, Salvia

Childhood: Buttercup (Kingscup), Sweet William

Childish ingratitude: Buttercup (Kingscup)

Childishness: Buttercup (Kingscup), Geranium (Cranesbill), Narcissus

Chivalry: Aconite (Wolf's Bane), Buttercup (Kingscup), Carnation, Cherry, Daffodil (Jonquil, Lent Lily), Dianthus (Pinks), Great Yellow Daffodil, Monkshood, Sweet William

Choice: Apple Blossom

Chosen one: Pimpernel, Scarlet Pimpernel

Christmas joy: Holly Berries

Church unity: Scarlet Verbena

Civil service: Laurel Tree (Bay, Sweet Bay)

Clarity: Bilberry

Clarity of thought: Pennyroyal

Cleanliness: Hyssop

Cleansing: Camphor, Canary Grass, Nicotiana (Flowering Tobacco)

Cleverness: Baby's Breath, Saxifrage, Strawberry Begonia

Clinging affection: Irish Ivy

Coarseness: Pumpkin

Cold-hearted: Lettuce

Coldness: Chaste Bush, Fig Marigold, Icicle Plant

Come down to me: Jacob's Ladder

Comeliness: Cowslip (Primrose)

Come to me: Balsam, Bridal-wreath (Spirea)

Comfort/Comforting: Chamomile, Geranium (Cranesbill), Ginger, Pear Blossom, Pear Tree, Scarlet Geranium, Tea

Comfort to those who mourn: Sage

Coming of age: Mayflower

Communication: Bilberry, Mullein, Scabiosa (Pincushion Flower)

Communication with Spirits: Staghorn Sumac

Compassion: Allspice, Bee Balm (Monarda), Elder Tree, Elderberry, Japanese Rose,

Passionflower

Compensation: Poor Robin

Compliance: Reed

Concealed love: Acacia, Almond Tree, Motherwort

Concealed merit: Coriander (Chinese Parsley, Cilantro)

Conceited: Bridal-wreath (Spirea), Coxcomb, Cockscomb Amaranth, Pomegranate

Conception: Mugwort

Concert: Nettle, Nettle Tree (Lote Tree)

Concord: Apple, Nettle Tree (Lote Tree)

Confessed love/Confession of love: Moss Rose, Moss Rosebud, Red Tulip

Confidence: Bird's Nest Fern, Coxcomb, Fern, Hepatica, Liverwort

Confidence in Heaven: Flowering Reed, Lilac Polyanthus

Confiding love: Fuchsia

Conflict: Blackthorn

Congeniality: Jasmine

Conjugal affection: Geranium (Cranesbill), Ivy, Lime Tree, Linden Tree

Conjugal love: Lime Tree, Linden Tree

Conquest: Nasturtium

Consistency: Baby's Breath, Bellflower, Bluebell, Blue Hyacinth, Canterbury Bells, Forget-Me-Not (Myosotis), Globe Amaranth, Hyacinth, Scarlet Zinnia

Consolation: Geranium (Cranesbill), Poppy, Red Field Poppy, Red Poppy, Snowdrop, White Poppy

Constancy: Blue Hyacinth, Bluebell, Bluebottle, Boxwood (Box Tree), Calendula (Pot Marigold), Canterbury Bells, Cedar Tree, Century Plant, Dogwood Tree, Forget-Me-Not (Myosotis), Ivy, Pyramidal Bellflower, Scarlet Zinnia, Wild Geranium

Constancy in friendship: Boxwood (Box Tree)

Constancy in love: Cedar Tree

Constant: Globe Amaranth

Consumed by love: Althea (Rose of Sharon), Althea Frutes (Syrian Mallow), Mallow

Contempt: Rue, Yellow Carnation, Yellow Sultan

Content: Houstonia, Moss Fern

Contentment: Aster (September Flower), Bluets, Camelia, Houstonia, Hoyabella

Contrition: Peony

Coquetry: Asphodel (Lily), Dame's Gillyflower (Dame's Rocket, Dame's Violet, Dame's Wort), Dandelion, Daylily, Morning Glory (Major Convolvulus), Mother of the Evening, Night-scented Gillyflower, Roque's Gillyflower, Summer Lilac, Sweet Rocket, Yellow Lily

Cordiality: Peppermint, Woodruff

Could you bear poverty?: Amethyst Flower

Counterfeit: Mock Orange

Courage: Aspen Tree, Black Cohosh, Black Poplar Tree, Borage, Chelone (Turtlehead), Chives, Columbine, Edelweiss, Everlasting Pea, Fennel, Garlic, Gladiolus (Abyssinian Sword Lily), Grass Pea, Laurel Tree (Bay, Sweet Bay), Masterwort, Mullein, Pine Tree, Pokeweed, Protea (Sugarbush), Ragweed, Sweet

Pea, Tea, Thyme, Yarrow (Milfoil, Sneezewort)

Courtliness: Geranium (Cranesbill)

Courtship: Heather

Creation of beauty: Laurel Tree (Bay, Sweet Bay)

Creative force: Red and White Rose

Creativity: Alder Tree, Aspen Tree, Basil, Beardtongue (Pentsemon), Clematis, Elecampane, Mistletoe, Mock Orange

Crime: Tamarisk

Criticism: Cucumber

Crucifixion: Dogwood Tree

Cruelty: Burning Nettle, Marigold, Nettle

Cruelty in love: Burning Nettle, Marigold, Nettle

Cure: Balm of Gilead

Cure for heartache: Cranberry, Swallow-wart, Yarrow (Milfoil, Sneezewort)

Curiosity: Asparagus Fern, Sycamore Tree

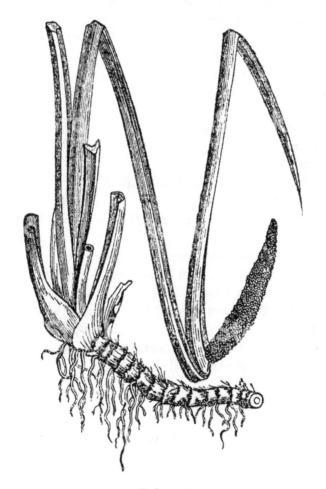

Calamus

Daily remembrance: Yellow Zinnia

Daintiness: American Starwort, Aster (September Flower), Bachelor's Button (Cornflower, Hurtsickle), Michaelmas Daisy, Sweet Sultan

Dainty pleasures: Coral Bells

Dance with me: Campion Rose, Magic Lily, Maltese Cross, Naked Lady (Belladonna Lily), Ragged-robin, Spider Lily

Danger/Dangerous: Henbane (Henbit), Red Hot Poker (Torch Lily), Rosebay (Rhododendron), Tuberose

Dangerous pleasures: Tuberose

Dangerous pride: Blackberry

Daring: Pine Tree

Dark thoughts: Begonia, Nightshade

Daughter's sweetness: Wisteria

Dauntlessness: Statice

Dead hope: Morning Glory (Major Convolvulus)

Deadly foe is near: Monkshood

Death: Belladonna, Black Rose, Chinaberry, Cypress Tree, Irish Cypress Tree, Italian Cypress Tree, Poppy

Death preferable to loss of innocence: Dried White Rose

Deceit: Angel's Trumpet, Apocynum (Dogbane), Arum (Wake-Robin), Cypress Tree, Devil's Cucumber, Devil's Trumpet, Fennel, Geranium (Cranesbill), Flytrap, Jewel Weed, Jimson Weed, Mock Orange, Prickly Burr, Thorn Apple, Venus Flytrap

Deceitful charms: Datura, Larch Fir, Thorn Apple

Deception: Cherry Tree, Linaria, Monkshood, Snapdragon, Toadflax, White Cherry, Winter Cherry

Decisions: Foxglove (Digitalis)

Declaration of love: Red Tulip

Decrease of love: Yellow Rose, Yellow Sweetbriar

Dedication: Hyacinth

Deep, pure love: Red Carnation

Deep romance: Red Canterbury Bells

Deep thoughts: Begonia

Defense: Holly, Rowan Tree

Deformity: Begonia

Deign to smile: Oak-leaf Geranium

Dejection: Aloe, Auricula (Bear's Ears), Lichen, Lupine, Yellow Chrysanthemum

Delay: Ageratum, Eupatorium, Joe Pye Weed, White Snakeroot

Delicacy/Delicate: Bachelor's Button (Cornflower, Hurtsickle), Bluebottle, Bottlebrush, Century Plant, Corn Bottle, Dusty Miller, Love-in-a-Mist (Nigella), Saint Bridgid de Caen, Sweet Sultan, Wisteria

Delicate beauty: Althea (Rose of Sharon), Flower-of-an-Hour, Hibiscus, Lavatera, Mallow, Malva Rose, Muskmallow, Orchid, Rose Mallow, Venetian Mallow

Delicate feelings: Sensitive Plant (Mimosa)

Delicate love connection: African Violet

Delicate pleasures: Everlasting Pea, Grass Pea, Sweet Pea

Delight/Delightful: Caladium, Cinchona, Cineraria

Delusion: Marjoram

Delusive hopes: Black Prince Geranium

Democracy: White Carnation

Departure: Everlasting Pea, Grass Pea, Morning Glory (Major Convolvulus), Pea, Sweet Pea

Departure of love: Yellow Rose

Desertion: Anemone (Zephyr Flower), Columbine, Japanese Anemone (Windflower)

Desire: Cactus, Coral Rose, Hawthorn Tree, Jonquil (Daffodil, Lent Lily), Orange Rose, Peach Rose, Rose

Desire for riches: Buttercup (Kingscup), Marsh Marigold

Desire to please: Mezereon, Daphne Odora

Desire to travel: Bridal-wreath (Spirea)

Desolate heart: Chrysanthemum (Bloom, Mum)

Despair: Cypress Tree, Marigold, Marigold and Cypress

Despair not: White Julienne

Despondency: Bindweed (Minor Convolvulus), Humble Plant, Morning Glory (Major Convolvulus), Marigold

Destiny: Ash Tree

Determined/Determination: Canary Grass, Red Hot-Poker (Torch Lily)

Devoted affection: Heliotrope

Devoted love: Honeysuckle, Monthly Honeysuckle

Devotion: Alstroemeria (Peruvian Lily), Carnation, Dianthus (Pinks), Heliotrope, Hosta, Hydrangea, Lavender, Night-scented Stock, Orange, Peruvian Heliotrope, Sunflower, White Carnation

Dexterity: Sweet William

Difficulty: Blackthorn

Diffidence: Cyclamen, Persian Violet

Dignity: Apple of Peru (Shoo-Fly Plant), Ash Tree, Clove, Dahlia, Elm Tree, Imperial Lily, Laurel-leaved Magnolia, Magnolia Tree

Dignity of mind: Hundred-leaved Rose

Diligence: Red Clover
Directness: Borage
Disagreement: Broken Corn Straw
Disappointed expectation: Fish Geranium
Disappointed in love: Weeping Willow Tree
Disappointment: Carolina Syringa, Yellow Carnation
Discipline: Bayberry (Wax Myrtle)
Discretion: Citron, Lemon Blossom, Maidenhair Fern
Disdain: Rue, Yellow Carnation
Disguise: Thorn Apple
Disgust: Frog Lily, Fungus
Dislike: Tansy
Dispassion: Hydrangea
Disquietude: Calendula (Pot Marigold)
Dissension: Pride of China
Distaste: Yellow Dahlia
Distinction: Cardinal Flower, Scarlet Lobelia
Distress: Marigold
Distrust: Apricot, Lavender
Diversity: Aster (September Flower)
Divination: Apocynum (Dogbane), Broom, Camphor, Cherry, Corn, Dandelion, Dittany of Crete, Dodder, Fig, Goldenrod (Solidago), Ground Ivy, Hibiscus, Lettuce, Meadowsweet, Mullein, Orris Root, Pansy, Pomegranate, Roots, Rose, Rue, Saint John's Wort, Weeping Willow Tree
Divine beauty: Cowslip (Primrose)
Divine guidance: Goldenrod (Solidago)
Divinity/Divine: Cowslip (Primrose)
Division: Broken Straw
Docility: Rush (Bulrush)
Do me justice: Chestnut, Chestnut Tree
Domestic duties: Meadow Saffron, Meadow Sage, Sage
Domestic happiness: Flax, Grape, Holly, Honeysuckle, Sage
Domestic industry: Flax, Hothouse Leek, Houseleek
Domestic virtues: Flax, Meadow Saffron, Meadow Sage, Sage
Do not abuse: Saffron
Do not forget me: Forget-Me-Not (Myosotis), Mouse-eared Scorpion Grass
Do not go away: Sweet Pea
Do not hurt me: Mimosa (Sensitive Plant)
Do not refuse me: Carrot flower, Escholzia (California Poppy), Queen Anne's Lace
Do not stand still: Kudzu
Dormant affection: White Poppy
Doubt: Apricot, Apricot Blossom
Do you love me?: Honeysuckle
Do you still love me?: Lilac

Drama: Amaryllis, Belladonna, Naked Lady (Belladonna Lily, Surprise Lily)
Dread: Dragon Plant
Dream magic: Holly, Huckleberry
Dreaminess: Pink Tulip, Poppy, Variegated Poppy
Dreams: Forget-Me-Not (Myosotis), Gentian, Huckleberry, Osmunda, Pimpernel, Texas Mountain Laurel
Dreams of fantasy: Mauve Carnation
Drunk and blousy: Valerian
Drunkenness: Vine
Duplicity: Venus Flytrap
Durability: Apocynum (Dogbane), Dogwood Tree, Flowering Dogwood
Duration: Cherry Tree, Corn Cockle, Cornel Tree
Dying love: Yellow Rose

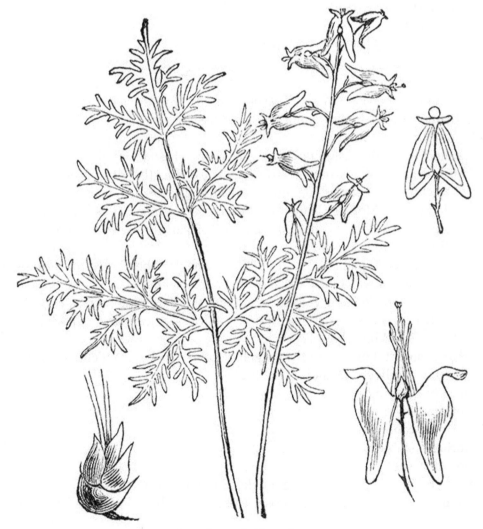

Dutchman's Breeches

Eagerness: Heliotrope, Pelargonium
Early attachment: Blue Periwinkle, Thornless Rose
Early friendship: Blue Periwinkle, Vinca (Periwinkle)
Early youth: Primrose (Cowslip)
Ease: Gooseberry
Eases cares and worries: Stitchwort
Economy: Chicory
Ecstasy: Gardenia
Education: Celandine, Cherry Blossom, Cherry Tree, Clover
Egotism: Daffodil (Jonquil, Lent Lily), Narcissus
Elation: Fir Tree, Pine Tree
Elegance: Asphodel (Lily), Birch Tree, Bleeding Heart (Lyre Flower, Venus' Car),
      Carolina Jasmine, Crepe Myrtle, Dahlia, Diosma (Breath of Heaven),
      Dutchman's Breeches, Geranium (Cranesbill), Jasmine, Locust Tree, Lotus,
      Maple Tree, Monk's Head, Pink Acacia, Pomegranate, Rose Acacia, Soldier's
      Cap, Squirrel Corn, White Acacia, White Hearts, Yellow Jasmine
Elevation: Fir Tree, Scotch Fir
Elope with me/Elopement: Basket Lily, Cleome, Ismene, Peruvian Daffodil, Sea
      Daffodil, Spider Lily, Spider Flower, Scorpion Orchid
Eloquence: Apostle Plant, Aspen Tree, Cape Myrtle, Crepe Myrtle, Flags Iris,
      Fleur-de-Lis Iris, Indian Lagerstroemia, Iris, Mexican Sage, Walking Iris,
      Waterlily, White Waterlily
Embarrassment: Love-in-a-Mist (Nigella), Love-in-a-Puzzle (Fennel Flower)
Eminence: Bindweed (Minor Convolvulus)
Emotion: Weeping Willow Tree
Emotional balance: Chamomile
Emotional calmness: Nettle
Emotional stability: Elecampane
Emotions: Rue
Employment: Devil's Shoestring, Lucky Hand, Pecan Tree
Enchantment: Holly, Lavender Rose, Monthly Rosebud, Purple Rose, Verbena,
      Vervain
Encouragement: Black-eyed Susan, Galax (Wandflower), Goldenrod (Solidago),

Grape Hyacinth, John Hopper Rose, Mugwort, Pink Carnation, Sagebrush, Wormwood

Endearment: White Carnation

Ending relationships: Turnip

Endings: Cyclamen, Yew

Endurance: Cactus, Dock, Ilex, Oak Tree, Pine Tree

Enduring affection: Furze (Gorse)

Enduring beauty: Gillyflower, Queen Anne's Thimbles

Enduring purity: Gerbera Daisy

Enemy: Orange Lily

Energy: Chamomile, Columbine, Dandelion, Dog Fennel, Gooseberry, Marguerite, Mayweed, Red Sally, Snapdragon, Thyme

Energy in adversity: Chamomile

Engagement: Grape Hyacinth

Enjoyment: Double Daisy, Gooseberry

Enlightenment: Hazel (Filbert), Lotus

Ennui: Guelder Rose, Moss, Mosses, Snowball (Snowberry)

Entertainment: Parsley

Enthusiasm: Asphodel (Lily), Blazing Star, Bouvardia, Button Snakeroot, Coral Rose, Day Lily, Elecampane, Fir Tree, Gay Feather (Kansas Feather), Orange Rose, Peach Rose, Pine Tree, Scabiosa (Pincushion Flower), Snakeroot

Envy: Blackberry, Bramble, Briar, Crowsbill, Geranium (Cranesbill), Wild Geranium

Error: Bumble Bee Orchid, Fly Orchid, Orchid

Escape: Celandine

Esteem: Daffodil (Jonquil, Lent Lily), Geranium (Cranesbill), Garden Sage, Meadow Saffron, Meadow Sage, Pineapple Sage, Sage

Esteem but not love: Spiderwort (Tradescantia), Strawberry Tree (Arbutus)

Estranged love: Anemone (Zephyr Flower), Lotus, Lotus Flower

Eternal love: Heliotrope, Orange Blossom, Rose, White Rose

Eternal sleep: Poppy

Eternal youth: Fern

Eternity: Everlasting

Evanescent pleasure: Poppy

Evening: Dame's Gillyflower (Dame's Rocket, Dame's Violet, Dame's Wort), Lilac, Mother of the Evening, Night-scented Gillyflower, Roque's Gillyflower, Sweet Rocket, Summer Lilac (Butterfly Bush)

Ever bright: Cineraria

Ever changing: Virginia Creeper (American Ivy)

Everlasting friendship: Arbor-Vitae

Everlasting love: Baby's Breath, Cedar Tree

Evil: Hemlock

Excellence: Camellia, Mignonette

Excellence beyond beauty: Alyssum, Aurinia

Excellence in women: White Camellia Japonica

Excess is dangerous: Saffron

Excessive self-love: Narcissus
Excess of sensibility: Aspen Tree
Excitement: Bronze Chrysanthemum, Red and yellow Rose together
Exile: Hothouse Leek
Exorcism: Frankincense, Fumitory, Juniper Tree, Leek
Expectancy/Expectation: Anemone (Zephyr Flower), Gooseberry, Hawthorn Tree, Japanese Anemone (Windflower)
Expected meeting: Nutmeg Geranium
Extent: Gourd
Extinguished hopes: Bindweed (Minor Convolvulus), Morning Glory (Major Convolvulus)
Extravagance: Poppy
Extreme amiability: White Jasmine
Extreme betrayal: Yellow Rose
Extremes: Striped Carnation
Exuberance: Crocus

Eglantine

Facility: Apple Geranium, Germander Speedwell, Speedwell, Valerian

Fading love: Anemone (Zephyr Flower)

Failure: Lavender

Fairies' Fire: Pyrus Japonica (Japanese Andromeda)

Faith: Anemone (Zephyr Flower), Apostle Plant, Compass Flower, Dogwood Tree, Flags Iris, Garden Anemone, Huckleberry, Iris, Mustard Seed, Pasque Flower, Passionflower, Walking Iris, Violet

Faithful: Croton

Faithful heart: Frankincense

Faithful in misfortune: Wallflower

Faithful love: Ageratum, Coxcomb

Faithfulness: African Violet, Arbutus (Strawberry Tree), Bay Leaf, Bird of Paradise (Crane Flower), Bluebell, Blue Violet, Carnation, Dahlia, Daisy, Dandelion, Dogwood Tree, Gillyflower, Heliotrope, Lemon Blossom, Madrone Tree, Pinks (Dianthus), Verbena, Violet

Faithfulness in adversity: Wallflower

Falsehood: Apocynum (Dogbane), Bugloss, Manchineel Tree, Nightshade, Yellow Lily

False love: White Rose

False riches: Sunflower

Fame: Apple Blossom, Apple Tree, Begonia, Climbing Lily (Flame Lily, Gloriosa, Glory Lily), Creeping Lilyturf, Daphne, Fire Lily, Trumpet Flower, Tulip, Tulip Poplar

Fame speaks him great and gold: Apple Blossom

Fame speaks well of him: Apple

Family union: Pink Verbena, Verbena

Fanciful: Rose Lupine

Fanciful nature: Begonia

Fantastic extravagance: Scarlet Poppy

Fantasy: Crimson Poppy, Queen Anne's Lace

Farewell: Black Rose, Cyclamen, Michaelmas Daisy, Spruce Tree

Farsightedness: Holly, Hollyhock

Fascination: Asparagus, Boston Fern, Canterbury Bells, Carnation, Dianthus

(Pinks), Enchanter's Nightshade, Flowering Fern, Fern, Honesty (Lunaria), Money Plant, Nightshade, Orange Rose, Red Carnation, Yellow Carnation

Fashion: Queen's Rocket

Fastidiousness: Lilac

Fate: Ash Tree, Flax, Hemp

Fault: Henbane (Henbit)

Favors: Chickweed, Chicory

Fealty: Ivy

Fear: Aspen Tree, Hawthorn Tree

Feasting: Parsley

Fecundity: Fig, Hollyhock

Felicity: Bachelor's Button (Cornflower, Hurtsickle), Balsam, Century Plant, Dusty Miller, Impatiens (Busy Lizzie), Sweet Sultan

Fellowship: Balm, Melissa

Female ambition: Double Narcissus, Hollyhock, White Hollyhock

Female attraction: Henbane (Henbit)

Female charm: Gardenia

Female fidelity: Speedwell, Veronica

Feminine modesty: Calla Lily

Femininity: Aster (September Flower), Azalea, Queen Anne's Lace

Ferocity: Arum (Wake Robin)

Fertility: Agaric, Banana, Bistort, Bodhi, Carrot, Chaste Tree (Agnus Castus), Chickweed, Cuckoo Flower, Cucumber, Cyclamen, Daffodil (Jonquil, Lent Lily), Date Palm, Dock, Fig, Geranium (Cranesbill), Grape, Hawthorn Tree, Hazel (Filbert), Hollyhock, Horsetail, Lotus, Mandrake, Mistletoe, Mustard, Nuts, Olive Tree, Orange Blossom, Palm Tree, Patchouli, Peach, Persian Violet, Pine Tree, Pinecone, Pomegranate, Poppy, Rice, Sunflower, Verbena, Wheat

Festivity/Festivities: Baby's Breath, Parsley

Fickleness: Delphinium, Larkspur, Lady's Slipper Orchid, Pink Larkspur

Fidelity: Aster (September Flower), Bleeding Heart (Lyre Flower, Venus' Car), Bluebell, Chili Pepper, China Aster, Clover, Dutchman's Breeches, Honeysuckle, Ivy, Lemon Blossom, Licorice, Magnolia Tree, Monk's Head, Plum Blossom, Plum Tree, Rhubarb, Rosemary, Ryegrass, Rye Skullcap, Skullcap, Soldier's Cap, Speedwell, Squirrel Corn, Veronica, Vetch, Wallflower, White Hearts

Fidelity in adversity: Wallflower

Fidelity in love: Citron, Lemon Blossom

Fiery love: Althea (Rose of Sharon)

Figment: Apocynum (Dogbane)

Filial love: Clematis (Leather Flower, Virgin's Bower)

Finding other ways of doing things: Scabosia (Pincushion Flower)

Finding your own way: Daisy

Fine Arts: Acanthus

Finesse: Carnation, Dianthus (Pinks), Sweet William

Fire: Fleur-de-lis Iris, Fraxinella, Horehound

Firmness: Boxwood (Box Tree)

First emotions of love: Purple Lilac
First love: Lilac, Purple Lilac, Purple Lily
Fishing magic: Cotton, Hawthorn Tree
Fitness: Flags Iris, Sweet Flag
Flame: Fleur-de-lis Iris, German Iris, Red Camellia Japonica, Red Carnation
Flashy: Red Carnation
Flattery: Fennel, Venus' Looking Glass
Flee away: Pennyroyal
Fleeting life: Grass
Flexibility: Honesty (Lunaria)
Flights of fancy: Delphinium, Larkspur
Flirt/Flirtation/Flirting: Dandelion, Day Lily, Feverfew, Mezereon, Variegated Poppy, Yellow Lily
Flower of the gladiators: Gladiolus (Abyssinian Sword Lily)
Flying: Basil, Poplar Tree
Fly with me: Venus' Car (Bleeding Heart, Lyre Flower)
Folly: Columbine, Geranium (Cranesbill), Pomegranate
Fond caresses: Anemone (Zephyr Flower), Fairy Lily, Rain Lily
Fond memories: Ginkgo Tree
Foolishness: Columbine, Pomegranate
Foppery: Amaranth, Cockscomb Amaranth, Coxcomb
Forbearance: Azalea
For once may pride befriend me: Tiger Flower
Force: Fennel
Foresight: Crocus, Holly, Saffron, Strawberry, Strawberry Blossom
Forever yours: Dahlia, Red Sally
Forgetfulness: Honesty (Lunaria), Money Plant, Moonwort, White Poppy
Forget me not: Forget-Me-Not (Myosotis), Garden Forget-Me-Not, Mouse-eared Scorpion Grass, Purple and yellow Pansy
Forgive and forget: Blue Scilla, Yellow Rose
Forgiveness: Asphodel (Lily), Creeping Jennie, Gooseneck Loosestrife, Loosestrife, Lysimachia
Forgiveness of injuries: Cinnamon
Formality: Narcissus
Fornication: Lime Blossom
Forsaken: Anemone (Zephyr Flower), Common Willow, Garden Anemone, Laburnum, Weeping Willow Tree, Willow Tree
Fortitude: Chamomile
Fortune: Peruvian Lily (Alstromeria)
Fragile: Anemone (Zephyr Flower), Azalea
Fragile and ephemeral passion: Indian Azalea
Fragile passion: Azalea, Indian Azalea
Fragrance remembered: Tussie Mussie
Frankness: Osier

Fraternal affection: Honeysuckle, Lilac, Woodbine
Fraternal love: Woodbine
Fraternal regard: Lilac
Freedom: Water Willow (Shrimp Plant), Willow Tree
Freshness: Damask Rose
Friendliness: Wheat
Friendship: Acacia, Apostle Plant, Arbutus (Strawberry Tree), Chrysanthemum (Bloom, Mum), Citron, Everlasting Pea, Freesia, Galax (Wandflower), Geranium (Cranesbill), Gerbera Daisy, Grass Pea, Iris, Ivy, Light Pink Rose, Lucky Hand, Pasque Flower, Passionflower, Peruvian Lily (Alstromeria), Pink Carnation, Pink Rose, Pussy Willow, Red Lucky Seed, Rose, Rose Acacia, Sweet Pea, Walking Iris, Wheat, White Acacia, Willow Tree, Zinnia
Friendship in adversity: Snowdrop, Wallflower
Frigidity: Chickweed, Chicory, Hydrangea
Frivolity: Bladder Nut Tree, London Pride
Frivolous: Columbine
Frugality: Chicory, Endive, Fuchsia, Nightshade
Fruitfulness: Hollyhock
Fulfillment: Raspberry
Fun: Delphinium, Foxtail Grass, Larkspur, Lemon Balm, Pansy, Tiger Lily
Funerals: Hawthorn Tree
Funny: Sorrel (Oxalis)
Future: Apple Blossom
Future joy: Celandine, Figwort, Pilewort
Future promise: Strawberry

Fuchsia

Gaiety: Baby's Breath, Butterfly Orchid, Delphinium, Larkspur, Yellow Lily

Gallantry: Carnation, Dianthus (Pinks), Nosegay, Sweet William, Yellow Daffodil

Gambling: Devil's Shoestring

Games: Hyacinth

Garden magic: Apple, Grape

General love: Furze (Gorse)

Generosity: Bubby Bush (Calycanthus), Carolina Allspice, Cottonweed, Gladiolus (Abyssinian Sword Lily), Globeflower (Trollius), Honeysuckle, Orange, Orange Tree, Sweet Betsy, Sweet Shrub

Generous and devoted love: Honeysuckle

Genius: Eglantine (European Sweetbriar), Pencil-leaved Geranium, Plane Tree, Plum Tree, Sycamore Tree

Gentility: Corn Cockle, Geranium (Cranesbill)

Gentle-heartedness: Raspberry

Gentleness: Lamb's Ears, Provence Rose

Giddiness: Almond

Gift of Mother Nature: Corn

Gifts of the Holy Spirit: Columbine

Gift to a Man: Camellia

Gilding the Lily: Daphne

Girlhood: Short-stemmed Rose, White Rosebud

Give me a break: Gladiolus (Abyssinian Sword Lily)

Give me an account of yourself: Chickweed

Give me your good wishes: Basil

Gladness: Cicely, Crocus, Morning Glory (Major Convolvulus), Myrrh, Rose, Saffron, Tea

Glorious beauty: Gloriosa (Climbing Lily, Flame Lily, Glory Lily), Morning Glory (Major Convolvulus)

Glory: Blood Flower (Bloedblom), Blood Lily, Cape Tulip, Catherine Wheel Pincushion, Daphne, Fireball Lily, Laurel Tree (Bay, Sweet Bay), Poison Root, Red Cape Lily

Glory and success: Laurel Tree (Bay, Sweet Bay)

Go: Rue

Goals: Helleborus (Lenten Rose), Oriental Helleborus, Wild Violet

Good-bye: Cyclamen, Everlasting Pea, Grass Pea, Persian Violet, Sweet Pea

Good cheer: Poinsettia

Good education: Cherry, Cherry Tree

Good fortune: Goldenrod (Solidago), Paper Birch Tree

Good government: Pear

Good health: Feverfew

Good health and long life: Sage

Good luck: Aloe, Bayberry (Wax Myrtle), Bells of Ireland, Clover, Garlic, Heather, Job's Tears, Mugwort, Stephanotis, White Heather

Good luck in the new year: Rosemary

Good natured: Forsythia, Mullein, White Mullein

Goodness: Carnation, Flowering Laurel, Gooseberry, Goosefoot, Mercury, Strawberry, White Zinnia

Good news: Guelder Rose

Good perspective: Bird of Paradise (Crane Flower)

Good taste: Daffodil (Jonquil, Lent Lily), Dahlia, Fuchsia, Single Daffodil, Single Dahlia

Goodwill: Holly

Good wishes: Sweet Basil, Holly

Good works: Cherry

Gossip: Canterbury Bells, Cobaea, Cup-and-Saucer Vine

Gossip stopper: Slippery Elm Tree

Grace: Asparagus Fern, Aster (September Flower), Bamboo, Birch Tree, China Rose, Cowslip (Primrose), Jasmine, Multiflora Rose, Pink Acacia, Pink Rose, Yellow Jasmine

Gracefulness: Carolina Jasmine, Daffodil (Jonquil, Lent Lily), Multiflora Rose, Red Pelargonium, White Geranium

Graciousness: Anthurium (Flamingo Flower), Camellia, Painter's Palette, Snapdragon

Grandeur: Ash Tree, Cactus

Grant me a smile: Carnation, Dianthus (Pinks), Sweet William

Gratitude: Agrimony, Bellflower, Bluebell, Bouquet of Roses, Camellia, Campanula, Canterbury Bells, Dahlia, Globeflower (Trollius), Parsley, Pink Carnation, Purple-leaf Sage, Small White Bellflower, Statice

Gratitude to parents: White Dahlia

Great beauty: Canna Lily

Great despair: Cypress Tree and Marigold

Great joy: Caladium

Greeting: Holly Berries

Grief: Aloe, Bellflower, Calendula (Pot Marigold), Canterbury Bells, Common Thistle, Harebell, Lady's Thimble, Marigold, Purple Hyacinth

Grounding: Cuckoo Flower

Growing indifference: Yellow Waterlily

Growing old: Gloire de Dijon Rose, Meadow Saffron

Growth: Acorn, Ash Tree, Ivy

Haiku: Japanese Maple

Hands full of cash: Peony

Hanging onto old ways: Lichen

Happiness: Adam and Eve Root, Baby's Breath, Catnip, Celandine, Coreopsis (Tickseed), Cumin, Cyclamen, Dandelion, Dusty Miller, Hawthorn Tree, High John the Conqueror, Honeysuckle, Hyacinth, Lavender, Lily-of-the-Valley, Madwort, Marjoram, Meadowsweet, Mugwort, Peony, Purslane, Quince, Raspberry, Rose, Saffron, Sagebrush, Saint John's Wort, Sunflower, Sweet Sultan, Wormwood, Yellow Lily

Happiness in marriage: Bridal-wreath (Spirea), Pea, Rosemary, Stephanotis

Happy love: Bridal Rose

Happy thoughts: Johnny Jump Up (Heartsease, Wild Pansy)

Happy years: Tulip

Hardness: Cranberry, Fennel

Hard work: Clover, Coral Bells

Harmony: Pimpernel

Harshness: Common Thistle

Hatred: Basil, Black Rose, Fumitory, Orange Lily

Haughtiness: Amaryllis, Delphinium, Purple Larkspur, Sunflower, Tall Sunflower

Have pity on my passion: Jonquil (Daffodil, Lent Lily)

Head over heels in love: Vine

Healing: Achillea, Adder's Tongue, Allspice, Aloe, Althea Frutes (Syrian Mallow), Amaranth, Angelica, Apple, Apple Blossom, Bachelor's Button (Cornflower, Hurtsickle), Balm of Gilead, Barley, Basil, Bay (Laurel Tree, Sweet Bay), Bay Leaf, Bittersweet, Blackberry, Black Samson, Bracken, Broom, Buddleia, Butterfly Bush, Calams, Carnation, Cedar Tree, Cinnamon, Citron, Columbine, Common Thistle, Coriander (Chinese Parsley, Cilantro), Coneflower (Echinacea), Cotton, Cowslip (Primrose), Cucumber, Cypress Tree, Dock, Eucalyptus, Fennel, Fern, Flax, Foxglove (Digitalis), Gardenia, Garlic, Ginseng, Goat's Rue, Golden Seal, Heliotrope, Hemp, Henna, Hops, Horehound, Horse Chestnut, Ivy, Job's Tears, Lemon Balm, Marsh Mallow, Mesquite, Mignonette, Mint, Mugwort, Myrrh, Nettle, Onion, Peony, Pepper

Tree, Peppermint, Persimmon, Pine Tree, Plantain, Plum, Potato, Rose, Rosemary, Rowan Tree, Rue, Sacred Plant, Saffron, Sandalwood, Sorrel (Oxalis), Spearmint, Thyme, Tobacco, Vervain, Violet, Weeping Willow Tree, Wintergreen, Wood Sorrel, Yarrow (Milfoil, Sneezewort)

Healing and charm: Digitalis

Healing of the spirit: Gentian

Healing properties: Bachelor's Button (Cornflower, Hurtsickle)

Heals conflicts: Currant

Heals indifference: Scabiosa (Pincushion Flower)

Health: Anemone (Zephyr Flower), Apple Blossom, Ash Tree, Blue Ginger, Calendula (Pot Marigold), Camphor, Caraway, Carob, Coriander (Chinese Parsley, Cilantro), Fern, Figwort, Furze (Gorse), Geranium (Cranesbill), Goat's Rue, Iceland Moss, Juniper Tree, Knotweed, Larkspur, Mandrake, Marigold, Marjoram, Mistletoe, Mullein, Pear, Pear Tree, Pimpernel, Rue, Saint John's Wort, Sainfoin, Sassafras, Sorrel (Oxalis), Sunflower, Tansy, Thyme, Walnut

Health and energy: Mixed colors Carnation

Heart: Anthurium (Flamingo Flower)

Heartache ease: Butterfly Weed, Yarrow (Milfoil, Sneezewort)

Heart ignorant of love: Rosebud, White Rosebud

Heart innocent of love: Red Rosebud

Heart is agitated: Hazel (Filbert)

Heartlessness: Hydrangea, Love-Lies-Bleeding

Heart's comfort: Marigold

Heart's mystery: Crimson Polyanthus, Primrose (Cowslip)

Heart's riches: Crimson Polyanthus

Heaven: Coleus, Snowball (Snowberry)

Heavenly: White Rose

Heedlessness: Almond

Help against weariness: Chamomile

Helpfulness: Black Bryony, Juniper Tree, Lady's Seal

Helpless: Wisteria

Hermitage: Milkwort

Her smile is the soul of witchery: White Pelargonium

Hex breaking: Toadflax

Hidden love: Acacia

Hidden worth: Coriander (Cilantro, Chinese Parsley)

Higher learning: Scabiosa (Pincushion Flower)

High of soul: Scarlet Lily

Holiness: Bramble, Fir Tree, Mistletoe

Holy wishes: Plumbago

Homage: Lignum Vitae, Sunflower

Home sweet home: Comfrey

Honesty: Althea Frutes (Syrian Mallow), Balloon Flower, Chinese Bellflower, Honesty (Lunaria), Marsh Mallow, Money Plant, White Verbena

Honor: Asphodel (Lily), Cardinal Flower, Climbing Lily (Flame Lily, Glorisoa, Glory Lily), Creeping Lilyturf, Fire Lily, Mandrake, Scarlet Lobelia

Honoring the dead: Umbrella Pine Tree

Hope: Almond, Almond Tree, Apostle Plant, Apple Blossom, Flags Iris, Florists' Nightmare (Ornithogalum), Flowering Almond, Forget-Me-Not (Myosotis), Hawthorn Tree, Iris, Pine Tree, Pretty Face, Snowdrop, Star of Bethlehem, Starflower, Walking Iris, Wild Hyacinth

Hope for better days: Marianthus

Hope in adversity: Spruce Tree

Hope in love: Bachelor's Button (Cornflower, Hurtsickle), Yellow Tulip

Hopeless: Love-Lies-Bleeding

Hopeless love: Yellow Tulip

Hopelessness: Fountain Plant, Joseph's Coat, Love-Lies-Bleeding, Prince of Wales Feather, Tampala

Hopeless not heartless: Love-Lies-Bleeding

Horror: Creeping Cereus, Dragonwort (Tarragon), Mandrake, Snakesfoot

Hospitality: American Starwort, Oak Sprig, Oak Tree, Pineapple, Pineapple Sage

Humanity: French Willow

Humble love: Fuchsia

Humiliation: Elder Tree

Humility: Allium, Bellflower, Bindweed (Minor Convolvulus), Bluebell, Blue Woodruff, Broom, Canterbury Bells, Field Lilac, Grass, Ground Ivy, Lily-of-the-Valley, Small Bindweed

Humor: Celosia, Coxcomb, Delphinium, Larkspur, Marjoram

Hunting: Fuzzy Weed, Prarie Clover (Parosela), Yellow Primrose

Hush: Belladonna

Hypocrisy: Foxglove (Digitalis)

Holly

I adore you: Heliotrope
I am...: Laurel Leaf, twisted around bouquet
I am dazzled by your charms: Buttercup (Kingscup), Globe Ranunculus, Ranunculus
I am deeply in love: Althea Frutes (Syrian Mallow)
I am happy that you love me: Yellow Dahlia
I am hurt: Mustard
I am not sure you've been faithful: Aster (September Flower)
I am really sincere: Gladiolus (Abyssinian Sword Lily)
I am sorry: Purple Hyacinth
I am still available: White Carnation
I am too happy: Cape Jasmine
I am unyielding: Lantana
I am worthy of you: White Rose
I am your captive: Peach Blossom
I attach myself to you: Indian Jasmine, Ipomaea
I await your pleasures: Orchid
I believe in your constancy: Boxwood (Box Tree)
I blush for you: Kiss Me Over the Garden Gate, Lady's Thumb, Prince's Feather
I burn for you: Fleur-de-lis Iris, German Iris, Prickly Pear
I cannot be with you: Striped Carnation
I cannot give you up: Columbine
I can't forget you: Pheasant's Eye
I change but in death: Bay Leaf
I cling to you: Chickweed, Vetch, Virginia Creeper (American Ivy), Wisteria
I cling to you in both sunshine and shade: Virginia Creeper (American Ivy)
I dare you to love me: Tiger Lily
I declare against you: Wild Licorice
I declare war against you: Belvedere (Summer Cypress), Tansy, Wild Tansy
I desire a return of affection: Daffodil (Jonquil, Lent Lily)
I desire to please: Wild Geranium
I die if neglected: Laurestina, Laurustinus, Viburnum
Idleness: Florists' Nightmare (Star of Bethlehem), Fig Marigold, Icicle Plant

I do not believe you: Yellow Carnation

I doubt you: Apocynum (Dogbane)

I dream of you: Osmunda

I fall into a trap laid for me: Red Catchfly

I fear no longer; I hope: Thornless Rosebud with leaves

I feel my obligations: Lint

I feel your kindness: Flax

I forgive you: Sultan Lilac

If you love me, you will find it out: Maiden Blush Rose

I have…: Ivy Leaf folded together

I have a message for you: Iris

I have cause: Marigold

I have lost all: Mourning Bride, Pincushion Flower (Scabiosa)

I have loved you and you have not known it: Clove

I keep my secrets: Fig

I like you only as a friend: Lavender

I live for you: Cedar Leaf, Cedar Tree, Mignonette

I long for your company: Balm

I look to Heaven: Fringed Gentian

I love: Red Chrysanthemum

I love you: Morning Glory (Major Convolvulus), Red Chrysanthemum, Rose, Single Rose

I love you in secret: Gardenia

I love you too: Red Chrysanthemum

I love your mind: Clematis

I mourn your absence: Zinnia

I offer you: Geranium (Cranesbill), Virginia Creeper leaf

I offer you my all: Shepherd's Purse

I offer you my fortune: Calceolaria

I offer you pecuniary assistance: Calceolaria

I only dream of you: Moonflower (Moon Vine)

I only love you: Arbutus (Strawberry Tree)

I oppose you: Tansy

I partake your sentiments: Double China Aster, Garden Daisy

I prefer you: Geranium (Cranesbill), Pink Geranium, Rose-scented Geranium

I promise: White Clover

I seek glory: Hollyhock

I shall die tomorrow: Gum Cistus

I shall not survive you: Black Mulberry Tree

I share your sentiments: Double China Aster, English Daisy, Garden Daisy

I still love you: Single Rose

I surmount all difficulties/obstacles: Mistletoe

I think of you: Blue Salvia, Everlasting

I think of you constantly: Variegated Dahlia

I turn to you: Heliotrope
I understand you: Cyclamen
I weep for you: Purple Verbena
I will always remember: Tea Rose
I will always remember you: Long-stemmed Rose
I will never change: Arbor-Vitae
I will never forget you: Pink Carnation
I will not economize: Red Cyclamen
I will pray for you: White Hyacinth
I will return: Queen Anne's Lace
I will still be waiting: False Goat's Beard (Astilbe), False Spirea
I will think about it: Daisy, Daisy Wreath, Single China Aster, Wild Daisy
I will think of you: China Aster
I will try again: Blazing Star, Button Snakeroot, Gay Feather (Kansas Feather), Liatris, Snakeroot
I wish I was rich: Buttercup (Kingscup)
I wish to speak to you: Bellflower
I would not have you otherwise: Daphne
I wound but to heal: European Sweetbriar (Eglantine)
Ill-natured: Crabapple Blossom
Ill-natured beauty: Citron
Ill-tempered: Crabapple blossom
Ill-timed wit: Wild Sorrel
Illusion: Marjoram
Image magic: Bryony, Potato, Straw
Imagination: Bluebonnet, Lupine, Poppy, Snowdrop, White Violet
Immortality: Amaranth, Apple, Daphne, Everlasting, Globe Amaranth, Sage
Immortal love: Amaranth, Globe Amaranth
Immunity: Coneflower (Echinacea)
Immutability: Yew
Impartiality: Brown-eyed Susan, Gloriosa Daisy, Rudbeckia (Black-eyed Susan)
Impatience: Balsam, Impatiens (Busy Lizzie), Jewel Weed, Our Lady's Earrings, Patient Lucy, Policeman's Helmet, Sultana, Touch-Me-Not, Yellow Balsam
Impatient of absence: Corchorus
Impatient resolves: Red Balsam
Imperfection: Henbane (Henbit)
Impermanence: Cherry Blossom
Impetuous love: Nasturtium
Importune me not: Green-edged Auricula
Importunity: Burdock, Fuller's Teasel, Great Bindweed
Imprudence: Almond, Plum Tree, Reed, White Oak
Impulsiveness: Hyacinth
Inconstancy: Columbine, Evening Primrose (Suncups, Sundrops), Honeysuckle, Wild Ranunculus (Wild Buttercup)

Inconstancy in love: Wild Honeysuckle

Incorruptible: Cedar Tree, Cedar of Lebanon

Indecision: Single China Aster, Striped Carnation, Wild Daisy

Independence: Bachelor's Button (Cornflower, Hurtsickle), Basket Flower, Bluebottle, Boutonniere Flower, Common Thistle, Love-in-a-Mist (Nigella), Plum Tree, Reed, White Oak, Wild Plum

Indifference/Indifferent: Candytuft, Chaste Bush, Everflowering Candytuft, Dogwood Tree, Marigold flower placed face-up, Mustard, Mustard Seed, Pigeonberry, Senvy (Mustard)

Indigence: Evergreen

Indignation: Peony

Indiscretion: Almond, Almond Blossom, Almond Tree, Bellflower, Bulrush (Rush), Canterbury Bells, Common Almond, Split Reed

Industrious/Industry: Bumble Bee Orchid, Clover, Dried Flax, Dusty Miller, Red Clover

Infatuation: Dwarf Sunflower, Nephitos Rose (White Climbing Rose)

Infertility: Walnut

Infidelity: Walnut, Yellow Rose

Infidelity prevented: Caraway

Ingeniousness: White Pink

Ingenious simplicity: Chickweed, Mouse-eared Chickweed

Ingenuity: Clematis, Geranium (Cranesbill), Pencil-leaved Geranium

Ingratitude: Buttercup (Kingscup), Crow Foot, Wild Ranunculus, Yellow Gentian

Injustice: Hops

In my thoughts: Johnny Jump Up (Wild Pansy, Heartsease)

Innate warmth: Red Camellia Japonica, Red Carnation

Inner beauty: Delphinium, Larkspur

Inner power: Daffodil (Jonquil, Lent Lily), Dracaena

Inner self: Sage

Inner wisdom: Sage

Innocence: Acacia, African Daisy (Cape Marigold), Asphodel (Lily), Baby's Breath, Chrysanthemum (Bloom, Mum), Daisy, English Daisy, Freesia, Fritillary, Gerbera Daisy, Houstonia, Orange Blossom, White Carnation, White Daisy, White Rose, White Rosebud, White Violet

Inquietude: Marigold

Insight: Snowdrop

Insincerity: Cherry, Foxglove (Digitalis), Morning Glory (Major Convolvulus)

Insinuation: Bindweed (Minor Convolvulus), Great Bindweed

Inspiration: Alder Tree, Angelica, Apostle Plant, Bindweed (Minor Convolvulus), Columbine, Hazel (Filbert), Iris, Walking Iris

Instability: Dahlia, Moonflower (Moon Vine)

Instruction: Bayberry (Wax Myrtle)

Integrity: Aloe, Gentian

Intellect: Daisy, Walnut Tree

Intellectual excellence: Sumac, Venice Sumac, Walnut
Intelligence: Clematis, Kennedia, Mountain Ash, Walnut
Intense emotions: Yellow Rose
Intoxicated with joy: Heliotrope
Intoxication: Grape, Grapevine, Vine
Intrinsic worth: Gentian
Intuition: Pansy, Weeping Willow Tree
Invincibility: Aaron's Beard
Invisibility: Aconite (Wolf's Bane), Amaranth, Chickweed, Chicory, Edelweiss,
    Heliotrope, Poppy
Invocation: Water Lily
Ire: Furze (Gorse)
Irony: Sardonyx
Irresistible: Dill
Irritability: Crabapple Blossom
It's time: Portulaca

Iris

Jealous/Jealousy: Adder's Tongue, Calendula (Pot Marigold), French Marigold, Marigold, Purple Hyacinth, Yellow Hyacinth, Yellow Rose

Jest: Southernwood

Joke: Balm, Melissa

Jovial/Joviality: Chrysanthemum (Bloom, Mum), Crocus, Saffron

Joy: Blanket Flower, Burnet, Calendula (Pot Marigold), Chrysanthemum (Bloom, Mum), Coreopsis (Tickseed), Crocus, Currant, Gaillardia, Gardenia, Lesser Celandine, Myrtle, Oregano, Ox-eye Daisy, Painted Daisy, Parsley, Pink Hyacinth, Red Dahlia, Red Hyacinth, Red and White Rose, Rose, Shamrock, Sorrel (Oxalis), Stitchwort, Umbrella Pine Tree, White Gardenia, Wood Sorrel, Yellow Rose, Yellow Tulip

Joy in love and life: Cosmos

Joy in sorrow: Shamrock

Joys to come: Celandine, Lesser Celandine

Judgment: Linden Tree

Justice: Black-eyed Susan (Rudbeckia), Coltsfoot

Justice shall be done to you: Coltsfoot, Sweet-scented Tussilage

Jimson Weed

Keep this for my sake: Calceolaria, Veronica Speciosa
Keep your promises: Plum
Keys: Maple Tree
Kindness: Bluebell, Cherry Blossom, Czar Violet, Elderberry, Marsh Mallow
Kindness and worth: Czar Violet
Kiss me: Mistletoe
Kiss me across the garden gate: Kiss-Me-Across-the-Garden-Gate
Kiss me twice before I rise: Love-in-a-Mist (Nigella)
Knot magic: Dodder
Knowledge: Hazel (Filbert)

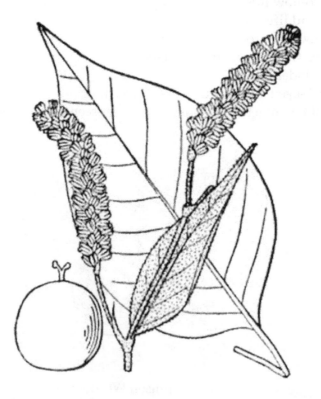

Kiss-Me-Over-the-Garden-Gate

Lady: Oak-leaf Geranium
Lamentation: Aspen Tree
Lasting affection: Magenta Zinnia
Lasting beauty: Gillyflower, Stock
Lasting friendship: Freesia
Lasting love: China Primrose
Lasting pleasure: Everlasting Pea
Laugh at trouble: Galax (Wandflower), Harlequin Flower
Learning: Cherry Blossom
Legal matters: Buckthorn, Cascara, Celandine, Hickory Tree, Marigold, Skunk
     Cabbage
Lenient: Linden Tree
Let me go: Bloodflower (Bloedblom), Butterfly Weed, Red Swallow-wort
Let me love you: Parma Violet
Let's meet: Everlasting Pea, Grass Pea, Sweet Pea
Let's take a chance: White Tulip
Let's take a chance on happiness: White Violet
Letting go: Skullcap
Let us forget: Yellow Sweetbriar
Let us pray for each other: Heliotrope
Levity: Delphinium, Larkspur
Liberty: Bird of Paradise (Crane Flower), Live Oak
Lies: Yellow Lily
Life: Lucerne, Lungwort, Pinecone
Life direction: Camphor, Canary Grass, Snowdrop
Life is sweet: Pyxie
Light-heartedness: Shamrock
Lightness: Larkspur
Lightning protection: Holly
Links: Tendrils of Climbing Plants
Literary debut: White Tulip
Little apple of death: Manchineel Tree
Live for me: Arbor-Vitae
Live life in the fast lane: Kudzu

Lively and pure affection: Pink Carnation

Living for love: White Carnation

Logical functioning: Chamomile

Loneliness: Anemone (Zephyr Flower), Fungus, Heather

Long beautiful: Begonia

Longevity: Bamboo, Citron, Cypress Tree, Fig, Floss Flower, Lavender, Maple Tree, Peach, Sage, Tansy

Longing: Pink Camellia Japonica

Long life: Chrysanthemum (Bloom, Mum), Euonymus (Spindle Tree), Meadow Saffron, Meadow Sage, Orchid, Sage

Look up and kiss me: London Pride

Loss of what could have been: Day Lily

Lost love: Anemone (Zephyr Flower), White Tulip

Love: Adam and Eve Root, Althea (Rose of Sharon), American Starwort, Anemone (Zephyr Flower), Apple, Apricot, Aster (September Flower), Avens, Avocado, Bachelor's Button (Cornflower, Hurtsickle), Balm of Gilead, Barley, Basil, Bean, Bedstraw, Beet, Black Cohosh, Black Snakeroot, Bleeding Heart (Lyre Flower, Venus' Car), Bloodroot, Blue Violet, Brazil Nut, Canterbury Bells, Cardamom, Catnip, Chamomile, Cherry, Chestnut Tree, Chickweed, Chili Pepper, China Berry, Cinnamon, Citron, Clove, Clover, Coltsfoot, Columbine, Copal Tree, Coriander (Chinese Parsley, Cilantro), Cowslip (Primrose), Crepe Myrtle, Crocus, Cymbidium Orchid, Daffodil (Jonquil, Lent Lily), Devil's Bit, Dodder, Dragon's Blood, Dutchman's Breeches, Elecampane, Elm Tree, Endive, Eryngo, Fairy Lily, Fern, Fig, Four-leaf Clover, Fuzzy Weed, Gardenia, Gentian, Geranium (Cranesbill), Ginger, Ginseng, Grains of Paradise, Grass of Paradise, Heather, Hemp, Hibiscus, High John the Conqueror, Honeysuckle, Hothouse Leek, Hyacinth, Indian Paintbrush, Japanese Anemone (Windflower), Japonica, Jasmine, Joe Pye Weed, Juniper Tree, Jupiter's Beard, Keys of Heaven, Lady's Mantle, Lavender, Leek, Lemon Balm, Lemon Verbena, Lettuce, Licorice, Lilac, Liverwort, Lovage, Love-in-a-Mist (Nigella), Maidenhair Fern, Male Fern, Mallow, Malva Rose, Mandrake, Maple Tree, Marjoram, Meadowsweet, Michaelmas Daisy, Milfoil (Sneezewort, Yarrow), Mimosa (Sensitive Plant), Mint, Mistletoe, Moonwort, Moss Rose, Mullein, Myrtle, Nuts, Orange, Orange Blossom, Orchid, Orris Root, Pansy, Papaya, Parsley, Pea, Peach, Pear, Peppermint, Periwinkle (Vinca), Pimento, Plumeria, Poppy, Prickly Ash, Primrose (Cowslip), Purslane, Quince, Rain Lily, Raspberry, Red Lucky Seed, Red Rose, Red Tulip, Rose, Rose Mallow, Rosemary, Rue, Ryegrass, Saffron, Saint John's Wort, Sarsaparilla, Skullcap, Spearmint, Spiderwort (Tradescantia), Strawberry, Sugar Cane, Tamarind, Thyme, Tulip, Valerian, Vanilla, Venus Flytrap, Vervain, Vetivert, Violet, Weeping Willow Tree, Wild Violet, Willow Tree, Wormwood, Yarrow (Milfoil, Sneezewort)

Love at first sight: Coreopsis Arkansa, False Goat's Beard (Astilbe), Gladiolus (Abyssinian Sword Lily), Gloxinia, Lavender Rose, Love-in-Idleness, Pyrus Japonica (Japanese Andromeda), Rose, Thornless Red Rose

Love attraction: Bleeding Heart, Dutchman's Breeches, Monk's Head, Soldier's Cap,

Squirrel Corn, White Hearts

Love for all seasons: Gorse (Furze)

Love forsaken: Creeping Willow

Love from a son or daughter: Clematis

Love from a woman to a man: African Daisy (Cape Marigold)

Love in absence: Myrtle

Love in idleness: Heartsease (Johnny Jump Up, Wild Pansy), Wild Violet

Love is dangerous: Carolina Rose

Love is reciprocated: Ragweed

Love letters: Agapanthus (African Blue Lily), Lily of the Nile

Love of nature: Magnolia Tree

Love of variety: China Aster

Love returned: Bitterweed, Bloodweed, Ragweed

Love sweet and secret: Honeyflower

Love that will not last: Field Anemone, Red Anemone

Love undiminished by adversity: Flowering Dogwood

Loveliness: Dogwood Tree, Gardenia, Gentian, Smilax

Lovely: White Carnation

Lover: Cuckoo Flower

Lovers: Heather

Lover's charm: Almond

Lovers' tryst: Beech Tree

Love's oracle: Dandelion, Moon Daisy

Lowliness: Bramble

Loyal love: Chrysanthemum (Bloom, Mum), Daisy

Loyalty: Bamboo, Bluebell, Daisy, Ivy, Shamrock, Sunflower

Luck: Allspice, Aloe, Anise, Apple Blossom, Bamboo, Banyan Tree, Bells of Ireland, Bluebell, Cabbage, Calamus, Camellia, Capers, Cinchona, Corn, Cotton, Daffodil (Jonquil, Lent Lily), Daisy, Devil's Shoestring, Dill, Fern, Four-leaved Clover, Grains of Paradise, Hazel (Filbert), Heather, Holly, Hothouse Leek, Huckleberry, Irish Moss, Job's Tears, Kava-Kava, Lavender, Lucky Hand, Male Fern, Moss, Nuts, Orange, Orange Blossom, Persimmon, Pineapple, Pomegranate, Poppy, Purslane, Snakeroot, Straw, Strawberry, Vetivert, Violet, White Clover

Luck in fishing: Hawthorn Tree

Luck in love: Aster (September Flower)

Lust: Aloe, Avocado, Black Snakeroot, Blue Ginger, Capers, Cardamom, Caraway, Carrot, Cattail, Celery, Cyclamen, Daisy, Deer's Tongue, Devil's Bit, Dill, Endive, Eryngo, Furze (Gorse), Garlic, Ginseng, Grains of Paradise, Hibiscus, Lemongrass, Licorice, Lime Blossom, Maguey, Mastic Tree, Mint, Nettle, Olive Tree, Onion, Patchouli, Pear, Periwinkle (Vinca), Persian Violet, Purple Rose, Radish, Saffron, Sesame, Sugar Cane, Vanilla, Violet

Luster: Aconite-leaved Crow Foot, Crow Foot

Lust protection: Cinnamon

Luxury: Chestnut Tree, Cymbidium Orchid, Horse Chestnut

Magic: Angelica, Bird's Nest Fern, Fern
Magnanimous: Delphinium
Magnificence: Bird of Paradise (Crane Flower), Cymbidium Orchid, Orchid
Magnificent beauty: Calla Lily
Majesty: Crown Imperial, Elm Tree, First Rose of Summer, Fritillary, Imperial Lily
Make haste: Dianthus (Pinks)
Male luck/Maleness: Camellia
Malevolence: Asthma Weed (Sticky-Weed), Indian Tobacco, Lobelia, Tobacco
Malicious representation: Helleborus (Lenten Rose)
Manifestations: Dittany of Crete, Mastic Tree
Manners: Rue
Man's footsteps: White Plantain
Many children: Orchid
Many interests: Begonia
Marital affection: Lime
Marriage: Ivy, Lime Tree, Linden Tree, Orange Blossom, Peony, Safflower, Saffron, Stephanotis, Verbena
Maternal affection: Cinquefoil, Pink Carnation
Maternal love: Moss, Nasturtium
Maternal tenderness: Wood Sorrel
Matrimony: American Linden
Mature charm: Cattleya Orchid
Mature elegance: Pomegranate Flower
Mature grace: Cattleya Orchid
Maturity: Oak Tree
Meanness: Cuscuta, Dodder of Thyme
Meditation: Bodhi, Chamomile, Daffodil (Jonquil, Lent Lily), Flowering Maple Tree (Abutilon), Gotu-Kola, Hemp
Meekness: Broom, Paper Birch Tree
Meet me: Sweet Pea
Meet me by moonlight: La France Rose
Melancholy: Autumn Leaves, Dark Geranium (Dark Cranesbill), Dead Leaves, Geranium (Cranesbill), Weeping Willow Tree, Wild Daisy

Memories: Colchicum, Everlasting, Forget-Me-Not (Myosotis), Meadow Saffron, Sweet William, Vinca (Periwinkle)

Memories of childhood: Buttercup (Kingscup)

Memory: Rosemary, Syringa, Tulip

Mental ability: Lily-of-the-Valley

Mental anguish: Marigold flower, placed face-down

Mental beauty: Clematis, Kennedia

Mental powers: Burnet, Caraway, Celery, Eyebright, Grape, Horehound, Mace, Mustard, Periwinkle (Vinca), Rosemary, Rue, Summer Savory, Spearmint, Vanilla, Walnut

Mercy: Elder Tree

Merriment: Southernwood

Merry heart: Apostle Plant, Burnet

Message: Apostle Plant, Flags Iris, Fleur-de-Lis Iris, Iris, Walking Iris, Winged Seeds

Mildness: Althea (Rose of Sharon), Hibiscus, Mallow, Malva Rose, Rose Mallow

Mirth: Broom, Chrysanthemum (Bloom, Mum), Crocus, Hops, Poinsettia, Saffron, Saffron Crocus, Wild Grape

Misanthropy: Aconite (Wolf's Bane), Fuller's Teasel, Fuller's Thistle, Teasel

Misery: Calendula (Pot Marigold)

Misplaced devotion: Aloe

Misrepresentation: Dahlia

Mistrust: Lavender, Mushroom (Champignon)

Missive: Apostle Plant, Flags Iris, Iris, Walking Iris

Mixed feelings: Dog Rose

Mobility: Kudzu, Pine Tree, Walking Fern

Moderating anger: Alyssum

Moderation: Azalea

Modest beauty: Throatwort (Trachelium), Trillium Pictum

Modest genius: Creeing Celandine, Creeping Cereus

Modest love: Blue Violet

Modesty: African Violet, Alyssum, Asphodel (Lily), Aurinia, Calla Lily, Cosmos, Cyclamen, Heartsease (Johnny Jump Up, Wild Pansy), Jasmine, Lilac, Mimosa (Sensitive Plant), Pale Peach Rose, Sweet Alison (Sweet Alyssum), Sweet Violet, Unique Rose, Violet, White Lily, White Violet, Woad (Glastum)

Momentary happiness: Spiderwort, Virginia Spiderwort

Money: Alfalfa, Allspice, Almond, Bergamont, Blackberry, Black Snakeroot, Blue Ginger, Blue Iris, Bromeliad, Bryony, Buckwheat, Calamus, Cascara, Cashew Nut, Cedar Tree, Chamomile, Cinquefoil, Clove, Clover, Comfrey, Dill, Dock, Fenugreek, Flax, Flowering Kale, Fumitory, Furze (Gorse), Ginger, Golden Seal, Goldenrod (Solidago), Grains of Paradise, Grape, High John the Conqueror, Honesty (Lunaria), Honeysuckle, Horse Chestnut, Irish Moss, Jasmine, Lucky Hand, Mandrake, Maple Tree, Marjoram, May Apple, Millet, Mint, Moonwort, Moss, Oats, Onion, Orange, Orange Blossom, Oregon Grape, Patchouli, Pea, Pecan Tree, Periwinkle (Vinca), Peruvian Lily, Pine Tree, Pineapple, Poplar Tree,

Poppy, Rattlesnake Root, Rice, Sarsaparilla, Sassafras, Sesame, Snakeroot, Vervain, Vetivert, Wheat, Woodruff

Money management: Endive

Moonlight: Moonflower (Moon Vine)

Most lovable: Ajuga (Bugleweed)

Mother: Pussy Willow

Motherhood: Asphodel (Lily), Daylily

Motherly love: Balsam, Busy Lizzie (Impatiens), Hens and Chicks (Sedum), Jewel Weed, Our Lady's Earrings, Patient Lucy, Policeman's Helmet, Sultana, Touch-Me-Not

Motivation: Love-in-a-Mist (Nigella)

Mourning: Cypress Tree, Dark Crimson Rose, Dark Red Rose, Weeping Willow Tree

Music: Alder Tree, Oats, Reed, Reeds with their panicles

My best days are past: Autumn Crocus, Colchicum, Meadow Saffron

My compliments: Apostle Plant, Flags Iris, Fleur-de-Lis Iris, Iris, Walking Iris

My destiny is in your hands: Camellia

My fortune is yours: Cinnamon

My gratitude exceeds your care: Dahlia

My heart aches for you: Carnation, Dianthus (Pinks), Red Carnation

My heart breaks: Red Carnation

My heart is yours: Peach Blossom

My regrets follow you to the grave: Asphodel (Lily)

Mysterious: Camas, Quamash, Wild Hyacinth

Mystery: Blue Rose

Mysticism: Witch Hazel

Magnolia Tree

Natural beauty: Citron
Natural grace: Gladiolus (Abyssinian Sword Lily)
Nature: Magnolia Tree
Neatness: Broom
Needing protection: Gerbera Daisy
Neglected beauty: Throatwort (Trachelium)
Never-ceasing remembrance: Everlasting, Everlasting Pea, Statice
Never despair: Petunia
Never judge solely on appearances: Coriander (Cilantro, Chinese Parsley)
Never return: Rue
New beginnings: Daffodil (Jonquil, Lent Lily), Easter Lily, Sage
New ideas: Saxifrage
New love: Rosebud
Newborn baby: English Daisy
Night: Bindweed (Minor Convolvulus), Blue Minor Convolvulus, Moonflower
    (Moon Vine), Night Convolvulus
Nirvana: Bo Tree
No!: Bi-colored Carnation, Snapdragon, Yellow Carnation
No change until death: Bay Leaf
Nobility: Asphodel (Lily), Cherry, Clove, Edelweiss, Magnolia Tree
Noble courage: Edelweiss
Not as bad as I seem: Basket Lily, Ismene, Peruvian Daffodil, Sea Daffodil,
    Spider Lily
Not funny: Oxalis (Sorrel), Wood Sorrel
Novelty: Dahlia
Nuisance: Ragweed
Numerous progeny: Orchid

Obedience: Balloon Flower, Chinese Bellflower
Objectivity: Groundseal
Obligation: Canterbury Bells, Lint
Oblivion: Poppy, White Poppy
Obsession: Black Rose
Obstacles: Hawthorn Tree, Mistletoe
Of an equivalent: Poor Robin
Old age: Gloire de Dijon Rose, Tree of Life (Himalayan Moringa)
Old beau: Ice Plant
Omen: Cape Marigold (African Daisy)
One love: Arbutus (Strawberry Tree), Madrone Tree
Only deserve my love: Campion Rose, Dundee Rambler Rose
Only for you: Boule de Neige Rose
Only thee do I love: Arbutus (Strawberry Tree)
Open heart: Larkspur
Optimism/Optimistic: Chrysanthemum (Bloom, Mum), Eustoma (Lisanthus),
    Pinecone, Prairie Gentian, Prairie Rose, Texas Bluebell, Tulip Gentian
Order: Cone Fir
Organization: Broom
Ornament: Daphne, Hornbeam
Ostentation: Peony
Our souls are united: Phlox
Outgoing: Bluebell, Eustoma (Lisianthus), Prairie Rose, Prairie Gentian, Texas
    Bluebell
Overcoming difficulties: Mistletoe
Overcoming fear: Aspen Tree

Pain: Blackthorn, Harebell
Painful remembrance: Pheasant's Eye
Painting: Auricula (Bear's Ears)
Painting the lily: Daphne Ordora
Panache: Calla Lily
Parental affection: Sorrel (Oxalis)
Partiality: Apple Blossom
Participation: Double Daisy, Double Dahlia
Passion: Althea (Rose of Sharon), Apostle Plant, Asphodel (Lily), Arum (Wake Robin), Azalea, Bougainvillea, Dittany of Crete, Furze (Gorse), Hibiscus, Iris, Laced Carnation, Lily (Asphodel), Mallow, Orange Lily, Purple Rose, Red Camellia Japonica, Red Canterbury Bells, Red Carnation, Red Poppy, Red Rose, Red and yellow Rose together, Rose, Rose Mallow, Tulip, Walking Iris, White Dittany, Yellow Iris
Passionate interest: Orange Rose
Past: Meadow Saffron
Pastoral poetry: Amaryllis
Paternal error: Cardamom, Cuckoo Flower
Patience: Allium, Aster (September Flower), Bedstraw, Chamomile, Dock, Ox-Eye Daisy, Patience Dock, Shasta Daisy, Willow, Yew
Patriotism: American Elm Tree, Nasturtium
Peace: Bilberry, Blooming Sally, Buckbean, Cattail, Cumin, Currant, Eryngo, Gardenia, Geranium (Cranesbill), Gooseberry, Gooseneck, Hazel (Filbert), Lavender, Loosestrife, Meadowsweet, Mistletoe, Olive Tree, Oregano, Pennyroyal, Saxifrage, Skullcap, Vervain, Violet
Peace and prosperity: Fig, Gardenia
Peace and victory: Olive Tree
Peacefulness: Cosmos
Peerless and proud: Corn Cockle
Pensive beauty: Golden Chain Tree, Laburnum
Pensiveness: Cowslip (Primrose)
Perception of reality: Gentian
Perfected loveliness: Camellia, White Camellia Japonica

Perfect excellence: Strawberry

Perfect goodness: Strawberry

Perfect happiness: Pink Rose, Rose

Perfect lover: Camellia, Tulip

Perfection: Alyssum, Aurinia, Camellia, Carnation, Dianthus (Pinks), Japonica, Pineapple, Pomegranate Flower, Sweet Alyssum (Sweet Alison), Sweet William, White Camellia Japonica

Perfidy: Almond, Almond Laurel, Bay (Laurel Tree, Sweet Bay), Common Laurel

Perplexity: Love-in-a-Mist (Nigella)

Persecution: Checkered Fritillary, Mission Bells

Perseverance: Canary Grass, Ground Laurel, Hydrangea, Magnolia, Swamp Magnolia, Yew

Persistence: Cushion Spurge (Spurge, Euphorbia)

Personal achievement: Laurel Tree (Bay, Sweet Bay)

Personal relationships: Forget-Me-Not (Myosotis)

Persuasion: Althea (Rose of Sharon), Althea Frutes (Syrian Mallow), Marsh Mallow

Pertinacity: Clotbur, Xanthium

Philosophy: Pitch Pine

Physician Plant: Chamomile

Piety: Amaranth

Pilgrimage: Plantain

Piquancy: Citron

Pity: Camellia, Red Camellia Japonica, Red Carnation

Platonic love: Bittersweet, Black Locust Tree, Rose Acacia, White Acacia

Play/Playful: Eustoma (Lisanthus), Prairie Gentian, Prairie Rose, Texas Bluebell

Playfulness: Buttercup (Kingscup), Delphinium, Hyacinth, Pink Hyacinth, Red Hyacinth

Pleasant: Ginger

Pleasant recollections: White Periwinkle

Pleasant thoughts: Heartsease (Johnny Jump Up, Wild Pansy), Pansy

Pleasantness: Alstroemeria (Peruvian Lily)

Pleasantry: Gentle Balm

Please believe me: Pink Rose, Rose

Please forgive me: Purple Hyacinth

Pleasure: Red Poppy, Tuberose

Pleasure and pain: Dog Rose

Pleasure of hope: Crocus

Pleasure without alloy: Beardtongue (Penstemon), Chelone (Turtlehead), Siberian Squill (Siberian Scilla)

Pleasures of memory: Vinca (Periwinkle), White Periwinkle

Plenty: Grain, Grape

Poetry: Alder Tree, Amaryllis, Bean, Eglantine (European Sweetbriar), Japanese Maple, Wild Rose

Poise: Helleborus (Lenten Rose), Oriental Helleborus

Pomp: Dahlia, Red Sally

Poor but happy: Vernal Grass

Popular favor: Begonia, Cistus, Rock Rose

Popular oracle: English Daisy

Popularity: Widow's Thrill (Kalanchoe)

Positive outlook: Wild Violet

Positive perspectives: Sage

Positive self-image: Snowflake (Leucojum)

Positive thoughts: Pennyroyal

Potency: Banana, Bean, Black Cohosh, Capers, Date Palm, Dragon's Blood, Olive, Palm Tree

Poverty: Evergreen Clematis

Power: Cinnamon, Clubmoss, Cress, Crown Imperial, Devil's Shoestring, Ebony Tree, Gentian, Ginger, Imperial Montague, Roots, Saint John's Wort, Wormwood

Prayer: Blueberry, Gentian, Reed, White Hyacinth

Pray for me: Verbena, White Verbena

Precaution: Goldenrod (Solidago)

Prediction: Prophetic Marigold

Preference: Apple, Apple Blossom, Apple Geranium, Pink Geranium, Rose-scented Geranium

Presage: African Daisy (Cape Marigold)

Present preference: Apple Geranium

Presumption: Snapdragon, Toadflax

Presumptuous: Snapdragon, Toadflax

Pretend to love: Catchfly

Pretension: Amaranth, Coxcomb, Glasswort (Salicornia), Loosestrife, Spiked Willow Herb

Price: Carnation

Pride: Amaryllis, Apple of Peru (Shoo-Fly Plant), Asphodel (Lily), Auricula (Bear's Ears), Dianthus (Pinks), Ginger, Lilac, Hundred-leaved Rose, Pink Carnation, Santana Rose, Tall Sunflower

Pride and beauty: Mixed color Carnations

Pride of birth: Crown Imperial

Pride of riches: Polyanthus

Privation: Indian Plum, Myrobalan

Profit: Cabbage

Profits in business: Pea

Profuseness: Bindweed (Minor Convolvulus)

Progress: Oak Tree

Prohibition: Privet Hedge

Prolific: Fig Tree

Promise: Almond, Apostle Plant, Apple Blossom, Iris, Plum, Walking Iris

Promise of good things to come: Buds, Fleur-de-Lis Iris

Promptitude: Ten-week Stock

Promptness: Gillyflower, Queen Anne's Thimbles, Stock, Ten-week Stock

Prophecies: Linden Tree

Prophecy: Dandelion

Prophetic dreams: Bracken, Buchu, Cinquefoil, Heliotrope, Jasmine, Marigold, Mimosa (Sensitive Plant), Mugwort, Onion

Proposal of love: Phlox

Prosperity: Alfalfa, Alkanet, Allium, Almond, Ash Tree, Asphodel (Lily), Banana, Beech Tree, Bryony, Cattail, Grape, Jersey Lily, Lily of the Incas, Nuts, Oregon Grape, Peony, Wheat Stalk

Prosperity and plenty: Love-in-a-Mist (Nigella), Wheat

Protection: Aaron's Beard, Aconite (Wolf's Bane), Acacia, African Violet, Agrimony, Ague Root, Aloe, Althea (Rose of Sharon), Alum Root, Alyssum, Amaranth, Angelica, Arbutus (Strawberry Tree), Asafetida, Ash Tree, Aurinia, Balm of Gilead, Bamboo, Barley, Basil, Bay (Laurel Tree, Sweet Bay), Bean, Bearded Crepis, Benzion, Birch Tree, Bittersweet, Blackberry, Black Cohosh, Black False Hellebore, Bloodroot, Blooming Sally, Blueberry, Blue Ginger, Bodhi, Boneset, Bromeliad, Broom, Bryony, Buckthorn, Buckwheat, Burdock, Cactus, Calamus, Caraway, Carnation, Carob, Cascara, Castor Bean, Cedar Tree, Celandine, Chives, Chrysanthemum (Bloom, Mum), Cinchona, Cinquefoil, Clove, Clover, Clubmoss, Coconut, Common Thistle, Coral Bells, Corn, Cotton, Cuckoo Flower, Cumin, Curry, Cyclamen, Cypress Tree, Datura, Deer's Tongue, Devil's Bit, Devil's Shoestring, Dill, Dogwood Tree, Dragon's Blood, Ebony Tree, Elder Tree, Elecampane, Eucalyptus, Euphorbia (Cushion Spurge, Spurge), Fennel, Fern, Feverfew, Figwort, Fir Tree, Flax, Fleabane, Foxglove, Frankincense, Furze (Gorse), Garlic, Geranium (Cranesbill), Ginseng, Gooseberry, Gooseneck, Gourd, Grain, Grass, Hazel (Filbert), Heather, Holly, Holly Berries, Honeysuckle, Horehound, Hothouse Leek, Huckleberry, Hyacinth, Hypericum, Hyssop, Irish Moss, Ivy, Juniper Tree, Jupiter's Beard, Kava-Kava, Keys of Heaven, Lady's Seal, Lady's Slipper Orchid, Larch Tree, Larkspur, Lavender, Leek, Lettuce, Liverwort, Loosestrife, Lotus, Lucky Hand, Mallow, Mandrake, Marigold, Marjoram, Masterwort, Mimosa (Sensitive Plant), Mint, Mistletoe, Molukka Bean, Mugwort, Mulberry Tree, Mullein, Mustard, Myrrh, Nettle, Norway Spruce Tree, Oak Tree, Olive Tree, Onion, Orris Root, Papaya, Papyrus, Parsley, Pennyroyal, Peony, Pepper, Pepper Tree, Periwinkle (Vinca), Persian Violet, Pimpernel, Pine Tree, Plantain, Primrose (Cowslip), Purslane, Quince, Radish, Raspberry, Rattlesnake Root, Rhubarb, Rice, Roots, Rosemary, Rowan Tree, Sage, Saint John's Wort, Sandalwood, Snapdragon, Solomon's Seal, Spanish Moss, Spruce Tree, Sweet Alyssum (Sweet Alison), Sweet Gum Tree, Tamarisk, Toadflax, Turnip, Valerian, Venus Flytrap, Vervain, Walking Iris, Wax Plant (Hoya), Weeping Willow Tree, White Heather, Wintergreen, Witch Hazel, Woodruff, Wormwood, Yucca

Protection for ships: Hawthorn

Protection for travelers: Wormwood

Protection from danger: Heather

Protection from snakes: Juniper Tree

Providence: Purple Clover, Trefoil

Prudence: Ash Tree, Mountain Ash, Service Tree

Psychic powers: Acacia, Althea Frutes (Syrian Mallow), Anise, Bay (Laurel Tree, Sweet Bay), Bay Leaf, Bistort, Blue Ginger, Borage, Buchu, Celery, Cinnamon, Citron, Elder Tree, Elecampane, Eyebright, Flax, Grass, Honeysuckle, Lemongrass, Mace, Marigold, Mastic Tree, Mugwort, Peppermint, Rose, Rowan Tree, Saffron, Texas Mountain Laurel, Thyme, Wormwood, Yarrow (Milfoil, Sneezewort)

Psychic workings: Uva Urse

Pure: Daffodil (Jonquil, Lent Lily), Gardenia, Rosebud, Waterlily, White Rose

Pure affection: Dianthus (Pinks)

Pure and ardent love: Double Red Pink, White Carnation

Pure and deep love: Carnation, Dianthus (Pinks)

Pure and guileless: White Verbena

Pure and lovely: Red Rosebud

Pure love: Clematis, Cosmos, Single Pink, Red Carnation

Pure of heart: Baby's Breath

Purification: Alkanet, Asafetida, Avens, Bay (Laurel Tree, Sweet Bay), Benzion, Birch Tree, Bloodroot, Broom, Cedar Tree, Chamomile, Citron, Coconut, Copal Tree, Euphorbia (Cushion Spurge, Spurge), Fennel, Horseradish, Hyssop, Iris, Lavender, Lemon Verbena, Mimosa (Sensitive Plant), Parsley, Peppermint, Rosemary, Sagebrush, Shallot, Thyme, Tobacco, Turmeric, Valerian, Vervain, Yucca

Purifies negativity and evil: Gum Arabic

Purity: Althea Frutes (Syrian Mallow), Arum Lily, Asphodel (Lily), Baby's Breath, Bachelor's Buttons (Cornflower, Hurtsickle), Broom, Daisy, Edelweiss, Florists' Nightmare (Star of Bethlehem), Gardenia, Gladiolus (Abyssinian Sword Lily), Hyssop, Jupiter's Beard, Keys of Heaven, Lilac, Lily-of-the-Valley, Lotus, Marsh Mallow, Valerian, White Carnation, White Lily, White Violet, Wild Rose

Purity and modesty: White Lilac

Purity and sweetness: White Gardenia

Purity of heart: Waterlily

Quandary: Convolvulus
Quarrel: Broken Corn Straw, Broken Straw
Questioning: Love-in-a-Mist (Nigella)
Quick-sighted: Hawkweed

Queen Anne's Lace

Radiant: Ranunculus

Rain: Ajuga (Bugleweed), Cotton, Fern, Rice

Rain magic: Pansy

Rain-making: Fern, Heather, Toadstool

Rare beauty: Orchid

Rarity: Mandrake, White Ivy

Rashness: Buddleia, Butterfly Bush, Hyacinth

Readiness: Red Valerian

Ready armed: Gladiolus (Abyssinian Sword Lily)

Reason: Goat's Rue

Rebirth: Black Rose

Rebuff: Yellow Dahlia

Recall: Silver-leaved Geranium

Recantation: Lotus Leaf

Reckless: Mandevilla

Reciprocal love: Daffodil (Jonquil, Lent Lily)

Reciprocated love: Jerusalem Artichoke

Reciprocity: Double China Aster

Reconciliation: Bean, Florists' Nightmare (Star of Bethlehem), Hazel (Filbert)

Recovery from illness: Pussy Willow

Reduces fears: Saint John's Wort, Wormwood

Refined beauty: Orchid

Refinement: Bachelor's Button (Cornflower, Hurtsickle), Gardenia, Orchid, Sweet Sultan, White Geranium

Refusal: Japanese Anemone (Windflower), Lavender, Striped Carnation, Tansy, Variegated Pink

Regard: Buttercup (Kingscup), Cypress Tree, Daffodil (Jonquil, Lent Lily), Double Daffodil

Regret: Asphodel (Lily), Bluebell, Colchicum, Elder Tree, Meadow Saffron, Purple Verbena, Wisteria

Rejected: Ice Plant (Ficoides)

Rejected addresses: Ice Plant (Ficoides)

Rejected suitor: Ice Plant (Ficoides)

Rejection: Striped Carnation, Withered Flowers, Yellow Carnation

Rejoices and comforts the heart: Cicely

Rejuvenation: Lemon Balm

Relationships: Honesty (Lunaria)

Relaxation: Apple Blossom, Currant, Gooseberry, Stitchwort

Release of negativity: Forget-Me-Not (Myosotis)

Relief: Balm of Gilead, Lemon Balm

Relieve my anxiety: Christmas Rose, Helleborus (Lenten Rose)

Religion: Lychnis, Maltese Cross, Pasque Flower

Religious enthusiasm: Lychnis, Schinus

Religious fervor: Passionflower

Religious superstition: Aloe, Passionflower

Remember me/Remembrance: Calendula (Pot Marigold), Everlasting, Grass Pea, Forget-Me-Not (Myosotis), Hydrangea, Marigold, Pheasant's Eye, Pink Carnation, Rosemary, Statice, Sweet Pea, Tea Rose, White Carnation, White Chrysanthemum, White Clover, Yellow Zinnia

Remorse: Bramble, Raspberry

Removing obstacles: Chickweed, Chicory

Rendezvous: Chickweed, Pimpernel

Renewal: Yew

Repose: Blue Bindweed, Blue Minor Convolvulus

Resentment: Petunia

Reserve: Maple Tree, Sycamore Tree

Resignation: Cyclamen, Nasturtium, Persian Violet

Resilience: Birdsfoot Trefoil, Fungus

Resistance: Tansy, Tremella Nestoc

Resoluteness: Sumac

Resolution: Purple Columbine

Resolve: Sycamore Tree

Resolved to win: Columbine, Purple Columbine

Respect: Buttercup (Kingscup), Daffodil (Jonquil, Lent Lily), Joe Pye Weed, Pea, Sage, Umbrella Pine Tree

Responsibility: Lemon Verbena

Rest: Hops

Restfulness: Chrysanthemum (Bloom, Mum)

Restlessness: Marigold

Restoration: Knotweed, Persicaria

Retaliation: Scotch Thistle

Retirement: Tulip Poplar

Retirement happiness: African Blue Lily, Lily of the Nile

Retrospection: Silver-leaved Geranium

Return of a friend is desired: Balloon Flower, Bellflower, Delphinium

Return of happiness: Lily-of-the-Valley

Return quickly: Corchorus
Reunion: Hazel (Filbert)
Revenge: Birdsfoot Trefoil, Clover, Trefoil
Reverie: Flowering Fern, Osmunda
Reward: Berry Wreath
Reward of merit: Bay Wreath, Laurel Tree (Bay, Sweet Bay)
Reward of virtue: Crown of Roses, Garland of Roses
Rich in charms: Buttercup (Kingscup)
Riches: Buttercup (Kingscup), Camellia, Chrysanthemum (Bloom, Mum), Corn, Corn Blossom, Fern, Marigold, Tea, Tiger Lily, Wax Flower, Wheat
Righteousness: Gentian
Rigor: Branch of Thorns, Lantana
Risqué: Frilled Pansies
Rivalry: Rocket
Role reversal: Perilla
Romance: Azalea
Romantic love: Grape Hyacinth
Royalty: Angrec (Comet Orchid), Calla Lily, Purple Tulip
Rudeness: Bur, Clotbur, Xanthium
Rue: Yellow Carnation
Rune magic: Bracken
Rupture: Blue-flowered Greek Valerian
Rupture of a contract: Broken Straw
Rural happiness: Tulip Poplar, Yellow Violet
Rustic beauty: French Honeysuckle
Rustic oracle: Dandelion

Rosemary

Sacred affection: Marigold
Sad memories: Adonis
Sadness: Citron, Dead Leaves, Gerbera Daisy, Marigold, Purple Hyacinth, Yew
Safe: Ginger
Safety: Broom, Traveler's Joy
Safety during travel: Comfrey
Sanctuary: Rowan Tree
Satire: Prickly Pear
Scandal: Helleborus (Lenten Rose), Madder
Scholarship: Coral Bells, Cymbidium Orchid
Scorn: Carnation, Dianthus (Pinks), Sweet William
Sculpture: Hoya (Wax Plant)
Sea rituals: Ash Tree
Seclusion: Mosses
Secrecy: Maidenhair Fern, Rose, full-flown, placed over two buds, White Rose
Secret admirer: Yellow Chrysanthemum
Secret bond of love: Maidenhair Fern
Secret followers of Oscar Wilde: Green Canterbury Bells
Secret love: Acacia, Gardenia, Maidenhair Fern, Mimosa (Sensitive Plant),
    Motherwort, Pink Rose, White Gardenia, Yellow Acacia
Secret sweetness: Oxalis (Sorrel), Wood Sorrel
Seeking: Asparagus Fern
Self-assurance: Helleborus (Lenten Rose), Oriental Helleborus
Self-communication: Gentian
Self-confidence: Aspen Tree
Self-determination: Wormwood
Self-empowerment: Mullein
Self-esteem: Basil, Coxcomb, Gentian
Self-expression: Rue
Self-image: Rue
Self-knowledge: Honesty (Lunaria), Mullein
Self-love: Daffodil (Jonquil, Lent Lily), Narcissus
Self-sacrifice: Andromeda

Self-seeking: Clianthus
Self-understanding: Wild Violet
Selfishness: Narcissus
Semblance: Spiked Speedwell
Sense of self: Mistletoe, Mock Orange
Sensibility: Humble Plant, Mimosa (Sensitive Plant), Prayer Plant, Scarlet Verbena, Sleeping Grass
Sensitiveness: Mimosa (Sensitive Plant)
Sensitivity: Lavender, Mimosa (Sensitive Plant), Rue, Scarlet Verbena
Sensuality: Jasmine, Spanish Jasmine
Sentimental recollections: Artemisia
Separation: Ash-leaved Trumpet Flower, Blackthorn, Carolina Jasmine, Datura, Trumpet Flower, Virginia Jasmine
Serenity: Buckbean, Chamomile, Currant, Willow Tree
Severity: Branch of Thorns
Sexual liberation: Althea (Rose of Sharon), Pink Carnation
Sexual passion: Hibiscus, Mallow, Malva Rose, Rose Mallow
Shame: Hawthorn Tree, Peony
Shared secrets: African Daisy (Cape Marigold)
Sharpness: Barberry Tree, Laurel Tree (Bay, Sweet Bay)
Sharpness of temper: Barberry
Shelter: Bird's Nest Fern, Fern
Showy: Lisianthus (Eustoma)
Shyness: Everlasting Pea, Four O'clock (Marvel of Peru), Grass Pea, Mimosa (Sensitive Plant), Peony, Peach Rose, Sweet Pea, Violet
Shyness reduction: Helleborus (Lenten Rose), Oriental Helleborus
Sibling relationships: Nettle
Sickness: Anemone (Zephyr Flower), Field Anemone, Wood Anemone
Silence: Belladonna, Nightshade, White Rose
Silliness: Celosia, Coxcomb, Fool's Parsley (Poison Parsley), Geranium (Cranesbill), Scarlet Geranium
Simple pleasure: Huckleberry
Simplicity: American Sweetbriar, Anemone (Zephyr Flower), Cicely, Daisy, English Daisy, Fern, Honesty, Single Rose, Wild Rose
Sincerity: Anemone (Zephyr Flower), Bird's Nest Fern, Chervil, Cicely, Fairy Lily, Fern, Garden Chervil, Gladiolus (Abyssinian Sword Lily), Honesty (Lunaria), Hyacinth, Japanese Anemone (Windflower), Japonica, Money Plant, Rain Lily, Satin Flower
Singularity: Celosia, Coxcomb, Cockscomb Amaranth
Skill: Coneflower (Echinacea), Spider Orchid
Sky: Coleus
Slander: Burning Nettle, Helleborus (Lenten Rose)
Sleep: Agrimony, Chamomile, Cinquefoil, Datura, Hops, Lavender, Lettuce, Pasque Flower, Peppermint, Poppy, Purslane, Rosemary, Thyme, Valerian, Vervain

Sleep—my bane, my antidote: White Poppy
Slighted: Yellow Chrysanthemum
Slighted love: Yellow Chrysanthemum
Snake removing: Century Plant
Snake repelling: Lemongrass
Snare: Arum (Wake Robin), Catchfly, Dragon Plant
Softness: Lamb's Ears
Sociality: Walnuts
Solace in adversity: Evergreen Thorn
Solitude: Bachelor's Button (Cornflower, Hurtsickle), Basket Flower, Bluebottle, Boutonniere Flower, Fungus, Globeflower (Trollius), Heath, Heather, Lavender Heather, Lichen
Soothes the heart: Lavender
Soothing: Dill, Milk Vetch
Sophistication: Calla Lily
Sorcery: Enchanter's Nightshade, Nightshade
Sorrow: Aloe, Asphodel (Lily), Auricula (Bear's Ears), Bluebell, Citron, Dead Leaves, Hyacinth, Purple Hyacinth, Yellow Iris, Yew
Sorrowful memories: Adonis Flos, Asclepius, Blood Drops, Pheasant's Eye
Sorrowful recollections: Adonis Flos, Blood Drops
Sorrowful regret: Bluebell
Sorrowful remembrance: Asclepius
Sorry I can't be with you: Striped Carnation
Souls united: Phlox
Sourness of temper: Barberry
Sparkle: Amaryllis
Speak low if you speak love: Charles le Fievree Rose
Speak your mind: Borage
Spectacular: Mexican Sage
Spell: Circaea
Spell breaking: Bamboo
Spirit calling: Sweetgrass
Spirited: Freesia
Spiritual beauty: Cherry Blossom
Spiritual confidence: Snowdrop
Spiritual energy: Pine
Spirituality: African Violet, Cherry Blossom, Cinnamon, Frankincense, Gardenia, Gourd, Myrrh, Passionflower, Sandalwood
Spleen: Fumitory
Splendid beauty: Amaryllis
Splendor: Blood Flower (Bloedblom), Blood Lily, Cape Tulip, Cardinal Flower, Catherine Wheel Pincushion, Fireball Lily, Poison Root, Red Cape Lily, Turk's Cap Cactus, Venetian Sumac
Spontaneous: Begonia

Sport: Foxtail Grass, Hyacinth, Purple Grass, Spiked Willow Herb

Sporting: Calamus, Foxtail Grass, Long Purples, Purple Willow Herb, Red Sally, Rosy Strife, Sage Willow, Salicaire, Spiked Soldiers, Willow Weed

Stability: Cress

Stateliness: Foxglove (Digitalis)

Stay as sweet as you are: Narcissus

Stay out of my way: Kudzu

Steadfast/Steadfastness: Bamboo, Globe Amaranth, Dogwood Tree, Scarlet Zinnia, Wild Geranium, Wisteria

Steadfast piety: Wild Geranium

Stoicism: Box Tree (Boxwood)

Stratagem: Walnut Tree

Strategy: Walnut

Strength: Bamboo, Bay (Laurel Tree, Sweet Bay), Carnation, Cedar Tree, Chives, Common Thistle, Coneflower (Echinacea), Everlasting Pea, Fennel, Garlic, Ginger, Grass Pea, Lovage, Masterwort, Mugwort, Mulberry Tree, Oak Leaf, Oak Tree, Pennyroyal, Plantain, Saffron, Saint John's Wort, Snapdragon, Sweet Pea, Tea, Toadflax

Strength and health: Purple Coneflower

Strength of character: Gladiolus (Abyssinian Sword Lily)

Strength of mind: Walnut

Strength to grow thin: Fennel

Strengthening: Holly

Stress relief/Stress release: Dandelion, Helleborus, Nettle

Strong friendship: Virginia Creeper (American Ivy)

Studious pursuit: Olive Tree

Stupidity: Common Almond, Geranium (Cranesbill), Scarlet Geranium

Submission: Grass, Harebell, Lady's Thimble, Peach

Success: Apple of Peru (Shoo-Fly Plant), Bramble, Clover, Crown Vetch, Dogwood Tree, Ginger, Goldenrod (Solidago), High John the Conqueror, Laurel Tree (Bay, Sweet Bay), Lavender, Leadwort, Lemon Balm, Lungwort, Maple Tree, Marsh Rosemary, Palm Leaves, Palm Tree, Plumbago, Poinsettia, Rosemary, Rowan Tree, Sea Lavender (Sea Pinks, Sea Thrift), Statice, Yellow Poppy

Success everywhere: Baby Blue Eyes

Success to you: Crown Vetch

Succor: Juniper

Suffering: Indian Plum

Suffers from cold: Cupid's Bower, Magic Flower, Widow's Tears

Sun: Calendula (Pot Marigold), Marigold, Sunflower

Sunbeaming eyes: Scarlet Lychnis

Sunny disposition: Chamomile

Superior merit: Moss Rose

Superstition: Auricula (Bear's Ears), Hypericum, Saint John's Wort

Support: Black Bryony, Goldenrod (Solidago), Lady's Seal, Lamb's Ears

Surprise: Betony, Lamb's Ears, Truffle
Susceptibility: Hoya (Wax Plant)
Suspicion: Lavender, Mushroom (Champignon)
Sweet and lovely: White Carnation
Sweet be your dreams: Closed Gentian, Phlox
Sweet disposition: Daffodil (Jonquil, Lent Lily), Hibiscus, Honeysuckle, Lavatera
Sweet innocence: White Scilla
Sweet memories: Periwinkle (Vinca)
Sweet neglect: Virginia Creeper (American Ivy)
Sweet remembrance: Periwinkle (Vinca)
Sweet virtues: Bee Balm (Monarda)
Sweetheart: Short-stemmed Rose
Sweetness: Asphodel (Lily), Daphne Odora, Eschscholtzia, Gladiolus (Abyssinian Sword Lily), Lavatara, Lily-of-the-Valley, Magnolia, Mallow, Pink Rose, White Carnation, White Lily, White Sultan
Sweetness of character: Cherry, Delphinium
Swiftness: Larkspur
Sympathy: Balm, Daffodil (Jonquil, Lent Lily), Leadwort, Lemon Balm, Marsh Rosemary, Melissa, Plumbago, Sea Lavender (Sea Thrift, Sea Pinks), Statice, Thrift

Sage

Take a chance together: White Violet
Take care of yourself: Azalea
Take care while I'm away: Azalea, Begonia
Take courage: Mullein
Talent: Borage, White Pink
Tardiness: Flax-leaved Goldilocks
Tasteful fashion: Scarlet Fuchsia
Tears: Helenium
Technology: Red Clover
Temperance: Azalea
Temptation: Apple, Apple Blossom, Quince
Tenacity: Ivy
Tender and quick emotions: Verbena
Tender memories: Sweet Pea
Tenderness: Everlasting Pea, Grass Pea, Sweet Pea
Tension relief: Helleborus (Lenten Rose), Oriental Helleborus
Testing: Holly
Thank you: Deep Pink Rose, Fleabane
Thank you for a good time: Everlasting Pea, Grass Pea, Sweet Pea
Thankfulness: Agrimony, Bellflower, Canterbury Bells
Thanks: Parsley
The ambition of my love plagues itself: Fuchsia
The color of my fate: Coral Honeysuckle
The heart: Anthurium (Flamingo Flower)
The perfection of female loveliness: Water Willow (Shrimp Plant)
The start of a long and happy life together: White Clover
The sun is always shining when I'm with you: Daffodil (Jonquil, Lent Lily)
The variety of your conversation delights me: Clarkia
The witching soul of music: Oats
There's nothing to hope or fear: Thornless, Leafless Rosebud
There's sunshine in your smile: Yellow Tulip
Think of me: Cedar Leaf, Cedar Tree, Clover, Heartsease (Johnny Jump Up, Wild Pansy), Pansy, White Clover

Thinking of an absent friend: Barberton Daisy, Gerbera Daisy, Mixed Zinnia, Zinnia

Thinking of you: Bellflower, Pansy, Mixed Zinnia

Thinness: Fennel

Thoughtfulness: Almond Tree, Orchid

Thoughtlessness: Almond Tree, Mandevilla

Thoughts: Heartsease (Johnny Jump Up, Wild Pansy), Pansy

Thoughts of Heaven: Guelder Rose, Snowball (Snowberry), Viburnum

Thriftiness: Thyme

Thy smile I aspire to: Rose

Ties: Tendrils of Climbing Plants

Time: Fir Tree, Pine Tree, White Poplar Tree

Timid hope: Cyclamen

Timid love: Half-blown Rose, Maiden Blush Rose

Timidity: Amaryllis, Four-o'clock (Marvel of Peru)

Token of affection: Laurustinus, Ox-eye Daisy, Viburnum

Tolerance: Cuckoo Flower, Daphne

Touch me not: Burdock, Red Balsam, Touch-Me-Not

Transport of joy: Cape Jasmine, Gardenia, Jasmine

Tranquility: Madder, Madwort, Mudwort, Mugwort, Sagebrush, Sedum (Hens and Chicks), Stonecrop, Wormwood

Tranquilize my anxiety: Christmas Rose

Transformation: Ash Tree, Holly

Transience: Morning Glory (Major Convolvulus)

Transient beauty: Night-blooming Cereus

Transient impressions: White withered Rose

Transitions: Yew

Transmutation: Yucca

Travel: Lucky Hand, Mint, Stephanotis

Traveler's Luck: Eryngo

Treachery: Bilberry, Mountain Laurel, Whortleberry

Treason: Whortleberry

Treasure finding: Cowslip (Primrose)

Tree of life: Arbor-Vitae

Tree of mothers: Paper Birch Tree

Trials: Holly

Trinity: Three-leaf Clover

Triteness: Quince

Triumph over winter: Eastern Hemlock, Hemlock

Trouble: Garden Marigold, Marigold

True friendship: Oak-leaf Geranium

True love: Forget-Me-Not (Myosotis), Single Red Rose

True love forever: Forget-Me-Not (Myosotis)

True to the end: Indian Azalea

Trust/Trusting: Aster (September Flower), Daisy, Freesia, Red Tulip, White

Chrysanthemum
Trust me: Bronze Chrysanthemum
Trustfulness: Ivy
Trustworthiness: Honesty (Lunaria)
Truth: Anemone (Zephyr Flower), Bittersweet, Bittersweet Nightshade, Bluebell, Chrysanthemum (Bloom, Mum), Nightshade, White Bloom, White Chrysanthemum

Tulip

Unanimity: Phlox
Unbelief: Judas Tree
Unceasing remembrance: American Cudweed, Artemisia
Uncertainty: Bindweed (Minor Convolvulus), Convolvulus, Morning Glory
(Major Convolvulus), Mock Orange, Narcissus
Unchangeable: Amaranth, Globe Amaranth
Unchanged for eternity: Clematis
Unchanging friendship: Arbor-Vitae, Catchfly
Unchanging love: Arbor-Vitae, Balloon Flower, Chinese Bellflower
Unconscious: Red Daisy
Unconscious beauty: Burgundy Rose
Unconsciousness: Burgundy Rose
Understanding: Hydrangea, Lemon Balm, Mace
Understanding animal languages: Cloth of gold
Undying love: Umbrella Pine Tree
Uneasiness: Garden Marigold, Marigold
Unexpected meeting: Geranium (Cranesbill), Lemon Geranium
Unfading beauty: Carnation
Unfading love: Amaranth, Anemone (Zephyr Flower), Globe Amaranth
Unfaithful: Evening Primrose, Oenothera
Unforgettable: Pink Carnation
Unfortunate attachment: Mourning Bride
Unfortunate love: Pincushion Flower (Scabiosa)
Union: Lancaster Rose, Straw
Unite against evil: Scarlet Verbena
Unity: Allium, Phlox, Red and White Rose together, Rose
Unobtrusive loveliness: Grape Hyacinth, White Hyacinth
Unpatronized merit: Red Primrose
Unpretending excellence: Japonica, Red Camellia Japonica, Red Carnation
Unpretentiousness: Pasque Flower
Unreliable: Purple Carnation
Unrequited love: Begonia, Bleeding Heart, Buttercup (Kingscup), Cypress Tree,
Daffodil (Jonquil, Lent Lily)

Untiring energy: Red Sally
Uprightness: Bamboo
Useful knowledge: Parsley
Uselessness: Diosma (Breath of Heaven), Meadowsweet, Queen of the Meadows, Red Daisy
Utility: Dried Flax, Grass

Ulster Mary

Valor: Apostle Plant, Flags Iris, Iris, Oak Leaf, Walking Iris

Vanity: Cypress Tree

Variety: American Starwort, Aster (September Flower), Calico Plant, China Aster, Michaelmas Daisy, Mundi Rose

Varying course of life: Red-flowering Marigold

Venerable: Dusty Miller

Vengeance: Birdsfoot Trefoil

Verbal communication: Snapdragon

Verity: Nightshade

Vice: Ray-grass (Darnel)

Victory: Mountain Laurel, Nasturtium, Palm Leaves, Palm Tree, Spiraea (Bridal-wreath), Woodruff

Victory in battle: Nasturtium

Vigilance: Pretty Face, Starflower, Sunflower, Wild Hyacinth

Virtue: African Violet, Dame's Gillyflower (Dame's Rocket, Dame's Violet, Dame's Wort), Mint, Mother of the Evening, Night-scented Gillyflower, Pineapple Sage, Roque's Gillyflower, Summer Lilac, Sweet Rocket

Visions: Angelica, Coltsfoot, Crocus, Hemp, Kava-Kava

Vitality: Apple Blossom, Broom, Furze (Gorse)

Vivacity: Hothouse Leek, Houseleek

Voice of the heart: Mandevilla

Voluptuous love: Moss Rose

Voluptuousness: Moss Rose, Saffron, Tuberose

Voraciousness: Bluebonnet, Lupine

Vulgar minds: African Marigold

Vulgarity: Pumpkin

Wantonness: Butterfly Bush (Summer Lilac)

War: Achillea, York and Lancaster Rose, Yarrow (Milfoil, Sneezewort)

Warding: Mistletoe

Warlike trophy: Indian Cress

Warm feelings: Spearmint

Warmth: Cactus, Feverfew, Peppermint, Spearmint

Warmth of feeling: Peppermint

Warmth of heart: Rose, White Cyclamen

Warmth of sentiment: Spearmint

Warning: Aconite (Wolf's Bane), Begonia, Bellflower, Canterbury Bells, Friar's Cap, Ginger, Goldenrod (Solidago), Hand-Flower Tree, Ivy Berry, Monkshood, Rhododendron (Rosebay), Yarrow (Milfoil, Sneezewort)

Warrior spirit: Aspen Tree, Columbine

Watchfulness: Azalea, Dame's Gillyflower (Dame's Rocket, Dame's Violet, Dame's Wort), Pretty Face, Violet

We will die together: Gathered flowers

Weak but winning: Moschatel

Weakness: Moschatel, Musk Plant

Wealth: Basil, Chrysanthemum (Bloom, Mum), Heliotrope, Pomegranate, Ulster Mary, Yellow Poppy

Wealth is not always happiness: Auricula (Bear's Ears)

Wedded love: Ivy

Wedding: Stephanotis

Wedding will follow shortly: Honeysuckle

Welcome: Euphorbia (Cushion Spurge, Spurge), Mayflower, Mistletoe, Pineapple, Safflower, Wisteria

Welcome, fair stranger: Wisteria

Welcome home, drunk husband: Hens and Chicks (Sedum)

Welcome me: Daily Rose

Welcome to a new home: Juniper Tree

Welcome to a stranger: American Starwort

Well-being: Delphinium

Well-spoken: Eustoma (Lisanthus), Prairie Gentian, Prairie Rose, Texas Bluebell, Tulip Gentian

Well-trodden path: Plantain
Whimsical: Purple Carnation
Whimsy: Bells of Ireland, London Pride
Widowhood: Sweet Scabiosa
Will you accompany me?: Stephanotis
Will you dance with me?: Clarkia
Will your wish come true?: Verbena
Win me and wear me: Lady's Slipper Orchid
Wind: Broom, Saffron
Winning grace: Cowslip (Primrose)
Winter: Gloire de Dijon Rose, Guelder Rose
Wisdom: Almond, Aloe, Apostle Plant, Bilberry, Blue Salvia, Bodhi, Flags Iris, Hazel (Filbert), Iris, Meadow Saffron, Meadow Sage, Sage, Sunflower, Walking Iris, White Mulberry Tree
Wise administration: Pear
Wish/Wishes: Bamboo, Beech Tree, Buckthorn, Dandelion, Dogwood, Foxglove (Digitalis), Ginger, Ginseng, Grains of Paradise, Hazel (Filbert), Job's Tears, Peach, Pomegranate, Sage, Sunflower, Violet, Walnut, White Heather
Wishes come true: Coppertip, Crocosmia, Falling Star, Heather, Montbretia, Valentine Flower
Wishes granted: Loosestrife
Wistfulness: Blue Rose
Wit: Lemon Balm, Lenten Rose (Helleborus), Lychnis, Meadow Lychnis, Ragged-robin
Witchcraft: Enchanter's Nightshade
With love: Chrysanthemum (Bloom, Mum)
With me you are safe: Ash Tree, Mountain Ash
Withered hopes: Anemone (Zephyr Flower), Garden Anemone
Without hope: Cypress Tree
Womanhood: Azalea
Woman's love: Carnation, Pink Carnation, Dianthus (Pinks)
Wonder: Fir Tree, Pine Tree
Wonderful: Four O'clock (Marvel of Peru)
Work: Red Clover
Worldliness: Clianthus
Worldly goods: Wheat
Worried: Red Columbine
Worship: Heliotrope
Worth: Czar Violet, White Camellia Japonica
Worth beyond all beauty: Alyssum, Aurinia, Sweet Alison (Sweet Alyssum)
Worth sustained by judicious and tender affection: Pink Convolvulus
Worthy of all praise: Fennel

Yes!: Solid-colored Carnation
Yielding: Linden Tree, Lime Tree
You are a prophet: Hypericum
You are a wonderful friend: Chrysanthemum (Bloom, Mum)
You are all that is lovely: Austrian Rose
You are charming: Leschenaultia Splendens
You are cold: Hortensia, Hydrangea
You are dazzling, but dangerous: Snapdragon
You are delicious: Potato Vine, Strawberry
You are everything to me: Rose
You are fair: Gillyflower
You are false: Foxglove (Digitalis)
You are hard: Ebony Tree
You are lovely: Gardenia, White Gardenia
You are merry: Mundi Rose
You are my divinity: Cowslip (Primrose), Shooting Stars
You are my life: Lungwort
You are perfect: Pineapple
You are radiant with charms: Ranunculus
You are rich in attractions: Garden Ranunculus
You are spiteful: Common Stinging Nettle
You are splendid: Tall Sunflower
You are the only one: Daffodil (Jonquil, Lent Lily)
You are the only one I love: Arbutus (Strawberry Tree)
You are the queen of coquettes: Queen's Rocket
You are unfair: Gentian
You are unjust: Gentian
You are wonderful: Cowslip (Primrose)
You are young and beautiful: Red Rosebud
You boast too much: Stephanotis
You flatter me: Orchid
You have disappointed me: Yellow Carnation
You have listened to scandal: Helleborus (Lenten Rose)

You have made my life complete: Lily-of-the-Valley

You have no claims: Pasque Flower

You light up my life: Feverfew

You love yourself too much: Narcissus

You may hope: Rose Leaf

You occupy my thoughts: Heartsease (Johnny Jump Up, Wild Pansy), Pansy, Purple Pansy, Purple Violet

You pierce my heart: Gladiolus (Abyssinian Sword Lily)

You please all: Currant

You weary me: Bur

You will always be beautiful to me: Stock

You will be my death: Hemlock

You will succeed: Goldenrod (Solidago)

Your blush has won me: Azalea

Your charms are engraved on my heart: Spindle Tree (Euonymus)

Your friendship is agreeable and pleasing: Soy Bean

Your friendship is valued: Apostle Plant, Flags Iris, Iris, Walking Iris

Your frown will kill me: Currant

Your hand for the next dance: Ivy Geranium

Your image is engraved on my heart: Spindle Tree (Euonymus)

Your looks freeze me: Dark Geranium (Dark Cranesbill), Ice Plant (Ficoides)

Your love is returned: Bitterweed, Bloodweed, Ragweed

Your presence softens my pains: Milk Vetch

Your presence soothes me: Petunia

Your purity equals your loveliness: Orange Blossom

Your qualities, like your charms, are unequaled: Peach

Your qualities surpass your charms: Mignonette

Your simple elegance charms me: Diosma (Breath of Heaven)

Your smile I aspire to: Daily Rose

Your thoughts are dark: Nightshade

Your whims are unbearable: Bee Balm (Monarda), Bergamont

Your wiles are irresistible: Bergamont

Youth: Buttercup (Kingscup), Catchfly, Cowslip (Primrose), Damask Rose, Evening Primrose (Suncups, Sun Drops), Foxglove, Lilac, Rosebud, Rosemary, Vervain

Youthful: Red Rosebud

Youthful beauty: Daisy

Youthful gladness: Crocus, Spring Crocus

Youthful innocence: White Lilac

Youthful love: Red Catchfly

Zeal: Elderberry, Wake-robin (Arum)
Zealousness: Elder Tree
Zest: Citron

Zinnia

BIRTH MONTH FLOWERS

January – Carnation or Snowdrop
February – Primrose or Violet
March – Daffodil
April – Daisy or Sweet Pea
May – Hawthorn or Lily-of-the-Valley
June – Honeysuckle or Rose
July – Larkspur or Waterlily
August – Abyssinian Sword Lily or
    Poppy
September – Aster or Morning Glory
October – Cosmos or Pot Marigold
November – Chrysanthemum
December – Holly or Narcissus

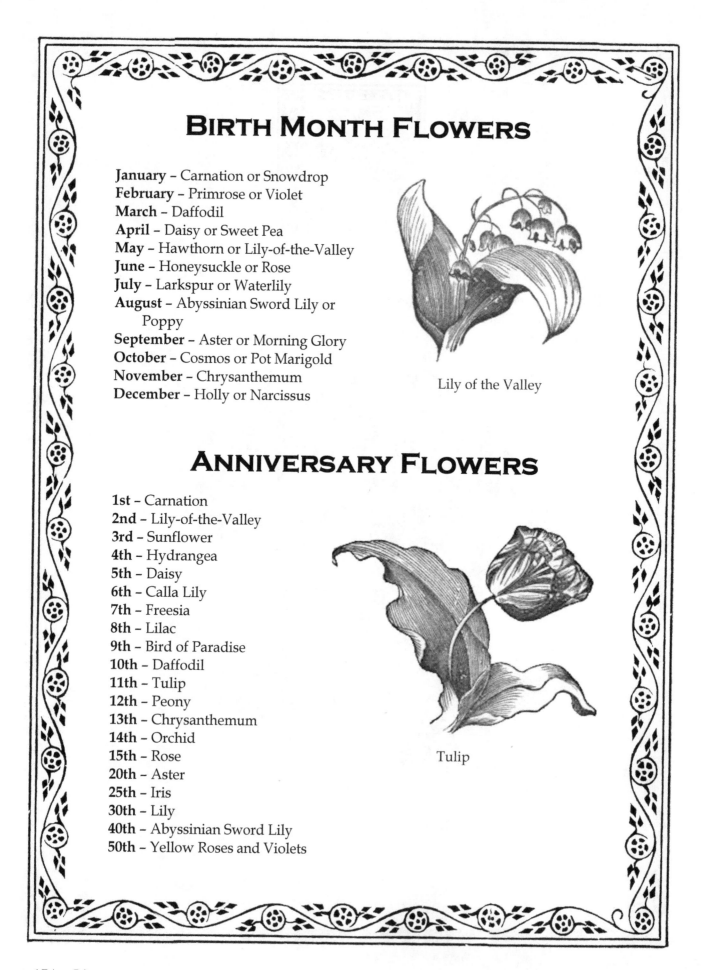

Lily of the Valley

ANNIVERSARY FLOWERS

1st – Carnation
2nd – Lily-of-the-Valley
3rd – Sunflower
4th – Hydrangea
5th – Daisy
6th – Calla Lily
7th – Freesia
8th – Lilac
9th – Bird of Paradise
10th – Daffodil
11th – Tulip
12th – Peony
13th – Chrysanthemum
14th – Orchid
15th – Rose
20th – Aster
25th – Iris
30th – Lily
40th – Abyssinian Sword Lily
50th – Yellow Roses and Violets

Tulip

COLOR CONNECTIONS

Black: Death, Infinity, Protection, Rebirth, Wisdom
Blue-black: Wounded pride
Blue: Peace, Poetry, Truth, Wisdom
Brown: Calmness, Earth, Security, Support
Gray: Friendship, Maturity, Responsibility, Sorrow
Green: Abundance, Forest, Healing, Hope, Money, New beginnings, Youth
Gold: Good health, Optimism, Wealth
Indigo: Spirituality, Wisdom
Lavender: Charity, Dreams, Peace, Serenity
Orange: Creativity, Happiness, Opportunities, Power
Pink: Beauty, Friendship, Harmony, Remembrance
Red: Action, Courage, Faith, Life, Passion, Strength
Silver: Endurance, Freedom, Reality, Restoration
Violet: Forgiveness, Humility, Intelligence, Justice, Religion, Truth
White: Kindness, Purity
Yellow: Creativity, Healing, Intelligence, Intuition, Life, Light

Green: Youth

FLOWERS FOR COURTSHIP

Abyssinian Sword Lily: Character, Courage, Generosity, "I'm really sincere", Love at first sight, Natural grace, Purity, Sincerity, Strength of character, "You pierce my heart"

Azalea: Abundance, Adoration, Caution, Femininity, Forbearance, Fragile, Fragile passion, Moderation, Passion, Romance, "Take care of yourself", "Take care while I'm away", Temperance, Watchfulness, Womanhood, "Your blush has won me"

Camellia: Admiration, Beauty, Contentment, Excellence, Graciousness, Gratitude, Luck, "My destiny is in your hands", Perfected loveliness, Perfect lover, Perfection

Garden Anemone: Beginnings, Belief, Faith

Mistletoe: Affection, Creativity, Fertility, Health, Holiness, Kiss me, Love, Peace, Protection, Welcome

Pink Geranium: "I prefer you", Preference

Primrose: Comeliness, Divine beauty, Grace, Healing, Heart's mystery, Love, Protection, Winning grace, "You are my divinity", "You are wonderful"

Violet Pansy: "You occupy my thoughts"

White Clover: "Be mine", "I promise", Luck, Remembrance, "The start of a long and happy life together", "Think of me"

White Gardenia: Purity and sweetness, secret love, joy, "You are lovely"

FLOWERS FOR LOVE AND AFFECTION

Acacia: Friendship, Chaste love
    Pink: Elegance
    Rose: Elegance, Platonic love
    White: Elegance, Platonic love
    Yellow: Secret love
Achimenes Cupreata: "Such worth is rare"
Adam and Eve Root: Love
African Blue Lily: Love letter
African Daisy (Cape Marigold): Love from a man to a woman
African Violet: Delicate love connection
Ageratum: Faithful love
Allspice: Compassion
Almond: Lover's charm
Almond Tree: Concealed love
Alstromeria (Peruvian Lily): Devotion
Althea (Rose of Sharon): Consumed by love, Fiery love, Love
Althea Frutes (Syrian Mallow): Consumed by love, "I am deeply in love"
Amaranth: Immortal love, Unfading love
Amaryllis: Splendid beauty
Ambrosia (Ragweed): Love is reciprocated, Love returned, "Your love is returned"
American Cudweed: Unceasing remembrance
American Starwort: Love, Welcome to a stranger
Amethyst Flower: Admiration
Apostle Plant: Friendship, "Your friendship is valued"
Apricot: Love
Arbor-Vitae: Everlasting friendship, Unchanging friendship, Unchanging love
Arbutus (Strawberry Tree): Faithfulness, Friendship, "I only love you", One love, "Only thee do I love", "You are the only one I love"
Aster (September Flower): Love, Luck in love
Astilbe (False Goat's Beard): "I will still be waiting", Love at first sight
Austrian Rose: "You are all that is lovely"
Avens: Love
Avocado: Love
Azalea: Temperance, Adoration, Moderation
    Indian: True to the end, Fragile and ephemeral passion
Baby's Breath: Everlasting love, Gaiety, Pure of heart
Bachelor's Button: Hope in love, Love

Balloon Flower: Unchanging love
Balm of Gilead: Love
Balsam: Ardent love, Motherly love
Barberton Daisy: "Thinking of an absent friend"
Barley: Love
Basil: Love
Bean: Love
Bedstraw: Love
Beech Tree: Lover's tryst
Beet: Love
Begonia: Unrequited love
Bittersweet: Platonic love
Bitterweed: Love returned, "Your love is returned"
Black Cohosh: Love
Black Locust Tree: Platonic love
Black Snakeroot: Love
Bleeding Heart (Lyre Flower, Venus' Car): Love, Love attraction, Unrequited love
Bloodweed: Love returned, "Your love is returned"
Bloodroot: Love
Bloom (Chrysanthemum, Mum): Friendship, Loyal love, "With love", "You are a wonderful friend"
   Red: "I love", "I love you", "I love you too"
Blue Violet: Love, Modest love
Brazil Nut: Love
Bridal Rose: Happy love
Bud of Rose, white: Heart ignorant of love
Busy Lizzie (Impatiens): Ardent and pure love, Motherly love
Buttercup (Kingscup): Unrequited love
Cabbage Rose: Ambassador of love
Cactus: Ardent love
Camellia: Perfect lover
Campion Rose: "You only deserve my love"
Canterbury Bells: Love
Cape Marigold (African Daisy): Love from a man to a woman
Cardamom: Love
Carnation: Ardent and pure love, Bonds of love, Pure and deep love, Woman's love
   Bouquet, one solid color: "Yes"
   Dark red: "Alas! my poor heart", Deep love and affection, "My heart aches for you"
   Light red: Friendship, "I admire you", Respect

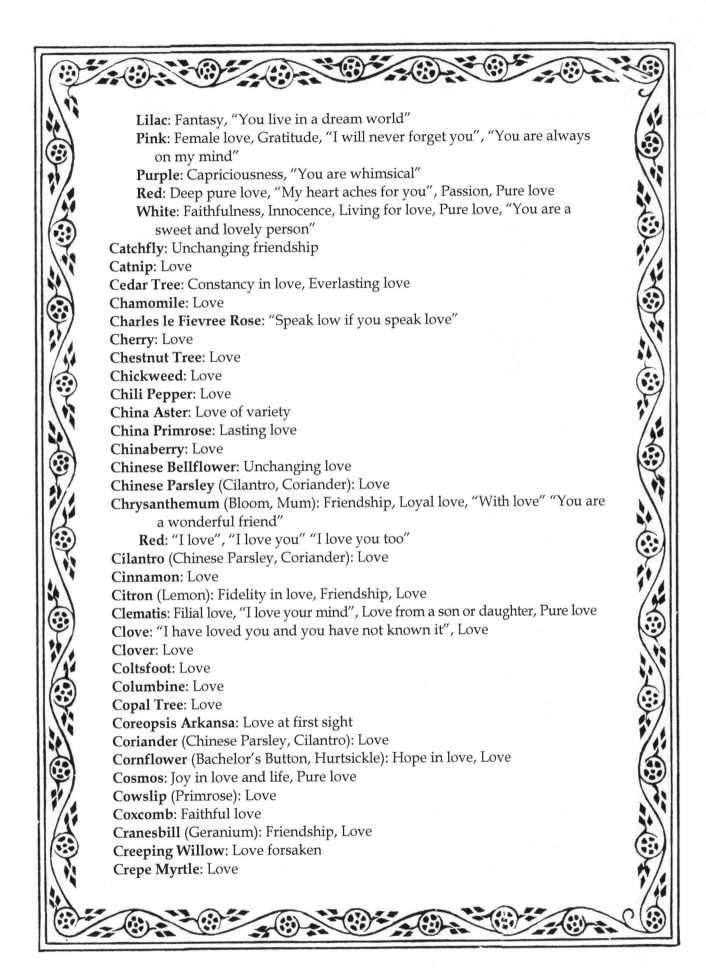

Lilac: Fantasy, "You live in a dream world"

Pink: Female love, Gratitude, "I will never forget you", "You are always on my mind"

Purple: Capriciousness, "You are whimsical"

Red: Deep pure love, "My heart aches for you", Passion, Pure love

White: Faithfulness, Innocence, Living for love, Pure love, "You are a sweet and lovely person"

Catchfly: Unchanging friendship

Catnip: Love

Cedar Tree: Constancy in love, Everlasting love

Chamomile: Love

Charles le Fievree Rose: "Speak low if you speak love"

Cherry: Love

Chestnut Tree: Love

Chickweed: Love

Chili Pepper: Love

China Aster: Love of variety

China Primrose: Lasting love

Chinaberry: Love

Chinese Bellflower: Unchanging love

Chinese Parsley (Cilantro, Coriander): Love

Chrysanthemum (Bloom, Mum): Friendship, Loyal love, "With love" "You are a wonderful friend"

   Red: "I love", "I love you" "I love you too"

Cilantro (Chinese Parsley, Coriander): Love

Cinnamon: Love

Citron (Lemon): Fidelity in love, Friendship, Love

Clematis: Filial love, "I love your mind", Love from a son or daughter, Pure love

Clove: "I have loved you and you have not known it", Love

Clover: Love

Coltsfoot: Love

Columbine: Love

Copal Tree: Love

Coreopsis Arkansa: Love at first sight

Coriander (Chinese Parsley, Cilantro): Love

Cornflower (Bachelor's Button, Hurtsickle): Hope in love, Love

Cosmos: Joy in love and life, Pure love

Cowslip (Primrose): Love

Coxcomb: Faithful love

Cranesbill (Geranium): Friendship, Love

Creeping Willow: Love forsaken

Crepe Myrtle: Love

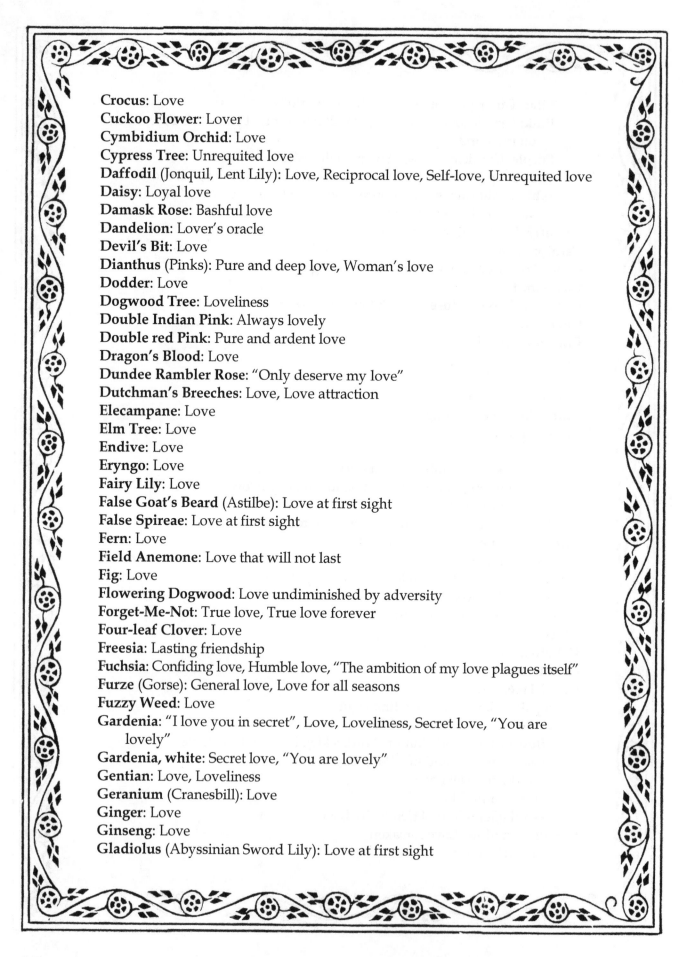

Crocus: Love
Cuckoo Flower: Lover
Cymbidium Orchid: Love
Cypress Tree: Unrequited love
Daffodil (Jonquil, Lent Lily): Love, Reciprocal love, Self-love, Unrequited love
Daisy: Loyal love
Damask Rose: Bashful love
Dandelion: Lover's oracle
Devil's Bit: Love
Dianthus (Pinks): Pure and deep love, Woman's love
Dodder: Love
Dogwood Tree: Loveliness
Double Indian Pink: Always lovely
Double red Pink: Pure and ardent love
Dragon's Blood: Love
Dundee Rambler Rose: "Only deserve my love"
Dutchman's Breeches: Love, Love attraction
Elecampane: Love
Elm Tree: Love
Endive: Love
Eryngo: Love
Fairy Lily: Love
False Goat's Beard (Astilbe): Love at first sight
False Spireae: Love at first sight
Fern: Love
Field Anemone: Love that will not last
Fig: Love
Flowering Dogwood: Love undiminished by adversity
Forget-Me-Not: True love, True love forever
Four-leaf Clover: Love
Freesia: Lasting friendship
Fuchsia: Confiding love, Humble love, "The ambition of my love plagues itself"
Furze (Gorse): General love, Love for all seasons
Fuzzy Weed: Love
Gardenia: "I love you in secret", Love, Loveliness, Secret love, "You are lovely"
Gardenia, white: Secret love, "You are lovely"
Gentian: Love, Loveliness
Geranium (Cranesbill): Love
Ginger: Love
Ginseng: Love
Gladiolus (Abyssinian Sword Lily): Love at first sight

Globe Amaranth: Immortal love, Unfading love

Gloxinia: Love at first sight

Gorse (Furze): General love, Love for all seasons

Grains of Paradise: Love

Grape Hyacinth: Romantic love, Unobtrusive loveliness

Grass of Paradise: Love

Half-blown Rose: Timid love

Heartsease (Johnny Jump Up, Wild Pansy): Love in idleness

Heather: Loveliness, Love, Lovers

Heliotrope: Eternal love

Hemp: Love

Hens and Chicks (Sedum): Motherly love

Hibiscus: Love

High John the Conqueror: Love

Honeyflower: Love sweet and secret

Honeysuckle: Bonds of love, Devoted love, "Do you love me?", Generous and
  devoted love, Love

   Monthly: Bonds of love, Devoted love

   Wild: Inconstancy in love

Hothouse Leek: Love

Hurtsickle (Bachelor's Button, Cornflower): Hope in love, Love

Hyacinth: Love

Impatiens (Busy Lizzie): Ardent and pure love, Motherly love

Indian Paintbrush: Love

Ivy: Wedded love

Japanese Andromeda (Pyrus Japonica): Love at first sight

Japanese Anemone (Windflower): Love

Japonica: Love

Jasmine: Love

Jerusalem Artichoke: Reciprocated love

Jewel Weed: Motherly love

Joe Pye Weed: Love

Johnny Jump Up (Heartsease, Wild Pansy): Love in idleness

Jonquil (Daffodil, Lent Lily): Love, Reciprocal love, Self-love, Unrequited love

Juniper Tree: Love

Jupiter's Beard: Love

Justicia: The perfection of female loveliness

Keys of Heaven: Love

Kingscup (Buttercup): Unrequited love

Lady's Mantle: Attract love, Love

Lavender: "I like you only as a friend", Love

Lavender Rose: Love at first sight

Leather Flower (Virgin's Bower): Fillial love, "I love your mind", Love from a
son or daughter, Pure love

Leek: Love

Lemon (Citron): Fidelity in love, Love

Lemon Balm: Love

Lemon Blossom: Fidelity in love

Lemon Verbena: Love

Lenten Lily (Daffodil, Jonquil): Love, Reciprocal love, Self-love, Unrequited
love

Lettuce: Love

Licorice: Love

Lilac: "Do you still love me?", First love, Love
  Purple: First emotions of love, First love

Lily of the Nile: Love letters

Lime Tree: Conjugal love

Linden Tree: Conjugal love

Liverwort: Love

Lotus: Estranged love

Lotus Flower: Estranged love

Lovage: Love

Love-in-a-Mist (Nigella): Love

Love-in-Idleness: Love at first sight

Lucky Seed: Love

Lyre Flower (Bleeding Heart, Venus' Car): Love, Love attraction, Unrequited
love

Madrone Tree: One love

Magnolia: Love of nature

Maiden blush Rose: "If you love me you will find it out", Timid love

Maidenhair Fern: Love, Secret bond of love, Secret love

Major Convolvulus (Morning Glory): "I love you"

Male Fern: Love

Mallow: Consumed by love, Love

Malva Rose: Love

Mandrake: Love

Maple Tree: Love

Marjoram: Love

Meadowsweet: Love

Michaelmas Daisy: Love

Milfoil (Sneezewort, Yarrow): Love

Mimosa (Sensitive Plant): Love, Secret love

Mint: Love

Mistletoe: Love

Monk's Head: Love attraction
Monthly Honeysuckle: Bond of love, Devoted love
Moon Daisy: Love's oracle
Moonwort: Love
Morning Glory (Major Convolvulus): "I love you"
Moss: Maternal love
Moss Rose: Confession of love, Love, Voluptuous love
Moss Rosebud: Confessed of love, Confession of love
Motherwort: Concealed love, Secret love
Mullein: Love
Mum (Bloom, Chrysanthemum): Loyal love, "With love"
    Red: "I love", "I love you", "I love you too"
Myosotis (Forget-Me-Not): True love, True love forever
Myrtle: Love, Love in absence
Nasturtium: Impetuous love, Maternal love
Nigella (Love-in-a-Mist): Love
Nosegay Tree (Plumaria): Love
Nuts: Love
Orange: Love
Orange Blossom: Eternal love, Love, "Your purity equals your loveliness"
Orchid: Love
Orris Root: Love
Our Lady's Earrings: Motherly love
Pansy: Love
Papaya: Love
Parma Violet: "Let me love you"
Parsley: Love
Patient Lucy: Motherly love
Pea: Love
Peach: Love
Pear: Love
Peppermint: Love
Periwinkle (Vinca): Love
Phlox: Proposal of love
Pimento: Love
Pincushion Flower (Scabiosa): Unfortunate love
Pinks (Dianthus): Woman's love
Pink Carnation: Woman's love
Pink Rose: Secret love
Pistachio: Breaking love spells
Plumeria (Nosegay Tree): Love
Policeman's Helmet: Motherly love

Poppy: Love
Prickly Ash: Love
Primrose (Cowslip): Love
Purple Lilac: First emotions of love, First love
Purple Lily: First love
Purslane: Love
Pyrus Japonica (Japanese Andrometda): Love at first sight
Quince: Love
Ragweed (Ambrosia): Love returned, "Your love is returned"
Rain Lily: Love
Raspberry: Love
Red Anemone: Love that will not last
Red Carnation: Deep pure love, Pure love
Red Catchfly: Youthful love
Red Chrysanthemum: "I love", "I love you", "I love you too"
Red Rose: Love
Red Rosebud: Pure and lovely
Red Tulip: Confession of love, Declaration of love
Red Rosebud: Heart innocent of love, Pure and lovely
Red thornless Rosebud: Love at first sight
Red Tulip: Confession of love, Declaration of love, Love
Rose Acacia: Platonic love
Rose Mallow: Love
Rose of Sharon (Althea): Consumed by love, Fiery love, Love
Rose: Eternal love, "I love you", Love, Love at first sight
    Austrian: "You are all that is lovely"
    Bridal: Happy love
    Cabbage: Ambassador of love
    Campion: "Only deserve my love"
    Carolina: Love is dangerous
    Charles le Fievree: "Speak low if you speak love"
    Damask: Bashful love
    Dundee Rambler: "Only deserve my love"
    Fifty, any color: "My love is unconditional"
    Half-blown: Timid love
    Lavender: Love at first sight
    Lilac: Love at first sight
    Maiden blush: "If you love me you will find it out", Timid love
    Malva: Love
    Moss: Confession of love, Love, Voluptuous love
    One red, one white: Mutual desire, Mutual love
    Pale pink: "You're so lovely"

Pink: Secret love
Pink, white, together: "I love you still and always will"
Red: Love
Seven, any color: "I am infatuated"
Single: "I love you", "I still love you"
Single, red: True love
Six, any color: "I want to be yours"
Tea: Always lovely
Ten, any color: "You are perfect"
Thornless, red: Love at first sight
Three red: "I love you"
Twelve, any color: "Be mine"
White: A heart unacquainted with love, Eternal love, False love
White, withered: Loss of innocence
Yellow: "Welcome back", "Remember me", Joy, Friendship,
Rosebud: Heart ignorant of love, New love
Rosebud, moss: Confessed love, Confession of love
Rosebud, red: Heart ignorant of love, Pure and lovely
Rosebud, white: Heart ignorant of love
Rosemary: Love
Rue: Love
Ryegrass: Love
Saffron: Love
Saint John's Wort: Love
Sarsaparilla: Love
Scabiosa (Pincushion Flower): Unfortunate love
Sedum (Hens and Chicks): Motherly love
Sensitive Plant (Mimosa): Love, Secret love
September Flower (Aster): Love, Luck in love
Shrimp Plant (Water Willow): "The perfection of female loveliness"
Single Pink: Pure love
Single Rose: "I love you", "I still love you"
Single red Rose: True love
Skullcap: Love
Smilax: Loveliness
Sneezewort (Milfoil, Yarrow): Love
Soldier's Cap: Love attraction
Spearmint: Love
Spiderwort: "Esteem but not love", Love
Squirrel Corn: Love attraction
Strawberry: Love
Strawberry Tree (Arbutus): "Esteem but not love", Friendship, "I only love

you", One love, "Thee only do I love", "You're the only one I love"

Sugar Cane: Love
Sultana: Motherly love
Syrian Mallow (Althea Frutes): Consumed by love, "I am deeply in love"
Tamarind: Love
Tea Rose: Always lovely,
Thornless red Rose: Love at first sight
Thyme: Love
Tiger Lily: "I dare you to love me"
Touch-Me-Not: Motherly love
Tradescantia (Spiderwort): Esteem but not love, Love
Tulip: Love, Perfect lover
Orange: Desire, Energy, Enthusiasm, Passion
Purple: Royalty
Pink: Affection, Best wishes, "I care about you", Perfect happiness
Red: Confession of love, Declaration of love, Love
Variegated: "You have beautiful eyes"
Violet: Modesty
White: Forgiveness, Heaven, Humility, Innocence, Lost love, Purity
Yellow: Friendship, Hope in love, Hopeless love, "You have a radiant smile"
Umbrella Pine Tree: Undying love
Valerian: Love
Vanilla: Love
Venus' Car (Bleeding Heart, Lyre Flower): Love, Love attraction, Unrequited love
Venus Flytrap: Love
Vervain: Love
Vetiver: Love
Vinca (Periwinkle): Love
Vine: Head over heels in love
Violet: Happiness, Innocence, Kindness, Love, Modesty, Purity, Worth
    African: Delicate love connection
    Blue: Love, Modest love
    Czar: Kindness and worth
    Parma: "Let me love you"
    Purple: "You occupy my thoughts"
    White: Innocence, "Let's take a chance on happiness", Modesty, Purity
    Wild: Love, Love in idleness
Virgin's Bower: Filial love, "I love your mind", Love from a son or daughter, Pure love
Water Willow (Shrimp Plant): "The perfection of female loveliness"
Weeping Willow Tree: Disappointed in love, Love

White Acacia: Platonic love

White Camellia Japonica: Perfected loveliness

White Carnation: Living for love, Lovely, Pure and adrdent love, Sweet and lovely

White Gardenia: Secret love, "You are lovely"

White Hearts: Love attraction

White Hyacinth: Unobtrusive loveliness

White Rose: "A heart unacquainted with love", Eternal love, False love

White Rosebud: "Heart ignorant of love"

White Tulip: Lost love

Wild Honeysuckle: Inconstancy in love

Wild Pansy (Heartease, Johnny Jump Up): Love in idleness

Wild Violet: Love, Love in idleness

Willow Tree: Love

Windflower (Japanese Anemone): Love

Woodbine: Fraternal love

Wormwood: Love

Yarrow (Milfoil, Sneezewort): Love

Yellow Acacia: Secret love

Yellow Chrysanthemum: Slighted love

Yellow Dahlia: "I am happy you love me"

Yellow Tulip: Hope in love, Hopeless love

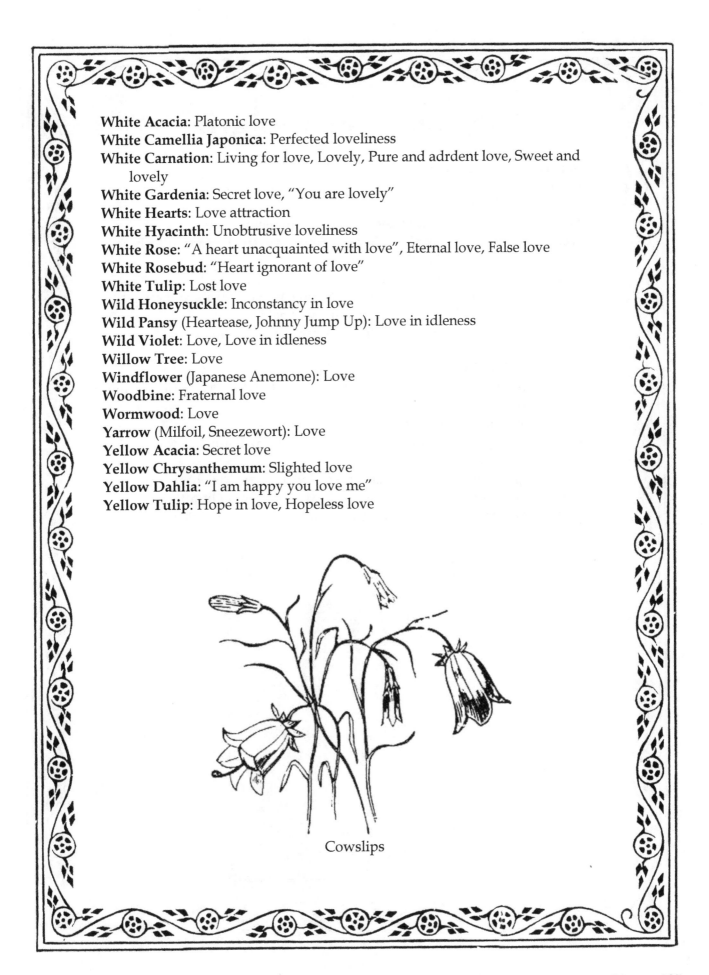

Cowslips

FLOWERS FOR BEAUTY

Amaryllis: Radiant beauty, Worth beyond beauty
Cherry Blossom: Beauty, Female power, "Life is beautiful but transient" (Japan), Sexuality (China)
Daisy: Beauty, Loyal love, Patience, Purity, Simplicity,
Iris: A message promising love, Beauty, Faith, Majesty, Perfection, "My compliments", Valor, Wisdom
Jasmine: Beauty, Elegance, Friendliness, Grace, Sensuality
Lily: Charm against evil, Death of a loved one, Female beauty and sexual attractiveness, Fertility, Majesty, Purity, Wealth
    Orange: "I burn for you", "There's a flame in my heart"
    Pink: "You are pretty"
    Tiger: Pride, Riches
    White: "It's heavenly to be with you", Majesty, Modesty, Perfect beauty, Purity
    Yellow: Fun, "I am walking on air", Happiness
Orchid: Beauty, Love, Many children, Mature charm, Refinement, Thoughtfulness
Snowdrop: Beauty of spirit, Consolation, Hopefulness, New beginnings
Violet: Faithfulness, "I return your love", Modesty, Sweet beauty
Water Lily: Beauty, Enlightenment, Love, Mental purity, Mystic powers, Purity of heart

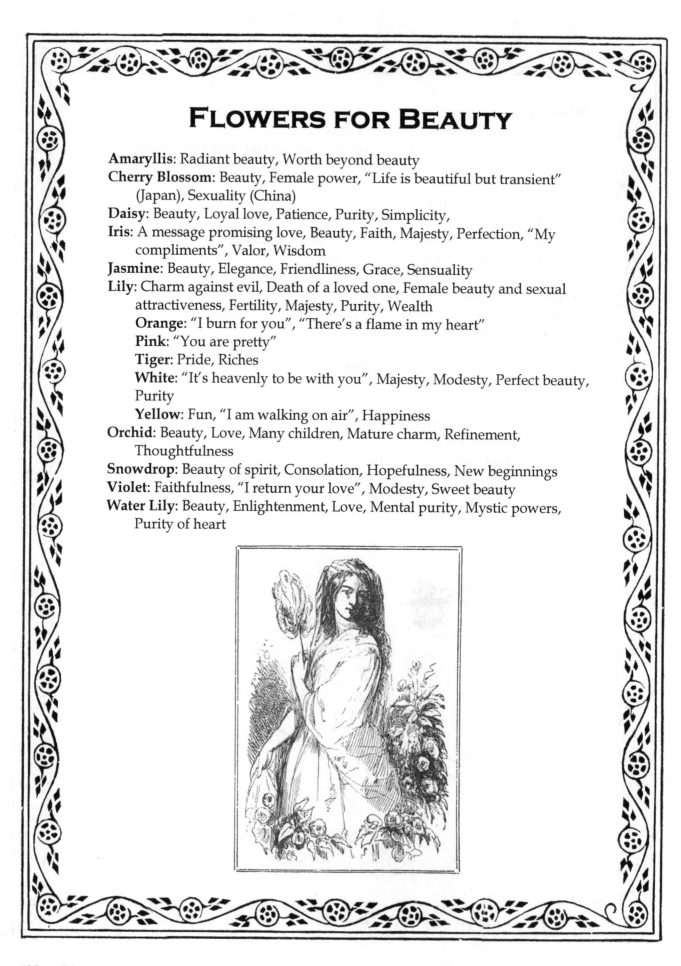

FLOWERS FOR FRIENDSHIP

Acacia: Friendship
Alstroemeria (Peruvian Lily): Friendship
American Ivy (Virginia Creeper): Strong friendship
Apostle Plant: Everlasting friendship, Unchanging friendship
Arbor-Vitae: Live for me, Unchanging friendship
Arbutus (Strawberry Tree): Friendship
Balloon Flower: "Return of a friend is desired"
Barberton Daisy: "Thinking of an absent friend"
Bellflower: "Return of a friend is desired"
Bloom (Chrysanthemum, Mum): Friendship, "You are a wonderful friend"
Blue Periwinkle: Early friendship
Boxwood (Box Tree): Constancy in friendship
Catchfly: Unchanging friendship
Chrysanthemum (Bloom, Mum): Friendship, "You are a wonderful friend"
Citron (Lemon): Friendship
Cranesbill (Geranium): Friendship
Delphinium: "Return of a friend is desired"
Everlasting Pea: Friendship
Flags Iris: "Your friendship is valued"
Freesia: Friendship, Lasting friendship
Galax (Wandflower): Friendship
Geranium (Cranesbill): Friendship
Gerbera Daisy: Friendship, "Thinking of an absent friend"
Grass Pea: Friendship
Iris: Friendship, "Your friendship is valued"
Ivy: Friendship
Lavender: "I like you only as a friend"
Lemon (Citron): Friendship
Light pink Rose: Friendship
Lucky Hand: Friendship
Lucky Seed: Friendship
Mixed Zinnia: Thinking of an absent friend, "Thinking of you"
Mum (Bloom, Chrysanthemum): Friendship, "You are a wonderful friend"
Oak-leaf Geranium: True friendship
Pasque Flower: Friendship
Passionflower: Friendship
Periwinkle (Vinca): Early friendship
Peruvian Lily (Alstroemeria): Friendship
Pink Carnation: Friendship

Pink Rose: Friendship
Pussy Willow: Friendship
Rose: Friendship
Rose Acacia: Friendship
Snowdrop: "A friend in adversity", Friendship in adversity
Soybean: "Your friendship is agreeable and pleasing"
Strawberry Tree (Arbutus): Friendship
Sweet Pea: Friendship
Tiger Flower: "For once may pride befriend me"
Vinca (Periwinkle): Early friendship
Virginia Creeper (American Ivy): Strong friendship
Walking Iris: Friendship, "Your friendship is valued"
Wallflower: Friendship in adversity
Wandflower (Galax): Friendship
Wheat: Friendliness, Friendship
White Acacia: Friendship
Willow Tree: Friendship
Zinnia: Absent friends, Friendship, "Thinking of an absent friend"

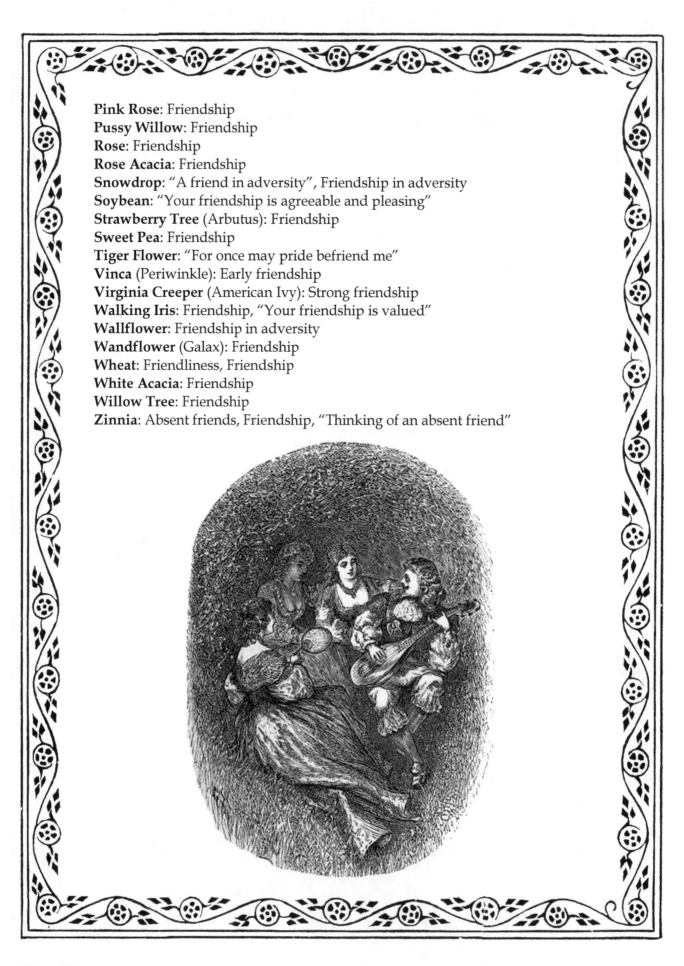

FLOWERS FOR REFUSAL

Agnus Castus: Coldness, Indifference
Almond, common: Indiscretion, Stupidity
Anemone, field: Abandonment, Love that will not last
Anemone, garden: Forsaken
Anemone, red: Abandonment, Love that will not last
Apricot blossom: Doubt
Ash-leaved Trumpet Flower: Separation
Balsam, red: Impatient resolves, "Touch me not"
Barberry: Sourness/Sharpness of temper
Basil: Hatred [Combined w/ Licorice, wild, or Belvedere]
Begonia: Caution, Dark thoughts, Deformity
Belladonna: Death, Hush, Silence
Belvedere: "I declare against you" [Used w/ Milfoil, Basil, or a York and
    Lancaster Rose]
Bilberry: Treachery
Birdsfoot Trefoil: Revenge, Vengeance
Black Prince Geranium: Delusive hopes
Bramble: Envy, Lowliness, Remorse
Broken Corn: Quarrel
Broken Corn Straw: Disagreement, Quarrel
Broken Straw: Division, Rupture of a contract
Bugloss: Falsehood
Bur: Rudeness, "You weary me"
Burdock: Importunity, "Touch me not"
Burning Nettle: Cruelty, Slander
Buttercup (Kingscup): Childishness, Desire for riches, Ingratitude
Butterfly Weed: "Let me go"
Candytuft: Indifference
Candytufy, everflowering: Indifference
Carnation, red: "My heart breaks"
Carnation, striped: Extremes, "I cannot be with you", Refusal
Carnation, yellow: Contempt, Disdain, "I do not believe you", No, Rejection,
    Rue, "You have disappointed me"
Carolina Syringa: Disappointment
Catchfly, white: Betrayal
Champignon (Mushroom): Suspicion
Cherry, white: Deception
Cherry, winter: Deception
China Pink: Aversion
Chrysanthemum, yellow: Slighted love

Clotbur: Pertinacity, Rudeness
Columbine: Desertion, Folly
Common Almond: Indiscretion, Stupidity
Common stinging Nettle: "You are spiteful"
Common Willow: Forsaken
Convolvulus, major: Extinguished hopes
Corn, broken: Quarrel
Corn, straw, broken: Disagreement, Quarrel
Creeping Willow: Love forsaken
Cypress and Marigold: Great despair
Daisy, Michaelmas: Afterthought, Farewell
Darnel (Ray-grass): Vice
Diosma: Uselessness
Dodder of Thyme: Baseness, Meanness
Dogsbane: Deceit
Dragon's Wort: Horror
Everflowering Candytuft: Indifference
Ficoides (Ice plant): Rejected addresses, "Your looks freeze me"
Field Anemone: Abandonment, Love that will not last
Fly Orchid: Error
Flytrap: Deceit
Flytrap, Venus: Deceit
Fool's Parsley: Silliness
Foxglove: Insincerity
Frog Lily: Disgust
Fuller's Thistle: Misanthropy
Garden Anemone: Forsaken
Garden Marigold: Uneasiness
Geranium, Black Prince: Delusive hopes
Geranium, scarlet: Silliness, Stupidity
Handflower Tree: Warning
Heath: Solitude
Hellebore: Calumny, Scandal
Hemlock: Black magic, Evil, "You will be my death"
Hortensia: "You are cold"
Hothouse Leek: Exile
Ice plant (Fidoides): Rejected addresses, "Your looks freeze me"
Indian Pink: Aversion
Ivy, berry: Warning
Japan Rose: "Beauty is your only attraction"
Judas Tree: Betrayal, Unbelief
Kingscup (Buttercup): Childishness, Desire for riches, Ingratitude
Laburnum: Forsaken

Lavender: Distrust, Failure, Mistrust
Lettuce: Cold-heartedness
Licorice, wild: "I declare against you" [used w/ Milfoil, Basil, or a York and Lancaster Rose]
Lily, Bee: Error
Lily, Frog: Disgust
Lily, yellow: Falsehood, Lies
Lobelia: Malevolence
Madder: Calumny
Major Convolvulus: Extinguished hopes
Manchineal Tree: Extinguished hopes
Mandrake: Horror
Marigold, garden: Uneasiness
Marigold, placed on bottom: Indifference
Marigold and Cypress: Great despair
Meadowsweet: Uselessness
Michaelmas Daisy: Farewell, Afterthought
Milfoil (Achillea Millefoilia): War [Combined w/ Licorice, wild or Belvedere]
Mock Orange: Counterfeit
Mourning Bride: "I have lost all", Unfortunate attachment
Mushroom (Champignon): Suspicion
Nettle, burning: Cruelty, Slander
Nettle, common, stinging: "You are spiteful"
Oleander: Beware
Orange, mock: Counterfeit
Orchid, Fly: Error
Parsley, Fool's: Silliness
Pasque flower: "You have no claims"
Pennyroyal: Flee away
Pigeonberry: Indifference
Pincushion Flower (Scabiosa): Unfortunate love
Pink, China: Aversion
Pink, Indian: Aversion
Pink, Indian, single: Aversion
Pink, variegated: Refusal
Plum, wild: Independence
Pomegranate: Folly, Foolishness
Quaking-grass: Agitation
Queen of the Meadows: Uselessness
Ray-grass (Darnel): Vice
Redbud: Betrayal
Red Anemone: Abandonment, Love that will not last

Red Carnation: "My heart breaks"
Rhododendron (Rosebay): Beware, Danger
Rose, Japan: "Beauty is your only attraction"
Rose, yellow: Decrease/Departure of love, Infidelity, Jealousy
Rose, York and Lancaster: War [Used w/ Milfoil and Belvedere]
Sainfoin: Agitation
Saint John's Wort: Animosity, Superstition
Scarlet Geranium: Silliness, Stupidity
Senvy: Indifference
Snakesfoot: Horror
Spiderwort: Esteem not love
Straw, broken: Rupture of a contract, Division
Stinging Nettle, common: "You are spiteful"
Striped Carnation: Extremes, "I cannot be with you", Refusal,
Sweetbriar, yellow: Decrease of love
Syringa, Carolina: Disappointment
Tansy, wild: "I declare war against you"
Teasel: Misanthropy
Thistle, Fuller's: Misanthropy
Thorn Apple: Deceitful charms
Thyme, dodder of: Baseness, Meanness
Trumpetflower, ash-leaved: Separation
Tulip, yellow: Hopeless love
Variegated Pink: Refusal
Venus Flytrap: Deceit
Whin: Anger
White Catchfly: Betrayal
White Cherry: Deception
Wild Plum: Independence
Willow, common: Forsaken
Willow, creeping: Love forsaken
Winter Cherry: Deception
Xanthium: Pertinacity, Rudeness
Yellow Carnation: Disdain
Yellow Chrysanthemum: Slighted love
Yellow Lily: Falsehood, Lies
Yellow Rose: Decrease/Departure of love, Infidelity, Jealousy
Yellow Sweetbriar: Decrease of love
Yellow Tulip: Hopeless love
Yew: Sorrow
York and Lancaster Rose: War [Used w/ Belvedere and Milfoil]

Gemstones
to
Meanings

Abalone Shell: Connection with the sea – tides of emotion, Easy flow of feelings, Family, Harmony in relationships, Motherhood, Sensitivity towards others, The beauty in the change of existence

Adamite: Awakens the joy of the inner child, Brings joy, creativity, and enthusiasm, Expression of playful spirit, Opens the heart to communication, Shields from psychic attacks and negativity, Stimulates creativity

African Jade (Butter Jade, Butterstone): Brings hope and healing, Brings resilience and versatility, Connects to the essence of life, Encourages steadfast persistence, Promotes grounding earth energy, Promotes stability

Agate: Attracts strength, Gives rich and variegated dreams, Logical thinking, Luck, New beginnings, Protection, Protects from bad dreams, Protects from stress and energy drains, Used to ward off storms

Agate varieties

    Blue Lace: Stone of calming

    Crazy Lace: Stone of laughter

    Dendrite: Stone of long life and prosperity

    Eye: Stone of protection against evil

    Fire: Stone of peace and serenity

    Moss: Stone of warriors

    Snakeskin: Stone of strength and stealth

    Tree: Stone of awareness and understanding

    Turritella: Stone of self-acceptance and inner peace

    White: Stone of protection

Alexandrite: Aids in accessing the highest realm of vibrations, Attracts wealth, Balances the heart chakra, Brings great fortune, Enhances physical capabilities, Expands one's adaptability, Opens one's perception to joy and love

Amazonite: Balances feminine and masculine energy, Gives physical stamina, Helps balance emotions, Intuition, Promotes kindness and practicality, Stone of artists and men, The Lucky Hope Stone

Amber: Brings a carefree, sunny disposition, Cheerfulness, Creativity, Dissolves oppositions, Fulfillment of desires, Increases motivation, Luck, Promotes good luck and success, Protection for travelers, Signifies the presence of the Lord

Amber varieties

    Far East cultures: Courage

    Asian Cultures: "Soul of the Tiger"

    Egypt: Ensures the dead remain whole

Amethyst: Combats insomnia, Cures headaches, Fights off nightmares if combined with Charoite, Grants pleasant dreams, Guards against drunkenness, Guards against guilty or deceptive emotions, Healing, Instills a sober mind, Intuition, Protection against witchcraft, Protection from poison, Readiness for action, Wisdom

    Green Amethyst (Prasiolite): Assists in bringing spiritual ideals into everyday life, Attracts prosperity, Brings good fortune and luck, Clears negativity, Closes the gap between the physical and spiritual, Fosters compassion, self-acceptance, and self-honor, Ignites love and compassion in one's heart, Protects wearer from intoxication, Strengthens emotions, mind, and will

    Amethyst Spirit Quartz (Cactus Quartz, Porcupine Quartz): Aids in merging with one's Higher Self, Aids in releasing fear, Balances the Crown chakra, Harmonizes aura, chakra points, and physical body, Purifies and protects

Ametrine (Bolivianite, Trystine): Aids in defeating depression, Brings inner peace and tranquility, Brings money, luck, protection and healing, Combats insomnia, Creativity, Cures headaches, Grants pleasant dreams, Guards against drunkenness, Increases self-esteem, Intuition, Luck, Opens the mind to new thoughts, Promotes clarity of thought, Protection against poison, Protects from negative energy, Readiness for action

Andalusite (Chiastolite, Cross Stone): Aids in defeating depression, Dispels negative thoughts and energies, Enhances energy of prosperity stones, Gateway to mysteries and out-of-body travel, Grounds energies, Overcomes feelings of loneliness and isolation, Protection, Protection for travelers, Psychic protection, Strengthens all chakras, Transmutes conflict into harmony

Angel Aura Quartz (Quartz Crystal): Channels higher knowledge, Finds one's personal purpose, Opens awareness to the angelic domain, Opens the Throat chakra, Promotes joy, light, and optimism, Used in deep meditation

Angelite (Anhydrite): Alleviates psychological pain, Communication with angels, Enhances astrological understanding, Gives protection in the area around one's body, Helps one speak the truth when it's difficult, Increases telepathy, Promotes compassion and understanding, Special focus on peace and brotherhood, Stone of heightened awareness

Apache Tears Obsidian: Clears one's auric field

Apatite: Assists in communicating with Nature's spirits, Assists in starting new adventures, Balances the wisdom of the mind and heart, Clarifies one's purpose in life, Clears confusion, Dissolves alienation, Draws negativity from oneself, Encourages extroversion, Helps overcome fears, Stimulates creativity and intellect, Stone of abundance, Stone of learning

Apophyllite: Brings recognition of one's true self, Deepens understanding of spiritual lessons, Enhances clarity of remote vision, Facilitates contact with angels, Increases inner vision, Increases psychic abilities if used with Cavansite, Releases mental blocks, Stone of Seeing, Stone of truth

Aqua Aura Quartz: Enhances ability to communicate inner truth, Expresses emotions in a positive way, Safeguards against psychological attacks, Stimulates Throat chakra

Aqua Blue Obsidian: Helps align one to their goals

Aquamarine: Brings peace and serenity, Calms nerves, Foresight, Gets in touch with one's spiritual being, Order, Picks up spirits, Protection for sailors, Protects against gossip, Stamina, Unfinished business, Used in deep meditation

Aragonite: Aids with stressful times, Centers and grounds physical energies, Intensifies emotional perception and joy, Promotes a sense of balance, Stabilizes Base chakra, Strengthens one's connection with the earth

Arfvedsonite: Aids with psychic visions and intuition, Assists in finding one's life purpose, Brings restful sleep and dreams, Clears insight for the best spiritual path forward, Crystal of fertility, Helps in understanding dream symbols, Psychic protection, Reduces negative thoughts

Astrophyllite: Activates and aligns chakra energy centers, Aids in communicating with other beings, Assists in astral travel, Assists in finding one's life purpose, Develops spiritual growth, Stone of personal knowledge

Atlantasite: Assists in regaining one's possessions, Brings peace to the environment, Encourages thinking before speaking, Grants access to past lives, Lowers stress levels, Promotes successful thinking in business, Stimulates spiritual development

Atlantis Stone (Dolphin Stone, Larimar, Stefilia's Stone): Awakens feminine power, Balances the energy of fire and water, Cleanses unhealthy emotional blocks, Releases attachments, Relieves stress for pregnant women and new mothers, Soothes the emotions, Stone of healing, Teaches love, respect, and nurturing

Aventurine: Enthusiasm, Lady Luck, Stone of opportunity

> **Blue Aventurine:** Assists in self-discipline, Develops inner strength, Increases vitality and positive outlook, Opens the Third Eye chakra, Powerful mental healer, Stone of Aries

> **Green Aventurine:** Increases perception and creative insight, Stone of luck and chance

> **Red Aventurine:** Aids in seeing the possibilities in opportunities, Assists in creativity, Opens the Root chakra

> **Yellow Aventurine:** Opens the Third Eye chakra, Used to balance emotions and energy

Axinite: Assists in avoiding power struggles and conflict, Enhances vitality and grounding, Harmonizes one's emotions, Helps with stamina for those who work hard, Increases access to spiritual planes, Stone of truth

Azurite: Assists in opening the mind, Excellent stone for students studying for exams, Increases intuition, creativity, and inspiration, Opens inner sight, Stimulates an increase in communication skills

Baryte: Aids in journeying to higher realms in meditation, Aids with entry to higher spiritual realms, Cleanses one's energy, Discovers dream patterns that reveal spiritual state, Opens the Third Eye and Crown chakras, Stone of inner vision

Benitoite: Aids in accessing and understand higher knowledge, Channels spiritual information, Opens the door to truth, Promotes synchronicity

Bismuth: Assists in finding answers to personal puzzles, Used in meditation to seek one's path

Black Diopside: Establishes connection, Grounds in the earth

Black Obsidian: Gets rid of negative energies

Black Tourmaline (Schorl): Brings luck and happiness, Logical thinking, Luck and happiness, Powerful stone of healing, Protection

Bloodstone (Heliotrope Stone): Brings change, Protects against evil, Symbol of justice

Blue Aventurine: Assists in self-discipline, Develops inner strength, Increases vitality and positive outlook, Opens the Third Eye chakra, Powerful mental healer, Stone of Aries

Blue Calcite: Psychic ability and astral travel

Blue Goldstone: Learning and communication

Blue Lace Agate: Stone of calming

Blue Quartz (Dumortierite): Assists in the ability to reach out to others, Assuages fear, Calms the mind, Helps one understand one's spiritual nature, Inspires hope, Soothing, stress-relief stone

Blue Tourmaline (Indicolite): Aids in developing psychic ability, Aids in exploring and understanding past lives, Facilitates deep meditation, Offers relief from stress, Opens doors and communication to the spiritual realm, Promotes a calming effect

Blue Zoisite (Tanzanite): Aids in speaking the truth, Brings a peaceful understanding of one's own heart, Calms an overactive mind, Promotes compassion, Raises consciousness in meditation, Stone of communication,

Used in deep meditation

Botryoidal Fluorite: Healing, Lightens rooms, Money, Personal power

Bronzite: Alleviates indecision and doubt, Beneficial for masculine energy, Increases self-esteem, Inspires courtesy, help, and acceptance, Restores harmony and self-confidence, Strengthens non-judgmental discernment

Butter Jade (African Jade, Butterstone): Brings hope and healing, Brings resilience and versatility, Connects to the essence of life, Encourages steadfast persistence, Promotes grounding earth energy, Promotes stability

Cacoxenite: Aligns oneself with the Divine, Assists in emotional upheaval, Assists with one's spiritual evolution, Cleanses, Cleanses one of negative attachments, Expands the consciousness, Stone of ascension

Cactus Quartz: Aids in merging with one's Higher Self, Aids in releasing fear, Balances the Crown chakra, Harmonizes aura, chakra points, and physical body, Purifies and protects

Calcite: Amplifies and cleanses energies, Opens energy channels, Self-confidence

    Blue Calcite: Psychic ability and astral travel

    Clear Calcite: Clarity, insight, and forgiveness

    Cobaltoan Calcite (Sphaerocobaltite): Aids in making friends and activating Heart chakra, Allows freer communication, Brings awareness of one's own body language, Coordinates release of buried emotions, Dispels negative emotions, Encourages positive emotions, Increases harmony when working in a group, Said to be crystals of joy, Stone of love

    Green Calcite: Emotional balance and stress relief

    Honey Calcite: Persistence and intellectual power

    Orange Calcite: Creativity, sexuality, and confidence

    Pink Calcite: Well-being, empathy, and health

    Red Calcite: Vitality

    White Calcite: Cleanses and heals

Calligraphy Stone: Healing, Lightens rooms, Money, Personal power

Candle Quartz: Brings abundance, Brings one's totem spirit guide closer, Helps focus on a true path and purpose, Promotes tranquility and certainty, Radiates love

Carnelian: Calms the temper, Gives energy to its carrier, Guards against poverty, Helps give a sense a humor, Passion, Protects from bad vibrations, Solving difficulties, Unfinished business

Cat's Eye: Brings a feeling of completeness, Brings good luck and protection, Combines with Topaz to bring wealth and money, Excellent in meditation, Grants insight, Makes one aware of one's own needs, Protection, Stone of the mind

Cavansite: Allows greater understanding, Beneficial for channeling spiritual information, Calms nerves and emotions, Grants clear insight and effective communication, Increases psychic abilities if used with Apophyllite, Opens the door to truth, Opens the Heart chakra if used with Stilbite, Unites Throat and Third Eye chakras

Celestite (Celestine): Cleanses the environment around it, Communication with angels, Raises one's awareness, Used to establish order

    Ohio Celestite: Enhances inspiration and learning skills, Gentle, yet strong, Increases discipline, Opens the Third Eye to higher dimensions, Strengthens psychic capabilities

Celestial Aura Quartz: Brings a sense of unity and self-understanding, Develops the ability to share and teach knowledge, Practice trust of others, Purifies, Remains true to one's spiritual path

Chalcedony: A stone sacred to Native American Indians, Absorbs negative energy and dissipates it, Harmonizes body, mind, and spirit, Instills generosity, Used to assist telepathy

Chalcopyrite (Peacock Ore): Increases ability to perceive, Makes an excellent meditation stone, Opens and cleans Crown chakra, Used to break up energy blockages

Champagne Tourmaline (Dravite): Aids in finding emotional strength, Brings self-acceptance, Calms and soothes, Grounds one's inner self, Inspires courage and persistence, Stone of self-healing

Charoite: Assists with deep sleep and powerful dreams, Fights off nightmares if combined with Amethyst, Grounds the spiritual self, Lifts energy when the physical body is exhausted, Opens and cleans the Crown chakra, Soul stone, Used to overcome fears, obsessions, and compulsions

Chiastolite (Andalusite, Cross Stone): Aids in defeating depression, Dispels negative thoughts and energies, Enhances energy of prosperity stones, Gateway to mysteries and out-of-body travel, Grounds energies, Overcome feelings of loneliness and isolation, Protection, Protection for travelers, Psychic protection, Strengthens all chakra, Transmutes conflict into harmony

Chinese Writing Stone (Porphyry): Accept and adjust to change, Access Akashic records, Promotes peaceful dreaming, Reaffirm relationships, commitments, and loyalties, Realigns goals towards a higher purpose, Sparks creativity, Stone of re-affirmation

Chlorite: Assists with inner balance, health and well-being, Powerful connection to nature, Stone of self-healing and regeneration

Chrysanthemum Stone: Aids in overcoming fear, Awakens one's true purpose in life, Brings joy, love, and abundance, Brings unexpected opportunities, Forges through obstacles, Lends support and courage to follow one's dreams

Chrysocolla: Brings about calm when upset, Can decrease nervousness and irritability, Encourages clarity of thought, Promotes levelheadedness, Stone of healing [American Indians], Stone of peace, increased wisdom, and discretion, Strengthens the body's resistance, Used to attract love

Chrysoprase: Encourages love and joy, Fertility, Helps clarify problems, Increases motivation, Logical thinking, Love, Luck, Positive attitude towards life, Protection on sea voyages, Readiness for action, Strengthens the workings of insight, Used as a cure for restlessness

Cinnabar: Activates and balances Root chakra, Aligns and clears blocks from chakra, Aligns personal will with Divine will, Assists in actualizing dreams, Called the "Magician Stone", Creates prosperity, Grants greater insight, Releases buried resentment, Stimulates the Third Eye, Stone of transformation

Cinnabrite: Personal power, Stone of emotional and spiritual growth, Willpower

Citrine: Brings money, luck, protection, and healing, Increases self-esteem, Known as the Merchant's Stone, Logical thinking, Opens the mind to new thoughts, Promotes clarity of thought, Protects from negative energy, Self-confidence

Clear Calcite: Clarity, forgiveness, and insight

Clintonite: Aids in personal growth and flexibility, Assists in gaining benefits from learning life lessons, Beneficial for self-examination, Helps one's inner vision, Used to cleanse one's aura and surrounding area

Cobaltoan Calcite (Sphaerocobaltite): Aids in making friends and activating Heart chakra, Allows freer communication, Brings awareness of one's own body language, Coordinates release of buried emotions, Dispels negative emotions, Encourages positive emotions, Increases harmony when working in a group, Said to be crystals of joy, Stone of love

Copper: Enhances energy fields, Enhances healing effects of other stones, Metal of healing, Used for arthritis and rheumatism

Coral: Believed to prevent ill fortune, Dreams of it foretold recovery from illness, Good for meditation and visualization, Protects from diseases, Symbolizes life and blood force energy

Covellite: Aids in developing psychic ability, Assists with past life work, Connects physical reality with higher realms, Develops one's inner intuition, Expresses knowledge through written word, Helpful during times of transition, Tunes into a muse or spirit guide

Crazy Lace Agate: Stone of laughter

Creedite: Energizes creative vision, Enhances creativity, Excellent meditation stone, Used to expand awareness

Cross Stone (Andalusite, Chiastolite): Aids in defeating depression, Dispels negative thoughts and energies, Enhances energy of prosperity stones, Gateway to mysteries and out-of-body travel, Grounds energies, Overcome feelings of loneliness and isolation, Protection, Protection for travelers, Psychic protection, Strengthens all chakra, Transmutes conflict into harmony

Crystal Quartz (Rock Crystal): Amplifies energies of other healing stones, Common but powerful, Excellent meditation stone, Said to have cooling powers, Stone of romance

Danburite: Aids in leaving the past behind, Excellent for relief of stress and worry, Facilitates deep change, Grants restful sleep and lucid dreaming, Karmic cleanser, Opens one to Divine Source, Promotes angelic communication, Stimulates the Heart chakra

Datolite: Connects with higher worlds, Expands the consciousness, Increases personal power, Relieves worries and fears, Retrieves lost memories

Dendrite Agate: Stone of long life and prosperity

Dendritic Limestone (Picture Stone): Symbolizes growth and chance

Diamond: Blocks negative energy flow from wearer, Constancy, Good for coughs and mucus problems, Healing, Innocence, Supplements energy of other gemstones

Diamond, Herkimer: Aids in communicating with other planes, Connects the astral plane with the earth plane, Used in out-of-body travel, Very strong

Diopside
>   **Black Diopside:** Establishes connection, Grounds in the earth
>   **Green Diopside:** Aids in exploration, Balances and heals, Energizes the Third Eye, Expands love on every level, Opens the mind to new concepts

Dioptase: Awakens love and compassion, Awakens the spiritual heart, Heals emotional distress, Heals emotional wounds, Releases emotional patterns, Stimulates forgiveness, Strengthens the physical heart, Supports the emotional heart

Dolomite: Aids in acclimating to new communities, Alleviates negative emotions, Assists with emotional balance and calm, Encourages self-realization, Promotes moderation

Dolphin Stone (Atlantis Stone, Larimar): Awakens feminine power, Balances the energy of fire and water, Cleanses unhealthy emotional blocks, Releases attachments, Relieves stress for pregnant women and new mothers, Soothes the emotions, Stone of healing, Teaches love, respect, and nurturing

Dragonstone (Septarian): Benefits overall health and well-being, Grants relief for muscle spasms, Nurtures and grounds, Opens psychic abilities, Stone of healing

Dravite (Champagne Tourmaline): Aids in finding emotional strength, Brings self-acceptance, Calms and soothes, Grounds one's inner self, Inspires courage and persistence, Stone of self-healing

Dream Stone (Lodalite): Induces visionary experiences and healing, No stone is alike, Stone of journeying

Dreamer's Crystal (Emma's Egg, Seer Stone, Window Quartz): Excellent meditation crystals. Composed of five stones: Amethyst, Clear Crystal, Labradorite, Rose Quartz, Smoky Quartz.

Dumortierite: Aids in overcoming tough situations, Opens the Third Eye chakra, Promotes mental discipline, Stone of learning, Study stone

Elestial Quartz (Orange Elestial): Brings a broader understanding of the past, Excellent meditation stone, Lightens the heart, Often attuned to the angelic realm, Relieves sorrow and depression

Emerald: Brings reason and wisdom, Faithfulness when given to a lover, Friendship, Gem of spring, Love, Sacred stone of the Goddess Venus, Stone of prophecy, Symbol of hope, Symbolizes faith and hope in Christianity, Symbolizes fertilizing rain, Thought to preserve love, Tranquilizes a troubled mind

Emma's Egg (Dreamer's Crystal, Seer Stone, Window Quartz): Excellent meditation crystals. Composed of five stones: Amethyst, Clear Crystal, Labradorite, Rose Quartz, Smoky Quartz.

Epidote (Pistacite, Unakite): Acts as an attraction stone, Brings more of what its wearer is, Cannot increase what is not present, Teaches "You reap what you sow"

Eudialyte: Amplifies the exchange of love, Brings harmony and balance, Dispels jealousy, Opens the mind to new insights, Opens the Root and Heart chakra, Stone of life and love

Eye Agate: Stone of protection against evil

Faden Quartz: Gives stability when working on deeper issues, Heals and repairs, Integrates and activates all chakras, Removes unhealthy emotional attachments, Repairs energy fields

Fairy Cross (Staurolite): Aids in finding lost objects, Good luck charm, Increases connection to other worlds, Opens the inner eye, Protects children from evil spirits

Fairy Stone: Brings good luck to fishermen and hunters, Brings health and prosperity, Lovers offer the most beautiful to their beloved, Protects against evil spirits

Falcon's Eye: Brings a feeling of completeness, Brings good luck and protection, Combines with Topaz to bring wealth and money, Excellent in meditation, Grants insight, Makes one aware of one's own needs, Protection, Stone of the mind

Fire Agate: Stone of peace and serenity

Fire Opal: Cheerfulness, Enthusiasm, Fulfillment of desires, Readiness for action

Fluorite: Absorbs and neutralizes negative emotions, Helps in decision-making, Increases concentration, Known as the "Genius Stone", Order, Self-confidence

Fool's Gold (Pyrite): Associated with the sun, Blocks negative energies, Energizes the area where it's placed, Fortifies and strengthens the mind, Helps one see through a facade, Overcomes inertia and feelings of inadequacy, Symbolizes money and good luck, Wonderful energy shield

Fuchsite (Green Muscovite): Decreases insomnia, Develops a quick wit, Improves self-worth, Inspiration, Intuition, Problem solving, Relieves emotional shock, Resilience

Fulgurite: Enhances the power of prayer, Joins with Divine energy, Opens a channel for intuition and psychic awareness, Purification, Surrenders to Divine intention through prayer

Galena: Assists in healing, Brings the ability to face difficult times, Helps recover personal power, Protection for spiritual journeys, Stone of transformation, Strength and courage, Used to recall past lives

Garnet: Constancy with friendships, Creativity, Enhances self-esteem, Enthusiasm, Luck, New beginnings, Popularity, Protection for travelers, Self-confidence, Solving difficulties, Stamina, Successful business stone

> **Mandarin Garnet** (Orange Garnet, Spessartine): Fortifies self-confidence, Grants hope, Lights one's path to dreams and goals, Provides courage, protections, and blessings, Symbolizes illumination for a dark soul

Gaspeite: Helps with weight loss, Rehabilitates self-love, Releases unhealthy attachments to possessions, Stimulates metabolism, Vision stone

Girasol Quartz: Allows one to clearly think things through, Amplifies one's ability to be creative, Brings a sense of relaxation, Brings balance to one's emotions, Grants calm, peace and optimism

Goethite: Awakens compassion and love, Brings emotional healing, Encourages deep inner journey, Enhances creativity, Stone of discovery, artists, and grief, Used by counselors

Gold Sheen Obsidian: Helps provide direction in life

Goldstone: Stone of energy

> **Blue Goldstone:** Learning and communication
> **Green Goldstone:** Growth and abundance
> **Red Goldstone:** Vitality and energy

Goshenite: Assists in gaining loyalty, Enhances dreams, Stimulates the mind

Green Amethyst (Prasiolite): Assists in bringing spiritual ideals into everyday life, Attracts prosperity, Brings good fortune and luck, Clears negativity, Closes the gap between the physical and spiritual, Fosters compassion, self-acceptance and self-honor, Ignites love and compassion in one's heart, Protects wearer from intoxication, Strengthens emotions, mind and will

Green Aventurine: Increases perception and creative insight, Stone of luck and

chance

Green Calcite: Emotional balance and stress relief

Green Diopside: Aids in exploration, Balances and heals, Energizes the Third Eye, Expands love on every level, Opens the mind to new concepts

Green Garnet (Tsavorite, Uvarovite): Enhances wealth in every respect, Stone of prosperity

Green Gold Gemstone (Lemon Quartz): Brings creativity and organization, Enhances focus on one's goals, Opens creativity and prosperity, Signifies optimism and well-being

Green Goldstone: Growth and abundance

Green Heulandite: Emotional healing of the heart, Overcomes grief and shock, Rekindles compassion, Releases unhealthy emotions

Green Muscovite (Fuchsite): Decreases insomnia, Develops a quick wit, Improves self-worth, Inspiration, Intuition, Problem solving, Relieves emotional shock, Resilience

Green Rhyolite (Rainforest Jasper): Alleviates depression and lethargy, Brings joy for the natural state of things, Celebrates the joy of life, Connects with nature, Used to invigorate or renew one's emotional state

Green Sardonyx: Abundance, fertility, and growth

Green Tourmaline (Verdelite): Attracts money and success in business, Brings a joy for life, Detoxifies and strengthens the heart, Encourages an interest in other human beings, Encourages patience and openness, Promotes an appreciation for life's many wonders, Stimulates creativity, Success

Green Watermelon Tourmaline: Feeds one's life-force

Grossularite: Calms and soothes, Draws away negative energy, Grounds emotions, Stone of health

Halite: Aids in bringing self-love, Aids in cleaning up unhealthy habits, Cleanses the heart of emotional wounds, Clears and resolves spiritual energy, Dissolves confusion and doubt

Hawk's Eye: Brings a feeling of completeness, Brings good luck and protection, Combines with Topaz to bring wealth and money, Excellent in meditation, Grants insight, Makes one aware of one's own needs, Protection, Stone of the mind

Heliotrope Stone (Bloodstone): Brings change, Protects against evil, Symbol of justice

Hematite: Fulfillment of desires, Good for increasing intuition, Has been used to prevent bleeding, Used to improve relationships, Worn when mourning

Hemimorphite: Aids in communicating inner feelings, Aids in seeing projects through to the end, Develops inner strength, Encourages compassion, Increases psychic or vision abilities, Stone of empathy

Herkimer Diamond: Aids in communicating with other planes, Connects the astral plane with the earth plane, Used in out-of-body travel, Very strong

Heulandite: Purifying crystal

    Green Heulandite: Emotional healing of the heart, Overcomes grief and shock, Rekindles compassion, Releases unhealthy emotions

Hiddenite: Aids in experiencing joy and bliss, Aids in mending a bad relationship, Helps soothe the heart, Releases negative energy between individuals, Restores love in one's heart

Himalayan Ice Quartz (Nirvana Quartz): Brings power and healing, Releases blocks and limitations imposed on oneself

Honey Calcite: Persistence and intellectual power

Howlite: Balances calcium levels, Excellent antidote to insomnia, Stone of calming, Strengthens teeth and bones, Teaches patience, Used to relieve all kinds of stress

Hypersthene: Alleviates shyness, Assists with emotional expression, Enhances self-esteem, Puts one at ease in social situations

Idocrase (Vesuvianite): Aids in finding one's true path in life, Aligns truth with daily life, Brings a sense of wholeness and integrity, Encourages enthusiasm for life, Imparts the courage to change, Releases hidden fears, Releases negative attachments

Ilvaite: Assists in developing patience, Can be used to seek truth, Often used to find one's center when meditating, Opens the door to increasing personal perseverance

Imperial Topaz: Fertility, Positive attitude towards life, Self-confidence

Inca Rose Stone (Manganese Spar, Raspberry Spar, Rhodochrosite): Benefits the creative process, Enthusiasm, Excellent conductor of energy, Industriousness, Love, Positive attitude towards life, Promotes intuition, Soothes the heart, Stimulates warm feelings of love and compassion

Indicolite (Blue Tourmaline): Aids in developing psychic ability, Aids in exploring and understanding past lives, Facilitates deep meditation, Offers relief from stress, Opens doors and communication to the spiritual realm, Promotes a calming effect

Infinite Stone (The Healer's Stone): Activates kundalini energy, Increases potency of reiki and other healing energies, Repatterns the auric field

Iolite: Believed to unlock creativity in an artist, Opens the path to one's inner self, Stone of vision and creative expression, Used as a compass

Jade: Brings money into one's life, Dreams, Stone of protection, Used to attract love

   New Jade (Serpentine): Aids in finding one's inner peace, Balances mood swings, Encourages conflict solving through peaceful means, Excellent meditation stone, Guards against disease and sorcery, Protects against poisonous creatures

Jasper

   Leopard Skin Jasper: Aids in healing, Associated with spiritual discovery, Grants emotional healing, Powerful protection stone, Shaman travel and spiritual discovery, Stone of protection

   Mookaite Jasper: Encourages desires for new experiences, Imparts calm while encouraging versatility, Keeps balances between external and internal, Shields wearer from difficult situations, Stone of strength and decision-making

   Ocean Jasper (Orbicular Jasper): Brings a sense of relaxation and peace, Focuses on positive aspects in one's life, Stone of joy, Ups expression of love in words and actions

   Picasso Jasper: Aids in finding the right path, Dissolves creative blocks, Renews lost friendships

   Picture Jasper: Aids in alleviating fear, Encourages creative vision, Promotes feelings of responsibility, Stone of grounding and harmonizing

   Polychrome Jasper: Aids in finding balance, Brings stability, Grounds one's self

   Rainbow Jasper: Protects against the hazards of the night, Stone of protection

   Rainforest Jasper (Green Rhyolite): Alleviates depression and lethargy, Brings joy for the natural state of things, Celebrates the joy of life, Connects with nature, Used to invigorate or renew one's emotional state

   Red Jasper: Balances emotional energy, Grants courage to speak out, Lucky for actors and actresses, Stamina, Stone of protection, Stone of stability

Shell Jasper: Brings relaxation, well-being, and serenity, Rejuvenates and strengthens, Used for balance, Used for protection and grounding

Snowflake Jasper: Reveals and removes hidden imbalances

Tiger Jasper: Brings a sense of personal independence, Courage to speak out, Eases emotional stress

Yellow Jasper: Channels positive energy, Protects during physical travel, Purifies toxins, Stone of protection

Zebra Jasper: Increases one's appreciation for the joys of life, Stimulates transition to the astral plane, Stone of meditating and centering, Stone of stability and grounding

Jet (Lignite): Draws and channels the earth's energies, Neutralizes negative energies, Purifies and protects, Used in magic rituals

Kunzite: Brings good fortune, Devotion, Emits exceptionally tranquil vibrations, Intuition, Logical thinking, Promotes a peaceful disposition, Releases tension, Sign of new life, Sometimes regarded as a symbol for pregnancy, Symbolizes purity

Kyanite: Creates stillness and tranquility, Excellent meditation stone, Restores energy balance

Labradorite: Aids in seeing clearly in meditation, Allows one to see through illusions, Creativity, Develops enthusiasm and new ideas, Enthusiasm, Excellent for strengthening intuition, Goal setting, Intuition, Stimulates imagination, Stone of power

Lapis Lazuli: Bestows wisdom and honesty, Clears the mind, Encourages self-awareness, Friendship, Reveals inner truth, Stone of friendship and love, Stone of meditation, Symbol of truth [Ancient Egypt]

Larimar (Atlantis Stone, Dolphin Stone): Awakens feminine power, Balances the energy of fire and water, Cleanses unhealthy emotional blocks, Releases attachments, Relieves stress for pregnant women and new mothers, Soothes the emotions, Stone of healing, Teaches love, respect, and nurturing

Lazulite: Aids in solving problems, Aids with headaches, migraines, and reduced vision, Helps one focus, Increases brain function, Increases one's psychic abilities, Makes dreams more vivid and meaningful, Strengthens one's self-discipline and focus, Strengthens self-discipline

Lazurite: Clears the mind, One of the most powerful stones, Used as a symbol of truth

Lemon Quartz (Green Gold Gemstone): Brings creativity and organization, Enhances focus on one's goals, Opens creativity and prosperity, Signifies optimism and well-being

Lemurian Seed Crystal: Brings a connection with the Divine Feminine, Imparts a sense of oneness and unity, Opens access to ancient wisdom and knowledge, Unifies the soul

Leopard Skin Jasper: Aids in healing, Associated with spiritual discovery, Grants emotional healing, Powerful protection stone, Shaman travel and spiritual discovery, Stone of protection

Leopardite: Aids in releasing the judgment of self and others, Assists in letting go of conflict and insecurity, Connects with one's inner wisdom, Promotes acceptance and understanding

Lepidocrocite: Attracts good luck to those who carry it, Calms symptoms of

ADHD and hyperactivity, Drives away negativity, Encourages independence, Goal setting, Helps in attaining goals inconspicuously, Logical thinking, Promotes restful sleep when placed near one's pillow, Protection, Protection from outside influences, Relieves everyday stress, Strengthens one's ability to let go of fear and anxiety

Lepidolite: Attracts good luck to those who carry it, Calms symptoms of ADHD and hyperactivity, Drives away negativity, Encourages independence, Goal setting, Helps in attaining goals inconspicuously, Logical thinking, Promotes restful sleep when placed near one's pillow, Protection, Protection from outside influences, Relieves every day stress, Strengthens one's ability to let go of fear and anxiety

Lignite (Jet): Draws and channels the earth's energies, Neutralizes negative energies, Purifies and protects, Used in magic rituals

Lithium Quartz: Activates the Heart and Third Eye chakra, Awakens one's Higher Self, Brings harmony to relationships, Enhances deep meditation, Releases one from tension

Lodalite (Dream Stone): Induces visionary experiences and healing, No stone is alike, Stone of journeying

Lodestone (Magnetite): Aids telepathy, meditation, and visualization, Attracts love, commitment, and loyalty, Balances the intellect with inner emotions, Brings about stability, Has a powerful positive-negative polarity, Offers relief from negative emotions, Strengthens trust in one's own intuitions

Luvulite (Sugilite): Aids forgiveness by eliminating hostility, Brings light and love to the darkest situations, Clears disappointments and relieves spiritual tension, Protects the soul from shock and trauma, Represents spiritual love and wisdom, Stone of love, Teaches and protects in matters of spiritual quests, Teaches and protects love and forgiveness

Magnetite (Lodestone): Aids telepathy, meditation and visualization, Attracts love, commitment, and loyalty, Balances the intellect with inner emotions, Brings about stability, Has a powerful positive-negative polarity, Offers relief from negative emotions, Strengthens trust in one's own intuitions

Mahogany Obsidian: Grounds and protects its owner

Malachite: Aids success in business, Friendship, Fulfillment of desires, Grants protection to travelers, Luck, Positive attitude towards life, Protects against undesirable business associations, Protects wearer from accidents, Reflects the inner feelings of the soul, Stone of balance for relationships, Strong protector of children

Mandarin Garnet (Orange Garnet, Spessartine): Fortifies self-confidence, Grants hope, Lights one's path to dreams and goals, Provides courage, protections, and blessings, Symbolizes illumination for a dark soul

Manganese Spar (Inca Rose Stone, Raspberry Spar, Rhodochrosite): Benefits the creative process, Enthusiasm, Excellent conductor of energy, Industriousness, Love, Positive attitude towards life, Promotes intuition, Soothes the heart, Stimulates warm feelings of love and compassion

Melody's Stone (Sacred Seven, Super Seven): Enhance the power of psychic abilities, Extremely powerful and special stone, Never needs cleansing, recharging, or energizing. Made of seven stones: Amethyst, Cacoxenite, Crystal Quartz, Goethite, Lepidocrocite, Rutilated Quartz, and Smoky Quartz.

Merlinite: Achieves balance between light and dark, Develops past life recall, Learns magic, Opens the door to communication with the deceased, Used in shamanic work, magic rituals, and healing

Mochi Marbles (Moqui, Shamatic Star Stones, Thunderballs): Excellent tools for vibrational healing, Excellent tools in Shamanic journeys, Helps in meditation, Helps unblock psychic visions, Relieves physical discomfort, Stones of harmony and balance

Moldavite: Accelerates one's spiritual path, Awakens the intelligence of the heart, Clears blockages, Disconnects one from unhealthy attachments, Increases synchronicity, Makes dreams more vivid and meaningful, Spiritual catalyst, Widely effective in metaphysical practice

Mookaite Jasper: Encourages desires for new experiences, Imparts calm while encouraging versatility, Keeps balances between external and internal, Shields wearer from difficult situations, Stone of strength and decision-making

Moonstone: Assists in telling the future, Brings good fortune, Brings success in love as well as business matters, Enhances intuition, Fertility, Gifts passion, Intuition, Love, Luck, Offers protection on land and at sea, Promotes inspiration

Moqui (Mochi Marbles, Shamanic Star Stones, Thunderballs): Excellent tools for vibrational healing, Excellent tools in Shamanic journeys, Helps in meditation, Helps unblock psychic visions, Relieves physical discomfort, Stone of harmony and balance

Morganite (Pink Beryl): Aids in developing trust, Attracts love and maintains it, Brings a sense of joy and inner strength, Helps release unhealthy emotional patterns, Stone of Divine Love

Moss Agate: Stone of warriors

Muscovite

    Green Muscovite (Fuchsite): Decreases insomnia, Develops a quick wit, Improves self-worth, Inspiration, Intuition, Problem solving, Relieves emotional shock, Resilience

    Yellow Muscovite (Star Mica): Decreases insomnia, Develops a quick wit, Improves self-worth, Increases resilience, Relieves emotional shock, Stone of inspiration, problem solving, and intuition

Moonstone

New Jade (Serpentine): Aids in finding one's inner peace, Balances mood swings, Encourages conflict solving through peaceful means, Excellent meditation stone, Guards against disease and sorcery, Protects against poisonous creatures, Protection

Nirvana Quartz (Himalayan Ice Quartz): Brings power and healing, Releases blocks and limitations imposed on oneself

Nuummite: Develops self-love and acceptance, Draws on deep earth energy, Enhances intuition, Facilitates journey to discovery of inner self, Increases opportunities for personal good fortune, Stone of personal power

Obsidian
  Apache Tears Obsidian: Clears one's auric field
  Aqua Blue Obsidian: Helps align one to their goals
  Black Obsidian: Gets rid of negative energies
  Gold Sheen Obsidian: Helps provide direction in one's life

Mahogany Obsidian: Grounds and protects its owner

Rainbow Obsidian: Grants protection, Sharpens the senses

Snowflake Obsidian: Reveals and removes hidden imbalances

Ocean Jasper (Orbicular Jasper): Brings a sense of relaxation and peace, Focuses on positive aspects in one's life, Stone of joy, Ups expression of love in words and actions

Ohio Celestite: Enhances inspiration and learning skills, Gentle, yet strong, Increases discipline, Opens the Third Eye to higher dimensions, Strengthens psychic capabilities

Onyx: Courage, Encourages a healthy ego, Fortifies self-confidence and responsibility, Releases negative emotions, Sharpens the senses, Used to end unhappy or bothersome relationships

Opal: Balances all chakras, Healing, Leads one to higher spiritual awareness, Most powerful healing stone, Queen of gems, Stone of hope, great achievement, and good luck, Stone of sexual attractiveness, Stone of the Gods

Fire Opal: Cheerfulness, Enthusiasm, Fulfillment of desires, Readiness for action

Opalite: Has a soft, gentle, and soothing effect, Placed on the Crown chakra to enhance vision, Stabilizes mood swings

Orange Calcite: Creativity, sexuality, and confidence

Orange Elestial (Elestial Quartz): Brings a broader understanding of the past, Excellent meditation stone, Lightens the heart, Often attuned to the angelic realm, Relieves sorrow and depression

Orange Garnet (Mandarin Garnet, Spessartine): Fortifies self-confidence, Grants hope, Lights one's path to dreams and goals, Provides courage, protections, and blessings, Symbolizes illumination for a dark soul

Orbicular Jasper (Ocean Jasper): Brings a sense of relaxation and peace, Focuses on positive aspects in one's life, Stone of joy, Ups expression of love in words and actions

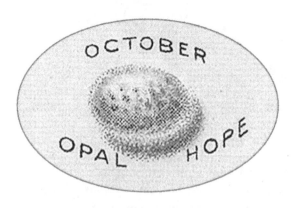

Peach Selenite: Brings self-awareness and understanding, Stone of emotional healing

Peacock Ore (Chalcopyrite): Increases ability to perceive, Makes an excellent meditation stone, Opens and cleans Crown chakra, Used to break up energy blockages

Pearl: Amplifies focus, meditation skills, and wisdom, Encloses oneself with a sense of calm and beauty, Helps balance the Solar Plexus chakra, Helps with stomach, digestion, and emotional stress, Peace, Promotes prosperity and success, Stimulates spiritual transformation, Used in deep meditation

Peridot: Considered a gift of Mother Nature, Considered sacred by early Christians, Friendship, Stone of springtime, Symbol of undying love and admiration, Symbolizes impending danger when dreamed of, Symbolizes purity and morality

Petalite: Brings about relaxation during meditation, Brings self-acceptance and self-love, Emits profound peace and joy, Heals emotional trauma, Protects and balances, Stone of vision

Petrified Wood: Aids in reaching troublesome goals, Connection with the earth, Good at relieving hip and back problems, Helps restore physical energy, Intuition, Powerful in removing obstacles, Smooths a path ridden with difficult obstacles

Phenacite: Activates psychic abilities, Facilitates inner vision, Increases prophetic vision, Links the Third eye and Crown chakras, Opens the path to new levels of growth and understanding, Promotes communication with angels, Stimulates prosperity and financial abundance, Used to clear the auric field

Picasso Jasper: Aids in finding the right path, Dissolves creative blocks, Renews lost friendships

Picture Jasper: Aids in alleviating fear, Encourages creative vision, Promotes feelings of responsibility, Stone of grounding and harmonizing

Picture Stone (Dendritic Limestone): Symbolizes growth and chance

Pietersite: Excellent meditation stone, Links daily consciousness to the spiritual, Recognizes truth, Stone of vision, Strengthens inner guidance, Supports willpower, The Tempest Stone

Pink Beryl (Morganite): Aids in developing trust, Attracts love and maintains it, Brings a sense of joy and inner strength, Helps to release unhealthy emotional patterns, Stone of Divine Love

Pink Calcite: Well-being, empathy, and health

Pink Tourmaline (Rubellite): Associated with feminine energies, Brings feelings of safety and comfort, Can heal emotional wounds, Gentle stone that directly touches the heart, Love and friendship, Relaxes and nurtures, Vibrates a deep resonance with Heart chakra

Pink Watermelon Tourmaline: Soothes and harmonizes

Pistacite (Epidote, Unakite): Acts as an attraction stone, Brings more of what its wearer is, Cannot increase what is not present, Teaches "You reap what you sow"

Polychrome Jasper: Aids in finding balance, Brings stability, Grounds one's self

Porcupine Quartz: Aids in merging with one's Higher Self, Aids in releasing fear, Balances the Crown chakra, Harmonizes aura, chakra points, and physical body, Purifies and protects

Porphyry (Chinese Writing Stone): Accepts and adjusts to change, Accesses Akashic records, Promotes peaceful dreaming, Reaffirms relationships, commitments, and loyalties, Realigns goals towards a higher purpose, Sparks creativity, Stone of re-affirmation

Prasiolite (Green Amethyst): Assists in bringing spiritual ideals into everyday life, Attracts prosperity, Brings good fortune and luck, Clears negativity, Closes the gap between the physical & spiritual, Fosters compassion, self-acceptance, and self-honor, Ignites love and compassion in one's heart, Protects wearer from intoxication, Strengthens emotions, mind, and will

Prehnite: Aids in recognizing truths, Connects the will and the heart, Enhances inner knowledge, Stone of meditation, Stone of unconditional love, Strengthens one's intuition

Purpurite: Aids in repairing mistakes and emotional damage, Encourages acceptance, Encourages insight and truth, Integrates skills with thoughts and ideas, Purifies energy fields, Stone of calming

Pyrite (Fool's Gold): Associated with the sun, Blocks negative energies, Energizes the area where it's placed, Fortifies and strengthens the mind, Helps one see through a facade, Overcomes inertia and feelings of inadequacy, Symbolizes money and good luck, Wonderful energy shield

Quantum Quattro Silica: Aids in finding love and money, Aligns all chakras, Bolsters the immune system, Brings mental clarity if placed on the Third Eye, Heals grief from past trauma

Quartz

Amethyst Spirit Quartz (Cactus Quartz, Porcupine Quartz): Aids in merging with one's Higher Self, Aids in releasing fear, Balances the crown chakra, Harmonizes aura, chakra points, and physical body, Purifies and protects

Angel Aura Quartz: Channels higher knowledge, Finds one's personal purpose, Opens awareness to the angelic domain, Opens the Throat chakra, Promotes joy, light, and optimism, Used in deep meditation

Aqua Aura Quartz: Enhances ability to communicate inner truth, Expresses emotions in a positive way, Safeguards against psychological attacks, Stimulates Throat chakra

Blue Quartz: Assists in the ability to reach out to others, Assuages fear, Calms the mind, Helps one understand one's spiritual nature, Inspires hope, Soothing, stress-relief stone

Cactus Quartz (Amethyst Spirit Quartz, Porcupine Quartz): Aids in merging with one's Higher Self, Aids in releasing fear, Balances the Crown chakra, Harmonizes aura, chakra points, and physical body, Purifies and protects

Candle Quartz: Brings abundance, Brings one's totem spirit guide closer, Helps focus on a true path and purpose, Promotes tranquility, Radiates love

Celestial Aura Quartz: Brings a sense of unity and self-understanding, Develops the ability to share and teach knowledge, Practice trust of others, Purifies, Remains true to one's path

Crystal Quartz (Rock Crystal): Amplifies energies of other healing stones, Common but powerful, Excellent meditation stone, Said to have cooling powers, Stone of romance

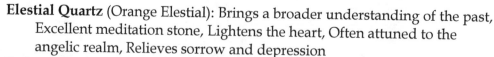

Elestial Quartz (Orange Elestial): Brings a broader understanding of the past, Excellent meditation stone, Lightens the heart, Often attuned to the angelic realm, Relieves sorrow and depression

Faden Quartz: Gives stability when working on deeper issues, Heals and repairs, Integrates and activates all chakras, Removes unhealthy emotional attachments, Repairs energy fields

Girasol Quartz: Allows one to clearly think things through, Amplifies one's ability to be creative, Brings a sense of relaxation, Brings balance to one's emotion, Calm, relaxed, hopeful and optimistic, Grants calm, peace, and optimism, Increases control over impulsive behavior

Himalayan Ice Quartz (Nirvana Quartz): Brings power and healing, Releases blocks and limitations imposed on oneself

Lemon Quartz (Green Gold Gemstone): Brings creativity and organization, Enhances focus on one's goals, Opens creativity and prosperity, Signifies optimism and well-being

Lithium Quartz: Activates the Heart and Third Eye chakra, Awakens one's Higher Self, Brings harmony to relationships, Enhances deep meditation, Releases one from tension

Nirvana Quartz (Himalayan Ice Quartz): Brings power and healing, Releases blocks and limitations imposed on oneself

Porcupine Quartz (Amethyst Spirit Quartz, Cactus Quartz): Aids in merging with one's Higher Self, Aids in releasing fear, Balances the Crown chakra, Harmonizes aura, chakra points, and physical body, Purifies and protects

Red Rutilated Quartz: Acts as an anti-depressant, Brings new hope, Helps develop vision for the bigger picture, Relief from anxiety

Rose Quartz: Aids in looking younger, Brings a strong feeling of self-worth, Fertility, Love, Stone of love in marriage, Stone of universal love

Smoky Quartz: Brings creativity in business, Harmony, Opens the path for perception and learning, Promotes personal pride and joy in living, Protection, Stone of endurance, Stone of protection against negative energies

Strawberry Quartz: Amplifies loving and generous intentions, Brings balance to one's emotions

Tangerine Aura Quartz: Directs energy to where it's most beneficial, Helps one recognize one's unique gifts, Leads one to a more positive outlook on life, Promotes drive and enthusiasm, Stone of healing with trauma and shock, Used in past life healing, Used to boost self confidence, Used to enhance sexuality and creativity

Tibetan Black Quartz: Activates and balances the chakras, Brings rapid expansion of the consciousness, Cleanses and purifies living spaces, Excellent meditation stone, Powerful stone of protection

Tourmalated Quartz: Assists with clear thinking, Clears energy patterns, Peace of mind, Protects from unhealthy energies, Super good luck

Window Quartz (Dreamer's Crystal, Emma's Egg, Seer Stone): Excellent meditation stone. Composed of five crystals: Amethyst, Clear Crystal, Labradorite, Rose Quartz, Smoky Quartz.

Quartz Crystal (Angel Aura Quartz): Channels higher knowledge, Finds one's personal purpose, Opens awareness to the angelic domain, Opens the Throat chakra, Promotes joy, light, and optimism, Used in deep meditation

Rainbow Jasper: Protects against the hazards of the night, Stone of protection

Rainbow Obsidian: Grants protection, Sharpens the senses

Rainforest Jasper (Green Rhyolite): Alleviates depression and lethargy, Brings joy for the natural state of things, Celebrates the joy of life, Connects with nature, Used to invigorate or renew one's emotional state

Raspberry Spar (Inca Rose Stone, Manganese Spar, Rhodochrosite): Benefits the creative process, Enthusiasm, Excellent conductor of energy, Industriousness, Love, Positive attitude towards life, Promotes intuition, Soothes the heart, Stimulates warm feelings of love and compassion

Red Aventurine: Aids in seeing the possibilities in opportunities, Assists in creativity, Opens the Root chakra

Red Calcite: Vitality

Red Goldstone: Vitality and energy

Red Jasper: Balances emotional energy, Grants courage to speak out, Lucky for actors and actresses, Stamina, Stone of protection, Stone of stability

Red Rutilated Quartz: Acts as an anti-depressant, Brings new hope, Helps develop vision for the bigger picture, Relief from anxiety

Rhodochrosite (Inca Rose Stone, Manganese Spar, Raspberry Spar): Benefits the creative process, Enthusiasm, Excellent conductor of energy, Industriousness, Love, Positive attitude towards life, Promotes intuition, Soothes the heart, Stimulates warm feelings of love and compassion

Rhodonite: Brings a sense of well-being, Fertility, Friendship, Promotes relaxation, Readiness for action, Soothes the nervous system, Stone of balance, Used to clear one's psychic centers, Vibrates with love

Rock Crystal (Crystal Quartz): Amplifies energies of other healing stones, Common but powerful, Excellent meditation stone, Said to have cooling powers, Stone of romance

Rose Quartz: Aids in looking younger, Brings a strong feeling of self-worth, Fertility, Love, Stone of love in marriage, Stone of universal love

Rubellite (Pink Tourmaline): Associated with feminine energies, Brings feelings of safety and comfort, Can heal emotional wounds, Gentle stone that directly touches the heart, Love and friendship, Relaxes and nurtures, Vibrates a deep resonance with Heart chakra

Ruby: Associated with many astral signs, Considered to be the most powerful gem, Contentment and peace, Courage to be one's best, Filled with love, Grants pleasant dreams, Helps sexual love be passionate, Love, Protection, Symbol of love and friendship when gifted, Symbol of vanity and royalty, Uses life-force to provide protection to wearer, Wards off bad dreams

Sacred Seven (Melody's Stone, Super Seven): Enhance the power of psychic abilities, Extremely powerful and special stone, Never needs cleansing, recharging, or energizing. Made of seven stones: Amethyst, Cacoxenite, Crystal Quartz, Goethite, Lepidocrocite, Rutilated Quartz, and Smoky Quartz.

Sapphire: Associated with Aquarius, Virgo, Libra, and Capricorn, Contributes to mental clarity and perception, Promotes financial rewards, Stone of destiny, Symbol of Heaven and devotion to God, Symbol of Saturn and Venus

Sardonyx: Attracts good friends and fortune, Believed to bring lasting happiness, Enhances willpower, integrity, stamina, and vigor, Prevents crime and misfortune, Protects

> **Green Sardonyx**: Abundance, fertility, growth

Scapolite: Aids in focusing on a goal and seeing it through, Assists in developing willpower, Develops self-discipline, Overcomes limitations in one's personal power, Stone of purpose and destiny

> **White Scapolite**: Clears Crown chakra, Used when working with astral planes

Schorl (Black Tourmaline): Brings luck and happiness, Logical thinking, Luck and happiness, Powerful stone of healing, Protection

Scolecite: Aids with lucid dreaming and restful sleep, Creates a heart-to-heart connection between lovers, Enhances one's dream state, Enhances the Heart chakra energies, Excellent meditation stone, Facilitates dream recall, Opens the door to spontaneous expressions of love, Promotes inner peace and deep relaxation

Sedona Vortex Stone: Enhances vitality and grounding, Excellent meditation stone, Harmonizes one's emotions, Helps with contacting spirit guides, Increases access to spiritual planes, Perfect dream-stones

Seer Stone (Dreamer's Crystal, Emma's Egg, Window Quartz): Excellent meditation stone. Composed of five crystals: Amethyst, Clear Crystal,

Labradorite, Rose Quartz, Smoky Quartz.

Selenite: Brings about reconciliation between lovers, Brings mental clarity, Helps one access angelic guidance, Instills a deep peace, Makes a wonderful protection stone, Quickly unblocks stagnant energy

Peach Selenite: Brings self-awareness and understanding, Stone of emotional healing

Septarian (Dragonstone): Benefits overall health and well-being, Grants relief for muscle spasms, Nurtures and grounds, Opens psychic abilities, Stone of healing

Seraphinite: Brings greater awareness of the Divine Feminine, Connects the physical and angelic realms, Encourages living from the heart, Promotes regeneration and self-healing, Restores health and balance, Used to establish connections to the angelic realm

Serpentine (New Jade): Aids in finding one's inner peace, Balances mood swings, Encourages conflict solving through peaceful means, Excellent meditation stone, Guards against disease and sorcery, Protects against poisonous creatures, Protection

Shamanic Star Stones (Mochi, Moqui Marbles, Thunderballs): Excellent tools for vibrational healing, Excellent tools in Shamanic journeys, Helps in meditation, Helps unblock psychic visions, Relieves physical discomfort, Stone of harmony and balance

Shattuckite: Aligns one's life with the truth, Gives greater intuition and oracle skills, Good for public speakers, attorneys, and teachers, Increases ability to receive and express truth, Stone of truth, wisdom, and communication

Shell Jasper: Brings relaxation, well-being, and serenity, Rejuvenates and strengthens, Used for balance, Used for protection and grounding

Shiva Lingam: Activates kundalini energy, Boosts vitality, Breaks up old patterns and opens the path for new life, Charges the chakra system, Enhances inner transformation

Shu Fa Stone: Healing, Lightens rooms, Money, Personal power

Shungite: Healing and antibacterial properties, Induces recovery, Promotes growth in living organisms, Protects from harmful electromagnetic radiation, Purifies water, Stone of life, Stone of rejuvenation

Silver: Blocks negative energies, Brings calm, peace, and focus, Brings one in tune with the vibrations of the universe, Facilitates calm and balance, Helps to manifest wealth, Resonates energies from other stones, Uses the moon's energy to protect against negativity, Wonderful energy shield

Smoky Quartz: Brings creativity in business, Harmony, Opens the path for perception and learning, Promotes personal pride and joy in living, Protection, Stone of endurance, Stone of protection against negative energies

Snakeskin Agate: Stone of strength and stealth

Snowflake Jasper: Reveals and removes hidden imbalances

Sodalite: Brings extra luck for writers, Brings inner peace, Harmonizes the inner being, Order, Promotes peace and harmony, Stimulates endurance, Stone of athletics

Spectrolite: Aids in seeing through illusions, Awakens one's magical power, Determines the actual form of one's dreams and goals, Enhances awareness of higher realms, Excellent at strengthening intuition, Promotes synchronicity and opportunity, Stone of power

Spessartine (Mandarin Garnet, Orange Garnet): Fortifies self-confidence, Grants hope, Lights one's path to dreams and goals, Provides courage, protection, and blessings, Symbolizes illumination for a dark soul

Sphaerocobaltite (Cobaltoan Calcite): Aids in making friends and activating Heart chakra, Allows freer communication, Brings awareness of one's own body language, Coordinates release of buried emotions, Dispels negative ones, Encourages positive emotions, Increases harmony when working in a group, Said to be crystals of joy, Stone of love

Sphalerite: Aids in sexual energy and creative pursuits, Enhances perceptions to determine the truth, Increases energy in athletes and physical training, Mineral of strength, vitality, and grounding, Used to balance and ground higher and lower chakras

Sphene (Titanite): Aids in removing negative energy, Aligns the spiritual, emotional, and mental bodies, Calm the emotions and soothes the heart, Good for calming the mind, Stimulates healing and improves health

Spinel (Often confused for a Ruby, but is not one): Friendship, Known as the Daughter of the Ruby, Protects wearer from harm, Reconciles differences, Soothes away sadness

Stalactites: Aids in the secret expansion of the inner self, Associated with hidden inner growth

Star Mica (Yellow Muscovite): Decreases insomnia, Develops a quick wit, Improves self-worth, Increases resilience, Relieves emotional shock, Stone of inspiration, problem solving, and intuition

Staurolite (Fairy Cross): Aids in finding lost objects, Good luck charm, Increases connection to other worlds, Opens the inner eye, Protects children from evil spirits

Stromatolites: Brings resilience and versatility, Brings steadfast persistence, Connects one to the essence of life, Record of emerging life, Stabilizes

Stibnite: Brings new opportunity, great wealth, and power, Emanates energies of rebirth and transformation, Stone of prosperity

Stichtite: Aids in emotional and physical resurgence to health, Brings love and compassion, Helps soften stubborn attitudes, Stone of forgiveness, rescue, and recovery

Stilbite: Aids in achieving mental balance, Assists in restful sleep and vivid dreaming, Balances and clears Heart chakra, Brings a calming influence, Brings inner peace during meditation, Discovers one's true dreams and desires, Enhances one's ability to learn, Opens the Heart chakra if used with Cavansite, Stimulates the expansion

of the mind

Strawberry Quartz: Amplifies loving and generous intentions, Brings balance to one's emotions

Sugilite (Luvulite): Aids forgiveness by eliminating hostility, Brings light and love to the darkest situations, Clears disappointments and relieves spiritual tension, Protects the soul from shocks and trauma, Represents spiritual love and wisdom, Stone of love, Teaches and protects in matters of spiritual quests, Teaches and protects love and forgiveness

Sulfur: A negative electrical charge, Absorbs negative emotions and energies, Assists in constructive change, Calms a rebellious or stubborn side of a personality, Removes negativity of any kind

Sunstone: Gives one extra energy when one is ill or under stress, Increases self-healing power, Luck, Magicians called upon the influences of the sun, Positive attitude towards life, Promotes harmony with one's body, Self-confidence, Stimulates sexual arousal and increases sexual energy, Stone of protection

Super Seven (Melody's Stone, Sacred Seven): Enhances the power of psychic abilities, Extremely powerful and special stone, Never needs cleansing, recharging, or energizing. Made of seven stones: Amethyst, Cacoxenite, Crystal Quartz, Goethite, Lepidocrocite, Rutilated Quartz, and Smoky Quartz.

Talc: Brings good fortune, Enhances purity of thought and clarity of the mind, Stone of good luck

Tangerine Aura Quartz: Directs energy to where it's most beneficial, Helps one recognize one's unique gifts, Leads one to a more positive outlook on life, Promotes drive and enthusiasm, Stone of healing with trauma and shock, Used in past life healing, Used to boost self confidence, Used to enhance sexuality and creativity

Tanzanite (Blue Zoisite): Aids in speaking the truth, Brings a peaceful understanding of one's own heart, Calms an overactive mind, Promotes compassion, Raises consciousness in meditation, Stone of communication, Used in deep meditation

Tektite: Brings financial prosperity, increased sales and profits, Grants good luck, Heightens psychic sensitivity and psychic travel, Increases energy fields, Inspires new ideas, Opens and clears the lower chakras

Thunderballs (Mochi, Moqui Marbles, Shamanic Star Stones): Excellent tools for vibrational healing, Excellent tools in Shamanic journeys, Helps in meditation, Helps unblock psychic visions, Relieves physical discomfort, Stone of harmony and balance

Tibetan Black Quartz: Activates and balances the chakras, Brings rapid expansion of the consciousness, Cleanses and purifies living spaces, Excellent meditation stone, Powerful stone of protection

Tiger's Eye: Brings a feeling of completeness, Brings good luck and protection, Combines with Topaz to bring wealth and money, Excellent in meditation, Grants insight, Makes one aware of one's own needs, Protection, Stone of the mind

Tiger Iron: Encourages creative expression, Excellent for those building strength, Focuses one's will and mental clarity, Reinforces health patterns, Stone of courage, strength, and stamina, Very powerful grounding and protecting stone

Tiger Jasper: Brings a sense of personal independence, Courage to speak out,

Eases emotional stress

Titanite (Sphene): Aids in removing negative energy, Aligns the spiritual, emotional, and mental bodies, Calm the emotions and soothes the heart, Good for calming the mind, Stimulates healing and improves health

Topaz: Aids against negative magic and death, Bestows charisma, Combines with Tiger's Eye to bring wealth and money, Draws in love, Encourages self-realization and confidence, Grants pleasant dreams, Protects wearer against envy and disease, Quiets wild emotions, Wards off bad dreams

    Imperial Topaz: Fertility, Positive attitude towards life, Self-confidence

Tourmalated Quartz: Assists with clear thinking, Clears energy patterns, Peace of mind, Protects from unhealthy energies, Super good luck

Tourmaline: Creativity, Devotion

    Black Tourmaline (Schorl): Brings luck and happiness, Logical thinking, Luck and happiness, Powerful stone of healing, Protection

    Blue Tourmaline (Indicolite): Aids in developing psychic ability, Aids in exploring and understanding past lives, Facilitates deep meditation, Offers relief from stress, Opens doors and communication to the spiritual realm, Promotes a calming effect

    Champagne Tourmaline (Dravite): Aids in finding emotional strength, Brings self-acceptance, Calms and soothes, Grounds one's inner self, Inspires courage and persistence, Stone of self-healing

    Green Tourmaline (Verdelite): Attracts money and success in business, Brings a joy for life, Detoxifies and stregthens the heart, Encourages an interest in other human beings, Encourages patience and openness, Promotes an appreciation for life's many wonders, Stimulates creativity, Success

    Green Watermelon Tourmaline: Feeds one's life-force

    Pink Tourmaline (Rubellite): Associated with feminine energies, Brings feelings of safety and comfort, Can heal emotional wounds, Gentle stone that directly touches the heart, Love and friendship, Relaxes and nurtures, Vibrates a deep resonance with the Heart chakra

    Pink Watermelon Tourmaline: Soothes and harmonizes

    Watermelon Tourmaline: Attracts love, Balances the male and feminine energies within, Friendship, Goal setting, Love, Protection, Removes imbalances and guilt

Tree Agate: Stone of awareness and understanding

Tsavorite (Green Garnet, Uvarovite): Enhances wealth in every respect, Stone of prosperity

Turritella Agate: Stone of self-acceptance and inner peace

Turquoise: Brings great fortune, Brings peace to one's home, Brings strength and protection from harm, Carries wisdom of basic truth, Foresight, Increases psychic sensitivity, Intuition, Luck, Protection, Protects wearer from negative energy, Readiness for action, Serenity, Symbol of friendship, Takes on properties of its owner

Ulexite: Clears fatigue and double vision, Element of wind, Gives one a clear vision of all levels of reality, Helps heal and balance natural psychic vision, Helps unblock psychic visions, Stimulates creativity and the imagination, Stone of clairvoyance

Unakite (Epidote, Pistacite): Acts as an attraction stone, Brings more of what its wearer is, Cannot increase what is not present, Teaches "You reap what you sow"

Uvarovite (Green Garnet, Tsavorite): Enhances wealth in every respect, Stone of prosperity

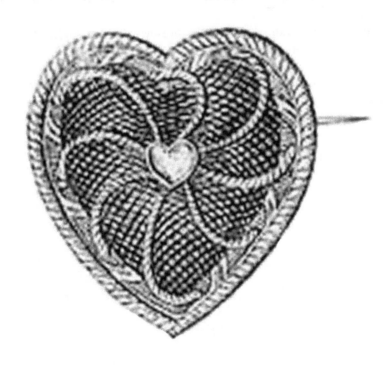

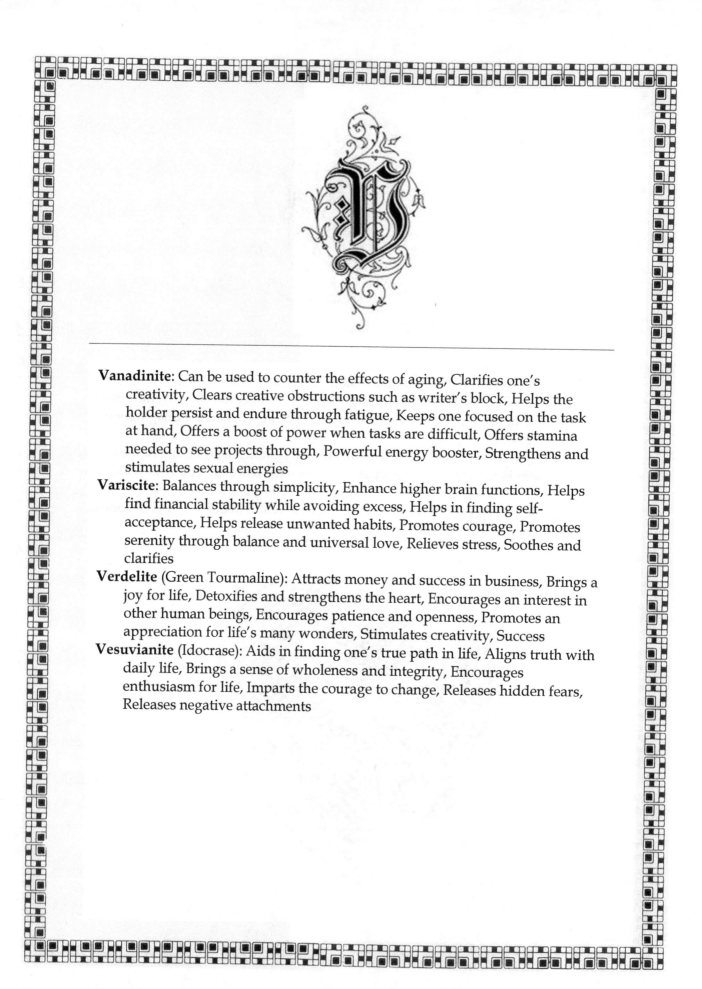

Vanadinite: Can be used to counter the effects of aging, Clarifies one's creativity, Clears creative obstructions such as writer's block, Helps the holder persist and endure through fatigue, Keeps one focused on the task at hand, Offers a boost of power when tasks are difficult, Offers stamina needed to see projects through, Powerful energy booster, Strengthens and stimulates sexual energies

Variscite: Balances through simplicity, Enhance higher brain functions, Helps find financial stability while avoiding excess, Helps in finding self-acceptance, Helps release unwanted habits, Promotes courage, Promotes serenity through balance and universal love, Relieves stress, Soothes and clarifies

Verdelite (Green Tourmaline): Attracts money and success in business, Brings a joy for life, Detoxifies and strengthens the heart, Encourages an interest in other human beings, Encourages patience and openness, Promotes an appreciation for life's many wonders, Stimulates creativity, Success

Vesuvianite (Idocrase): Aids in finding one's true path in life, Aligns truth with daily life, Brings a sense of wholeness and integrity, Encourages enthusiasm for life, Imparts the courage to change, Releases hidden fears, Releases negative attachments

Watermelon Tourmaline: Attracts love, Balances the male and feminine energies within, Friendship, Goal setting, Love, Protection, Removes imbalances and guilt
　Green Watermelon Tourmaline: Feeds one's life-force
　Pink Watermelon Tourmaline: Soothes and harmonizes
Wavellite: Balances one's energy flow, Enhances and improves decision-making, Helps energy flow freely, Improves intuition, Supports decisions that require attention to detail
White Agate: Stone of protection
White Calcite: Cleanses and heals
White Scapolite: Clears Crown chakra, Used when working with astral planes
Window Quartz (Emma's Egg, Dreamer's Crystal, Seer Stone): Excellent meditation stone. Composed of five crystals: Amethyst, Clear Crystal, Labradorite, Rose Quartz, Smoky Quartz.
Wulfenite: Boosts one's creativity as an artist, Brings new ideas and concepts, Enhances sexual function and pleasure, Heals past-life relationships and issues, Helps stimulate metabolism, Stone of originality

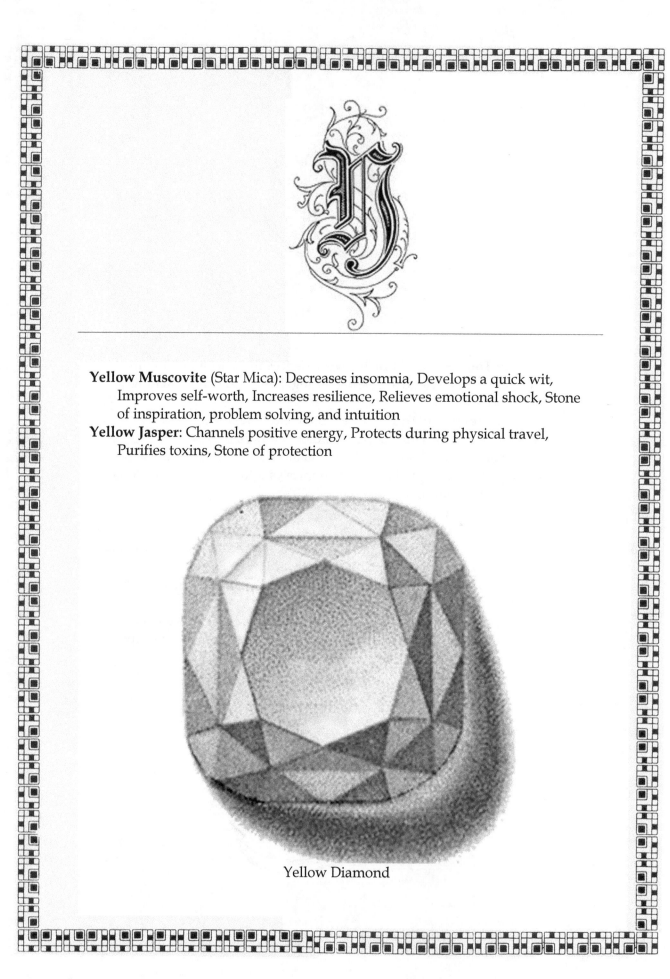

Yellow Muscovite (Star Mica): Decreases insomnia, Develops a quick wit, Improves self-worth, Increases resilience, Relieves emotional shock, Stone of inspiration, problem solving, and intuition

Yellow Jasper: Channels positive energy, Protects during physical travel, Purifies toxins, Stone of protection

Yellow Diamond

Zebra Jasper: Increases one's appreciation for the joys of life, Stimulates transition to the astral plane, Stone of meditating and centering, Stone of stability and grounding

Zeolite: Absorbs toxins and odors, Assists garden fertility when buried, Creates fields of protection, Detoxifies, Enhances healing responses

Zincite: Aids in effective communication, Grants clear insight and creativity, Stone of creativity and imagination

Zircon: Aids in overcoming depleted energy, Balances dreams with reality, Cleanses toxins from the body, Energizes all chakras, Harmonizes one's dreams and goals with reality, Helps one focus on maintaining goals, Powerful grounding stone, Provides spiritual protection

Meanings
to
Gemstones

Absorbs and neutralizes negative emotions: Fluorite
Absorbs negative emotions and energies: Sulfur
Absorbs negative energy and dissipates it: Chalcedony
Absorbs toxins and odors: Zeolite
Accelerates one's spiritual path: Moldavite
Accepts and adjusts to change: Porphyry (Chinese Writing Stone)
Accesses Akashic records: Porphyry (Chinese Writing Stone)
Achieves balance between light and dark: Merlinite
Activates and aligns chakra energy centers: Astrophyllite
Activates and balances Root chakra: Cinnabar
Activates and balances the chakras: Tibetan Black Quartz
Activates kundalini energy: Infinite Stone, Shiva Lingam
Activates psychic abilities: Phenacite
Activates the Heart and Third Eye chakra: Lithium Quartz
Acts as an anti-depressant: Red Rutilated Quartz
Acts as an attraction stone: Epidote (Pistacite, Unakite)
Aids against negative magic and death: Topaz
Aids forgiveness by eliminating hostility: Luvulite (Sugilite)
Aids in accessing and understanding higher knowledge: Benitoite
Aids in accessing the highest realm of vibrations: Alexandrite
Aids in acclimating to new communities: Dolomite
Aids in achieving mental balance: Stilbite
Aids in alleviating fear: Picture Jasper
Aids in bringing self-love: Halite
Aids in cleaning up unhealthy habits: Halite
Aids in communicating inner feelings: Hemimorphite
Aids in communicating with other beings: Astrophyllite
Aids in communicating with other planes: Herkimer Diamond
Aids in defeating depression: Ametrine, Andalusite (Chiastolite, Cross Stone)

Aids in developing psychic ability: Covellite, Indicolite (Blue Tourmaline)

Aids in developing trust: Morganite (Pink Beryl)

Aids in effective communication: Zincite

Aids in emotional and physical resurgence to health: Stichtite

Aids in experiencing joy and bliss: Hiddenite

Aids in exploration: Green Diopside

Aids in exploring and understanding past lives: Indicolite (Blue Tourmaline)

Aids in finding balance: Polychrome Jasper

Aids in finding emotional strength: Champagne Tourmaline (Dravite)

Aids in finding lost objects: Staurolite (Fairy Cross)

Aids in finding love and money: Quantum Quattro Silica

Aids in finding one's inner peace: Serpentine (New Jade)

Aids in finding one's true path in life: Vesuvianite (Idocrase)

Aids in finding the right path: Picasso Jasper

Aids in focusing on a goal and seeing it through: Scapolite

Aids in healing: Leopard Skin Jasper

Aids in journeying to higher realms in meditation: Baryte

Aids in leaving the past behind: Danburite

Aids in looking younger: Rose Quartz

Aids in making friends and activating Heart chakra: Sphaerocobaltite (Cobaltoan Calcite)

Aids in mending a bad relationship: Hiddenite

Aids in merging with one's higher self: Amethyst Spirit Quartz (Cactus Quartz, Porcupine Quartz)

Aids in overcoming depleted energy: Zircon

Aids in overcoming fear: Chrysanthemum Stone

Aids in overcoming tough situations: Dumortierite

Aids in personal growth and flexibility: Clintonite

Aids in reaching troublesome goals: Petrified Wood

Aids in recognizing truths: Prehnite

Aids in releasing fear: Amethyst Spirit Quartz (Cactus Quartz, Porcupine Quartz)

Aids in releasing judgment of self and others: Leopardite

Aids in removing negative energy: Sphene (Titanite)

Aids in repairing mistakes and emotional damage: Purpurite

Aids in seeing clearly in meditation: Labradorite

Aids in seeing projects through to the end: Hemimorphite

Aids in seeing the possibilities in opportunities: Red Aventurine

Aids in seeing through illusions: Spectrolite

Aids in sexual energy and creative pursuits: Sphalerite

Aids in solving problems: Lazulite

Aids in speaking the truth: Tanzanite (Blue Zoisite)

Aids in the secret expansion of the inner self: Stalactites

Aids success in business: Malachite

Aids telepathy, meditation, and visualization: Magnetite (Lodestone)

Aids with entry to higher spiritual realms: Baryte

Aids with headaches, migraines, and reduced vision: Lazulite

Aids with lucid dreaming and restful sleep: Scolecite

Aids with psychic visions and intuition: Arfvedsonite

Aids with stressful times: Aragonite

Aligns all chakra systems: Quantum Quattro Silica

Aligns and clears blocks from chakras: Cinnabar

Aligns one's life with the truth: Shattuckite

Aligns oneself with the Divine: Cacoxenite

Aligns truth with daily life: Vesuvianite (Idocrase)

Aligns personal will with Divine will: Cinnabar

Aligns the spiritual, emotional, and mental bodies: Sphene (Titanite)

Alleviates depression and lethargy: Rainforest Jasper (Green Rhyolite)

Alleviates indecision and doubt: Bronzite

Alleviates negative emotions: Dolomite

Alleviates psychological pain: Angelite (Anhydrite)

Alleviates shyness: Hypersthene

Allows one to clearly think things through: Girasol Quartz

Allows one to see through illusions: Labradorite

Allows freer communication: Sphaerocobaltite (Cobaltoan Calcite)

Allows greater understanding: Cavansite

Amplifies ability to be creative: Girasol Quartz

Amplifies and cleanses energies: Calcite

Amplifies energies of other healing stones: Crystal Quartz (Rock Crystal)

Amplifies focus, meditation skills, and wisdom: Pearl

Amplifies loving and generous intentions: Strawberry Quartz

Amplifies one's ability to be creative: Girasol Quartz

Amplifies the exchange of love: Eudialyte

A negative electrical charge: Sulfur

Assists garden fertility when buried: Zeolite

Assists in actualizing dreams: Cinnabar

Assists in astral travel: Astrophyllite

Assists in avoiding power struggles and conflict: Axinite

Assists in bringing spiritual ideals into everyday life: Prasiolite (Green Amethyst)

Assists in communicating with Nature's spirits: Apatite

Assists in constructive change: Sulfur

Assists in creativity: Red Aventurine

Assists in developing patience: Ilvaite

Assists in developing willpower: Scapolite

Assists in emotional upheaval: Cacoxenite

Assists in finding answers to personal puzzles: Bismuth

Assists in finding one's life purpose: Arfvedsonite, Astrophyllite

Assists in gaining benefits from learning life lessons: Clintonite

Assists in gaining loyalty: Goshenite

Assists in healing: Galena
Assists in letting go of conflict and insecurity: Leopardite
Assists in opening the mind: Azurite
Assists in regaining one's possessions: Atlantasite
Assists in restful sleep and vivid dreaming: Stilbite
Assists in self-discipline: Blue Aventurine
Assists in starting new adventures: Apatite
Assists in telling the future: Moonstone
Assists in the ability to reach out to other: Blue Quartz
Assists with clear thinking: Tourmalated Quartz
Assists with deep sleep and powerful dreams: Charoite
Assists with emotional balance and calm: Dolomite
Assists with emotional expression: Hypersthene
Assists with inner balance, health, and well-being: Chlorite
Assists with one's spiritual evolution: Cacoxenite
Assists with past life work: Covellite
Associated with Aquarius, Virgo, Libra, and Capricorn: Sapphire
Associated with feminine energies: Rubellite (Pink Tourmaline)
Associated with hidden inner growth: Stalactites
Associated with many astral signs: Ruby
Associated with spiritual discovery: Leopard Skin Jasper
Associated with the sun: Pyrite
Assuages fear: Blue Quartz
A stone sacred to American Indians: Chalcedony
Attracts good friends and fortune: Sardonyx
Attracts good luck to those who carry it: Lepidocrocite, Lepidolite
Attracts love: Watermelon Tourmaline
Attracts love and maintains it: Morganite (Pink Beryl)
Attracts love, commitment, and loyalty: Magnetite (Lodestone)
Attracts money and success in business: Verdelite (Green Tourmaline)
Attracts prosperity: Prasiolite (Green Amethyst)
Attracts strength: Agate
Attracts wealth: Alexandrite
Awakens compassion and love: Goethite
Awakens feminine power: Larimar (Atlantis Stone, Dolphin Stone)
Awakens love and compassion: Dioptase
Awakens one's Higher Self: Lithium Quartz
Awakens one's magical power: Spectrolite
Awakens one's true purpose in life: Chrysanthemum Stone
Awakens the intelligence of the heart: Moldavite
Awakens the joy of the inner child: Adamite
Awakens the spiritual heart: Dioptase

Balances all chakras: Opal
Balances and clears Heart chakra: Stilbite
Balances and heals: Green Diopside
Balances dreams with reality: Zircon
Balances emotional energy: Red Jasper
Balances feminine and masculine energy: Amazonite
Balances calcium levels: Howlite
Balances mood swings: Serpentine (New Jade)
Balances one's energy flow: Wavellite
Balances the Crown chakra: Amethyst Spirit Quartz (Cactus Quartz, Porcupine
    Quartz)
Balances the energy of fire and water: Larimar (Atlantis Stone, Dolphin Stone)
Balances the Heart chakra: Alexandrite
Balances the intellect with inner emotions: Magnetite (Lodestone)
Balances the male and female energies within: Watermelon Tourmaline
Balances the wisdom of the mind and heart: Apatite
Balances through simplicity: Variscite
Believed to bring lasting happiness: Sardonyx
Believed to prevent ill fortune: Coral
Believed to unlock creativity in an artist: Iolite
Beneficial for channeling spiritual energy: Cavansite
Beneficial for masculine energy: Bronzite
Beneficial for self-examination: Clintonite
Benefits the creative process: Rhodochrosite (Inca Rose Stone, Manganese Spar,
    Raspberry Spar)
Benefits overall health and well-being: Septarian (Dragonstone)
Bestows charisma: Topaz
Bestows wisdom and honesty: Lapis Lazuli
Blocks negative energy flow from wearer: Diamond
Blocks negative energies: Pyrite, Silver

Bolsters the immune system: Quantum Quattro Silica

Boosts one's creativity as an artist: Wulfenite

Boosts vitality: Shiva Lingam

Breaks up old patterns and opens the path for new life: Shiva Lingam

Brings a broader understanding of the past: Elestial Quartz (Orange Elestial)

Brings a calming influence: Stilbite

Brings a carefree, sunny disposition: Amber

Brings a connection with the Divine Feminine: Lemurian Seed Crystal

Brings a feeling of completeness: Cat's Eye, Falcon's Eye, Hawk's Eye, Tiger's Eye

Brings a joy for life: Verdelite (Green Tourmaline)

Brings a peaceful understanding of one's own heart: Tanzanite (Blue Zoisite)

Brings a sense of joy and inner strength: Morganite (Pink Beryl)

Brings a sense of personal independence: Tiger Jasper

Brings a sense of relaxation: Girasol Quartz

Brings a sense of relaxation and peace: Ocean Jasper (Orbicular Jasper)

Brings a sense of unity and self-understanding: Celestial Aura Quartz

Brings a sense of well-being: Rhodonite

Brings a sense of wholeness and integrity: Vesuvianite (Idocrase)

Brings a strong feeling of self-worth: Rose Quartz

Brings about calm when upset: Chrysocolla

Brings about reconciliation between lovers: Selenite

Brings about relaxation during meditation: Petalite

Brings about stability: Magnetite (Lodestone)

Brings abundance: Candle Quartz

Brings awareness of one's own body language: Sphaerocobaltite (Cobaltoan Calcite)

Brings balance to one's emotions: Girasol Quartz, Strawberry Quartz

Brings calm, peace, and focus: Silver

Brings change: Bloodstone (Heliotrope Stone)

Brings creativity in business: Smoky Quartz

Brings creativity and organization: Lemon Quartz (Green Gold Gemstone)

Brings emotional healing: Goethite

Brings extra luck for writers: Sodalite

Brings feelings of safety and comfort: Rubellite (Pink Tourmaline)

Brings financial prosperity, increased sales, and profits: Tektite

Brings good fortune: Kunzite, Moonstone, Talc

Brings good fortune and luck: Prasiolite (Green Amethyst)

Brings good luck and protection: Cat's Eye, Falcon's Eye, Hawk's Eye, Tiger's Eye

Brings good luck to fishermen and hunters: Fairy Stone

Brings great fortune: Alexandrite, Turquoise

Brings greater awareness of the Divine Feminine: Seraphinite

Brings harmony and balance: Eudialyte

Brings harmony to relationships: Lithium Quartz

Brings health and prosperity: Fairy Stone

Brings hope and healing: Butterstone (Butter Jade, African Jade)

Brings inner peace: Sodalite

Brings inner peace and tranquility: Ametrine

Brings inner peace during meditation: Stilbite

Brings joy, creativity, and enthusiasm: Adamite

Brings joy for the natural state of things: Rainforest Jasper (Green Rhyolite)

Brings joy, love, and abundance: Chrysanthemum Stone

Brings light and love to the darkest situations: Luvulite (Sugilite)

Brings love and compassion: Stichtite

Brings luck and happiness: Schorl (Black Tourmaline)

Brings mental clarity: Selenite

Brings mental clarity if placed on the Third Eye: Quantum Quattro Silica

Brings money into one's life: Jade

Brings money, luck, protection, and healing: Ametrine, Citrine

Brings more of what its wearer is: Epidote (Pistacite, Unakite)

Brings new hope: Red Rutilated Quartz

Brings new ideas and concepts: Wulfenite

Brings new opportunity, great wealth, and power: Stibnite

Brings one in tune with the vibrations of the universe: Silver

Brings one's totem spirit guide closer: Candle Quartz

Brings peace and serenity: Aquamarine

Brings peace to one's home: Turquoise

Brings peace to the environment: Atlantasite

Brings power and healing: Nirvana Quartz (Himalayan Ice Quartz)

Brings rapid expansion of the consciousness: Tibetan Black Quartz

Brings reason and wisdom: Emerald

Brings recognition of one's true self: Apophyllite

Brings relaxation, well-being, and serenity: Shell Jasper

Brings resilience and versatility: Butterstone (African Jade, Butter Jade), Stromatolites

Brings restful sleep and dreams: Arfvedsonite

Brings self-acceptance: Champagne Tourmaline (Dravite)

Brings self-acceptance and self-love: Petalite

Brings self-awareness and understanding: Peach Selenite

Brings stability: Polychrome Jasper

Brings steadfast persistence: Stromatolites

Brings strength and protection from harm: Turquoise

Brings success in love as well as business matters: Moonstone

Brings the ability to face difficult times: Galena

Brings unexpected opportunities: Chrysanthemum Stone

Called the "Magician Stone": Cinnabar
Calm, relaxed, hopeful, and optimistic: Girasol Quartz
Calms a rebellious or stubborn side of a personality: Sulfur
Calms an overactive mind: Tanzanite (Blue Zoisite)
Calms and soothes: Champagne Tourmaline (Dravite), Grossularite
Calms nerves: Aquamarine
Calms nerves and emotions: Cavansite
Calms symptoms of ADHD and hyperactivity: Lepidocrocite, Lepidolite
Calms the emotions and soothes the heart: Sphene (Titanite)
Calms the mind: Blue Quartz
Calms the temper: Carnelian
Can be used to counter the effects of aging: Vanadinite
Can be used to seek truth: Ilviate
Can decrease nervousness and irritability: Chrysocolla
Can heal emotional wounds: Rubellite (Pink Tourmaline)
Cannot increase what is not present: Epidote (Pistacite, Unakite)
Carries wisdom of basic truth: Turquoise
Celebrates the joy of life: Rainforest Jasper (Green Rhyolite)
Centers and grounds physical energies: Aragonite
Channels higher knowledge: Angel Aura Quartz (Quartz Crystal)
Channels positive energy: Yellow Jasper
Channels spiritual information: Benotoite
Charges the chakra system: Shiva Lingam
Cheerfulness: Amber, Fire Opal
Clarifies one's creativity: Vanadinite
Clarifies one's purpose in life: Apatite
Clarity, insight, and forgiveness: Clear Calcite
Cleanses: Cacoxenite
Cleanses and heals: White Calcite
Cleanses and purifies living spaces: Tibetan Black Quartz

Cleanses one of negative attachments: Cacoxenite

Cleanses one's energy: Baryte

Cleanses the environment around it: Celestite (Celestine)

Cleanses the heart of emotional wounds: Halite

Cleanses toxins from the body: Zircon

Cleanses unhealthy emotional blocks: Larimar (Atlantis Stone, Dolphin Stone)

Clears and resolves spiritual energy: Halite

Clears blockages: Moldavite

Clears confusion: Apatite

Clears creative obstructions such as writers block: Vanadinite

Clears Crown chakra: White Scapolite

Clears disappointments and relieves spiritual tension: Luvulite (Sugilite)

Clears energy patterns: Tourmalated Quartz

Clears fatigue and double vision: Ulexite

Clears insight for the best spiritual path forward: Arfvedsonite

Clears negativity: Prasiolite (Green Amethyst)

Clears one's auric field: Apache Tears Obsidian

Clears the mind: Lapis Lazuli, Lazurite

Closes the gap between the physical and spiritual: Prasiolite (Green Amethyst)

Combats insomnia: Amethyst, Ametrine

Combines with Tiger's Eye's to bring wealth and money: Topaz

Combines with Topaz to bring wealth and money: Cat's Eye, Falcon's Eye, Hawk's Eye, Tiger's Eye

Common but powerful: Crystal Quartz (Rock Crystal)

Communication with angels: Angelite (Anhydrite), Celestite (Celestine)

Connection with the Earth: Petrified Wood

Connection with the sea – tides of emotion: Abalone Shell

Connects one to the essence of life: Stromatolites

Connects physical reality with higher realms: Covellite

Connects the astral plane with the earth plane: Herkimer Diamond

Connects the physical and the angelic realms: Seraphinite

Connects the will and the heart: Prehnite

Connects to the essence of life: Butterstone (African Jade, Butter Jade)

Connects with higher worlds: Datolite

Connects with nature: Rainforest Jasper (Green Rhyolite)

Connects with one's inner wisdom: Leopardite

Considered a gift of Mother Nature: Peridot

Considered sacred by early Christians: Peridot

Considered to be the most powerful gem: Ruby

Constancy: Diamond

Constancy with friendships: Garnet

Contentment and peace: Ruby

Contributes to mental clarity and perception: Sapphire

Coordinates release of buried emotions: Sphaerocobaltite (Cobaltoan Calcite)

Courage: Onyx
Courage [Far East]: Amber
Courage to be one's best: Ruby
Courage to speak out: Tiger Jasper
Creates a heart-to-heart connection between lovers: Scolecite
Creates fields of protection: Zeolite
Creates prosperity: Cinnabar
Creates stillness and tranquility: Kyanite
Creativity: Amber, Ametrine, Garnet, Labradorite, Tourmaline
Creativity, sexuality, and confidence: Orange Calcite
Crystal of fertility: Arfvedsonite
Cures headaches: Amethyst, Ametrine

Decreases insomnia: Fuchsite (Green Muscovite), Star Mica (Yellow Muscovite)

Deepens understanding of spiritual lessons: Apophyllite

Determines the actual form of one's dreams and goals: Spectrolite

Detoxifies: Zeolite

Detoxifies and strengthens the heart: Green Tourmaline (Verdelite)

Develops a quick wit: Fuchsite (Green Muscovite), Star Mica (Yellow Muscovite)

Develops enthusiasm and new ideas: Labradorite

Develops inner strength: Blue Aventurine, Hemimorphite

Develops one's inner intuition: Covellite

Develops past life recall: Merlinite

Develops self-discipline: Scapolite

Develops self-love and acceptance: Nuummite

Develops spiritual growth: Astrophyllite

Develops the ability to share and teach knowledge: Celestial Aura Quartz

Devotion: Kunzite, Tourmaline

Directs energy to where it's most beneficial: Tangerine Aura Quartz

Disconnects one from unhealthy attachments: Moldavite

Discovers dream patterns that reveal spiritual state: Baryte

Discovers one's true dreams and desires: Stilbite

Dispels jealousy: Eudialyte

Dispels negative emotions: Sphaerocobaltite (Cobaltoan Calcite)

Dispels negative thoughts and emotions: Andalusite (Chiastolite, Cross Stone)

Dissolves alienation: Apatite

Dissolves confusion and doubt: Halite

Dissolves creative blocks: Picasso Jasper

Dissolves oppositions: Amber

Draws and channels the earth's energies: Jet (Lignite)

Draws away negative energy: Grossularite

Draws in love: Topaz

Draws on deep earth energy: Nuummite
Draws negativity from oneself: Apatite
Dreams: Jade
Dreams of it foretold recovery from illness: Coral
Drives away negativity: Lepidocrocite, Lepidolite

Eases emotional stress: Tiger Jasper
Easy flow of feelings: Abalone Shell
Element of wind: Ulexite
Emanates energies of rebirth and transformation: Stibnite
Emits exceptionally tranquil vibrations: Kunzite
Emits profound peace and joy: Petalite
Emotional balance and stress relief: Green Calcite
Emotional healing of the heart: Green Heulandite
Encloses oneself with a sense of calm and beauty: Pearl
Encourages a healthy ego: Onyx
Encourages an interest in other human beings: Verdelite (Green Tourmaline)
Encourages acceptance: Purpurite
Encourages clarity of thought: Chrysocolla
Encourages compassion: Hemimorphite
Encourages conflict solving through peaceful means: Serpentine (New Jade)
Encourages creative expression: Tiger Iron
Encourages creative vision: Picture Jasper
Encourages deep inner journey: Goethite
Encourages desires for new experiences: Mookaite Jasper
Encourages enthusiasm for life: Vesuvianite (Idocrase)
Encourages extroversion: Apatite
Encourages independence: Lepidocrocite, Lepidolite
Encourages insight and truth: Purpurite
Encourages living from the heart: Seraphinite
Encourages love and joy: Chrysoprase
Encourages patience and openness: Verdelite (Green Tourmaline)
Encourages positive emotions: Sphaerocobaltite (Cobaltoan Calcite)
Encourages self-awareness: Lapis Lazuli
Encourages self-realization: Dolomite
Encourages self-realization and confidence: Topaz

Encourages steadfast persistence: Butterstone (African Jade, Butter Jade)

Encourages thinking before speaking: Atlantasite

Energizes all chakras: Zircon

Energizes creative vision: Creedite

Energizes the area where it's placed: Pyrite

Energizes the Third Eye: Green Diopside

Enhances ability to communicate inner truth: Aqua Aura Quartz

Enhances and improves decision-making: Wavellite

Enhances astrological understanding: Angelite (Anhydrite)

Enhances awareness of higher realms: Spectrolite

Enhances clarity of remote vision: Apophyllite

Enhances creativity: Creedite, Goethite

Enhances deep meditation: Lithium Quartz

Enhances dreams: Goshenite

Enhances energy fields: Copper

Enhances energy of prosperity stones: Andalusite (Chiastolite, Cross Stone)

Enhances focus on one's goals: Lemon Quartz (Green Gold Gemstone)

Enhances healing effects of other stones: Copper

Enhances healing properties: Zeolite

Enhances higher brain functions: Variscite

Enhances inner knowledge: Prehnite

Enhances inner transformation: Shiva Lingam

Enhances inspiration and learning skills: Ohio Celestite

Enhances intuition: Moonstone, Nuummite

Enhances one's ability to learn: Stilbite

Enhances one's dream state: Scolecite

Enhances perceptions to determine the truth: Sphalerite

Enhances physical capabilities: Alexandrite

Enhances purity of thought and clarity of the mind: Talc

Enhances self-esteem: Garnet, Hypersthene

Enhances sexual function and pleasure: Wulfenite

Enhances the Heart chakra energies: Scolecite

Enhances the power of prayer: Fulgurite

Enhances the power of psychic abilities: Super Seven (Melody's Stone, Sacred Seven)

Enhances vitality and grounding: Axinite, Sedona Vortex Stone

Enhances wealth in every respect: Tsavorite (Green Garnet, Uvarovite)

Enhances willpower, integrity, stamina, and vigor: Sardonyx

Ensures the dead remain whole [Egypt only]: Amber

Enthusiasm: Aventurine, Fire Opal, Garnet, Labradorite, Rhodochrosite (Inca Rose Stone, Manganese Spar, Raspberry Spar)

Establishes connection: Black Diopside

Excellent antidote to insomnia: Howlite

Excellent at strengthening intuition: Spectrolite

Excellent conductor of energy: Rhodochrosite (Inca Rose Stone, Manganese Spar, Raspberry Spar)

Excellent for relief of stress and worry: Danburite

Excellent for strengthening intuition: Labradorite

Excellent for those building strength: Tiger Iron

Excellent in meditation: Cat's Eye, Falcon's Eye, Hawk's Eye, Tiger's Eye

Excellent meditation stone: Creedite, Crystal Quartz (Rock Crystal), Elestial Quartz (Orange Elestial), Kyanite, Pietersite, Scolecite, Sedona Vortex Stone, Serpentine (New Jade), Tibetan Black Quartz, Window Quartz (Emma's Egg, Seer Stone, Dreamer's Crystal)

Excellent stone for students studying for exams: Azurite

Excellent tools for vibrational healing: Moqui Marbles (Mochi Marbles, Shamanic Star Stones, Thunderballs)

Excellent tools in Shamanic journeys: Moqui Marbles (Mochi Marbles, Shamanic Star Stones, Thunderballs)

Expands love on every level: Green Diopside

Expands one's adaptability: Alexandrite

Expands the consciousness: Cacoxenite, Datolite

Expresses emotions in a positive way: Aqua Aura Quartz

Expresses knowledge through written word: Covellite

Expression of playful spirit: Adamite

Extremely powerful and special stone: Super Seven (Melody's Stone, Sacred Seven)

Facilitates calm and balance: Silver
Facilitates contact with angels: Apophyllite
Facilitates deep change: Danburite
Facilitates deep meditation: Indicolite (Blue Tourmaline)
Facilitates dream recall: Scolecite
Facilitates inner vision: Phenacite
Facilitates journey to discovery of inner self: Nuummite
Faithfulness when given to a lover: Emerald
Family: Abalone Shell
Feeds one's life-force: Green Watermelon Tourmaline
Fertility: Chrysoprase, Imperial Topaz, Moonstone, Rhodonite, Rose Quartz
Filled with love: Ruby
Fights off nightmares if combined with Amethyst: Charoite
Fights off nightmares if combined with Charoite: Amethyst
Finds one's personal purpose: Angel Aura Quartz (Quartz Crystal)
Focuses on positive aspects in one's life: Ocean Jasper (Orbicular Jasper)
Focuses one's will and mental clarity: Tiger Iron
Foresight: Aquamarine, Turquoise
Forges through obstacles: Chrysanthemum Stone
Fortifies and strengthens the mind: Pyrite
Fortifies self-confidence: Spessartine (Mandarin Garnet, Orange Garnet)
Fortifies self-confidence and responsibility: Onyx
Fosters compassion, self-acceptance, and self-honor: Prasiolite (Green Amethyst)
Friendship: Emerald, Lapis Lazuli, Malachite, Peridot, Rhodonite, Spinel, Watermelon Tourmaline
Fulfillment of desires: Amber, Fire Opal, Hematite, Malachite

Gateway to mysteries and out-of-body travel: Andalusite (Chiastolite, Cross Stone)

Gem of spring: Emerald

Gentle stone that directly touches the heart: Rubellite (Pink Tourmaline)

Gentle, yet strong: Ohio Celestite

Gets in touch with one's spiritual being: Aquamarine

Gets rid of negative energies: Black Obsidian

Gifts passion: Moonstone

Gives energy to its carrier: Carnelian

Gives greater intuition and oracle skills: Shattuckite

Gives one a clear vision on all levels of reality: Ulexite

Gives one extra energy when one is ill or under stress: Sunstone

Gives physical stamina: Amazonite

Gives protection in the area around one's body: Angelite (Anhydrite)

Gives rich and variegated dreams: Agate

Gives stability when working on deeper issues: Faden Quartz

Goal setting: Labradorite, Lepidocrocite, Lepidolite, Watermelon Tourmaline

Good at relieving hip and back problems: Petrified Wood

Good for calming the mind: Sphene (Titanite)

Good for coughs and mucus problems: Diamond

Good for increasing intuition: Hematite

Good for meditation and visualization: Coral

Good for public speakers, attorneys, and teachers: Shattuckite

Good luck charm: Staurolite (Fairy Cross)

Grants access to past lives: Atlantasite

Grants calm, peace, and optimism: Girasol Quartz

Grants clear insight and creativity: Zincite

Grants clear insight and effective communication: Cavansite

Grants courage to speak out: Red Jasper

Grants emotional healing: Leopard Skin Jasper

Grants good luck: Tektite
Grants greater insight: Cinnabar
Grants hope: Spessartine (Mandarin Garnet, Orange Garnet)
Grants insight: Cat's Eye, Falcon's Eye, Hawk's Eye, Tiger's Eye
Grants pleasant dreams: Amethyst, Ametrine, Ruby, Topaz
Grants protection: Rainbow Obsidian
Grants protection to travelers: Malachite
Grants relief for muscle spasms: Septarian (Dragonstone)
Grants restful sleep and lucid dreaming: Danburite
Grounds and protects its owners: Mahogany Obsidian
Grounds emotions: Grossularite
Grounds energies: Andalusite (Chiastolite, Cross Stone)
Grounds in the earth: Black Diopside
Grounds one's inner self: Champagne Tourmaline (Dravite)
Grounds one's self: Polychrome Jasper
Grounds the spiritual self: Charoite
Growth and abundance: Green Goldstone
Growth, fertility, and abundance: Green Sardonyx
Guards against disease and sorcery: Serpentine (New Jade)
Guards against drunkenness: Amethyst, Ametrine
Guards against guilty or deceptive emotions: Amethyst
Guards against poverty: Carnelian

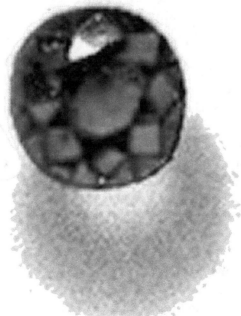

Garnet

Harmonizes aura, chakra points, and psychical body: Amethyst Spirit Quartz (Cactus Quartz, Porcupine Quartz)

Harmonizes body, mind, and spirit: Chalcedony

Harmonizes one's dreams and goals with reality: Zircon

Harmonizes one's emotions: Axinite, Sedona Vortex Stone

Harmonizes the inner being: Sodalite

Harmony: Smoky Quartz

Harmony in relationships: Abalone Shell

Has a powerful positive-negative polarity: Magnetite (Lodestone)

Has a soft, gentle, and soothing effect: Opalite

Has been used to prevent bleeding: Hematite

Healing: Amethyst, Botryoidal Fluorite, Calligraphy Stone, Diamond, Opal, Shu Fa Stone

Healing and antibacterial properties: Shungite

Heals and repairs: Faden Quartz

Heals emotional distress: Dioptase

Heals emotional trauma: Petalite

Heals emotional wounds: Dioptase

Heals grief from past trauma: Quantum Quattro Silica

Heals past-life relationships and issues: Wulfenite

Heightens psychic sensitivity and psychic travel: Tektite

Helpful during times of transition: Covellite

Helps align one to their goals: Aqua Blue Obsidian

Helps balance emotions: Amazonite

Helps balance the Solar Plexus chakra: Pearl

Helps clarify problems: Chrysoprase

Helps develop vision for the bigger picture: Red Rutilated Quartz

Helps energy flow freely: Wavellite

Helps find financial stability while avoiding excess: Variscite

Helps focus on a true path and purpose: Candle Quartz

Helps give a sense of humor: Carnelian

Helps heal and balance natural psychic vision: Ulexite

Helps in attaining goals inconspicuously: Lepidocrocite, Lepidolite

Helps in decision-making: Fluorite

Helps in finding self-acceptance: Variscite

Helps in meditation: Moqui Marbles (Mochi Marbles, Shamanic Star Stones, Thunderballs)

Helps in understanding dream symbols: Arfvedsonite

Helps one access angelic guidance: Selenite

Helps one focus: Lazulite

Helps one focus on maintaining goals: Zircon

Helps one recognize one's unique gifts: Tangerine Aura Quartz

Helps one see through a facade: Pyrite

Helps one speak the truth when it's difficult: Angelite (Anhydrite)

Helps one understand one's spiritual nature: Blue Quartz

Helps one's inner vision: Clintonite

Helps overcome fears: Apatite

Helps provide direction in life: Gold Sheen Obsidian

Helps recover personal power: Galena

Helps release unhealthy emotional patterns: Morganite (Pink Beryl)

Helps release unwanted habits: Variscite

Helps restore physical energy: Petrified Wood

Helps sexual love be passionate: Ruby

Helps soften stubborn attitudes: Stichtite

Helps soothe the heart: Hiddenite

Helps stimulate metabolism: Wulfenite

Helps the holder persist and endure through fatigue: Vanadinite

Helps to manifest wealth: Silver

Helps unblock psychic visions: Moqui Marbles (Mochi Marbles, Shamanic Star Stones, Thunderballs), Ulexite

Helps with contacting spirit guides: Sedona Vortex Stone

Helps with stamina for those who work hard: Axinite

Helps with stomach, digestion, and emotional stress: Pearl

Helps with weight loss: Gaspeite

Ignites love and compassion in one's heart: Prasiolite (Green Amethyst)

Imparts a sense of oneness and unity: Lemurian Seed Crystal

Imparts calm while encouraging versatility: Mookaite Jasper

Imparts the courage to change: Vesuvianite (Idocrase)

Improves intuition: Wavellite

Improves self-worth: Fuchsite (Green Muscovite), Star Mica (Yellow Muscovite)

Increases ability to perceive: Chalcopyrite (Peacock Ore)

Increases ability to receive and express truth: Shattuckite

Increases access to spiritual planes: Axinite, Sedona Vortex Stone

Increases brain function: Lazulite

Increases concentration: Fluorite

Increases connection to other worlds: Staurolite (Fairy Cross)

Increases control over impulsive behavior: Girasol Quartz

Increases discipline: Ohio Celestite

Increases energy fields: Tektite

Increases energy in athletes and physical training: Sphalerite

Increases harmony when working in a group: Sphaerocobaltite (Cobaltoan Calcite)

Increases inner vision: Apophyllite

Increases intuition, creativity, and inspiration: Azurite

Increases motivation: Amber, Chrysoprase

Increases one's appreciation for the joys of life: Zebra Jasper

Increases one's psychic abilities: Lazulite

Increases opportunities for personal good fortune: Nuummite

Increases perception and creative insight: Green Aventurine

Increases personal power: Datolite

Increases potency of reiki and other healing energies: Infinite Stone

Increases prophetic vision: Phenacite

Increases psychic abilities if used with Apophyllite: Cavansite

Increases psychic abilities if used with Cavansite: Apophyllite
Increases psychic or vision abilities: Hemimorphite
Increases psychic sensitivity: Turquoise
Increases resilience: Star Mica (Yellow Muscovite)
Increases self-esteem: Ametrine, Bronzite, Citrine
Increases self-healing power: Sunstone
Increases synchronicity: Moldavite
Increases telepathy: Angelite (Anhydrite)
Increases vitality and positive outlook: Blue Aventurine
Induces recovery: Shungite
Induces visionary experiences and healing: Lodalite (Dream Stone)
Industriousness: Rhodochrosite (Inca Rose Stone, Manganese Spar, Raspberry Spar)
Innocence: Diamond
Inspiration: Fuchsite (Green Muscovite)
Inspires courage and persistence: Champagne Tourmaline (Dravite)
Inspires courtesy, help, and acceptance: Bronzite
Inspires hope: Blue Quartz
Inspires new ideas: Tektite
Instills a deep peace: Selenite
Instills a sober mind: Amethyst
Instills generosity: Chalcedony
Integrates and activates all chakras: Faden Quartz
Integrates skills with thoughts and ideas: Purpurite
Intensifies emotional perception and joy: Aragonite
Intuition: Amazonite, Amethyst, Ametrine, Fuchsite (Green Moscovite), Kunzite, Labradorite, Moonstone, Petrified Wood, Turquoise

Joins with Divine energy: Fulgurite

Karmic cleanser: Danburite
Keeps balances between external and internal: Mookaite Jasper
Keeps one focused on the task at hand: Vanadinite
Known as the Daughter of the Ruby: Spinel
Known as the Genius Stone: Fluorite
Known as the Merchant's Stone: Citrine

Lady Luck: Aventurine
Leads one to a more positive outlook on life: Tangerine Aura Quartz
Leads one to higher spiritual awareness: Opal
Learns magic: Merlinite
Learning and communication: Blue Goldstone
Lends support and courage to follow one's dreams: Chrysanthemum Stone
Lifts energy when the psychical body is exhausted: Charoite
Lightens rooms: Botryoidal Fluorite, Calligraphy Stone, Shu Fa Stone
Lightens the heart: Elestial Quartz (Orange Elestial)
Lights one's path to dreams and goals: Spessartine (Mandarin Garnet, Orange Garnet)

Links daily consciousness to the spiritual: Pietersite
Links the Third Eye and Crown chakras: Phenacite
Logical thinking: Agate, Black Tourmaline (Schorl), Chrysoprase, Citrine, Kunzite, Lepidocrocite, Lepidolite
Love: Chrysoprase, Emerald, Moonstone, Rhodochrosite (Inca Rose Stone, Manganese Spar, Raspberry Spar), Rose Quartz, Ruby, Watermelon Tourmaline
Love and friendship: Pink Tourmaline
Lovers offer the most beautiful to their beloved: Fairy Stone
Lowers stress levels: Atlantasite
Luck: Agate, Amber, Ametrine, Chrysoprase, Garnet, Malachite, Moonstone, Sunstone, Turquoise
Luck and happiness: Black Tourmaline (Schorl)
Lucky for actors and actresses: Red Jasper

Magicians called upon the influences of the sun: Sunstone
Makes a wonderful protection stone: Selenite
Makes an excellent meditation stone: Chalcopyrite (Peacock Ore)
Makes dreams more vivid and meaningful: Lazulite, Moldavite
Makes one aware of one's own needs: Cat's Eye, Falcon's Eye, Hawk's Eye, Tiger's Eye
Metal of healing: Copper
Mineral of strength, vitality, and grounding: Sphalerite
Money: Botryoidal Fluorite, Calligraphy Stone, Shu Fa Stone
Most powerful healing stone: Opal
Motherhood: Abalone Shell

New beginnings: Agate, Garnet
Neutralizes negative energies: Jet (Lignite)
Never needs cleansing, recharging, or energizing: Super Seven (Melody's Stone, Sacred Seven)
No stone is alike: Lodalite (Dream Stone)
Nurtures and grounds: Septarian (Dragonstone)

Offers a boost of power when tasks are difficult: Vanadinite
Offers protection on land and at sea: Moonstone
Offers relief from negative emotions: Magnetite (Lodestone)
Offers relief from stress: Indicolite (Blue Tourmaline)
Offers stamina needed to see projects through: Vanadinite
Often attuned to the angelic realm: Elestial Quartz (Orange Elestial)
Often used to find one's center when meditating: Ilviate
One of the most powerful stones: Lazurite
Opens a channel for intuition and psychic awareness: Fulgurite
Opens access to ancient wisdom and knowledge: Lemurian Seed Crystal

Opens awareness to the angelic domain: Angel Aura Quartz (Quartz Crystal)

Opens and cleans Crown chakra: Chalcopyrite (Peacock Ore), Charoite

Opens and clears the lower chakras: Tektite

Opens creativity and prosperity: Lemon Quartz (Green Gold Gemstone)

Opens doors and communication to the spiritual realm: Indicolite (Blue Tourmaline)

Opens energy channels: Calcite

Opens inner sight: Azurite

Opens one to Divine Source: Danburite

Opens one's perception to joy and love: Alexandrite

Opens psychic abilities: Septarian (Dragonstone)

Opens the door to communication with the deceased: Merlinite

Opens the door to increasing personal perseverance: Ilviate

Opens the door to spontaneous expressions of love: Scolecite

Opens the door to truth: Benitoite, Cavansite

Opens the Heart chakra if used with Canvasite: Stilbite

Opens the Heart chakra if used with Stilbite: Cavansite

Opens the heart to communication: Adamite

Opens the inner eye: Staurolite (Fairy Cross)

Opens the mind to new concepts: Green Diopside

Opens the mind to new insights: Eudialyte

Opens the mind to new thoughts: Ametrine, Citrine

Opens the path for perception and learning: Smoky Quartz

Opens the path to new levels of growth and understanding: Phenacite

Opens the path to one's inner self: Iolite

Opens the Root chakra: Red Aventurine

Opens the Root and Heart chakra: Eudialyte

Opens the Third Eye chakra: Blue Aventurine, Dumortierite, Yellow Aventurine

Opens the Third Eye and Crown chakras: Baryte

Opens the Third Eye to higher dimensions: Ohio Celestite

Opens the Throat chakra: Angel Aura Quartz (Quartz Crystal)

Order: Aquamarine, Fluorite, Sodalite

Overcomes inertia and feelings of inadequacy: Pyrite

Overcomes feelings of loneliness and isolation: Andalusite (Chiastolite, Cross Stone)

Overcomes grief and shock: Green Heulandite

Overcomes limitations in one's personal power: Scapolite

OCTOBER OPAL HOPE

Passion: Carnelian
Peace: Pearl
Peace of mind: Tourmalated Quartz
Perfect dream-stones: Sedona Vortex Stone
Persistence and intellectual power: Honey Calcite
Personal power: Botryoidal Fluorite, Calligraphy Stone, Cinnabrite, Shu Fa Stone
Picks up spirits: Aquamarine
Placed on the Crown chakra to enhance vision: Opalite
Popularity: Garnet
Positive attitude towards life: Chrysoprase, Imperial Topaz, Malachite, Rhodochrosite (Inca Rose Stone, Manganese Spar, Raspberry Spar), Sunstone
Powerful connection to nature: Chlorite
Powerful energy booster: Vanadinite
Powerful grounding stone: Zircon
Powerful in removing obstacles: Petrified Wood
Powerful mental healer: Blue Aventurine
Powerful protection stone: Leopard Skin Jasper
Powerful stone of healing: Schorl (Black Tourmaline)
Powerful stone of protection: Tibetan Black Quartz
Practice trust of others: Celestial Aura Quartz
Prevents crime and misfortune: Sardonyx
Problem solving: Fuchsite (Green Muscovite)
Promotes a calming effect: Indicolite (Blue Tourmaline)
Promotes a peaceful disposition: Kunzite
Promotes a sense of balance: Aragonite
Promotes an appreciation for life's many wonders: Verdelite (Green Tourmaline)
Promotes acceptance and understanding: Leopardite
Promotes angelic communication: Danburite
Promotes clarity of thought: Ametrine, Citrine
Promotes communication with angels: Phenacite

Promotes compassion: Tanzanite (Blue Zoisite)

Promotes compassion and understanding: Angelite (Anhydrite)

Promotes courage: Variscite

Promotes drive and enthusiasm: Tangerine Aura Quartz

Promotes feelings of responsibility: Picture Jasper

Promotes financial rewards: Sapphire

Promotes good luck and success: Amber

Promotes grounding earth energy: Butterstone (African Jade, Butter Jade)

Promotes growth in living organisms: Shungite

Promotes harmony with one's body: Sunstone

Promotes inner peace and deep relaxation: Scolecite

Promotes inspiration: Moonstone

Promotes intuition: Rhodochrosite (Inca Rose Stone, Manganese Spar, Raspberry Spar)

Promotes joy, light, and optimism: Angel Aura Quartz (Quartz Crystal)

Promotes kindness and practicality: Amazonite

Promotes levelheadedness: Chrysocolla

Promotes mental discipline: Dumortierite

Promotes moderation: Dolomite

Promotes peace and harmony: Sodalite

Promotes peaceful dreaming: Porphyry (Chinese Writing Stone)

Promotes personal pride and joy in living: Smoky Quartz

Promotes prosperity and success: Pearl

Promotes regeneration and self-healing: Seraphinite

Promotes relaxation: Rhodonite

Promotes restful sleep when placed near one's pillow: Lepidocrocite, Lepidolite

Promotes serenity through balance and universal love: Variscite

Promotes stability: Butterstone (African Jade, Butter Jade)

Promotes successful thinking in business: Atlantasite

Promotes synchronicity: Benitoite

Promotes synchronicity and opportunity: Spectrolite

Promotes tranquility and certainty: Candle Quartz

Protection: Agate, Andalusite (Chiastolite, Cross Stone), Black Tourmaline (Schorl), Cat's Eye, Falcon's Eye, Hawk's Eye, Lepidocrocite, Lepidolite, Ruby, Smoky Quartz, Serpentine (New Jade), Turquoise, Watermelon Tourmaline

Protection against witchcraft: Amethyst

Protection against poison: Amethyst, Ametrine

Protection for sailors: Aquamarine

Protection for spiritual journeys: Galena

Protection for travelers: Amber, Andalusite (Chiastolite, Cross Stone), Garnet

Protection from outside influences: Lepidocrocite, Lepidolite

Protection on sea voyages: Chrysoprase

Protects: Sardonyx

Protects against evil: Bloodstone (Heliotrope Stone)

Protects against evil spirits: Fairy Stone

Protects against evil: Bloodstone (Heliotrope Stone)
Protects against gossip: Aquamarine
Protects against poisonous creatures: Serpentine (New Jade)
Protects against the hazards of the night: Rainbow Jasper
Protects against undesirable business associations: Malachite
Protects and balances: Petalite
Protects children from evil spirits: Staurolite (Fairy Cross)
Protects during physical travel: Yellow Jasper
Protects from bad dreams: Agate
Protects from bad vibrations: Carnelian
Protects from diseases: Coral
Protects from harmful electromagnetic radiation: Shungite
Protects from negative energy: Ametrine, Citrine
Protects from stress and energy drains: Agate
Protects from unhealthy energies: Tourmalated Quartz
Protects the soul from shock and trauma: Luvulite (Sugilite)
Protects wearer from accidents: Malachite
Protects wearer against envy and disease: Topaz
Protects wearer from harm: Spinel
Protects wearer from intoxication: Prasiolite (Green Amethyst)
Protects wearer from negative energy: Turquoise
Provides courage, protection, and blessings: Spessartine (Mandarin Garnet, Orange Garnet)
Provides spiritual protection: Zircon
Psychic ability and astral travel: Blue Calcite
Psychic protection: Andalusite (Chiastolite, Cross Stone), Arfvedsonite
Purification: Fulgurite
Purifies: Celestial Aura Quartz
Purifies and protects: Amethyst Spirit Quartz, Cactus Quartz, Porcupine Quartz, Jet (Lignite)
Purifies energy fields: Purpurite
Purifies toxins: Yellow Jasper
Purifies water: Shungite
Purifying crystal: Heulandite
Puts one at ease in social situations: Hypersthene

Queen of Gems: Opal
Quickly unblocks stagnant energy: Selenite
Quiets wild emotions: Topaz

Radiates love: Candle Quartz
Raises consciousness in meditation: Tanzanite (Blue Zoisite)
Raises one's awareness: Celestite (Celestine)
Readiness for action: Amethyst, Ametrine, Chrysoprase, Fire Opal, Rhodonite, Turquoise
Reaffirms relationships, commitments, and loyalties: Porphyry (Chinese Writing Stone)
Realigns goals towards a higher purpose: Porphyry (Chinese Writing Stone)
Recognizes truth: Pietersite
Reconciles differences: Spinel
Record of emerging life: Stromatolites
Reduces negative thoughts: Arfvedsonite
Reflects the inner feelings of the soul: Malachite
Rehabilitates self-love: Gaspeite

Rejuvenates ands strengthens: Shell Jasper

Rekindles compassion: Green Heulandite

Reinforces health patterns: Tiger Iron

Relaxes and nurtures: Rubellite (Pink Tourmaline)

Releases attachments: Larimar (Atlantis Stone, Dolphin Stone)

Releases blocks and limitations imposed on oneself: Nirvana Quartz (Himalayan Ice Quartz)

Releases buried resentment: Cinnabar

Releases emotional patterns: Dioptase

Releases hidden fears: Vesuvianite (Idocrase)

Releases mental blocks: Apophyllite

Releases negative attachments: Vesuvianite (Idocrase)

Releases negative emotions: Onyx

Releases negative energy between individuals: Hiddenite

Releases one from tension: Lithium Quartz

Releases tension: Kunzite

Releases unhealthy attachments to possessions: Gaspeite

Releases unhealthy emotions: Green Heulandite

Relief from anxiety: Red Rutilated Quartz

Relieves emotional shock: Fuchsite (Green Muscovite), Star Mica (Yellow Muscovite)

Relieves everyday stress: Lepidocrocite, Lepidolite

Relieves physical discomfort: Moqui Marbles (Mochi Marbles, Shamanic Star Stones, Thunderballs)

Relieves sorrow and depression: Elestial Quartz (Orange Elestial)

Relieves stress: Variscite

Relieves stress for pregnant women and new mothers: Larimar (Atlantis Stone, Dolphin Stone)

Relieves worries and fears: Datolite

Remains true to one's spiritual path: Celestial Aura Quartz

Removes imbalances and guilt: Watermelon Tourmaline

Removes negativity of any kind: Sulfur

Removes unhealthy emotional attachments: Faden Quartz

Renews lost friendships: Picasso Jasper

Repairs energy fields: Faden Quartz

Repatterns the auric field: Infinite stone

Represents spiritual love and wisdom: Luvulite (Sugilite)

Resilience: Fuchsite (Green Muscovite)

Resonates energies from other stones: Silver

Restores energy balance: Kyanite

Restores harmony and self-acceptance: Bronzite

Restores health and balance: Seraphinite

Restores love in the heart: Hiddenite

Retrieves lost memories: Datolite

Reveals and removes hidden imbalances: Snowflake Obsidian

Reveals inner truth: Lapis Lazuli

Sacred stone of the Goddess Venus: Emerald
Safeguards against psychological attacks: Aqua Aura Quartz
Said to be crystals of joy: Sphaerocobaltite (Cobaltoan Calcite)
Said to have cooling powers: Crystal Quartz (Rock Crystal)
Self-confidence: Calcite, Citrine, Fluorite, Garnet, Imperial Topaz, Sunstone
Sensitivity towards others: Abalone Shell
Serenity: Turquoise
Shaman travel and spiritual discovery: Leopard Skin Jasper
Sharpens the senses: Onyx, Rainbow Obsidian
Shields from psychic attacks and negativity: Adamite
Shields wearer from difficult situations: Mookaite Jasper
Sign of new life: Kunzite
Signifies optimism and well-being: Lemon Quartz (Green Gold Gemstone)
Signifies the presence of the Lord: Amber
Smooths a path ridden with difficult obstacles: Petrified Wood
Solving difficulties: Carnelian, Garnet
Sometimes regarded as a symbol of pregnancy: Kunzite
Soothes and clarifies: Variscite
Soothes and harmonizes: Pink Watermelon Tourmaline
Soothes away sadness: Spinel
Soothes the emotions: Larimar (Atlantis Stone, Dolphin Stone)
Soothes the heart: Rhodochrosite (Inca Rose Stone, Manganese Spar, Raspberry Spar)
Soothes the nervous system: Rhodonite
Soothing, stress-relief stone: Blue Quartz
Soul of the tiger [Asia]: Amber
Soul stone: Charoite
Sparks creativity: Porphyry (Chinese Writing Stone)
Special focus on peace and brotherhood: Angelite (Anhydrite)
Spiritual catalyst: Moldavite
Stabilizes: Stromatolites
Stabilizes Base chakra: Aragonite

Stabilizes mood swings: Opalite
Stamina: Aquamarine, Garnet, Red Jasper
Stimulates an increase in communication skills: Azurite
Stimulates creativity: Adamite, Verdelite (Green Tourmaline)
Stimulates creativity and intellect: Apatite
Stimulates creativity and the imagination: Ulexite
Stimulates endurance: Sodalite
Stimulates forgiveness: Dioptase
Stimulates the Heart chakra: Danburite
Stimulates healing and improves health: Sphene (Titanite)
Stimulates imagination: Labradorite
Stimulates metabolism: Gaspeite
Stimulates prosperity and financial abundance: Phenacite
Stimulates sexual arousal and increases sexual energy: Sunstone
Stimulates spiritual development: Atlantasite
Stimulates spiritual transformation: Pearl
Stimulates the expansion of the mind: Stilbite
Stimulates the mind: Goshenite
Stimulates the Third Eye: Cinnabar
Stimulates Throat chakra: Aqua Aura Quartz
Stimulates transition to the astral plane: Zebra Jasper
Stimulates warm feelings of love and compassion: Rhodochrosite (Inca Rose Stone, Manganese Spar, Raspberry Spar)
Stone of abundance: Apatite
Stone of Aries: Blue Aventurine
Stone of artists and men: Amazonite
Stone of ascension: Cacoxenite
Stone of athletics: Sodalite
Stone of awareness and understanding: Tree Agate
Stone of balance: Rhodonite
Stone of balance for relationships: Malachite
Stone of calming: Blue Lace Agate, Howlite, Purpurite
Stone of clairvoyance: Ulexite
Stone of communication: Tanzanite (Blue Zoisite)
Stone of courage, strength, and stamina: Tiger Iron
Stone of creativity and imagination: Zincite
Stone of destiny: Sapphire
Stone of discovery, artists, and grief: Goethite
Stone of Divine Love: Morganite (Pink Beryl)
Stone of emotional healing: Peach Selenite
Stone of empathy: Hemimorphite
Stone of emotional and spititual growth: Cinnabrite
Stone of energy: Goldstone
Stone of endurance: Smoky Quartz

Stone of friendship and love: Lapis Lazuli

Stone of forgiveness, rescue, and recovery: Stichtite

Stone of good luck: Talc

Stone of grounding and harmonizing: Picture Jasper

Stone of harmony and balance: Moqui Marbles (Mochi Marbles, Shamanic Star Stones, Thunderballs)

Stone of healing: Larimar (Atlantis Stone, Dolphin Stone), Septarian (Dragonstone)

Stone of healing [American Indians]: Chrysocolla

Stone of healing with trauma and shock: Tangerine Aura Quartz

Stone of health: Grossularite

Stone of heightened awareness: Angelite (Anhydrite)

Stone of hope, great achievement, and good luck: Opal

Stone of inner vision: Baryte

Stone of inspiration, problem solving, and intuition: Star Mica (Yellow Muscovite)

Stone of journeying: Lodalite (Dream Stone)

Stone of joy: Ocean Jasper (Orbicular Jasper)

Stone of laughter: Crazy Lace Agate

Stone of learning: Apatite, Dumortierite

Stone of life: Shungite

Stone of life and love: Eudialyte

Stone of long life and prosperity: Dendrite Agate

Stone of love: Luvulite (Sugilite), Sphaerocobaltite (Cobaltoan Calcite)

Stone of love in marriage: Rose Quartz

Stone of luck and chance: Green Aventurine

Stone of mediating and centering: Zebra Jasper

Stone of meditation: Lapis Lazuli, Prehnite

Stone of opportunity: Aventurine

Stone of originality: Wulfenite

Stone of peace and serenity: Fire Agate

Stone of peace, increased wisdom, and discretion: Chrysocolla

Stone of personal knowledge: Astrophyllite

Stone of personal power: Nuummite

Stone of power: Labradorite, Spectrolite

Stone of prophecy: Emerald

Stone of prosperity: Stibnite, Tsavorite (Green Garnet, Uvarovite)

Stone of protection: Jade, Leopard Skin Jasper, Rainbow Jasper, Red Jasper, Sunstone, White Agate, Yellow Jasper

Stone of protection against evil: Eye Agate

Stone of protection against negative energies: Smoky Quartz

Stone of purpose and destiny: Scapolite

Stone of re-affirmation: Porphyry (Chinese Writing Stone)

Stone of rejuvenation: Shungite

Stone of romance: Crystal Quartz (Rock Crystal)

Stone of seeing: Apophyllite

Stone of self-acceptance and inner peace: Turritella Agate

Stone of self-healing: Champagne Tourmaline (Dravite)
Stone of self-healing and regeneration: Chlorite
Stone of sexual attractiveness: Opal
Stone of springtime: Peridot
Stone of stability: Red Jasper
Stone of stability and grounding: Zebra Jasper
Stone of strength and decision-making: Mookaite Jasper
Stone of strength and stealth: Snakeskin Agate
Stone of the Gods: Opal
Stone of the mind: Cat's Eye, Falcon's Eye, Hawk's Eye, Tiger's Eye
Stone of transformation: Cinnabar, Galena
Stone of truth: Apophyllite, Axinite
Stone of truth, wisdom, and communication: Shattuckite
Stone of unconditional love: Prehnite
Stone of universal love: Rose Quartz
Stone of vision: Petalite, Pietersite
Stone of vision and creative expression: Iolite
Stone of warriors: Moss Agate
Strength and courage: Galena
Strengthens all chakras: Andalusite (Chiastolite, Cross Stone)
Strengthens and stimulates sexual energies: Vanadinite
Strengthens emotions, mind, and will: Prasiolite (Green Amethyst)
Strengthens inner guidance: Pietersite
Strengthens non-judgmental discernment: Bronzite
Strengthens one's ability to let go of fear and anxiety: Lepidocrocite, Lepidolite
Strengthens one's connection with the earth: Aragonite
Strengthens one's intuition: Prehnite
Strengthens one's self-discipline and focus: Lazulite
Strengthens psychic capabilities: Ohio Celestite
Strengthens self-discipline: Lazulite
Strengthens teeth and bones: Howlite
Strengthens the body's resistance: Chrysocolla
Strengthens the physical heart: Dioptase
Strengthens the workings of insight: Chrysoprase
Strengthens trust in one's own intuitions: Magnetite (Lodestone)
Strong protector of children: Malachite
Study stone: Dumortierite
Success: Green Tourmaline (Verdelite)
Successful business stone: Garnet
Super good luck: Tourmalated Quartz
Supplements energy of other gemstones: Diamond
Supports decisions that require attention to detail: Wavellite
Supports the emotional heart: Dioptase
Supports willpower: Pietersite
Surrenders to Divine intention through prayer: Fulgurite

Symbol of friendship: Turquoise
Symbol of Heaven and devotion to God: Sapphire
Symbol of hope: Emerald
Symbol of justice: Bloodstone (Heliotrope Stone)
Symbol of love and friendship when gifted: Ruby
Symbol of Saturn and Venus: Sapphire
Symbol of truth [Ancient Egypt]: Lapis Lazuli
Symbol of undying love and admiration: Peridot
Symbol of vanity and royalty: Ruby
Symbolizes faith and hope in Christianity: Emerald
Symbolizes fertilizing rain: Emerald
Symbolizes growth and chance: Dendritic Limestone (Picture Stone)
Symbolizes illumination for a dark soul: Spessartine (Mandarin Garnet, Orange Garnet)
Symbolizes impending danger when dreamed of: Peridot
Symbolizes life and blood force energy: Coral
Symbolizes money and good luck: Pyrite
Symbolizes purity: Kunzite

Takes on properties of its owner: Turquoise
Teaches and protects in matters of spiritual quests: Luvulite (Sugilite)
Teaches and protects love and forgiveness: Luvulite (Sugilite)
Teaches love, respect, and nurturing: Larimar (Atlantis Stone, Dolphin Stone)
Teaches patience: Howlite
Teaches "you reap what you sow": Epidote (Pistacite, Unakite)
The beauty in the change of existence: Abalone Shell
The Lucky Hope Stone: Amazonite
The Tempest Stone: Pietersite
Thought to preserve love: Emerald
Tranquilizes a troubled mind: Emerald
Transmutes conflict into harmony: Andalusite (Chiastolite, Cross Stone)
Tunes into a muse or spirit guide: Covellite

Unfinished business: Aquamarine, Carnelian

Unifies the soul: Lemurian Seed Crystal

Unites Throat and Third Eye chakras: Cavansite

Ups expression of love in words and actions: Ocean Jasper (Orbicular Jasper)

Used as a compass: Iolite

Used as a cure for restlessness: Chrysoprase

Used as a symbol of truth: Lazurite

Used by counselors: Goethite

Used for arthritis and rheumatism: Copper

Used for balance: Shell Jasper

Used for protection and grounding: Shell Jasper

Used in deep meditation: Angel Aura Quartz (Quartz Crystal), Aquamarine, Pearl, Tanzanite (Blue Zoisite)

Used in magic rituals: Jet (Lignite)

Used in meditation to seek one's path: Bismuth

Used in out-of-body travel: Herkimer Diamond

Used in past life healing: Tangerine Aura Quartz

Used in shamanic work, magic rituals, and healing: Merlinite

Used to assist telepathy: Chalcedony

Used to attract love: Chrysocolla, Jade

Used to balance and ground higher and lower chakras: Sphalerite

Used to balance emotions and energy: Yellow Aventurine

Used to boost self-confidence: Tangerine Aura Quartz

Used to break up energy blockages: Chalcopyrite (Peacock Ore)

Used to cleanse one's aura and surrounding area: Clintonite

Used to clear one's psychic centers: Rhodonite

Used to clear the auric field: Phenacite

Used to end unhappy or bothersome relationships: Onyx

Used to enhance sexuality and creativity: Tangerine Aura Quartz

Used to establish connections to the angelic realm: Seraphinite

Used to establish order: Celestite (Celestine)

Used to expand awareness: Creedite

Used to improve relationships: Hematite

Used to invigorate or renew one's emotional state: Rainforest Jasper (Green Rhyolite)

Used to overcome fears, obsessions, and compulsions: Charoite

Used to recall past lives: Galena

Used to relieve all kinds of stress: Howlite

Used to ward off storms: Agate

Used when working with astral planes: White Scapolite

Uses life-force to provide protection to wearer: Ruby

Uses the moon's energy to protect against negativity: Silver

Very powerful grounding and protecting stone: Tiger Iron

Very strong: Herkimer Diamond

Vibrates a deep resonance with Heart chakra: Rubellite (Pink Tourmaline)

Vibrates with love: Rhodonite

Vision stone: Gaspeite

Vitality: Red Calcite

Vitality and energy: Red Goldstone

Wards off bad dreams: Ruby, Topaz
Well-being, empathy, and health: Pink Calcite
Widely effective in metaphysical practice: Moldavite
Willpower: Cinnabrite
Wisdom: Amethyst
Wonderful energy shield: Pyrite, Silver
Worn when mourning: Hematite

Gemstones of Protection

Absorbs and neutralizes negative emotions: Fluorite
Absorbs negative emotions and energies: Sulfur
Absorbs negative energy and dissipates it: Chalcedony
Absorbs toxins and odors: Zeolite
Aids against negative magic and death: Topaz
Aids in removing negative energy: Sphene (Titanite)
Blocks negative energy flow from wearer: Diamond
Blocks negative energies: Pyrite, Silver
Brings strength and protection from harm: Turquoise
Cleanses and purifies living spaces: Tibetan Black Quartz
Creates fields of protection: Zeolite
Dispels negative emotions: Sphaerocobaltite (Cobaltoan Calcite)
Dispels negative thoughts and emotions: Andalusite (Chiastolite, Cross Stone)
Dissolves oppositions: Amber
Draws away negative energy: Grossularite
Drives away negativity: Lepidocrocite, Lepidolite
Gets rid of negative energies: Black Obsidian
Guards against disease and sorcery: Serpentine (New Jade)
Neutralizes negative energies: Jet (Lignite)
Offers protection on land and at sea: Moonstone
Offers relief from negative emotions: Magnetite (Lodestone)
Powerful protection stone: Leopard Skin Jasper
Powerful stone of protection: Tibetan Black Quartz
Protection: Agate, Andalusite (Chiastolite, Cross Stone), Black Tourmaline (Schorl), Cat's Eye, Falcon's Eye, Hawk's Eye, Lepidocrocite, Lepidolite, Ruby, Serpentine (New Jade), Smoky Quartz, Turquoise, Watermelon Tourmaline
Protection against witchcraft: Amethyst
Protection against poison: Amethyst, Ametrine
Protection for sailors: Aquamarine
Protection for spiritual journeys: Galena
Protection for travelers: Amber, Andalusite (Chiastolite, Cross Stone), Garnet
Protection from outside influences: Lepidocrocite, Lepidolite
Protection on sea voyages: Chrysoprase
Protects: Sardonyx
Protects against evil: Bloodstone (Heliotrope Stone)
Protects against evil spirits: Fairy Stone

Protects against poisonous creatures: Serpentine (New Jade)
Protects against the hazards of the night: Rainbow Jasper
Protects children from evil spirits: Staurolite (Fairy Cross)
Protects during physical travel: Yellow Jasper
Protects from harmful electromagnetic radiation: Shungite
Protects from negative energy: Ametrine, Citrine
Protects from stress and energy drains: Agate
Protects from unhealthy energies: Tourmalated Quartz
Protects the soul from shock and trauma: Luvulite (Sugilite)
Protects wearer from accidents: Malachite
Protects wearer against envy and disease: Topaz
Protects wearer from harm: Spinel
Protects wearer from negative energy: Turquoise
Shields from psychic attacks and negativity: Adamite
Stone of protection: Jade, Leopard Skin Jasper, Rainbow Jasper, Red
    Jasper, Sunstone, White Agate, Yellow Jasper
Stone of protection against evil: Eye Agate
Stone of protection against negative energies: Smoky Quartz
Strong protector of children: Malachite
Used to ward off storms: Agate
Very powerful grounding and protecting stone: Tiger Iron

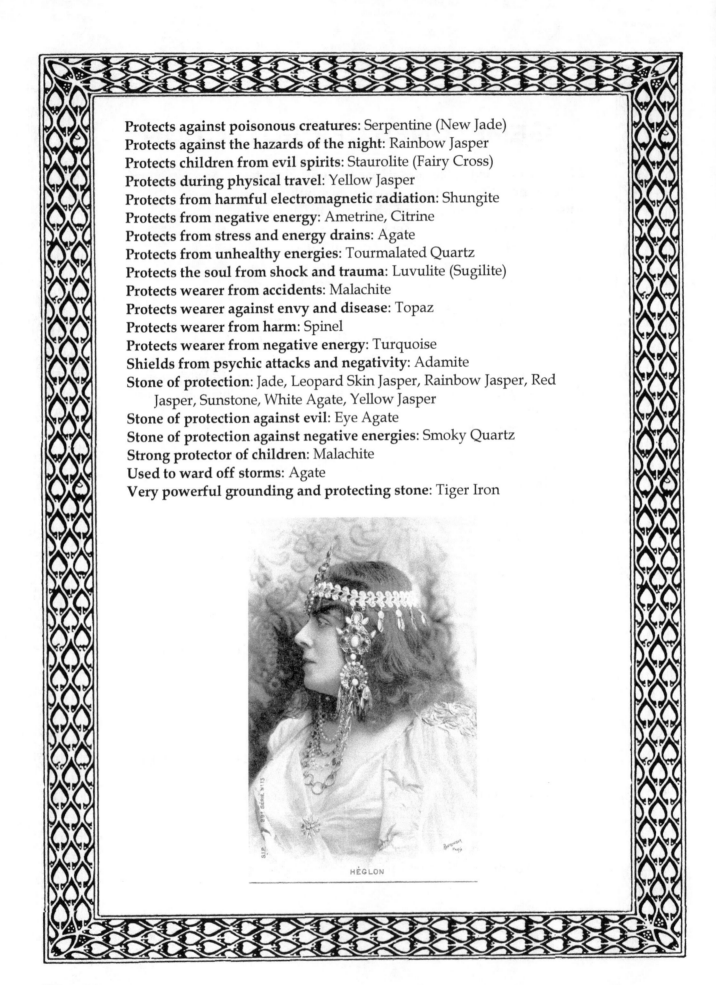

HÉGLON

GEMSTONES TO AID CHAKRAS

Activates and aligns chakra energy centers: Astrophyllite
Activates and balances Root chakra: Cinnabar
Activates and balances the chakras: Tibetan Black Quartz
Activates the Heart and Third Eye chakra: Lithium Quartz
Aids in making friends and activating Heart chakra: Sphaerocobaltite
    (Cobaltoan Calcite)
Aligns all chakra systems: Quantum Quattro Silica
Aligns and clears blocks from chakras: Cinnabar
Balances all chakras: Opal
Balances and clears Heart chakra: Stilbite
Balances the Crown chakra: Amethyst Spirit Quartz (Cactus Quartz,
    Porcupine Quartz)
Balances the Heart chakra: Alexandrite
Brings mental clarity if placed on the Third Eye: Quantum Quattro Silica
Charges the chakra system: Shiva Lingam
Clears Crown chakra: White Scapolite
Energizes all chakras: Zircon
Harmonizes aura, chakra points, and psychical body: Amethyst Spirit
    Quartz (Cactus Quartz, Porcupine Quartz)
Helps balance the Solar Plexus chakra: Pearl
Links the Third Eye and Crown chakras: Phenacite
Opens and cleans Crown chakra: Chalcopyrite (Peacock Ore), Charoite
Opens and clears the lower chakras: Tektite
Opens the Heart chakra if used with Canvasite: Stilbite
Opens the Heart chakra if used with Stilbite: Cavansite
Opens the Root chakra: Red Aventurine
Opens the Root and Heart chakra: Eudialyte
Opens the Third Eye chakra: Blue Aventurine, Dumortierite, Yellow
    Aventurine
Opens the Third Eye and Crown chakras: Baryte
Opens the Throat chakra: Angel Aura Quartz (Quartz Crystal)
Placed on the Crown chakra to enhance vision: Opalite
Stabilizes Base chakra: Aragonite
Stimulates the Heart chakra: Danburite
Stimulates Throat chakra: Aqua Aura Quartz
Strengthens all chakras: Andalusite (Chiastolite, Cross Stone)
Unites Throat and Third Eye chakras: Cavansite
Used to balance and ground higher and lower chakras: Sphalerite
Vibrates a deep resonance with Heart chakra: Rubellite (Pink Tourmaline)

GEMSTONES FOR GOOD LUCK

Attracts good luck to those who carry it: Lepidocrocite, Lepidolite
Believed to prevent ill fortune: Coral
Brings extra luck for writers: Sodalite
Brings good luck and protection: Cat's Eye, Falcon's Eye, Hawk's Eye, Tiger's Eye
Brings good luck to fishermen and hunters: Fairy Stone
Brings luck and happiness: Black Tourmaline (Schorl)
Good luck charm: Staurolite (Fairy Cross)
Grants good luck: Tektite
Lady Luck: Aventurine
Luck: Agate, Amber, Ametrine, Chrysoprase, Garnet, Malachite, Moonstone, Sunstone, Turquoise
Luck and happiness: Black Tourmaline (Schorl)
Lucky for actors and actresses: Red Jasper
Promotes good luck and success: Amber
Stone of good luck: Talc
Stone of luck and chance: Green Aventurine
Super good luck: Tourmalated Quartz
The Lucky Hope Stone: Amazonite

GEMSTONES FOR MAGIC AND SPIRITUAL USE

Accelerates one's spiritual path: Moldavite
Accesses Akashic records: Porphyry (Chinese Writing Stone)
Activates kundalini energy: Infinite Stone, Shiva Lingam
Activates psychic abilities: Phenacite
Aids in accessing the highest realm of vibrations: Alexandrite
Aids in communicating with other beings: Astrophyllite
Aids in communicating with other planes: Herkimer Diamond
Aids in developing psychic ability: Covellite, Indicolite (Blue Tourmaline)
Aids in exploring and understanding past lives: Indicolite (Blue Tourmaline)
Aids in journeying to higher realms in meditation: Baryte
Aids in seeing clearly in meditation: Labradorite
Aids telepathy, meditation, and visualization: Magnetite (Lodestone)
Aids with entry to higher spiritual realms: Baryte
Aids with psychic visions and intuition: Arfvedsonite
Aligns oneself with the Divine: Cacoxenite
Aligns personal will with Divine will: Cinnabar
Aligns the spiritual, emotional, and mental bodies: Sphene (Titanite)
Assists in astral travel: Astrophyllite
Assists in communicating with Nature's spirits: Apatite
Assists in telling the future: Moonstone
Assists with one's spiritual evolution: Cacoxenite
Assists with past life work: Covellite
Associated with many astral signs: Ruby
Awakens one's magical power: Spectrolite
Beneficial for channeling spiritual energy: Cavansite
Brings inner peace during meditation: Stilbite
Brings one in tune with the vibrations of the universe: Silver
Brings one's totem spirit guide closer: Candle Quartz
Channels higher knowledge: Angel Aura Quartz (Quartz Crystal)
Channels spiritual information: Benotoite
Clears one's auric field: Apache Tears Obsidian
Communication with angels: Angelite (Anhydrite), Celestite (Celestine)
Connects physical reality with higher realms: Covellite
Connects the astral plane with the earth plane: Herkimer Diamond
Connects the physical and the angelic realms: Seraphinite
Connects with higher worlds: Datolite
Develops past life recall: Merlinite
Develops spiritual growth: Astrophyllite

Discovers dream patterns that reveal spiritual state: Baryte
Energizes the Third Eye: Green Diopside
Enhances astrological understanding: Angelite (Anhydrite)
Enhances awareness of higher realms: Spectrolite
Enhances the power of psychic abilities: Super Seven (Melody's Stone, Sacred Seven)
Expands the consciousness: Cacoxenite, Datolite
Facilitates contact with angels: Apophyllite
Gateway to mysteries and out-of-body travel: Andalusite (Chiastolite, Cross Stone)
Grants access to past lives: Atlantasite
Heals past-life relationships and issues: Wulfenite
Heightens psychic sensitivity and psychic travel: Tektite
Helps one access angelic guidance: Selenite
Helps with contacting spirit guides: Sedona Vortex Stone
Increases access to spiritual planes: Axinite, Sedona Vortex Stone
Increases connection to other worlds: Staurolite (Fairy Cross)
Increases one's psychic abilities: Lazulite
Increases psychic abilities if used with Apophyllite: Cavansite
Increases psychic abilities if used with Cavansite: Apophyllite
Increases psychic or vision abilities: Hemimorphite
Increases telepathy: Angelite (Anhydrite)
Joins with Divine energy: Fulgurite
Leads one to higher spiritual awareness: Opal
Learns magic: Merlinite
Lifts energy when the psychical body is exhausted: Charoite
Links daily consciousness to the spiritual: Pietersite
Often attuned to the angelic realm: Elestial Quartz (Orange Elestial)
Opens doors and communication to the spiritual realm: Indicolite (Blue Tourmaline)
Opens one to Divine Source: Danburite
Opens awareness to the angelic domain: Angel Aura Quartz (Quartz Crystal)
Opens psychic abilities: Septarian (Dragonstone)
Opens the door to communication with the deceased: Merlinite
Opens the Third Eye to higher dimensions: Ohio Celestite
Promotes angelic communication: Danburite
Promotes communication with angels: Phenacite
Psychic ability and astral travel: Blue Calcite
Psychic protection: Andalusite (Chiastolite, Cross Stone), Arfvedsonite
Repatterns the auric field: Infinite stone
Shaman travel and spiritual discovery: Leopard Skin Jasper
Signifies the presence of the Lord: Amber

Stimulates spiritual development: Atlantasite
Stimulates transition to the astral plane: Zebra Jasper
Stone of clairvoyance: Ulexite
Stone of Divine Love: Morganite (Pink Beryl)
Strengthens psychic capabilities: Ohio Celestite
Surrenders to Divine intention through prayer: Fulgurite
Symbol of Heaven and devotion to God: Sapphire
Tunes into a muse or spirit guide: Covellite
Used in magic rituals: Jet (Lignite)
Used in out-of-body travel: Herkimer Diamond
Used in past life healing: Tangerine Aura Quartz
Used in shamanic work, magic rituals, and healing: Merlinite
Used to assist telepathy: Chalcedony
Used to establish connections to the angelic realm: Seraphinite
Used to recall past lives: Galena
Used when working with astral planes: White Scapolite
Uses life-force to provide protection to wearer: Ruby
Uses the moon's energy to protect against negativity: Silver
Widely effective in metaphysical practice: Moldavite

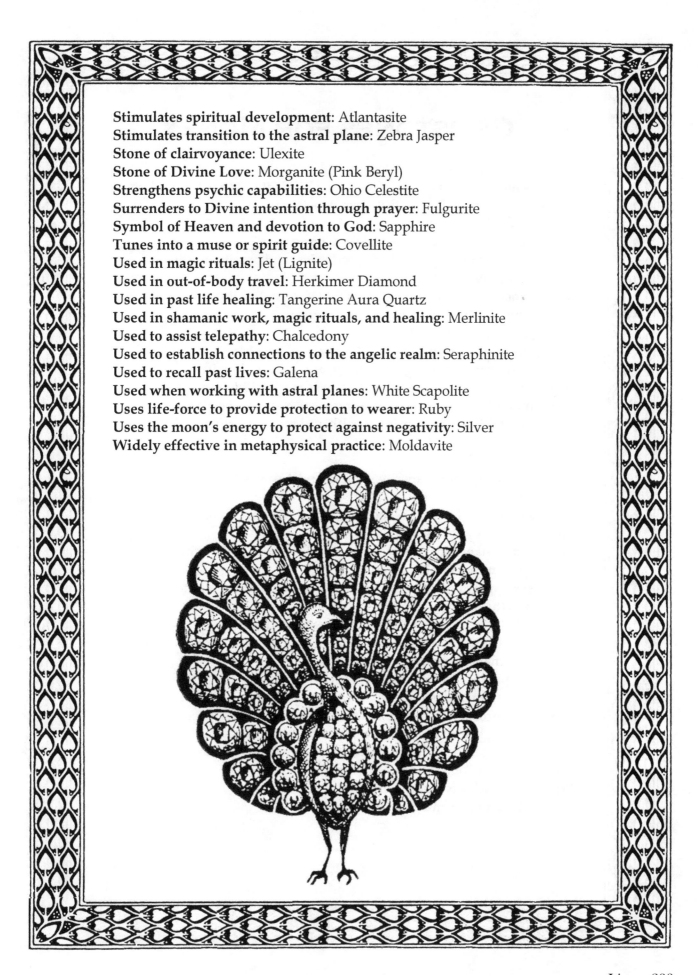

Gemstones for Money

Aids success in business: Malachite
Attracts money and success in business: Verdelite (Green Tourmaline)
Attracts prosperity: Prasiolite (Green Amethyst)
Attracts wealth: Alexandrite
Brings creativity in business: Smoky Quartz
Brings financial prosperity, increased sales, and profits: Tektite
Brings good fortune: Kunzite, Moonstone, Talc
Brings good fortune and luck: Prasiolite (Green Amethyst)
Brings great fortune: Alexandrite, Turquoise
Brings money into one's life: Jade
Brings money, luck, protection, and healing: Ametrine, Citrine
Brings new opportunity, great wealth, and power: Stibnite
Brings success in love as well as business matters: Moonstone
Combines with Tiger's Eye's to bring wealth and money: Topaz
Combines with Topaz to bring wealth and money: Cat's Eye, Falcon's Eye, Hawk's Eye, Tiger's Eye
Creates prosperity: Cinnabar
Enhances energy of prosperity stones: Andalusite (Chiastolite, Cross Stone)
Enhances wealth in every respect: Tsavorite (Green Garnet, Uvarovite)
Guards against poverty: Carnelian
Helps find financial stability while avoiding excess: Variscite
Helps to manifest wealth: Silver
Increases opportunities for personal good fortune: Nuummite
Known as the Merchant's Stone: Citrine
Money: Botryoidal Fluorite, Calligraphy Stone, Shu Fa Stone
Opens creativity and prosperity: Lemon Quartz (Green Gold Gemstone)
Promotes financial rewards: Sapphire
Promotes prosperity and success: Pearl
Protects against undesirable business associations: Malachite
Stimulates prosperity and financial abundance: Phenacite
Stone of long life and prosperity: Dendrite Agate
Stone of prosperity: Stibnite, Tsavorite (Green Garnet, Uvarovite)
Success: Green Tourmaline (Verdelite)
Successful business stone: Garnet
Symbolizes money and good luck: Pyrite

GEMSTONES FOR LOVE AND FRIENDSHIP

Aids in finding love and money: Quantum Quattro Silica
Aids in mending a bad relationship: Hiddenite
Aids in sexual energy and creative pursuits: Sphalerite
Amplifies loving and generous intentions: Strawberry Quartz
Amplifies the exchange of love: Eudialyte
Attracts good friends and fortune: Sardonyx
Attracts love: Watermelon Tourmaline
Attracts love and maintains it: Morganite (Pink Beryl)
Attracts love, commitment, and loyalty: Magnetite (Lodestone)
Awakens compassion and love: Goethite
Awakens love and compassion: Dioptase
Brings about reconciliation between lovers: Selenite
Brings love and compassion: Stichtite
Brings success in love as well as business matters: Moonstone
Creates a heart-to-heart connection between lovers: Scolecite
Crystal of fertility: Arfvedsonite
Dispels jealousy: Eudialyte
Draws in love: Topaz
Encourages love and joy: Chrysoprase
Enhances sexual function and pleasure: Wulfenite
Expands love on every level: Green Diopside
Faithfulness when given to a lover: Emerald
Fertility: Chrysoprase, Imperial Topaz, Moonstone, Rhodonite, Rose Quartz
Filled with love: Ruby
Harmony in relationships: Abalone Shell
Helps sexual love be passionate: Ruby
Ignites love and compassion in one's heart: Prasiolite (Green Amethyst)
Love: Chrysoprase, Emerald, Moonstone, Rhodochrosite (Inca Rose Stone, Manganese Spar, Raspberry Spar), Rose Quartz, Ruby, Watermelon Tourmaline
Love and friendship: Pink Tourmaline
Lovers offer the most beautiful to their beloved: Fairy Stone
Opens the door to spontaneous expressions of love: Scolecite
Passion: Carnelian
Radiates love: Candle Quartz
Reaffirms relationships, commitments, and loyalties: Porphyry (Chinese Writing Stone)
Rehabilitates self-love: Gaspeite

Renews lost friendships: Picasso Jasper

Restores love in the heart: Hiddenite

Stimulates sexual arousal and increases sexual energy: Sunstone

Stimulates warm feelings of love and compassion: Rhodochrosite (Inca Rose Stone, Manganese Spar, Raspberry Spar)

Stone of friendship and love: Lapis Lazuli

Stone of life and love: Eudialyte

Stone of love: Luvulite (Sugilite), Sphaerocobaltite (Cobaltoan Calcite)

Stone of love in marriage: Rose Quartz

Stone of romance: Crystal Quartz (Rock Crystal)

Stone of sexual attractiveness: Opal

Stone of unconditional love: Prehnite

Stone of universal love: Rose Quartz

Strengthens and stimulates sexual energies: Vanadinite

Symbol of friendship: Turquoise

Symbol of love and friendship when gifted: Ruby

Symbol of undying love and admiration: Peridot

Teaches and protects love and forgiveness: Luvulite (Sugilite)

Teaches love, respect, and nurturing: Larimar (Atlantis Stone, Dolphin Stone)

Thought to preserve love: Emerald

Ups expression of love in words and actions: Ocean Jasper (Orbicular Jasper)

Used to attract love: Chrysocolla, Jade

Used to end unhappy or bothersome relationships: Onyx

Used to enhance sexuality and creativity: Tangerine Aura Quartz

Vibrates with love: Rhodonite

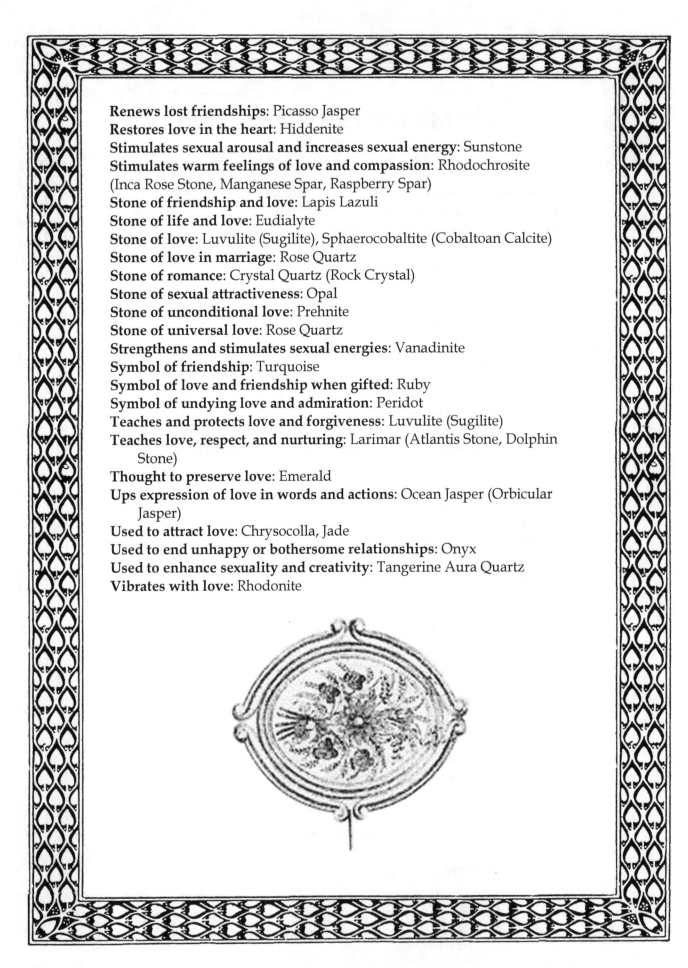

GEMSTONES FOR HEALTH

Aids with headaches, migraines, and reduced vision: Lazulite
Aids with lucid dreaming and restful sleep: Scolecite
Alleviates depression and lethargy: Rainforest Jasper (Green Rhyolite)
Alleviates psychological pain: Angelite (Anhydrite)
Assists in healing: Galena
Assists in restful sleep and vivid dreaming: Stilbite
Assists with deep sleep and powerful dreams: Charoite
Assists with inner balance, health, and well-being: Chlorite
Balances and heals: Green Diopside
Benefits overall health and well-being: Septarian (Dragonstone)
Bolsters the immune system: Quantum Quattro Silica
Brings emotional healing: Goethite
Brings health and prosperity: Fairy Stone
Brings power and healing: Nirvana Quartz (Himalayan Ice Quartz)
Brings restful sleep and dreams: Arfvedsonite
Calms nerves: Aquamarine
Calms nerves and emotions: Cavansite
Calms symptoms of ADHD and hyperactivity: Lepidocrocite, Lepidolite
Can be used to counter the effects of aging: Vanadinite
Can decrease nervousness and irritability: Chrysocolla
Can heal emotional wounds: Rubellite (Pink Tourmaline)
Cleanses and heals: White Calcite
Cleanses toxins from the body: Zircon
Clears fatigue and double vision: Ulexite
Combats insomnia: Amethyst, Ametrine
Cures headaches: Amethyst, Ametrine
Decreases insomnia: Fuchsite (Green Muscovite), Star Mica (Yellow Muscovite)
Enhances healing effects of other stones: Copper
Enhances healing properties: Zeolite
Excellent antidote to insomnia: Howlite
Excellent for those building strength: Tiger Iron
Gives one extra energy when one is ill or under stress: Sunstone
Gives physical stamina: Amazonite
Good at relieving hip and back problems: Petrified Wood
Good for coughs and mucus problems: Diamond
Grants relief for muscle spasms: Septarian (Dragonstone)
Grants restful sleep and lucid dreaming: Danburite
Has been used to prevent bleeding: Hematite
Healing: Amethyst, Botryoidal Fluorite, Calligraphy Stone, Diamond, Opal,

Shu Fa Stone

Healing and antibacterial properties: Shungite

Heals and repairs: Faden Quartz

Heals emotional distress: Dioptase

Heals emotional trauma: Petalite

Heals emotional wounds: Dioptase

Heals grief from past trauma: Quantum Quattro Silica

Helps restore physical energy: Petrified Wood

Helps stimulate metabolism: Wulfenite

Helps with stomach, digestion, and emotional stress: Pearl

Helps with weight loss: Gaspeite

Increases brain function: Lazulite

Increases potency of reiki and other healing energies: Infinite Stone

Increases self-healing power: Sunstone

Metal of healing: Copper

Most powerful healing stone: Opal

Powerful stone of healing: Black Tourmaline (Schorl)

Promotes restful sleep when placed near one's pillow: Lepidocrocite, Lepidolite

Protects from diseases: Coral

Protects wearer from intoxication: Prasiolite (Green Amethyst)

Rejuvenates ands strengthens: Shell Jasper

Reinforces health patterns: Tiger Iron

Relieves physical discomfort: Moqui (Mochi Marbles, Shamanic Star Stones, Thunderballs)

Relieves sorrow and depression: Elestial Quartz (Orange Elestial)

Relieves stress for pregnant women and new mothers: Larimar (Atlantis Stone, Dolphin Stone)

Stimulates healing and improves health: Sphene (Titanite)

Stimulates metabolism: Gaspeite

Stone of healing: Larimar (Atlantis Stone, Dolphin Stone), Septarian (Dragonstone)

Stone of healing [American Indians]: Chrysocolla

Stone of healing with trauma and shock: Tangerine Aura Quartz

Stone of health: Grossularite

Stone of self-healing: Champagne Tourmaline (Dravite)

Stone of self-healing and regeneration: Chlorite

Strengthens teeth and bones: Howlite

Strengthens the body's resistance: Chrysocolla

Strengthens the physical heart: Dioptase

Used for arthritis and rheumatism: Copper

Well-being, empathy, and health: Pink Calcite

GEMSTONES

BY MONTH

JANUARY

Garnet: Constancy with friendships, Creativity, Enhances self-esteem, Enthusiasm, Luck, New beginnings, Popularity, Protection for travelers, Self-confidence, Solving difficulties, Stamina, Successful business stone

FEBRUARY

Amethyst: Combats insomnia, Cures headaches, Fights off nightmares if combined with Charoite, Grants pleasant dreams, Guards against drunkenness, Guards against guilty or deceptive emotions, Healing, Instills a sober mind, Intuition, Protection against witchcraft, Protection from poison, Readiness for action, Wisdom

MARCH

Aquamarine: Brings peace and serenity, Calms nerves, Foresight, Get in touch with your spiritual being, Order, Picks up spirits, Protection for sailors, Protects against gossip, Stamina, Unfinished business, Used in deep meditation

APRIL

Diamond: Blocks negative energy flow from wearer, Constancy, Good for coughs and mucus problems, Healing, Innocence, Supplements energy of other gemstones

MAY

Emerald: Brings reason and wisdom, Faithfulness when given to a lover, Friendship, Gem of spring, Love, Sacred stone of Goddess Venus, Stone of prophecy, Symbol of hope, Symbolizes faith and hope in Christianity, Symbolizes fertilizing rain, Thought to preserve love, Tranquilizes a troubled mind

JUNE

Alexandrite: Aids in accessing the highest realm of vibrations, Attracts wealth, Balances the Heart chakra, Brings great fortune, Enhances physical capabilities, Expands one's adaptability, Opens one's perception to joy and love

Pearl: Amplifies focus, meditation skills, and wisdom, Encloses oneself with a sense of calm and beauty, Helps balance the Solar Plexus chakra, Helps with stomach, digestion, and emotional stress, Peace, Promotes prosperity and success, Stimulates spiritual transformation, Used in deep meditation

JULY

Ruby: Associated with many astral signs, Considered to be the most powerful gem, Contentment and peace, Courage to be one's best, Filled with love, Grants pleasant dreams, Helps sexual love be passionate, Love, Protection, Symbol of love and friendship when gifted, Symbol of vanity and royalty, Uses life-force to provide protection to wearer, Wards off bad dreams

AUGUST

Peridot: Considered a gift of Mother Nature, Considered sacred by early Christians, Friendship, Stone of springtime, Symbol of undying love and admiration, Symbolizes impending danger when dreamed of, Symbolizes purity and morality

Spinel (Often confused for a Ruby, but is not one): Friendship, Known as the Daughter of the Ruby, Protects wearer from harm, Reconciles differences, Soothes away sadness

SEPTEMBER

Sapphire: Associated with Aquarius, Virgo, Libra, and Capricorn, Contributes to mental clarity and perception, Promotes financial rewards, Stone of Destiny, Symbol of Heaven and devotion to God, Symbol of Saturn and Venus

OCTOBER

Opal: Balances all chakras, Healing, Leads one to higher spiritual awareness, Most powerful healing stone, Queen of Gems, Stone of hope, great achievement, and good luck, Stone of sexual attractiveness, Stone of the Gods

NOVEMBER

Citrine: Brings money, luck, protection, and healing, Increases self-esteem, Known as the Merchant's Stone, Logical thinking, Opens the mind to new thoughts, Promotes clarity of thought, Protects from negative energy, Self-confidence

Topaz: Aids against negative magic and death, Bestows charisma, Combines with Tiger's Eye to bring wealth and money, Draws in love, Encourages self-realization and confidence, Grants pleasant dreams, Protects wearer against envy and disease, Quiets wild emotions, Wards off bad dreams

December

Tanzanite (Blue Zoisite): Aids in speaking the truth, Brings a peaceful understanding of one's own heart, Calms an overactive mind, Promotes compassion, Raises consciousness in meditation, Stone of communication, Used in deep meditation

Turquoise: Brings great fortune, Brings peace to one's home, Brings strength and protection from harm, Carries wisdom of basic truth, Foresight, Increases psychic sensitivity, Intuition, Luck, Protection, Protects wearer from negative energy, Readiness for action, Serenity, Symbol of friendship, Takes on properties of its owner

Zircon: Aids in overcoming depleted energy, Balances dreams with reality, Cleanses toxins from the body, Energizes all chakras, Harmonizes one's dreams and goals with reality, Helps one focus on maintaining goals, Provides spiritual protection

BIBLIOGRAPHY

Anonymous, "Birthstone Jewelry Guide," *Wixon Jewelers*, http://www.wixonjewelers.com/education/gemstones/birthstones/, accessed Feb. 11, 2017.

Anonymous, "Gemstones: Meanings and Properties," *Emily Gems*, https://crystal-cure.com/gemstone-meanings.html, accessed Feb. 11, 2017.

Connolly, Shane. *The Secret Language of Flowers: Rediscovering Traditional Meanings*. New York: Rizzoli International Publications, 2004.

Crowell, Robert L. *The Lore and Legends of Flowers*. New York: Thomas Crowell, 1982.

DK Publishing, Inc. *Gem: The Definitive Visual Guide*. New York: DK, 2016.

Gips, Kathleen M. *Flora's Dictionary: The Victorian Language of Herbs and Flowers*. Chagrin Falls, Ohio: TM Publications, 1995.

Gray, Samantha. *The Secret Language of Flowers*. London: Circo, 2011.

Greenaway, Kate. *The Language of Flowers*. London: G. Routledge and Sons, 1884.

Karlsen, Kathleen. *Flower Symbols: The Language of Love: Discovering the Meaning of Flowers in Folklore, Religion and Popular Culture*. Bozeman, Mont.: Living Arts Enterprises, 2011.

Kirkby, Mandy and Vanessa Diffenbaugh. *A Victorian Flower Dictionary: The Language of Flowers Companion*. New York: Ballantine, 2011.

Kleager, Brenda Jenkins. *The Secret Meanings of Flowers*. Huntsville, Ala.: Treasured Secrets Publishing, 2013.

Laufer, Geraldine Adamich. *Tussie-mussies: The Victorian Art of Expressing Yourself in the Language of Flowers*. New York: Workman Pub., 1993.

Lehner, Ernst, and Johanna Lehner. *Folklore and Symbolism of Flowers, Plants, and Trees: All Times and Countries, Legendary Stories and Secret Meanings*. New York: Tudor Publishing, 1960.

McCabe, James. *The Language and Sentiment of Flowers*. Applewood Books, 2003.

Mitchell, Richard Scott. *Mineral Names: What Do They Mean?* New York: Van Nostrand Reinhold, 1979.

Pickston, Margaret. *The Language of Flowers*. New York: Viking, 1987.

Scoble, Gretchen and Ann Field. *The Meaning of Flowers: Myth, Language and Lore*. San Francisco: Chronicle Books, 1998.

Turner, R.G. *Botanica: The Illustrated A-Z Guide of Over 10,000 Garden Plants*. New York: Random House, 1999.

Waterman, Catharine. *Flora's Lexicon: An Interpretation of the Language and Sentiment of Flowers*. Forgotten Books, 2015.

AUTHOR'S NOTE

Oh, hello, you've reached the back of the book with my "bio." Yes, that's in quotes for a reason. I'm a bit of a private person and also very shy, so don't expect too much.

My name is Skye, and no, it's not my real name, but it's the one I go by more often than not. If you've noticed that it's somewhat familiar, it's probably because you've stumbled across my Twitter or Tumblr, Earth_Fire_Skye. If not, then don't worry too much about it.

I'm twenty-one, though not for long if the passage of time has anything to say about that, and I enjoy many hobbies, which range from reading and writing, to drawing and crocheting random stuff. Currently, I live in a town in somewhat southern Pennsylvania with my dog and cat who I love very much, even if they do have the tendency of driving me nuts.

MORE FROM PESCHEL PRESS

Home of the History Behind the Mystery

The Complete, Annotated Series

Return to your favorite novels by Agatha Christie & Dorothy L. Sayers, republished with plenty of extras, such as footnotes describing people, places, events, and idioms, and essays about the author, their creations, and historical events. They deepen your enjoyment and understanding of the novel and its world.

The Complete, Annotated Whose Body?

Dorothy L. Sayers

Her first novel featuring Lord Peter Wimsey comes with 3 maps of London, 10 essays on notorious crimes, anti-Semitism, Sayers and Wimsey, plus a timeline of his cases and Sayers' life. *282 pages.*

The Complete, Annotated Mysterious Affair at Styles

Agatha Christie

Hercule Poirot's debut, updated with revised art, explanation of the murder method, and essays on Poirot, Christie, strychnine, women during the war, plus chronology and book lists. *352 pages.*

The Complete, Annotated Deluxe Secret Adversary

Agatha Christie

Tommy and Tuppence battle socialists plotting to destroy England! This deluxe edition has illustrations from the newspaper edition, plus essays on thrillers, Christie's vanishing and more! *478 pages.*

Suburban Stockade

Strengthening Your Life Against an Uncertain Future

"Suburban Stockade" is Teresa Peschel's manifesto memoir about her quest to drop out of the rat race, embrace her peasant ancestry, and prepare her family for an uncertain future. She describes how our emphasis on a consumer economy and cheap goods blinded us to the personal and moral costs of economic growth. To pursue material wealth, we're taught to ignore the value of family, friends, and community, and the pleasures of a comfortable home and good food. Peschel dares you to build your suburban stockade by not playing the game where the rules are set by corporations and economists and rigged by politicians and the media.

Don't miss future Peschel Press books: Visit Peschelpress.com and sign up for our newsletter. We publish only when we have something to say and we will never sell or trade your personal information.

The 223B Casebook Series

In Trade Paperback and Ebook editions

Reprints of classic and newly discovered fanfiction written during Arthur Conan Doyle's lifetime, with original art and extensive historical notes.

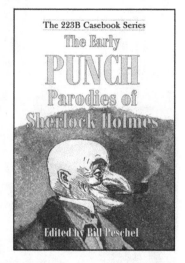

The Early Punch Parodies of Sherlock Holmes

• More than 50 parodies, pastiches, book reviews, cartoons, and jokes from 1890 to 1928 culled from the pages of *Punch*, the classic British humor magazine.

• Includes 17-story cycle by R.C. Lehmann.

• Two parodies by P.G. Wodehouse, and a story by Arthur Conan Doyle.

• Exclusive essays on *Punch*, Lehmann, Wodehouse, and an interview with Conan Doyle. Plus a bonus story featuring Sherlock Holmes and Mark Twain! *281 pages.*

Victorian Parodies & Pastiches: 1888-1899	**Edwardian Parodies & Pastiches I: 1900-1904**	**Edwardian Parodies & Pastiches II: 1905-1909**	**Great War Parodies and Pastiches I: 1910-1914**	**Great War Parodies and Pastiches II: 1915-1919**	**Jazz Age Parodies and Pastiches I: 1920-1924**
More than 60 pieces with stories by Arthur Conan Doyle, Robert Barr, Jack Butler Yeats, John Kendrick Bangs, and J.M. Barrie. *279 pages.*	More than 55 pieces with stories by Mark Twain, Finley Peter Dunn, John Kendrick Bangs, and P.G. Wodehouse. *390 pages.*	More than 40 pieces with stories by 'Banjo' Paterson, Max Beerbohm, Carolyn Wells, and Lincoln Steffens. *401 pages.*	More than 40 pieces with stories by O. Henry, Maurice Baring, Carolyn Wells, Edmund Pearson, & Stephen Leacock. *362 pages.*	More than 35 pieces with stories by Ring Lardner, Carolyn Wells, John Kendrick Bangs, and a young George Orwell. *390 pages.*	More than 35 pieces with stories by Dashiell Hammett, James Thurber, Vincent Starrett, Gardner Rea, and Arthur Conan Doyle. *353 pages.*

The Casebook of Twain & Holmes

Bill Peschel Seven new stories featuring Mark Twain in Sherlock Holmes' world. Guest appearances by Mycroft Holmes, Irene Adler, and John Watson.

The History Behind the Mystery

PESCHEL PRESS; P.O. BOX 132, HERSHEY, PA., PA 17033

WWW.PESCHELPRESS.COM

The Rugeley Poisoner Series

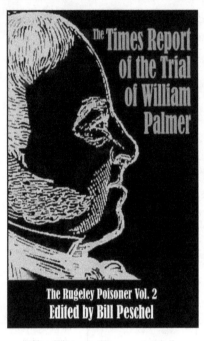

The Illustrated Life and Career of William Palmer

(1856)

● Gossip about Palmer, racing scams, and London's stews.

● More than 50 restored woodcuts.

● Excerpts from Palmer's love letters.

225 pages.

The Times Report of the Trial of William Palmer

(1856)

● The *Times'* trial transcript edited, corrected, & annotated.

● More than 50 original woodcuts restored to better-than-new condition.

● An account of Palmer's execution and medical glossary

426 pages.

The Life and Career of Dr. William Palmer of Rugeley

(1925)

● Written by a doctor who interviewed witnesses and jurors.

● Rare photos and art.

● Essays on Palmer's impact on culture, strychnine, and Rugeley. *227 pages.*

THE PESCHEL PRESS was created by Bill Peschel, a former journalist and co-holder of a Pulitzer Prize for his newspaper's coverage of the Joe Paterno case. In addition to the books listed here, Bill plans on finishing the 223B Casebook series and will publish original fiction by himself and others.

He lives with his family and animal menagerie in Hershey, where the air really does smell like chocolate.